Seventeenth Century
Lyrics

ELIZABETHAN LYRICS

From the Original Texts
Chosen, Edited and Arranged by
NORMAN AULT

Seventeenth Century Lyrics

FROM THE

ORIGINAL TEXTS 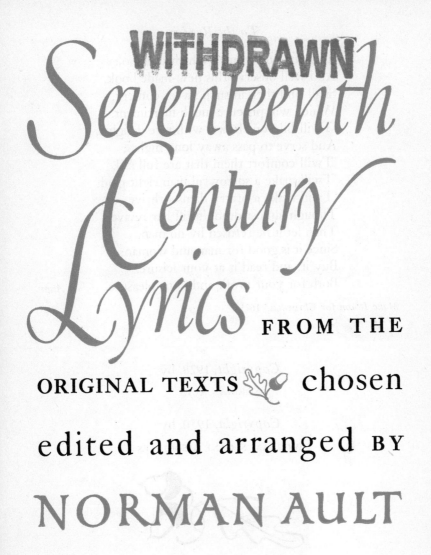 chosen

edited and arranged BY

NORMAN AULT

PUBLISHED IN New York
by WILLIAM SLOANE ASSOCIATES

To the Reader

That man or woman which will look
And well observe this new-made book,
Shall find therein such sweet content,
Which will procure much merriment.
'Twill fill your hearts with rare delights,
And serve to pass away long nights;
'Twill comfort them that are full sad,
'Twill make a sorrowful man right glad;
'Twill make a pretty damsel thrive,
Though almost dead, 'twill her revive.
Then let it be refused by no man,
Since it is good for man and woman;
Buy it, and read it at your leisure,
Both for your profit and your pleasure.   *Anon.*

'*Make Room for Christmas,*' 1675.

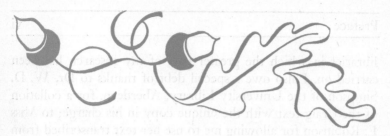

PREFACE

As with my previous anthology, *Elizabethan Lyrics*, recently revised and reissued, the printing of a new edition of the present work has provided opportunity for its revision. I have thus been able to incorporate in the text the few corrections and readjustments, chiefly of date and position, which modern scholarship has made possible. In addition, five poems of the original collection have for various reasons been substituted by others; and several pieces, hitherto anonymous, are now assigned to their authors, real or putative. I have also taken advantage of the resetting to follow more strictly the alphabetical order of the authors within the year-groups, and to include in the Notes fresh matter not only relating to the new changes, but also touching a number of old problems of text, source, or occasion. For convenience of reference, the two volumes of lyrics have now been made uniform in details of arrangement as well as plan, so that students moving from one to the other will find the same system obtaining in both. Nevertheless, like its companion volume, this edition of *Seventeenth Century Lyrics*, in purpose, scope, and selection, remains essentially the same book as that which was first published in 1928.

I must again express my appreciation of the unfailing courtesy and assistance of the Librarians and Staffs of the various

libraries in which the greater part of my research has been
carried on. I also owe a special debt of thanks to Dr. W. D.
Simpson of the University Library, Aberdeen, for a collation
of the Craig text with the unique copy in his charge; to Miss
E. Robinson for allowing me to use her text transcribed from
Beaumont's autograph MS. (now in America) for the two
poems of his here printed; and to the Governing Body of
Christ Church, Oxford, for permission to transcribe and include five poems from MSS. in their library.

For more recent kindnesses I am very grateful to those
friends, both here and in the United States, who in various
ways have assisted in the preparation of the present edition;
amongst whom I would especially mention Mr. T. T. Dom-
bras who has contributed the missing line of one of Carew's
lyrics ('Celia Singing'), and not a few of the additional bibliographical details now incorporated in the notes; Miss
Marion Howe who again—as in *Elizabethan Lyrics*—has
helped me with the new biographical appendix; and Mr. C. H.
Wilkinson who has discovered not only the unknown author
(W. Wasse) of one of my anonymous pieces, but also the unknown first edition of a famous poem by L'Estrange.

N. A.

Oxford, 1927–1950

CONTENTS

CONTENTS

INTRODUCTION

THE plan of illustrating the movement of poetic thought within a period by arranging poems according to the dates at which they became known to the author's public, employed (I believe for the first time) in my *Elizabethan Lyrics*, is followed in this sequel to it. This makes it possible to trace step by step the series of changes in the development of the lyric, from the last songs of Fletcher to the first of Pope; and to perceive that, great as are the changes, there is nowhere any abrupt break in the poetic tradition—late *Elizabethan, Caroline, Restoration*, and *Augustan* merging imperceptibly into each other in a natural progression. By this means also the student of literature is enabled to see each poem in its original environment, against its historical background of contemporary song; it is at times unexpectedly illuminating to find side by side in the same year, poets like Jonson and Milton, Dekker and Cowley, Waller and Bunyan.

For Seventeenth Century verse the field is very wide. The printed volumes I have examined run into thousands, the MSS. into hundreds. The 565 poems here printed represent the final result of the sifting and re-sifting of a provisional selection of over 3000 made in the course of that examination; and they comprise the work of 214 named poets besides much that is anonymous.

In working through the MSS. I found some hundreds of poems which have never been printed. Out of a large number that I transcribed, I include twenty-eight as being of outstanding merit. These are indicated by a dagger (†) in the *Index of First Lines*. To me it was sufficient reward for weeks of tedious search to light on a poem like 'Sickness, not Sleep' (p. 304); or 'Sleep, sleep, my soul' (p. 68); or in another kind, 'Oh, England!' (p. 400). Of special interest is the discovery of a MS. volume of lyrics—four of which I print—by the Duke of Newcastle, written to his wife while she was still Margaret Lucas (pp. 180–182 and note). Except the few songs in their plays, nothing of the Duke's lyric writing has hitherto been known; and the discovery of love poems in his own hand explains, if it does not justify, the Duchess's statement, which has often puzzled scholars, that he was 'the best Lyrick and Dramatick Poet of the Age.' The MSS. have also yielded up several entirely unknown Seventeenth Century poets, among them Thomas Beaumont, from whose volume of poems, probably autograph, I print three pieces (pp. 239–241); and Clement Paman and John Cobbes, each represented here by a lyric of more than average quality.

Nearly one-third of this volume consists of poems undeservedly forgotten because they have never been reprinted since the Seventeenth Century. For this period the number of such poems, often of exceptional beauty or interest, is very large. It is strange that such charming things as Baron's aubade (p. 232) Clerke's bitter-sweet song (p. 343), and the anonymous 'The Goddesses' Glory' (p. 424), should have been overlooked for nearly three hundred years.

I have found evidence enabling me to restore to their rightful authors some well-known pieces until now wrongly assigned or anonymous. Felltham wrote what has alway been regarded as one of Suckling's best poems (p. 320). No the famous bishop, Lancelot Andrewes, but a Dr. Franci

Andrewes, wrote the charming trifle 'Phyllis Inamorata' (p. 53), now printed for the first time in full from the MS.; while Bishop Morley and Dr. T. Bonham have each assigned to them, on MS. authority, a well-known poem hitherto anonymous. Students of the period will be interested in the new evidence for W. Browne's authorship of the famous epitaph on the Countess of Pembroke; and also in a text printed in the second year after her death—the earliest hitherto recorded being dated 1629 (p. 2, and note).

The bibliography of the Seventeenth Century, subsequent to 1640, is notoriously in a state of chaos. And I have been urged by scholars of my acquaintance to print, after the Notes, a chronological list of the anonymous collections of songs and poems which—often at the cost of days, and sometimes of weeks, of search—I have tracked down and read for this volume. In addition to the Ballad Collections mentioned therein, it includes upwards of 260 titles or editions, among them numerous books now of the utmost rarity, and many not noticed in 'Hazlitt' or similar works. On the other hand, I have omitted a large number of chap-books and the like of little or no poetic merit. Had such a bibliography already existed when I began work on this period, the labour involved in the production of this anthology would have been halved.* This *Short-Title List* has also a use other than bibliographical. In these collections the same pieces frequently appear in different volumes, and where these are the sole sources of a poem, a knowledge of the various places where it is to be found is essential for the textual critic. For the poems here included this information is supplied by references to the *List* in the Notes.

While at work on these collections I came to realise that the continual or occasional reappearance of certain poems was

---

* For a fuller list, see my bibliography of poetical collections of all kinds published subsequently in the *C.B.E.L.*, Vol. II, pp. 173–260.

significant. Some poems persisted throughout the period, others suddenly cropped up in contemporary volumes and then as suddenly vanished. Pondering these facts, after my own selection had gone to press, it struck me that I held in my hands the key to a historical study of poetic appreciation in the period: for together these collections reflect the taste of the century as nothing else could do. The reaction of the public in any age to different types of poetry, is an unexplored region of literary history—so much so that further investigation seemed well worth making. Accordingly I again worked through every single volume in the *List*, checking carefully every occurrence of each of the poems of my selection. Complete references are given in the Notes, which are, I hope, as accurate as was humanly possible in this re-examination of several thousands of poems, of which probably ninety per cent bear no author's name. It is of interest to note that, within our period, Herrick's 'Gather ye rose-buds' (p. 173) was easily the most popular poem of the century; that Strode's 'On Chloris walking in the Snow' (p. 81) came next; then Suckling's 'Ballad upon a Wedding' (p. 153); the fourth place rather surprisingly was filled by an anonymous song 'The Contented Lover' (p. 173); the fifth by Shirley's 'The glories of our blood and state' (p. 319); and the sixth by an anonymous Catch, 'The Wisemen were but seven' (p. 176). Space precludes further summary in this place, but it may be remarked that while the lyrics in general of Dryden, Etherege, Herrick, Suckling, Carew, Davenant, and Cowley, in approximately that order of favour, were very highly esteemed, other poets like Jonson (writing *after* 1620), Lovelace, Wade, W. Pope, Jordan, Duffett, May, R. Brome, and Wycherley, wrote each only one poem which hit the public taste—but then with resounding success. Milton makes but one appearance in these collections, late in the century and in an insignificant volume, with a song from 'Comus.'

By rights the longer lyric poems of Milton and Dryden should have been represented in this volume. But, space being limited, this would have meant the exclusion of much new matter not available elsewhere, whereas copies of poems like 'Lycidas,' and 'Alexander's Feast,' are an almost universal possession. But, to preserve the idea of a chronological survey of the century's best pieces, I have indicated in their proper years, such of these longer poems as I should otherwise have printed in full. The rules governing the chronology are the same as in *Elizabethan Lyrics*. Poems from printed books are normally dated by the first edition; but where printing was delayed, they are placed either according to the real or approximate date of writing, or, in the case of songs from plays, in the year of first performance. For poems from the MSS. I have, when other evidence is lacking, adopted the date assigned to the actual transcription of the MS. by the experts in the libraries concerned.

The Texts

By going back to the earliest or most authentic sources, I have been able in perhaps fifty or sixty cases, to reinstate an original reading which had disappeared from modern printed texts. Where the existence of a poem in MS. was known to me, I have myself collated it (with one exception mentioned in the Preface). For all other poems I have collated the text of the first, or oldest extant, edition with all the available subsequent editions (if any) published during the author's lifetime. Where the author had revised it, I print the text of his *last* revision with the date; otherwise I print the text of the first edition without comment.

With regard to emendations I adhere to the principle stated in *Elizabethan Lyrics*. If a mistake is obviously a trifling misprint, or slip of the pen, which can be corrected in one way only, and about the meaning of which there can be no possible doubt, I have made the necessary correction silently. Otherwise I print no emendation nor alternative reading, without giving the earliest authority for it and the date (or, where I am myself responsible for it, my own initials) in a note, together with the unemended reading. Thus the student is never at the mercy of the subjective judgments of editors past or present, but always has before him the actual text of the MS., or that of the printed edition which is either the first or the oldest extant, or which represents the author's own final revision.

The old erratic spellings and punctuation I have modernized, as in the former volume, *except* where these have some inherent significance—a shade of meaning, vowel sound, pronunciation or emphasis, different from ours—and have similarly normalized the excessive, inconsistent, and often meaningless, use of capitals and italics. Archaic words are left untouched, but glossed, if necessary, in a footnote. Vowels now mute but formerly sounded, are indicated by a diaeresis: affectïon, lovëd; and an antique stress, when not obvious, by an accent: Jùly, envỳ. As is well known, elision and abbreviation abound in the prosody and typography of the period. They were, in fact, used with a licence that often presents real difficulties to the modern ear and speech—and, not seldom, understanding—and many people regard them as an aesthetic blemish in lyric quality. But blemish or not, no representative selection of the century's best poems could be made which excluded them; and such forms as *to 't* and *ith'*, *sh 'hath* and *'has, b'w'y', at's* and *th'owe*, appear in these pages often enough to please the most fervid lover of old-time quaintness. Moreover, contemporary methods of translating these and other abbreviations into print show little or no desire for uniformity. For instance, the frequent use of a more or less elided dactyl for a trochee, or iambus for an anapaest, is represented, in MS. and print alike, with the utmost inconsistency. The forms *watery* and *wat'ry* actually occur in the same poem and the same scansion, and *watry* elsewhere. Milton prints *amorous* in a position where others print *am'rous;* Crashaw has *glistering* and *suffring,* and Vaughan *lingring* and *glimmering,* not only in the same poem, but within a few lines and in the same scansion. Such examples could be multipled a hundredfold; and the same applies to the indiscriminate use of *t'admire, to'admire, to admire,* and *th' empire, the' empire, the empire,* and so on. Such variation having no possible significance, I have printed the words in full where the ear cannot fail to indicate this partial elision; where at first sight the scansion might otherwise appear doubtful, the apostrophe has been retained. Again in the case of the auxiliaries, we find *w' are, we're,* and *we are* actually occurring in the same line of the repeated chorus of a poem; while *y' ave* and *you've, th' are* and *they're, th' art* (used also for 'the art') and *thou 'rt,* etc. jostle each other continually. Here I have printed the usage most agreeable to modern ears, giving, if it differs, the original reading in a footnote; but, in conclusion, it should be remarked that nowhere have I used any form lacking contemporary sanction.

Seventeenth Century Lyrics

Seventeenth Century Lyrics

GIPSY SONGS

I

The faery beam upon you,
The stars to glister on you;
 A moon of light
 In the noon of night,
Till the fire-drake hath o'ergone you!
The wheel of fortune guide you,
The boy with the bow beside you;
 Run aye in the way
 Till the bird of day,
And the luckier lot betide you!

II

To the old, long life and treasure,
To the young, all health and pleasure;
 To the fair, their face
 With eternal grace,
And the foul to be loved at leisure!
To the witty, all clear mirrors,
To the foolish, their dark errors;
 To the loving sprite,
 A secure delight;
To the jealous, his own false terrors!   *Jonson.*

The Metamorphosed Gipsies, in *Masques*, 1640. (Performed 1621.)

1

ON THE DEATH OF MARIE, COUNTESS OF PEMBROKE

Underneath this marble hearse
Lies the subject of all verse:
Sidney's sister, Pembroke's mother:
Death, ere thou hast killed another,
Fair, and learn'd, and good as she,
Time shall throw a dart at thee.

Marble piles let no man raise
To her name, for after days;
Some kind woman born as she
Reading this, like Niobe
Shall turn marble, and become
Both her mourner and her tomb.   *W. Browne.*

W. Camden's *Remains, Concerning Britain,* 1623. And Bodley MS. Ashm.
781.* (The Countess died 1621.)

THE BOUNTY OF OUR AGE

To see a strange outlandish fowl,
A quaint baboon, an ape, an owl,
A dancing bear, a giant's bone,
A foolish engine move alone,
A morris dance, a puppet-play,
Mad Tom to sing a roundelay,
A woman dancing on a rope,
Bull-baiting also at the *Hope,*
A rhymer's jests, a juggler's cheats,
A tumbler showing cunning feats,
Or players acting on the stage,—
There goes the bounty of our age:

marble hearse] 1623; sable hearse, MS.   piles] 1623; pillars, MS.

But unto any pious motion
There 's little coin and less devotion.   *Farley.*

St. Paul's Church, 1621.

SONNET OF BLACK BEAUTY

Black beauty, which above that common light,
    Whose power can no colours here renew
    But those which darkness can again subdue,
Dost still remain unvaried to the sight,
And like an object equal to the view,
    Art neither changed with day, nor hid with night;
    When all those colours which the world calls bright,
And which old poetry doth so pursue,
Are with the night so perishëd and gone
    That of their being there remains no mark,
Thou still abidest so entirely one,
    That we may know thy blackness is a spark
Of light inàccessible, and alone
    Our darkness which can make us think it dark.

                        Herbert of Cherbury.

B.M. Add. MS. 37157, (Autograph). (Printed in *Occasional Verses,* 1665.
Poem written 1621 ?)*

LOVE, WHAT ART THOU?

Love, what art thou?   A vain thought,
    In our minds by fancy wrought;
        Idle smiles did thee beget,
        While fond wishes made the net
Which so many fools has caught.

Dost] 1665;   Doth, MS.   has caught] E. Arber, 1899;   have caught, 1621.

Love, what art thou?   Light, and fair,
Fresh as morning, clear as the air:
    But too soon thy evening change
    Makes thy worth with coldness range;
Still thy joy is mixed with care.

Love, what art thou?   A secret flower,
Once full blown, dead in an hour.
    Dust in wind as staid remains
    As thy pleasure, or our gains,
If thy humour change to lour.

Love, what art thou?   Childish, vain,
Firm as bubbles made by rain;
    Wantonness thy greatest pride;
    These foul faults thy virtues hide;
But babes can no staidness gain.

Love, what art thou?   Causeless curst,
Yet, alas, these not the worst.
    Much more of thee may be said;
    But thy law I once obeyed,
Therefore say no more at first.   *Wroath.*

The Countess of Montgomery's Urania, 1621.

SONNET

If, of a wretched state and all forlorn,
That be the wretched'st, not at all to be—
Since in condemnèd prisoners we may see
Though they must die they 'd not not have been born,—
Then, by oblivion, to be slowly torn,
Or vexed with absence in extremity,

Or plagued with rage of restless jealousy,
These nothing are to not being loved, (a scorn).
He that 's forgotten, yet a being had;
He that is absent may return again;
He that is jealous may find constancy.
But still to follow shadows, love in vain,
Still to be hopeless (worse than to be mad),
That never was, is, or shall happy be.   *Digges.*

Gerado, 1622.

DEAREST, DO NOT YOU DELAY ME

Dearest, do not you delay me,
   Since, thou knowest, I must be gone;
Wind and tide, 'tis thought, doth stay me,
   But 'tis wind that must be blown
     From that breath, whose native smell
     Indian odours far excel.

Oh, then speak, thou fairest fair!
   Kill not him that vows to serve thee;
But perfume this neighbouring air,
   Else dull silence, sure, will starve me:
     'Tis a word that 's quickly spoken,
     Which being restrained, a heart is broken.

J. Fletcher(?)*

The Spanish Curate, in *Fifty Comedies and Tragedies*, 1679. (Licensed 1622.)

TO TIME

Time, I ever must complain
   Of thy craft and cruel cunning;
Seeming fixed here to remain,
   When thy feet are ever running;

And thy plumes
Still resumes
Courses new, repose most shunning.

Like calm winds thou passest by us;
Lined with feathers are thy feet:
Thy downy wings with silence fly us,
Like the shadows of the night;
Or the stream
That no beam
Of sharpest eye discerns to fleet.

Therefore mortals, all deluded
By thy grave and wrinkled face,
In their judgements have concluded
That thy slow and snail-like pace
Still doth bend
To no end
But to an eternal race.

Budding Youth's vain blooming wit
Thinks the spring shall ever last,
And the gaudy flowers that sit
On Flora's brow, shall never taste
Winter's scorn,
Nor, forlorn,
Bend their heads with chilling blast.

Riper Age expects to have
Harvests of his proper toil;
Times to give and to receive
Seeds and fruits from fertile soil:
But, at length,
Doth his strength,
Youth, and beauty, all recoil.

Cold December hope retains
That the spring, each thing reviving,
Shall throughout his aged veins
Pour fresh youth, past joys repriving:
But thy scythe
Ends his strife,
And to Lethe sends him driving.   *Hagthorpe.*

Divine Meditations, and Elegies, 1622.

SONG

Now do the birds in their warbling words
Welcome the year;
While sugared notes they chirrup through their throats,
To win a pheare:
Sweetly they breathe the wanton love
That Nature in them warms:
And each to gain a mate doth prove
With sweet enchanting charms.

He sweetly sings, and stays the nimble wings
Of her in the air,
She hovering stays, to hear his loving lays
Which woo her there:
She becomes willing, hears him woo,
Gives ear unto his song;
And doth as Nature taught her do,
Yields, sued unto not long.

But Celia stays, she feeds me with delays,
Hears not my moan:
She knows the smart in time will kill my heart

pheare] fere, mate.

To live alone:
Learn of the birds to choose thee a pheare,
    But not like them to range:
They have their mate but for a year,
    But, sweet, let 's never change.

The turtle-dove let 's imitate in love,
    That still loves one:
Dear, do not stay, youth quickly flies away,
    Then desire 's gone.
Love is kindest, and hath most length,
    The kisses are most sweet,
When it 's enjoyed in heat of strength,
    Where like affections meet.   *Hannay.*

The Nightingale, &c., 1622.*

A MAID ME LOVED

A maid me loved; her love I not respected;
She mourned, she sighed, nay, sued, yet I neglected:
Too late! too late! alas, I now repent,
For Cupid with her love hath me infected.

As erst he hers, so love my heart now burneth;
As I at her, she laughs at me that mourneth:
Too late! too late! alas, I now repent,
Since her disdainëd love to hatred turneth.

On her alone doth health and hope rely,
Yet still she scorns and doth me love deny:
Too late! too late! alas, I now repent,
Since she joys in my death, I for her die.   *Hannay.*

Ibid.

sighed] Saintsbury, 1905;   signed, 1622.

I WANDERED OUT

I wandered out, a while agone,
And went I know not whither;
But there do Beauties, many a one,
Resort, and meet together:
And Cupid's power will there be shown,
If ever you come thither.

For, like two suns, two Beauties bright
I shining saw together;
And, tempted by their double light,
My eyes I fixed on either;
Till both at once so thralled my sight,
I loved, and knew not whether.

Such equal sweet, Venus gave,
That I preferred not either;
And when for love I thought to crave,
I knew not well of whether:
For one while, this I wished to have;
And then I, that, had liefer.

A lover of the curious'st eye
Might have been pleased in either;
And so, I must confess, might I,
Had they not been together.
Now both must love, or both deny;
In one, enjoy I neither.

But yet at last I 'scaped the smart
I feared at coming thither:
For, seeing my divided heart,
I choosing, knew not whether,

whether] which.

Love angry grew, and did depart:
And now I care for neither.   *Wither.*

Fair Virtue, the Mistress of Phil'arete, 1622. *

A STOLEN KISS

Now gentle sleep hath closëd up those eyes
Which, waking, kept my boldest thoughts in awe;
And free access unto that sweet lip lies,
From whence I long the rosy breath to draw.
Methinks no wrong it were, if I should steal
From those two melting rubies one poor kiss;
None sees the theft that would the thief reveal,
Nor rob I her of aught which she can miss;
Nay, should I twenty kisses take away,
There would be little sign I had done so;
Why then should I this robbery delay?
Oh! she may wake, and therewith angry grow.
  Well, if she do, I 'll back restore that one,
  And twenty hundred thousand more for loan.

Ibid.
                                           Wither.

SILVY

On a time the amorous Silvy
Said to her shepherd, 'Sweet, how do you?
Kiss me this once, and then God b' wi' you,
                    My sweetest dear!
Kiss me this once and then God b' wi' you,
For now the morning draweth near.'

With that, her fairest bosom showing,
Opening her lips, rich perfumes blowing,

---

b' wi' you] b' wee you, 1622.

She said, 'Now kiss me and be going,
      My sweetest dear!
Kiss me this once and then be going,
For now the morning draweth near.'

With that the shepherd waked from sleeping,
And, spying where the day was peeping,
He said, 'Now take my soul in keeping,
      My sweetest dear!
Kiss me, and take my soul in keeping,
Since I must go, now day is near.'   *Anon.*

J. Attey's *The First Book of Airs*, 1622.

THE MISERY OF MAN

The life of man is full of grief and sorrow:
First at our birth we breathe, and next we mourn.
As day to night, and night succeeds to morrow,
Woe follows woe, to earth till we return.
  Euripides did well and wisely say
  Man's life and care are twins, and born one day.

The Poetical Recreations, 1623.   *Craig.*

A HYMN TO GOD THE FATHER

Wilt thou forgive that sin where I begun,
 Which was my sin, though it were done before?
Wilt thou forgive that sin, through which I run,
 And do run still, though still I do deplore?
  When thou hast done, thou hast not done,
    For I have more.

Wilt thou forgive that sin which I have won
 Others to sin, and made my sin their door?

Wilt thou forgive that sin which I did shun
   A year or two, but wallowed in, a score?
      When thou hast done, thou hast not done,
         For I have more.

I have a sin of fear, that when I have spun
   My last thread, I shall perish on the shore;
But swear by thyself, that at my death thy Son
   Shall shine, as he shines now and heretofore:
      And, having done that, thou hast done,
         I fear no more.   *Donne.*

Poems, 1633. (Poem written 1623.)*

SONNETS

Of this fair volume which we World do name,
If we the sheets and leaves could turn with care,
Of him who it corrects, and did it frame,
We clear might read the art and wisdom rare:
Find out his power which wildest powers doth tame,
His providence extending everywhere,
His justice which proud rebels doth not spare,
In every page, no, period of the same.
But silly we, like foolish children, rest
Well pleased with coloured vellum, leaves of gold,
Fair dangling ribbons, leaving what is best,
On the great Writer's sense ne'er taking hold;
   Or if by chance our minds do muse on aught,
   It is some picture on the margin wrought.

                                                      Drummond.

Flowers of Sion, 1623, and 1630.

our minds do muse] 1630;   we stay our minds, 1623.

Look how the flower which lingeringly doth fade,
The morning's darling late, the summer's queen,
Spoiled of that juice which kept it fresh and green,
As high as it did raise, bows low the head:
Right so my life, contentments being dead
Or in their còntraries but only seen,
With swifter speed declines than erst it spread,
And, blasted, scarce now shows what it hath been.
As doth the pilgrim therefore, whom the night
By darkness would imprison on his way,
Think on thy home, my soul, and think aright
Of what yet rests thee of life's wasting day;
    Thy sun posts westward, passëd is thy morn,
    And twice it is not given thee to be born.

Drummond.

Ibid.

THE DEAD HOST'S WELCOME

'Tis late and cold, stir up the fire;
Sit close, and draw the table nigher;
Be merry, and drink wine that 's old,
A hearty medicine 'gainst a cold.
Your bed 's of wanton down the best,
Where you shall tumble to your rest;
I could wish you wenches too,
But I am dead, and cannot do.
Call for the best, the house may ring,
Sack, white, and claret, let them bring,
And drink apace while breath you have;
You 'll find but cold drink in the grave.

As doth . . . therefore] 1630;   Therefore as doth the pilgrim, 1623.
By darkness would] 1630;   Hastes darkly to, 1623.

Plover, partridge, for your dinner,
And a capon for the sinner,
You shall find ready, when you are up,
And your horse shall have his sup:
   Welcome, welcome, shall fly round,
   And I shall smile, though under ground.

J. Fletcher.

The Lover's Progress, in *Comedies and Tragedies,* 1647. (Licensed 1623.)*

COME FOLLOW ME, YOU COUNTRY LASSES

Come follow me, you country lasses,
And you shall see such sport as passes:
You shall dance and I will sing;
Pedro, he shall rub the string;
Each shall have a loose-bodied gown
Of green, and laugh till you lie down.
    Come follow me, &c.

You shall have crowns of roses, daisies,
Buds where the honey-maker gazes;
You shall taste the golden thighs,
Such as in wax-chamber lies:
What fruit please you, taste, freely pull,
Till you have all your bellies full.
    Come follow me, &c.

J. Fletcher or W. Rowley.

The Maid in the Mill, in *Comedies and Tragedies,* 1647. (Licensed 1623.)*

TRIP IT, GIPSIES

Trip it, gipsies, trip it fine,
Show tricks and lofty capers;

Welcome, welcome] 1679; Welcome, 1647.

At threading-needles we repine,
   And leaping over rapiers:
Pindy-pandy rascal toys,
   We scorn cutting purses;
Though we live by making noise,
   For cheating none can curse us.

Over high ways, over low,
   And over stones and gravel,
Though we trip it on the toe,
   And thus for silver travel:
Though our dances waste our backs,
   At night fat capons mend them;
Eggs well brewed in buttered sack,
   Our wenches say befriend them.

Oh, that all the world were mad!
   Then should we have fine dancing;
Hobby-horses would be had,
   And brave girls keep a-prancing;
Beggars would on cock-horse ride,
   And boobies fall a-roaring;
And cuckolds, though no horns be spied,
   Be one another goring.

Welcome, poet, to our ging!
   Make rhymes, we 'll give thee reason,
Canary bees thy brains shall sting,
   Mull-sack did ne'er speak treason;
Peter-see-me shall wash thy nowl,
   And Malaga glasses fox thee;

---

threading-needles] Old game, a little like 'Oranges and Lemons.'
ging] company.   Peter-see-me] *Pedro Ximenes*, a Spanish wine.

If, poet, thou toss not bowl for bowl,
Thou shalt not kiss a doxy.

Middleton or *W. Rowley.*

The Spanish Gipsy, 1653. (Acted 1623.)*

TELL ME NO MORE

Tell me no more how fair she is;
  I have no mind to hear
The story of that distant bliss
  I never shall come near:
By sad experience I have found
That her perfection is my wound.

And tell me not how fond I am
  To tempt a daring fate,
From whence no triumph ever came,
  But to repent too late:
There is some hope ere long I may
In silence dote myself away.

I ask no pity, Love, from thee,
  Nor will thy justice blame,
So that thou wilt not envy me
  The glory of my flame,
Which crowns my heart whene'er it dies
In that it falls her sacrifice.   *H. King.*

Poems, Elegies, Paradoxes, and Sonnets, 1657. (Poem written before 1624?)*

GO THOU, THAT VAINLY DOST MINE EYES INVITE

Go thou, that vainly dost mine eyes invite
To taste the softer comforts of the night,

And bid'st me cool the fever of my brain
In those sweet balmy dews which slumber pain;
Enjoy thine own peace in untroubled sleep,
Whilst my sad thoughts eternal vigils keep.

Oh, couldst thou for a time change breasts with me,
Thou in that broken glass shouldst plainly see
A heart, which wastes in the slow smothering fire
Blown by despair and fed by false desire,
Can only reap such sleeps as seamen have
When fierce winds rock them on the foaming wave.

H. King.

Ibid.

LIVE WITH ME STILL

Live with me still, and all the measures
    Played to by the spheres I 'll teach thee;
Let 's but thus dally, all the pleasures
    The moon beholds, her man shall reach thee.

Dwell in mine arms, aloft we 'll hover,
    And see fields of armies fighting:
Oh, part not from me!   I will discover
    There all but books of fancy's writing.

Be but my darling, age to free thee
    From her curse, shall fall a-dying;
Call me thy empress, Time to see thee
    Shall forget his art of flying.   *Dekker(?)*

The Sun's Darling, 1656. By Ford and Dekker. (Licensed 1624.)

thy empress] Mod. eds.;   their empress, 1656.

TO THE BLEST EVANTHE

Let those complain that feel Love's cruelty,
    And in sad legends write their woes;
With roses gently 'has corrected me,
    My war is without rage or blows:
My mistress' eyes shine fair on my desires,
And hope springs up inflamed with her new fires.

No more an exile will I dwell,
    With folded arms, and sighs all day,
Reckoning the torments of my hell,
    And flinging my sweet joys away:
I am called home again to quiet peace,
My mistress smiles, and all my sorrows cease.

Yet, what is living in her eye,
    Or being blessed with her sweet tongue,
If these no other joys imply?
    A golden gyve, a pleasing wrong:
To be your own but one poor month, I 'd give
My youth, my fortune, and then leave to live.

J. Fletcher.
A Wife for a Month, in *Comedies and Tragedies*, 1647. (Licensed 1624.)*

DROP GOLDEN SHOWERS, GENTLE SLEEP

Drop golden showers, gentle sleep;
And all the angels of the night,
Which do us in protection keep,
Make this queen dream of delight.
Morpheus, be kind a while, and be
Death's now true image, for 'twill prove

feel] 1679; feels, 1647.   'has] *i.e.* he has.   her eye] 1679; her eyes, 1647.

To her that sleeps here thou art he.
Her grave is made i' the bed of love:
Now when she looks her lord should come
She 's dreaming sent to Elysium.
Her marriage night she well may call
No wedding but a funeral.   *Goffe.*

Christ Church MS. 87, (dated 1624.) (Variant in *The Courageous Turk*, 1632.)*

CHORUS IN A MASQUE

Spring all the Graces of the age,
    And all the Loves of time;
Bring all the pleasures of the stage,
    And relishes of rhyme;
Add all the softnesses of courts,
The looks, the laughters, and the sports:
And mingle all their sweets and salts
That none may say, the Triumph halts.   *Jonson.*

Neptune's Triumph, in *Masques*, 1640. (Performed 1624.)

THE EXEQUY

Accept, thou shrine of my dead saint,
Instead of dirges this complaint;
And for sweet flowers to crown thy hearse,
Receive a strew of weeping verse
From thy grieved friend, whom thou might'st see
Quite melted into tears for thee.

    Dear loss! since thy untimely fate
My task hath been to meditate
On thee, on thee: thou art the book,
The library whereon I look,

Though almost blind.   For thee, loved clay,
I languish out, not live, the day,
Using no other exercise
But what I practise with mine eyes:
By which wet glasses I find out
How lazily time creeps about
To one that mourns; this, only this
My exercise and business is:
So I compute the weary hours
With sighs dissolvëd into showers.

   Nor wonder if my time go thus
Backward and most preposterous;
Thou hast benighted me, thy set
This eve of blackness did beget,
Who wast my day (though overcast
Before thou hadst thy noontide past),
And I remember must in tears,
Thou scarce hadst seen so many years
As day tells hours.   By thy clear sun
My love and fortune first did run;
But thou wilt never more appear
Folded within my hemisphere,
Since both thy light and motïon,
Like a fled star, is fall'n and gone,
And 'twixt me and my soul's dear wish
The earth now interposëd is,
Which such a strange eclipse doth make
As ne'er was read in almanake.

   I could allow thee for a time
To darken me and my sad clime;
Were it a month, a year, or ten,

I would thy exile live till then;
And all that space my mirth adjourn,
So thou wouldst promise to return;
And putting off thy ashy shroud
At length disperse this sorrow's cloud.

But woe is me! the longest date
Too narrow is to calculate
These empty hopes: never shall I
Be so much blessed as to descry
A glimpse of thee, till that day come
Which shall the earth to cinders doom,
And a fierce fever must calcine
The body of this world like thine,
My little World! That fit of fire
Once off, our bodies shall aspire
To our souls' bliss: then we shall rise,
And view ourselves with clearer eyes
In that calm region, where no night
Can hide us from each other's sight.

Meantime, thou hast her, earth: much good
May my harm do thee.   Since it stood
With Heaven's will I might not call
Her longer mine, I give thee all
My short-lived right and interest
In her, whom living I loved best:
With a most free and bounteous grief,
I give thee what I could not keep.
Be kind to her, and prithee look
Thou write into thy Doomsday book
Each parcel of this rarity
Which in thy casket shrined doth lie:

See that thou make thy reckoning straight,
And yield her back again by weight;
For thou must audit on thy trust
Each grain and atom of this dust,
As thou wilt answer him that lent,
Not gave thee, my dear Monument.

So close the ground, and 'bout her shade
Black curtains draw, my bride is laid.

Sleep on, my Love, in thy cold bed
Never to be disquieted!
My last good night!   Thou wilt not wake
Till I thy fate shall overtake:
Till age, or grief, or sickness must
Marry my body to that dust
It so much loves; and fill the room
My heart keeps empty in thy tomb.
Stay for me there; I will not fail
To meet thee in that hollow Vale.
And think not much of my delay;
I am already on the way,
And follow thee with all the speed
Desire can make, or sorrows breed.
Each minute is a short degree,
And every hour a step towards thee.
At night when I betake to rest,
Next morn I rise nearer my west
Of life, almost by eight hours' sail,
Than when sleep breathed his drowsy gale.

Thus from the sun my bottom steers,
And my day's compass downward bears:

hollow] Bod. MSS. Ashm. 36–7, & Mal. 22;   hallow, 1657.

Nor labour I to stem the tide,
Through which to thee I swiftly glide.

'Tis true, with shame and grief I yield,
Thou, like the van, first took'st the field,
And gotten hast the victory
In thus adventuring to die
Before me, whose more years might crave
A just precèdence in the grave.
But hark! my pulse like a soft drum
Beats my approach, tells thee I come;
And slow howe'er my marches be,
I shall at last sit down by thee.

The thought of this bids me go on,
And wait my dissolutïon
With hope and comfort. Dear (forgive
The crime) I am content to live
Divided, with but half a heart,
Till we shall meet and never part.   *H. King.*

Poems, Elegies, Paradoxes, and Sonnets, 1657. (Poem written c. 1624.)*

AS LIFE WHAT IS SO SWEET

As life what is so sweet,
What creature would not choose thee?
The wounded hart doth weep
When he is forced to lose thee:
The bruisëd worm doth strive 'gainst fear of death,
And all choose life with pain ere loss of breath.

The dove which knows no guilt
Weeps for her mate a-dying;
And never any blood was spilt

But left the loser crying:
If swans do sing, it is to crave of death
He would not reave them of their happy breath.

Anon.

B.M. MS. Harl. 6917. (Poem written c. 1624 ?)*

A PROPER NEW BALLAD, ENTITLED THE FAIRIES'
FAREWELL OR GOD-A-MERCY WILL; TO BE SUNG
OR WHISTLED TO THE TUNE OF THE MEADOW
BROW BY THE LEARNED; BY THE UNLEARNED,
TO THE TUNE OF FORTUNE

Farewell, rewards and fairies,
    Good housewives now may say,
For now foul sluts in dairies
    Do fare as well as they;
And though they sweep their hearths no less
    Than maids were wont to do,
Yet who of late for cleanliness
    Finds sixpence in her shoe?

Lament, lament old abbeys,
    The fairies lost command,
They did but change priests' babies,
    But some have changed your land;
And all your children stol'n from thence
    Are now grown puritanes
Who live as changelings ever since
    For love of your demaines.

At morning and at evening both,
    You merry were and glad;
So little care of sleep and sloth

These pretty ladies had;
When Tom came home from labour,
    Or Ciss to milking rose,
Then merrily went their tabor,
    And nimbly went their toes.

Witness those rings and roundelays
    Of theirs which yet remain,
Were footed in Queen Mary's days
    On many a grassy plain.
But since of late Elizabeth
    And later James came in,
They never danced on any heath
    As when the time had been.

By which we note the fairies
    Were of the old profession,
Their songs were *Ave Maries*,
    Their dances were procession;
But now, alas, they all are dead
    Or gone beyond the seas,
Or further from religion fled,
    Or else they take their ease.

A tell-tale in their company
    They never could endure,
And whoso kept not secretly
    Their mirth, was punished sure.
It was a just and Christian deed
    To pinch such black and blue;
Oh, how the commonwealth doth need
    Such justices as you!

Now they have left our quarters,
　　A register they have,
Who can preserve their charters,
　　A man both wise and grave.
A hundred of their merry pranks,
　　By one that I could name
Are kept in store; con twenty thanks
　　To William for the same.

I marvel who his cloak would turn
　　When Puck had led him round,
Or where those walking fires would burn
　　Where Cureton would be found;
How Broker would appear to be,
　　For whom this age doth mourn,
But that their spirits live in thee—
　　In thee, old William Churne.

To William Churne of Staffordshire
　　Give laud and praises due;
Who every meal can mend your cheer
　　With tales both old and true.
To William all give audience,
　　And pray you for his noddle;
For all the fairies' evidence
　　Were lost if it were addle.   *Corbet.*

Certain Elegant Poems, 1647. (With stz. 8 from *Poetica Stromata*, 1648. Poem
written before 1625.)*

BEAUTY CLEAR AND FAIR

Beauty clear and fair,
　　Where the air
Rather like a perfume dwells;

Where the violet and the rose
Their blue veins and blush disclose,
And come to honour nothing else;

Where to live near,
    And planted there,
Is to live, and still live new;
    Where to gain a favour is
    More than light, perpetual bliss,—
Make me live by serving you.

Dear, again back recall
    To this light,
A stranger to himself and all;
    Both the wonder and the story
    Shall be yours, and eke the glory:
I am your servant, and your thrall.   *J. Fletcher.*

The Elder Brother, 1637. (Written before 1625.)*

PRAYER TO VENUS

O Divinest Star of heaven!
Thou in power above the seven;
Thou sweet kindler of desires
Till they grow to mutual fires;
Thou, O gentle Queen, that art
Curer of each wounded heart;
Thou the fuel and the flame;
Thou, in heaven and here, the same;

---

veins and] B.M. Eg. MS. 1994; veins in, 1637 and 1679.   O Divinest]
Seward, 1750; O Divine, 1647.

Thou the wooer and the wooed;
Thou the hunger and the food;
Thou the prayër and the prayed;
Thou what is, or shall be, said;
Thou still young and golden tressëd,—
Make me by thy answer blessëd.   *J. Fletcher.*

The Mad Lover, in *Comedies and Tragedies,* 1647. (Written before 1625.)

HENCE, ALL YOU VAIN DELIGHTS

Hence, all you vain delights,
As short as are the nights
    Wherein you spend your folly!
There 's nought in this life sweet,
If man were wise to see 't,
    But only melancholy,
    Oh, sweetest melancholy!
Welcome, folded arms, and fixëd eyes,
A sigh that piercing mortifies,
A look that 's fastened to the ground,
A tongue chained up without a sound!
Fountain-heads, and pathless groves,
Places which pale passion loves;
Moonlight walks, when all the fowls
Are warmly housed, save bats and owls;
    A midnight bell, a parting groan,
    These are the sounds we feed upon;
Then stretch our bones in a still gloomy valley,
Nothing 's so dainty sweet as lovely melancholy.
                              J. Fletcher or *Strode.*

The Nice Valour, in *Comedies and Tragedies,* 1647. (Written before 1625 ?) *

sigh] 1647 and 1679;   sight, in several MSS.

LOVE WILL FIND OUT THE WAY

Over the mountains
  And under the waves,
Over the fountains
  And under the graves;
Over floods which are the deepest,
  Which do Neptune obey,
Over rocks which are the steepest
  Love will find out the way.

Where there is no place
  For the glow-worm to lie;
Where there is no space
  For the receipt of a fly;
Where the gnat she dares not venter,
  Lest herself fast she lay;
But if Love come, he will enter
  And will find out the way.

You may esteem him
  A child by his force;
Or you may deem him
  A coward, which is worse;
But if she whom Love doth honour
  Be concealed from the day,
Set a thousand guards upon her,
  Love will find out the way.

Some think to lose him,
  Which is too unkind;
And some do suppose him,
  Poor heart! to be blind;

---

if she] 1666; if he, Roxb.   upon her] 1666; upon him, Roxb.

If that he were hidden,
  Do the best that you may,
Blind Love, if so you call him,
  Will find out the way.

Well may the eagle
  Stoop down to the fist;
Or you may inveigle
  The phoenix of the east;
With fear the tiger 's movëd
  To give over his prey;
But never stop a lover,
  He will post on his way.

If the earth should part him,
  He would gallop it o'er;
If the seas should o'erthwart him,
  He would swim to the shore.
Should his love become a swallow,
  Through the air to stray,
Love would lend wings to follow,
  And will find out the way.

There is no striving
  To cross his intent,
There is no contriving
  His plots to prevent;
But if once the message greet him,
  That his true love doth stay,
If death should come and meet him,
  Love will find out the way.   *Anon.*

B.M. Roxb. Coll. I. 426–7. (Also J. Forbes' *Songs and Fancies*, 1666. Poem written c. 1625 ?)*

CAROL

All this night shrill chanticler,
Day's proclaiming trumpeter,
Claps his wings and loudly cries:
'Mortals! mortals! wake and rise!
        See a wonder,
        Heaven is under;
From the earth is risse a sun
Shines all night, though day be done.

'Wake, O earth! wake, every thing!
Wake and hear the joy I bring;
Wake and joy, for all this night
Heaven and every twinkling light
        All amazing
        Still stand gazing;
Angels, powers, and all that be,
Wake, and joy this sun to see.'

Hail, O sun! O blessèd light
Sent into the world by night!
Let thy rays and heavenly powers
Shine in this dark soul of ours,
        For most duly
        Thou art truly
God and man, we do confess:
Hail, O Sun of Righteousness!   *Austin.*

Certain Divine Hymns or Carols, 1626, in Bodley MS. Rawl. Poet. 61.*

SEE'ST NOT, MY LOVE

See'st not, my Love, with what a grace
The spring resembles thy sweet face?

---

risse] risen.

Here let us sit, and in these bowers
Receive the odours of the flowers,
For Flora, by thy beauty wooed, conspires thy good.

See how she sends her fragrant sweet,
And doth this homage to thy feet,
Bending so low her stooping head
To kiss the ground where thou dost tread,
And all her flowers proudly meet, to kiss thy feet.

Then let us walk, my dearest Love,
And on this carpet strictly prove
Each other's vow; from thy request
No other love invades my breast:
For how can I contemn that fire which gods admire?

To crop that rose why dost thou seek,
When there's a purer in thy cheek?
Like coral held in thy fair hands,
Or blood and milk that mingled stands:
To whom the powers all grace have given, a type of
                                            [Heaven.

Yon lily, stooping t'wards this place,
Is a pale shadow for thy face,
Under which veil doth seem to rush
Modest Endymion's ruddy blush:
A blush, indeed, more pure and fair than lilies are.

Glance on those flowers thy radiant eyes,
Through which clear beams they'll sympathise
Reflective love, to make them far
More glorious than the Hesperian star,
For every swain amazèd lies, and gazing dies.

See how these silly flowers twine
With sweet embracings, and combine,
Striving with curious looms to set
Their pale and red into a net,
To show how pure desire doth rest for ever blessed.

Why wilt thou then unconstant be
To infringe the laws of amity,
And so much disrespect my heart
To derogate from what thou art,
When in harmonious love there is Elysian bliss?

Bosworth.

The Chaste and Lost Lovers, 1651. (Written c. 1626.)

NOT HE THAT KNOWS

Not he that knows how to acquire,
    But to enjoy, is blessed.
Nor does our happiness consist
    In motion, but in rest.

The gods pass man in bliss, because
    They toil not for more height,
But can enjoy, and in their own
    Eternal rest delight.

Then, princes, do not toil, nor care;
    Enjoy what you possess;
Which whilst you do, you equalise
    The gods in happiness.

May.

The Tragedy of Cleopatra, 1639. (Acted 1626.)

OF MY DEAR SON, GERVASE BEAUMONT

Can I, who have for others oft compiled
The songs of death, forget my sweetest child,
Which, like a flower crushed, with a blast is dead,
And ere full time hangs down his smiling head,
Expecting with clear hope to live anew,
Among the angels fed with heavenly dew?
We have this sign of joy, that many days,
While on the earth his struggling spirit stays,
The name of Jesus in his mouth contains
His only food, his sleep, his ease from pains.
O may that sound be rooted in my mind,
Of which in him such strong effect I find!
Dear Lord, receive my son, whose winning love
To me was like a friendship, far above
The course of nature, or his tender age;
Whose looks could all my bitter griefs assuage:
Let his pure soul, ordained seven years to be
In that frail body which was part of me,
Remain my pledge in heaven, as sent to show
How to this port at every step I go.   *Sir J. Beaumont.*

Bosworth Field, 1629. (Written before 1627.)

A WELL-WISHING TO A PLACE OF PLEASURE

See that building, which, when my mistress living,
    Was pleasure's essence;
See how it droopeth, and how nakedly it looketh
    Without her presence;
Hark how the hollow wind doth blow
    And seems to murmur
    In every corner

For her being absent, from which doth chiefly grow
The cause that I do now this grief and sorrow show.

See that garden, where oft I had reward in
          For my true love;
See the places, where I enjoyed those graces
          The gods might move;
Oft in that arbour, while that she
          With melting kisses
          Distilling blisses
From her free lips, for joy did ravish me,
The pretty nightingale did sing melodiously.

Hail to those groves, where we enjoyed our loves
          So many days!
May trees there be springing and the pretty birds be singing
          Their roundelays.
Oh! may the grass grow ever green
          On which we lying
          Have oft been trying
More several ways of pleasure than that queen,
Which once in bed with Mars by all the gods was seen.

Anon.

B.M. Add. MS. 24665. (Poem written before 1627.)*

ART THOU THAT SHE

'Art thou that she than whom none fairer is,
Art thou that she desire so strives to kiss?'
          'Say I am: how then?
          Maids may not kiss
          Such wanton-humoured men.'

'Art thou that she the world commends for wit?
Art thou so wise and mak'st no use of it?'

> 'Say I am: how then?
> My wit doth teach me shun
> Such foolish foolish men.'   *Anon.*

Christ Church MS. 439. (Poem written before 1627.)*

THE HUNTER'S SONG

Long ere the morn
Expects the return
Of Apollo from the ocean queen,
Before the creak
Of the crow, and the break
Of the day in the welkin is seen,
Mounted he 'd hollo
And cheerfully follow
To the chase with his bugle clear:
Echo he makes
And the mountains shakes
With the thunder of his career.

Now bonny Bay
In his foam waxeth grey,
Dapple Grey waxeth bay in his blood;
White Lily stops
With the scent in her chops,
And Black Lady makes it good.
Poor silly Wat
In this wretched state
Forgets these delights for to hear;
Nimbly she bounds
From the cry of the hounds
And the music of their career.

Wat] name given to the hare.

Hills with the heat
Of the gallopers sweat,
Reviving their frozen tops;
Dales' purple flowers
They spring from the showers
That down from the rowels drops:
Swains their repast,
And strangers their haste
Neglect when the horns they do hear;
To see a fleet
Pack of hounds in a sheet,
And the hunter in his career.

Thus he careers
Over moors, over meres,
Over deeps, over downs, over clay,
Till he hath won
The noon from the morn,
And the evening from the day:
His sport then he ends,
And joyfully wends
Home again to his cottage, where
Frankly he feasts
Himself and his guests,
And carouses to his career.   *Basse.*

Sportive Wit, 1656. (And in Bodley MS. Rawl. Poet. 246. Poem written
c. 1627 ?)*

SIRENA

Near to the silver Trent
Sirena dwelleth;
She to whom Nature lent
All that excelleth;

By which the Muses late
   And the neat Graces
Have for their greater state
   Taken their places,
Twisting an anadem
   Wherewith to crown her,
As it belonged to them
   Most to renown her.
      On thy bank,
      In a rank,
      Let thy swans sing her,
      And with their music
      Along let them bring her.

Tagus and Pactolus
   Are to thee debtor,
Nor for their gold to us
   Are they the better:
Henceforth of all the rest
   Be thou the river
Which, as the daintiest,
   Puts them down ever:
For as my precious one
   O'er thee doth travel,
She to pearl paragon
   Turneth thy gravel.
      On thy bank, &c.

Our mournful Philomel,
   That rarest tuner,
Henceforth in Aperil
   Shall wake the sooner,
And to her shall complain
   From the thick cover,

Redoubling every strain
    Over and over:
For when my Love too long
    Her chamber keepeth,
As though it suffered wrong,
    The morning weepeth.
            On thy bank, &c.

Oft have I seen the sun,
    To do her honour,
Fix himself at his noon
    To look upon her;
And hath gilt every grove,
    Every hill near her,
With his flames from above
    Striving to cheer her;
And when she from his sight
    Hath herself turnéd,
He, as it had been night,
    In clouds hath mournéd.
            On thy bank, &c.

The verdant meads are seen,
    When she doth view them,
In fresh and gallant green
    Straight to renew them;
And every little grass
    Broad itself spreadeth,
Proud that this bonny lass
    Upon it treadeth;
Nor flower is so sweet
    In this large cincture,
But it upon her feet
    Leaveth some tincture.
            On thy bank, &c.

The fishes in the flood,
  When she doth angle,
For the hook strive a-good
  Them to entangle,
And leaping on the land
  From the clear water,
Their scales upon the sand
  Lavishly scatter,
Therewith to pave the mould
  Whereon she passes,
So herself to behold
  As in her glasses.
    On thy bank, &c.

When she looks out by night
  The stars stand gazing,
Like comets to our sight
  Fearfully blazing,
As wondering at her eyes
  With their much brightness,
Which so amaze the skies,
  Dimming their lightness.
The raging tempests are calm
  When she speaketh,
Such most delightful balm
  From her lips breaketh.
    On thy bank, &c.

In all our Brittany
  There 's not a fairer,
Nor can you fit any
  Should you compare her:
Angels her eyelids keep,

All hearts surprising,
　Which look, whilst she doth sleep,
　　Like the sun's rising:
She alone of her kind
　Knoweth true measure,
And her unmatchëd mind
　Is heaven's treasure.
　　　　On thy bank, &c.

Fair Dove and Darwen clear,
　Boast ye your beauties,
To Trent your mistress here
　Yet pay your duties:
My Love was higher born
　Towards the full fountains,
Yet she doth moorland scorn
　And the Peak mountains;
Nor would she none should dream
　Where she abideth,
Humble as is the stream
　Which by her slideth.
　　　　On thy bank, &c.

Yet my poor rustic Muse
　Nothing can move her,
Nor the means I can use,
　Though her true lover:
Many a long winter's night
　Have I waked for her,
Yet this my piteous plight
　Nothing can stir her:
All thy sands, silver Trent,
　Down to the Humber,

The sighs that I have spent
      Never can number.
          On thy bank,
          In a rank,
          Let thy swans sing her,
          And with their music
              Along let them bring her.   *Drayton.*

The Battle of Agincourt, &c., 1627.

MAN'S MORTALITY

Like as the damask rose you see,
Or like the blossom on the tree,
Or like the dainty flower of May,
Or like the morning to the day,
Or like the sun, or like the shade,
Or like the gourd which Jonas had—
Even such is man, whose thread is spun,
Drawn out, and cut, and so is done.
The rose withers, the blossom blasteth,
The flower fades, the morning hasteth,
The sun sets, the shadow flies,
The gourd consumes; and man he dies.

Like to the grass that 's newly sprung,
Or like a tale that 's new begun,
Or like the bird that 's here to-day,
Or like the pearlèd dew of May,
Or like an hour, or like a span,
Or like the singing of a swan—
Even such is man, who lives by breath,
Is here, now there: so life, and death.
The grass withers, the tale is ended,

The bird is flown, the dew 's ascended,
The hour is short, the span not long,
The swan 's near death; man's life is done.

Like to the bubble in the brook,
Or, in a glass, much like a look,
Or like a shuttle in weaver's hand,
Or like a writing on the sand,
Or like a thought, or like a dream,
Or like the gliding of the stream—
Even such is man, who lives by breath,
Is here, now there: so life, and death.
The bubble 's cut, the look 's forgot,
The shuttle 's flung, the writing 's blot,
The thought is past, the dream is gone,
The water glides; man's life is done.

Like to an arrow from the bow,
Or like swift course of watery flow,
Or like the time 'twixt flood and ebb,
Or like the spider's tender web,
Or like a race, or like a goal,
Or like the dealing of a dole—
Even such is man, whose brittle state
Is always subject unto fate.
The arrow 's shot, the flood soon spent,
The time no time, the web soon rent,
The race soon run, the goal soon won,
The dole soon dealt; man's life first done.

Like to the lightning from the sky,
Or like a post that quick doth hie,
Or like a quaver in short song,
Or like a journey three days long,

Or like the snow when summer 's come,
Or like the pear, or like the plum—
Even such is man, who heaps up sorrow,
Lives but this day and dies to-morrow.
The lightning 's past, the post must go,
The song is short, the journey 's so,
The pear doth rot, the plum doth fall,
The snow dissolves, and so must all.   *Anon.*

M. Sparke's *The Crumbs of Comfort*, 1628. (Poem written before 1628.)*

THE AUTHOR'S ABSTRACT OF MELANCHOLY

When I go musing all alone,
Thinking of divers things foreknown,
When I build castles in the air,
Void of sorrow and void of fear,
Pleasing myself with phantasms sweet,
Methinks the time runs very fleet.
    All my joys to this are folly,
    Naught so sweet as melancholy.

When I lie waking all alone,
Recounting what I have ill done,
My thoughts on me then tyrannize,
Fear and sorrow me surprise;
Whether I tarry still or go,
Methinks the time moves very slow,
    All my griefs to this are jolly,
    Naught so sad as melancholy.

When to myself I act and smile,
With pleasing thoughts the time beguile,
By a brook side, or wood so green,
Unheard, unsought for, or unseen,

A thousand pleasures do me bless,
And crown my soul with happiness.
 All my joys besides are folly,
 None so sweet as melancholy.

When I lie, sit, or walk alone,
I sigh, I grieve, making great moan,
In a dark grove, or irksome den,
With discontents and Furies then,
A thousand miseries at once,
Mine heavy heart and soul ensconce.
 All my griefs to this are jolly,
 None so sour as melancholy.

Methinks I hear, methinks I see,
Sweet music, wondrous melody,
Towns, palaces, and cities fine,
Here now, then there: the world is mine,
Rare beauties, gallant ladies, shine,
Whate'er is lovely or divine.
 All other joys to this are folly,
 None so sweet as melancholy.

Methinks I hear, methinks I see,
Ghosts, goblins, fiends; my phantasy
Presents a thousand ugly shapes,
Headless bears, black men, and apes;
Doleful outcries and fearful sights,
My sad and dismal soul affrights.
 All my griefs to this are jolly,
 None so damned as melancholy.

---

palaces] 1628;   places, 1632 and 1638.

Methinks I court, methinks I kiss,
Methinks I now embrace my mistris:
O blessëd days!   O sweet content!
In Paradise my time is spent;
Such thoughts may still my fancy move,
So may I ever be in love.
     All my joys to this are folly,
      Naught so sweet as melancholy.

When I recount love's many frights,
My sighs and tears, my waking nights,
My jealous fits; O mine hard fate!
I now repent, but 'tis too late.
No torment is so bad as love,
So bitter to my soul can prove.
     All my griefs to this are jolly,
      Naught so harsh as melancholy.

Friends and companions, get you gone!
'Tis my desire to be alone:
Ne'er well but when my thoughts and I
Do domineer in privacy.
No gem, no treasure, like to this;
'Tis my delight, my crown, my bliss.
     All my joys to this are folly,
      Naught so sweet as melancholy.

'Tis my sole plague to be alone,
I am a beast, a monster grown,
I will no light, nor company,
I find it now my misery.
The scene is turned; my joys are gone;
Fear, discontent, and sorrows come.

All my griefs to this are jolly,
Naught so fierce as melancholy.

I 'll not change life with any king;
I ravished am: can the world bring
More joy than still to laugh and smile,
In pleasant toys time to beguile?
Do not, oh, do not trouble me!
So sweet content I feel and see.
    All my joys to this are folly,
    None so divine as melancholy.

I 'll change my state with any wretch
Thou canst from jail or dunghill fetch:
My pain past cure, another Hell,
I may not in this torment dwell;
Now desperate, I hate my life,
Lend me a halter, or a knife.
    All my griefs to this are jolly,
    Naught so damned as melancholy.   *Burton.*

The *Anatomy of Melancholy*, 5th Ed., 1638. (Poem first printed, 3rd Ed., 1628.) *

FLY HENCE, SHADOWS

Fly hence, shadows, that do keep
Watchful sorrows charmed in sleep!
Though the eyes be overtaken,
Yet the heart doth ever waken
Thoughts, chained up in busy snares
Of continual woes and cares:
Love and griefs are so expressed
As they rather sigh than rest.

Fly hence, shadows, that do keep
Watchful sorrows charmed in sleep!   *J. Ford.*

The Lover's Melancholy, 1629. (Licensed 1628.)*

LOVE, A THOUSAND SWEETS DISTILLING

Love, a thousand sweets distilling,
And with pleasure bosoms filling,
Charm all eyes that none may find us,
Be above, before, behind us;
And, while we thy raptures taste,
    Compel time itself to stay,
Or by forelock hold him fast
    Lest occasion slip away.   *Shirley.*

The Witty Fair One, 1633. (Text 1646. Licensed 1628.)*

IN PRAISE OF ALE

When that the chill Charocco blows
    And winter tells a heavy tale,
When pies and daws and rooks and crows
Do sit and curse in frost and snows,
        Then give me ale.

Ale in a Saxon rumkin then,
    Such as will make grimalkin prate,
Bids valour burgeon in tall men,
Quickens the poet's wit and pen,
        Despises fate.

Ale, that the absent battle fights,
    And scorns the march of Swedish drum;

Disputes of princes, laws and rights;
What 's done and past tells mortal wights,
     And what 's to come.

Ale, that the ploughman's heart up keeps
    And equals it to tyrants' thrones;
That wipes the eye that fain would weep,
And lulls in sweet and dainty sleep
     The o'erwearied bones.

Grandchild of Ceres, barley's daughter,
    Wine's emulous neighbour if but stale,
Ennobling all the nymphs of water
And filling each man's mouth with laughter—
     Oh, give me ale!   *Bonham.*

The Academy of Compliments, 1650. (Poem written before 1629 ?)*

CELIA IS GONE

Celia is gone, and now sit I
    As Philomela on a thorn,
Turned out of Nature's livery,
    Mirthless, alone, and all forlorn;
Only she sings not, while my sorrows can
Afford such notes as fit a dying swan.

So shuts the marigold her leaves
    At the departure of the sun;
So from the honeysuckle sheaves
    The bee goes when the day is done;

So sits the turtle when she is but one,
So is all woe, as I, now she is gone.

   To some few birds, kind Nature hath
     Made all the summer as one day;
   Which once enjoyed, cold winter's wrath
     As night they sleeping pass away.
Those happy creatures are, that know not yet
The pains to be deprived or to forget.

   I oft have heard men say there be
     Some, that with confidence profess
   The helpful art of memory;
     But could they teach forgetfulness,
I 'd learn, and try what further art could do
To make me love her and forget her too.

   Sad melancholy, that persuades
     Men from themselves to think they be
   Headless or other bodies' shades,
     Hath long and bootless dwelt with me;
For could I think she some idea were,
I still might love, forget, and have her here.

   But such she is not: nor would I,
     For twice as many torments more,
   As her bereavëd company
     Hath brought to those I felt before;
For then no future time might hap to know
That she deserved, or I did love her so.

   Ye hours then but as minutes be,
     (Though so I shall be sooner old,)
   Till I those lovely graces see

Which but in her can none behold!
Then be an age that we may never try
More grief in parting, but grow old and die.

W. Browne.

B.M. Lansd. MS. 777. (Poem written before 1629 ?)*

LOVE WHO WILL

Love who will, for I 'll love none,
    There 's fools enough besides me:
Yet if each woman have not one,
    Come to me where I hide me,
And if she can the place attain,
For once I 'll be her fool again.

It is an easy place to find,
    And women sure should know it;
Yet thither serves not every wind,
    Nor many men can show it:
It is the storehouse, where doth lie
All women's truth and constancy.

If the journey be so long,
    No woman will adventer;
But dreading her weak vessel's wrong,
    The voyage will not enter:
Then may she sigh and lie alone,
In love with all, yet loved of none.   *W. Browne.*

Ibid.

A VISION

A rose, as fair as ever saw the north,
Grew in a little garden all alone;
A sweeter flower did Nature ne'er put forth,

Nor fairer garden yet was never known:
The maidens danced about it morn and noon,
And learned bards of it their ditties made;
The nimble fairies by the pale-faced moon
Watered the root and kissed her pretty shade.
But well-a-day, the gardener careless grew;
The maids and fairies both were kept away,
And in a drought the caterpillars threw
Themselves upon the bud and every spray.
    God shield the stock! if heaven send no supplies
    The fairest blossom of the garden dies.

W. Browne.

B.M. Lansd. MS. 777. (Poem written before 1629?)

TO CHLORIS

Fairer than the rosy east,
Sweeter than the phoenix' nest,
Lovelier than the starry sky,
Milder than heaven's lesser eye,
Gentler than the silver dove—
Why should I then fear to love?

Lively as the nimble roe,
Quick as arrow from the bow,
Clasping as the fruitful vine,
Breathing sweet as eglantine,
Billing like the gall-less dove—
How can I forbear to love?

Soft as is the beaver's down,
Cheering like the springing sun,
Tasting like the honey dew,
Lasting as the firmest yew,

Wanton as the Cyprian dove—
Heaven let me enjoy her love.
Moving like the western wind,
Pleasing as the gold refined,
Rising strongly as the want,
Tractive as the adamant,
Languishing like turtle dove—
Heaven it is to have her love.   *Cobbes.*

Bodley MS. Rawl. Poet. 166. (Written before 1629.) *

Milton's *Ode on the Nativity* (*Poems*, 1645) was written 1629.

PHYLLIS INAMORATA

Come, be my valentine!
I 'll gather eglantine,
Cowslips and sops-in-wine,
        With fragrant roses;
Down by thy Phyllis sit,
She will white lilies get,
And daffadillies fit
        To make thee posies.

I have a milk-white lamb
New taken from the dam,
It comes where'er I am
        When I call 'Willie.'
I have a wanton kid
Under mine apron hid,
A colt that ne'er was rid,
        A pretty filly.

want] mole (see *O.E.D.*).   Tractive] Attractive.   adamant] loadstone.

I bear, in sign of love,
A sparrow in my glove,
And in my breast a dove,
    These shall be all thine;
Besides, of sheep a flock
Which yieldeth many a lock,
And that shall be thy stock—
    Come, be my valentine!   *F. Andrewes.*

B.M. Harl. MS. 4955. (Poem written c. 1629 ?)*

SONG

Peace, wayward barne! O cease thy moan!
Thy far more wayward daddy 's gone:
And never will recallëd be
By cries of either thee or me:
    For should we cry
    Until we die,
We could not scant his cruelty.
        Ballow, Ballew, &c.

He needs might in himself foresee
What thou successively might'st be;
And could he then (though me forgo)
His infant leave, ere he did know
    How like the dad
    Would be the lad,
In time, to make fond maidens glad?
        Ballow, Ballew, &c.   *R. Brome.*

The Northern Lass, 1632. (Licensed 1629.)

barne] bairn.

IT WAS A BEAUTY THAT I SAW

It was a beauty that I saw
    So pure, so perfect, as the frame
    Of all the universe was lame,
To that one figure, could I draw,
Or give least line of it a law!

A skein of silk without a knot,
    A fair march made without a halt,
    A curious form without a fault,
A printed book without a blot,
All beauty, and without a spot!   *Jonson.*

The New Inn, 1631. (Acted 1629.)

TO HIMSELF

Where dost thou careless lie
    Buried in ease and sloth?
Knowledge, that sleeps, doth die;
And this security,
    It is the common moth
That eats on wits and arts, and so destroys them both.

Are all the Aonian springs
    Dried up? lies Thespia waste?
Doth Clarius' harp want strings,
That not a nymph now sings?
    Or droop they as disgraced,
To see their seats and bowers by chattering pies defaced?

and so destroys] Gifford, 1816;   and destroys, 1640.

If hence thy silence be,
　　As 'tis too just a cause,
Let this thought quicken thee:
Minds that are great and free,
　　Should not on fortune pause;
'Tis crown enough to virtue still, her own applause.

What though the greedy fry
　　Be taken with false baits
Of worded balladry,
And think it poesy?
　　They die with their conceits,
And only piteous scorn upon their folly waits.

Then take in hand thy lyre,
　　Strike in thy proper strain,
With Japhet's line, aspire
Sol's chariot for new fire,
　　To give the world again:
Who aided him, will thee, the issue of Jove's brain.

And since our dainty age
　　Cannot endure reproof,
Make not thyself a page
To that strumpet the stage,
　　But sing high and aloof,
Safe from the wolf's black jaw, and the dull ass's hoof.

Jonson.

Underwoods, 1640. (Poem written 1629.) *

A SONG OF PLEASURE

The blushing rose and purple flower,
　　Let grow too long, are soonest blasted.
Dainty fruits, though sweet, will sour

And rot in ripeness, left untasted.
　　Yet here is one more sweet than these:
　　The more you taste, the more she 'll please.

Beauty, though enclosed with ice,
　　Is a shadow chaste as rare;
Then how much those sweets entice
　　That have issue full as fair!
　　　　Earth cannot yield from all her powers
　　　　One equal, for Dame Venus' bowers.   *Massinger.*

The Picture, 1630. (Licensed 1629.)*

MY MIDNIGHT MEDITATION

Ill-busied man! why shouldst thou take such care
To lengthen out thy life's short calendar,
When every spectacle thou look'st upon
Presents and acts thy execution?
　　Each drooping season and each flower doth cry,
　　'Fool! as I fade and wither, thou must die.'

The beating of thy pulse (when thou art well)
Is just the tolling of thy passing bell:
Night is thy hearse, whose sable canopy
Covers alike deceasëd day and thee.
　　And all those weeping dews which nightly fall,
　　Are but the tears shed for thy funeral.

　　　　　　　　　　　　　　　　　　H. King or *J. King.*

Poems, etc., 1657. (Poem written before 1630.)*

A CONTEMPLATION UPON FLOWERS

Brave flowers—that I could gallant it like you,
　　And be as little vain!

You come abroad, and make a harmless shew,
    And to your beds of earth again.
You are not proud: you know your birth:
For your embroidered garments are from earth.

You do obey your months and times, but I
    Would have it ever spring:
My fate would know no winter, never die,
    Nor think of such a thing.
Oh, that I could my bed of earth but view
And smile, and look as cheerfully as you!

Oh, teach me to see death and not to fear,
    But rather to take truce!
How often have I seen you at a bier,
    And there look fresh and spruce!
You fragrant flowers, then teach me, that my breath
Like yours may sweeten and perfume my death.

                                            H. King(?)

B.M. Harl. MS. 6917. (Poem written before 1630?)*

LOVE'S PRIME

Dear, do not your fair beauty wrong
In thinking still you are too young;
The rose and lilies in your cheek
Flourish, and no more ripeness seek;
Your cherry lip, red, soft, and sweet,
Proclaims such fruit for taste most meet;
Then lose no time, for love has wings,
And flies away from aged things.   *May.*

The Old Couple, 1658. (Written before 1630?)*

DOWN IN A GARDEN

Down in a garden sat my dearest Love,
Her skin more soft and white than down of swan,
More tender-hearted than the turtle-dove,
And far more kind than bleeding pelican.
I courted her; she rose and blushing said,
'Why was I born to live and die a maid?'
With that I plucked a pretty marigold,
Whose dewy leaves shut up when day is done:
'Sweeting,' I said, 'arise, look and behold,
A pretty riddle I 'll to thee unfold:
These leaves shut in as close as cloistered nun,
Yet will they open when they see the sun.'
'What mean you by this riddle, sir?' she said,
'I pray expound it.'   Then I thus began:
'Know maids are made for men, man for a maid.'
With that she changed her colour and grew wan:
'Since that this riddle you so well unfold,
Be you the sun, I 'll be the marigold.'   *Anon.*

J. Cotgrave's *Wit's Interpreter*, 1655. (Before 1630, in Bod. MS. Eng.
Poet. e. 14.) *

TO HIS SON, VINCENT CORBET

What I shall leave thee none can tell,
But all shall say I wish thee well;
I wish thee, Vin, before all wealth,
Both bodily and ghostly health:
Nor too much wealth, nor wit, come to thee;
So much of either may undo thee.
I wish thee learning, not for show,
Enough for to instruct, and know;

Not such as gentlemen require,
To prate at table or at fire.
I wish thee all thy mother's graces,
Thy father's fortunes and his places.
I wish thee friends, and one at court,
Not to build on, but support;
To keep thee, not in doing many
Oppressions, but from suffering any.
I wish thee peace in all thy ways,
Nor lazy nor contentious days;
And when thy soul and body part,
As innocent as now thou art.   *Corbet.*

Certain Elegant Poems, 1647. (Poem written 1630?) *

THE NYMPHS' SONG

Behold, the rosy dawn
Rises in tinselled lawn,
And smiling seems to fawn
    Upon the mountains;
Awakèd from her dreams,
Shooting forth golden beams,
Dancing upon the streams,
    Courting the fountains.

These more than sweet showrets
Entice up these flowrets
To trim up our bowrets,
    Perfuming our coats;
Whilst the birds billing
Each one with his dilling,
The thickets still filling
    With amorous notes.

The bees up in honey rolled,
More than their thighs can hold,
Lapped in their liquid gold,
   Their treasure us bringing.
To these rillets purling,
Upon the stones curling
And oft about whirling,
   Dance toward their springing.

The wood-nymphs sit singing,
Each grove with notes ringing,
Whilst fresh Ver is flinging
   Her bounties abroad.
So much as the turtle
Upon the low myrtle,
To the meads fertile
   Her cares doth unload.

Nay, 'tis a world to see
In every bush and tree,
The birds with mirth and glee
   Wooed as they woo;
The robin and the wren,
Every cock with his hen:
Why should not we and men
   Do as they do?

The fairies are hopping,
The small flowers cropping,
And with dew dropping
   Skip thorough the greaves.
At Barley-break they play
Merrily all the day;

At night themselves they lay
　Upon the soft leaves.

The gentle winds sally
Upon every valley,
And many times dally
　And wantonly sport,
About the fields tracing
Each other in chasing,
And often embracing
　In amorous sort.

And Echo oft doth tell
Wondrous things from her cell,
As her what chance befel,
　Learning to prattle;
And now she sits and mocks
The shepherds and their flocks,
And the herds from the rocks
　Keeping their cattle.　　　　　　　*Drayton.*

The Muses' Elysium, 1630.*

SONG OF THE ASCENSION

Bright portals of the sky,
Embossed with sparkling stars,
Doors of eternity,
With diamantine bars,
Your arras rich uphold,
Loose all your bolts and springs,
Ope wide your leaves of gold,
That in your roofs may come the King of kings.

Scarfed in a rosy cloud,
He doth ascend the air;
Straight doth the moon him shroud
With her resplendent hair;
The next encrystalled light
Submits to him its beams,
And he doth trace the height
Of that fair lamp which flames of beauty streams.

He towers those golden bounds
He did to sun bequeath;
The higher wandering rounds
Are found his feet beneath;
The Milky Way comes near,
Heaven's axle seems to bend,
Above each turning sphere
That, robed in glory, heaven's King may ascend.

Now each ethereal gate
To him hath opened bin;
And glory's King in state
His palace enters in;
Now come is this high priest
In the most holy place,
Not without blood addressed,
With glory heaven, the earth to crown with grace.

Stars which all eyes were late,
And did with wonder burn,
His name to celebrate,
In flaming tongues them turn;
Their orby crystals move

Now come] Mod. eds.;   Now com'd, 1630.

More active than before,
And entheate from above,
Their sovereign Prince laud, glorify, adore.

The quires of happy souls,
Waked with that music sweet
Whose descant care controls,
Their Lord in triumph meet;
The spotless sprites of light
His trophies do extol,
And, arched in squadrons bright,
Greet their great Victor in his capitol.

O glory of the heaven!
O sole delight of earth!
To thee all power be given,
God's uncreated birth!
Of mankind lover true,
Indearer of his wrong,
Who dost the world renew,
Still be thou our salvation and our song!

Drummond.

Flowers of Sion, 1630. (Poem not in 1623 edition.)*

THE PASSING BELL

Come, list and hark! the bell doth toll
For some but new departing soul.
And was not that some ominous fowl—
The bat, the night-crow, or screech-owl?
To these I hear the wild wolf howl
In this black night that seems to scowl.
All these my black-book shall enroll,

---

entheate] divinely inspired.

For hark! still, still the bell doth toll
For some but now departing soul.   *Heywood.*

The Rape of Lucrece, 1630. (Song not in earlier editions.)*

NOW SLEEP, AND TAKE THY REST

Now sleep, and take thy rest,
    Once grieved and painëd wight,
Since she now loves thee best
    Who is thy heart's delight.
Let joy be thy soul's guest,
    And care be banished quite,
Since she hath thee expressed
    To be her favourite.   *Mabbe.*

The Spanish Bawd, 1631. (Registered 1630.)

ON SHAKESPEARE

What needs my Shakespeare for his honoured bones,
The labour of an age in pilëd stones,
Or that his hallowed reliques should be hid
Under a star-ypointing pyramid?
Dear son of memory, great heir of fame,
What need'st thou such weak witness of thy name?
Thou in our wonder and astonishment
Hast built thyself a live-long monument.
For whilst to the shame of slow-endeavouring art
Thy easy numbers flow, and that each heart
Hath from the leaves of thy unvalued book
Those Delphic lines with deep impression took,
Then thou our fancy of itself bereaving
Dost make us marble with too much conceiving;

And so sepùlchered in such pomp dost lie,
That kings for such a tomb would wish to die.

Milton.

Mr. William Shakespeare's Comedies, Histories and Tragedies, 1632. (Poem written 1630. Text from *Poems*, 1645.)*

SONNET

O nightingale! that on yon bloomy spray
   Warblest at eve, when all the woods are still,
   Thou with fresh hope the lover's heart dost fill,
While the jolly hours lead on propitious May:
Thy liquid notes that close the eye of day,
   First heard before the shallow cuckoo's bill,
   Portend success in love: oh, if Jove's will
Have linked that amorous power to thy soft lay,
   Now timely sing, ere the rude bird of hate
   Foretell my hopeless doom, in some grove nigh;
As thou from year to year hast sung too late
   For my relief, yet hadst no reason why:
Whether the Muse, or Love, call thee his mate,
   Both them I serve, and of their train am I.   *Milton.*

Poems, 1645. (Text 1673. Poem written c. 1630?)*

AT A SOLEMN MUSIC

Blest pair of sirens, pledges of Heaven's joy,
Sphere-born harmonious sisters, Voice and Verse,
Wed your divine sounds, and mixed power employ,
Dead things with inbreathed sense able to pierce;
And to our high-raised phantasy present
That undisturbëd song of pure concent
Aye sung before the sapphire-coloured throne

concent] 1673;   content, 1645.

To him that sits thereon,
With saintly shout and solemn jubilee;
Where the bright seraphim in burning row
Their loud uplifted angel-trumpets blow;
And the cherubic host in thousand quires
Touch their immortal harps of golden wires,
With those just spirits that wear victorious palms,
Hymns devout and holy psalms
Singing everlastingly:
That we on earth, with undiscording voice,
May rightly answer that melodious noise;
As once we did, till disproportioned sin
Jarred against nature's chime, and with harsh din
Broke the fair music that all creatures made
To their great Lord, whose love their motion swayed
In perfect diapason, whilst they stood
In first obedience, and their state of good.
O may we soon again renew that song,
And keep in tune with Heaven, till God ere long
To his celestial consort us unite,
To live with him, and sing in endless morn of light!

Milton.

Ibid.

DRINKING SONG

We care not for money, riches or wealth;
Old sack is our money, old sack is our health.
            Then let 's flock hither
            Like birds of a feather,
To drink, to fling,
To laugh and sing,

to fling] 1630;   to sling, 1668.

Conferring our notes together,
Conferring our notes together.

Come, let us laugh, let us drink, let us sing;
The winter with us is as good as the spring.
　　We care not a feather
　　For wind or for weather,
But night and day
We sport and play,
　　Conferring our notes together,
　　Conferring our notes together.　　*Randolph.*

Aristippus, 1630.*

SLEEP, SLEEP, MY SOUL

Sleep, sleep, my soul, let sorrow close thine eyes,
　Nurse fantasy records her lullabies:
Fold up thine arms and into sighs expire,
　Deep sighs, the drowsy pages of desire.

My restless heart, whom troublous thoughts molest,
　Shall cradle thee; thy cabin is my breast:
Where neither sun of joy, nor star of light
　Can break the mist of an affected night.

Here sadness rules; and here thy drooping head
　Instead of down shall have a frozen bed:
Love rocks thy panting cradle; and to bring
　Thy thoughts asleep, melancholy shall sing.

And when thou wakest, to appease thy cries,
　Sad grief with tears distilling from mine eyes
Shall feed thy passion, till that bitter food
　Do surfeit it, and in my death conclude.　　*Anon.*

*Uranus and Psyche.** B.M. Add. MS. 40145. (Written c. 1630.)

EPITHALAMIUM

       Rejoice,
   Ye woods and fountains,
   High rocks and mountains,
      And valleys low;
   Land and shore,
   And seas that roar,
      Murmuring clouds and winds that blow.
Come breathe your best music ye spheres on high,
    Whose eternal melody
Ravisheth heaven, and makes the Graces
Lustily trip in their circling embraces:
  Spend here these airs that wont to improve
  The merry banquets in the court of Jove.

      Bring, bring
   Your chirping noises,
   Ye woods, sweet voices;
      Come, Philomel,
   Leave thy song
   Of Tereus' wrong,
      And jolly tales of Hymen tell.
Come, Flora, bring hither the rosëd thorn,
    Violet filled with balmy morn,
Daisy enamoured on Phoebus' kisses,
Marigold sick when her lover she misses:
  Oh, bring and spread them under our feet,
  And Saba make them with thine odours sweet.

      Enwreathe
   White lily posies,
   And crimson roses,
      With myrtle twigs,

Olive calm,
And fruitful palm,
    Flourishing bay and oaken sprigs.
In pretty knots tie them with silken thread,
    Deck them with laces white and red,
Then crown with those chaplets, for comely beauty,
Majesty, glory, and submissive duty;
    Adorn their heads, whose coupled hands
    True love hath knit in undissolvëd bands.   *Anon.*

Uranus and Psyche, [c. 1630]. B.M. Add. MS. 40145.

THE THOUGHT

If you do love as well as I,
Then every minute from your heart
    A thought doth part;
And wingëd with desire doth fly
Till it hath met, in a straight line,
    A thought of mine
So like to yours, we cannot know
Whether of both doth come, or go,
    Till we define
Which of us two, that thought doth owe.

I say then, that your thoughts which pass,
Are not so much the thoughts you meant,
    As those I sent:
For as my image in a glass
Belongs not to the glass you see,
    But unto me;
So when your fancy is so clear
That you would think you saw me there,
    It needs must be
That it was I did first appear.

Likewise, when I send forth a thought,
My reason tells me, 'tis the same
    Which from you came,
And which your beauteous image wrought.
Thus while our thoughts by turns do lead,
    None can precede;
And thus, while in each other's mind
Such interchangëd forms we find,
    Our loves may plead
To be of more than vulgar kind.

May you then often think on me,
And by that thinking know 'tis true
    I thought on you;
I in the same belief will be:
While, by this mutual address,
    We will possess
A love must live, when we do die,
Which rare and secret property
    You will confess.
If you do love as well as I.   *Herbert of Cherbury.*

B.M. Add. MS. 37157, (Autograph). (Printed in *Occasional Verses*, 1665.
Poem written before 1631?)*

MY MISTRESS

Skin more pure than Ida's snow,
Whiter far than Moorish milk,
Sweeter than ambrosia too,
Softer than the Paphian silk,
Indian plumes or thistle-down,
Or may-blossoms newly blown—
Is my mistress, rosy-pale,
Adding beauty to her veil.   *Brathwaite.*

The English Gentlewoman, 1631.

OF MYSELF

This only grant me, that my means may lie
Too low for envy, for contempt too high.
　　Some honour I would have,
Not from great deeds, but good alone;
The unknown are better than ill known:
　　Rumour can ope the grave.
Acquaintance I would have, but when 't depends
Not on the number, but the choice, of friends.

Books should, not business, entertain the light,
And sleep, as undisturbed as death, the night.
　　My house a cottage more
Than palace, and should fitting be
For all my use, no luxury.
　　My garden painted o'er
With Nature's hand, not Art's, and pleasures yield,
Horace might envy in his Sabine field.

Thus would I double my life's fading space;
For he, that runs it well, twice runs his race.
　　And in this true delight,
These unbought sports, this happy state,
I would not fear nor wish my fate;
　　But boldly say each night,
To-morrow let my sun his beams display,
Or in clouds hide them; I have lived to-day.   *Cowley.*

Several Discourses by way of Essays, in *The Works,* 1668. (Poem written
1631; first printed 1636.)*

O SORROW, SORROW

O sorrow, sorrow, say where dost thou dwell?
　　In the lowest room of hell.

Art thou born of human race?
  No, no, I have a furier face.
Art thou in city, town, or court?
  I to every place resort.
Oh, why into the world is sorrow sent?
  Men afflicted best repent.
What dost thou feed on?
    Broken sleep.
What tak'st thou pleasure in?
    To weep,
    To sigh, to sob, to pine, to groan,
    To wring my hands, to sit alone.
Oh when, oh when shall sorrow quiet have?
    Never, never, never, never,
    Never till she finds a grave.   *Dekker* or *S. Rowley.**

The Noble Soldier, 1634. (Registered 1631.)

HYMN TO GOD, MY GOD, IN MY SICKNESS

Since I am coming to that holy room,
  Where with thy choir of saints for evermore
I shall be made thy music, as I come
  I tune the instrument here at the door,
  And what I must do then, think here before.

Whilst my physicians by their love are grown
  Cosmographers, and I their map, who lie
Flat on this bed, that by them may be shown
  That this is my south-west discovery,
  Per fretum febris, by these straits to die;

I joy, that in these straits I see my west;
  For, though those currents yield return to none,

Per fretum febris] Through the strait of fever.

What shall my west hurt me?   As west and east
   In all flat maps—and I am one—are one,
   So death doth touch the resurrection.

Is the Pacific sea my home?   Or are
   The eastern riches?   Is Jerusalem?
Anyan, and Magellan, and Gibraltar,
   All straits, and none but straits, are ways to them,
   Whether where Japhet dwelt, or Cham, or Shem.

We think that Paradise and Calvary,
   Christ's cross and Adam's tree, stood in one place;
Look, Lord, and find both Adams met in me;
   As the first Adam's sweat surrounds my face,
   May the last Adam's blood my soul embrace.

So, in his purple wrapped, receive me, Lord;
   By these his thorns, give me his other crown;
And as to others' souls I preached thy word,
   Be this my text, my sermon to mine own,
   'Therefore that he may raise, the Lord throws down.'

                                    Donne.

Poems, 1635. (Poem written 1631 ?)*

A SAD SONG

Why art thou slow, thou rest of trouble, Death,
   To stop a wretch's breath,
That calls on thee, and offers her sad heart
   A prey unto thy dart?
I am nor young nor fair, be therefore bold:
   Sorrow hath made me old,
Deformed, and wrinkled; all that I can crave
   Is quiet in my grave.
Such as live happy, hold long life a jewel;

But to me thou art cruel
If thou end not my tedious misery,
   And I soon cease to be.
Strike, and strike home, then; pity unto me,
   In one short hour's delay, is tyranny.   *Massinger.*

The Emperor of the East, 1632. (Licensed 1631.)

SONNET

How soon hath time, the subtle thief of youth,
Stol'n on his wing my three and twentieth year!
My hasting days fly on with full career,
But my late spring no bud or blossom shew'th.
Perhaps my semblance might deceive the truth,
That I to manhood am arrived so near,
And inward ripeness doth much less appear,
That some more timely-happy spirits indu'th.
Yet be it less or more, or soon or slow,
It shall be still in strictest measure even
To that same lot, however mean or high,
Toward which time leads me, and the will of Heaven:
All is, if I have grace to use it so,
As ever in my great Task-master's eye.   *Milton.*

Poems, 1645. (Text 1673. Poem written 1631.)

THE MAD-MERRY PRANKS OF ROBIN GOOD-FELLOW

From Oberon in fairyland,
   The king of ghosts and shadows there,
Mad Robin I, at his command,
   Am sent to view the night-sports here.
What revel rout is kept about,
   In every corner where I go

I will o'er-see, and merry be,
   And make good sport, with ho, ho, ho!

More swift than lightning can I fly
   About this airy welkin soon,
And in a minute's space descry
   Each thing that 's done beneath the moon.
There 's not a hag nor ghost shall wag,
   Nor cry 'Goblin!' where I do go,
But Robin I their feats will spy,
   And fear them home, with ho, ho, ho!

If any wanderers I meet,
   That from their night-sports do trudge home,
With counterfeiting voice I greet
   And cause them on with me to roam,
Through woods, through lakes, through bogs,
     through brakes,
   O'er bush and brier, with them I go,
I call upon them to come on,
   And wend me laughing, ho, ho, ho!

Sometimes I meet them like a man;
   Sometimes an ox, sometimes a hound;
And to a horse I turn me can,
   To trip and trot about them round.
But if to ride, my back they stride,
   More swift than wind away I go,
O'er hedge and lands, through pools and ponds
   I whirry, laughing, ho, ho, ho!

When lazy queans have naught to do,
   But study how to cog and lie;

---

fear] frighten, scare.   lands] ditch-divided ploughland.

To make debate and mischief too
    'Twixt one another secretly;
I mark their glose and do disclose
    To them that they had wrongëd so;
When I have done, I get me gone,
    And leave them scolding, ho, ho, ho!

When men do traps and engines set
    In loop-holes, where the vermin creep,
That from their folds and houses fet'
    Their ducks and geese, their lambs and sheep;
I spy the gin, and enter in,
    And seem a vermin taken so;
But when they there approach me near,
    I leap out laughing, ho, ho, ho!

By wells and gills in meadows green,
    We nightly dance our haydeguise,
And to our fairy king and queen
    We chant our moonlight harmonies.
When larks 'gin sing, away we fling,
    And babes new-born steal as we go;
An elf in bed we leave instead,
    And wend us laughing, ho, ho, ho!

From hag-bred Merlin's time have I
    Thus nightly revelled to and fro,
And for my pranks men call me by
    The name of Robin Good-fellow.
Fiends, ghosts and sprites, that haunt the nights,
    The hags and goblins, do me know;
And beldams old my feats have told,
    So *vale, vale*; ho, ho, ho!   *Anon.*

B.M. Roxb. Coll. I. 230–1. (Registered 1631.)*

DISDAIN RETURNED

He that loves a rosy cheek,
    Or a coral lip admires,
Or from star-like eyes doth seek
    Fuel to maintain his fires;
As old Time makes these decay,
So his flames must waste away.

But a smooth and steadfast mind,
    Gentle thoughts and calm desires,
Hearts with equal love combined,
    Kindle never-dying fires.
Where these are not, I despise
Lovely cheeks, or lips, or eyes.

No tears, Celia, now shall win
    My resolved heart to return;
I have searched thy soul within,
    And find nought but pride and scorn;
I have learned thy arts, and now
Can disdain as much as thou.
Some power, in my revenge convey
That love to her I cast away.   *Carew.*

Poems, 1640. (Stzs. 1 and 2, printed 1632.)*

OF HIS MISTRESS

Have you a desire to see
The glorious heaven's epitome?
Or an abstract of the spring?
Adonis' garden? or a thing
    Fuller of wonder, Nature's shop displayed,

Hung with the choicest pieces she has made?
Here behold it open laid.

Or else would you bless your eyes
With a type of paradise?
Or behold how poets feign
Jove to sit amidst his train?
    Or see (what made Actaeon rue)
    Diana 'mongst her virgin crew?
        Lift up your eyes and view.   *Hausted.*

The Rival Friends, 1632.*

HAVE PITY, GRIEF

Have pity, Grief; I cannot pay
    The tribute which I owe thee, tears;
        Alas, those fountains are grown dry,
        And 'tis in vain to hope supply
    From others' eyes; for each man bears
        Enough about him of his own
        To spend his stock of tears upon.

Woo then the heavens, gentle Love,
    To melt a cloud for my relief;
        Or woo the deep, or woo the grave;
        Woo what thou wilt, so I may have
    Wherewith to pay my debt, for Grief
        Has vowed, unless I quickly pay,
        To take both life and love away.   *Hausted.*

Ibid.

Milton's *L'Allegro* and *Il Penseroso* (*Poems*, 1645) were written in 1632.

A GOOD-NIGHT

Close now thine eyes, and rest secure;
Thy soul is safe enough; thy body sure;
    He that loves thee, he that keeps
And guards thee, never slumbers, never sleeps.
The smiling conscience in a sleeping breast
    Has only peace, has only rest:
    The music and the mirth of kings
Are all but very discords, when she sings:
    Then close thine eyes and rest secure;
No sleep so sweet as thine, no rest so sure.   *Quarles.*

Divine Fancies, 1632.*

ON THE INFANCY OF OUR SAVIOUR

Hail, blessëd Virgin, full of heavenly grace,
Blest above all that sprang from human race;
Whose heaven-saluted womb brought forth in one,
A blessëd Saviour, and a blessëd son:
Oh! what a ravishment 't had been to see
Thy little Saviour perking on thy knee!
To see him nuzzle in thy virgin breast,
His milk-white body all unclad, undressed!
To see thy busy fingers clothe and wrap
His spradling limbs in thy indulgent lap!
To see his desperate eyes, with childish grace,
Smiling upon his smiling mother's face!
And, when his forward strength began to bloom,
To see him diddle up and down the room!
Oh! what a ravishment 't had been to see
Should e'er be slain by a false-hearted kiss!
Had I a rag, if sure thy body wore it,

Pardon, sweet Babe, I think I should adore it:
Till then, O grant this boon (a boon far dearer),
The weed not being, I may adore the wearer.

                                                              Quarles.
Ibid.

A CHARM

Quiet, sleep! or I will make
Erinnys whip thee with a snake,
And cruel Rhadamanthus take
Thy body to the boiling lake,
Where fire and brimstone never slake;
Thy heart shall burn, thy head shall ache,
And every joint about thee quake;
And therefore dare not yet to wake!

Quiet, sleep! or thou shalt see
The horrid hags of Tartary,
Whose tresses ugly serpents be,
And Cerberus shall bark at thee,
And all the Furies that are three—
The worst is called Tisiphone,—
Shall lash thee to eternity;
And therefore sleep thou peacefully.   *Randolph.*

The Jealous Lovers, 1632.

ON CHLORIS WALKING IN THE SNOW

I saw fair Chloris walk alone,
Whilst feathered rain came softly down,
And Jove descended from his tower
To court her in a silver shower.

The wanton snow flew on her breast
Like little birds unto their nest;
But overcome with whiteness there,
For grief it thawed into a tear;
Thence falling on her garment's hem,
To deck her, froze into a gem.   *Strode.*

W. Porter's *Madrigals and Airs*, 1632.*

ON A SPARK OF FIRE FIXING ON A
GENTLEWOMAN'S BREAST

Fair Julia sitting by the fire,
An amorous spark, with hot desire,
Flew to her breast, but could not melt
The chaste snow there, which when it felt,
And that resistance it did bide,
For grief it blushed, and so it died.
Yet lest it should prove aught unkind,
It contrite ashes left behind.   *Philipott.*

Poems, 1646. (Poem written c. 1632 ?)*

MADRIGAL

Love in thy youth, fair maid; be wise,
    Old Time will make thee colder,
And though each morning new arise
    Yet we each day grow older.
Thou as heaven art fair and young,
    Thine eyes like twin stars shining:
But ere another day be sprung,
    All these will be declining.
Then winter comes with all his fears
    And all thy sweets shall borrow;

Too late then wilt thou shower thy tears,
And I too late shall sorrow.   *Anon.*

W. Porter's *Madrigals and Airs*, 1632.*

A MORISCO

The sky is glad that stars above
    Do give a brighter splendour:
The stars unfold their flaming gold,
    To make the ground more tender:
The ground doth send a fragrant smell,
    That air may be the sweeter:
The air doth charm the swelling seas
    With pretty chirping metre:
The sea with rivers water doth
    The plants and flowers dainty:
The plants do yield their fruitful seed,
    That beasts may live in plenty:
The beasts do give both food and cloth,
    That man high Jove may honour:
And so the world runs merrily round,
    When peace doth smile upon her.
Oh then, then oh: oh then, then oh:
    This jubilee last for ever,
That foreign spite or civil fight,
    Our quiet trouble never!   *Fisher.*

Fuimus Troes, 1633.

SONG TO A VIOL

So the silver-feathered swan,
Both by death and colour wan,

water doth] *i.e.* doth water.

Loves to sing before she die,
Leaving life so willingly.
But how can I sing a note
When dead hoarseness stops my throat?
Or how can I play a stroke
When my heart-strings are all broke?   *Fisher.*

Fuimus Troes, 1633.

NOW LOVE DIES

Oh, no more, no more! too late
  Sighs are spent; the burning tapers
Of a life as chaste as fate,
  Pure as are unwritten papers,
Are burnt out: no heat, no light
Now remains; 'tis ever night.
  Love is dead; let lovers' eyes,
    Locked in endless dreams,
    The extremes of all extremes,
  Ope no more, for now Love dies.
Now Love dies,—implying
Love's martyrs must be ever, ever dying.   *J. Ford.*

The Broken Heart, 1633.

UPON OUR VAIN FLATTERY OF OURSELVES THAT THE SUCCEEDING TIMES WILL BE BETTER THAN THE FORMER

How we dally out our days!
How we seek a thousand ways
To find death, the which if none
We sought out would show us one!

Why then do we injure Fate,
When we will impute the date
And expiring of our time
To be hers, which is our crime?

Wish we not our end? and worse,
Make it a prayer which is a curse?
Does there not in each breast lie
Both our soul and enemy?

Never was there morning yet
(Sweet as is the violet)
Which man's folly did not soon
Wish to be expired in noon;
As though such an haste did tend
To our bliss, and not our end.

Nay, the young ones in the nest
Suck this folly from the breast,
And no stammering ape but can
Spoil a prayer to be a man.

But suppose that he is heard,
By the sprouting of his beard,
And he hath what he doth seek,
The soft clothing of the cheek:
Would he yet stay here? or be
Fixed in this maturity?
Sooner shall the wandering star
Learn what rest and quiet are:
Sooner shall the slippery rill
Leave his motion and stand still.

Be it joy or be it sorrow,
We refer all to the morrow,
That we think will ease our pain,
That we do suppose again
Will increase our joy, and so
Events, the which we cannot know,

We magnify, and are (in sum)
Enamoured of the time to come.
   Well, the next day comes, and then
Another next, and so to ten,
To twenty we arrive, and find
No more before us than behind
Of solid joy, and yet haste on
To our consummation:
   Till the baldness of the crown,
Till that all the face do frown,
Till the forehead often have
The remembrance of a grave;
Till the eyes look in, to find
If that they can see the mind;
Till the sharpness of the nose,
Till that we have lived to pose
Sharper eyes, who cannot know
Whether we are men or no;
Till the tallow of the cheek,
Till we know not what we seek,
And at last of life bereaved,
Die unhappy, and deceived.   *Gomersal.*

Poems, 1633.

LIFE

I made a posy, while the day ran by:
Here will I smell my remnant out, and tie
            My life within this band;
But Time did beckon to the flowers, and they
By noon most cunningly did steal away,
            And withered in my hand.

My hand was next to them, and then my heart:
I took, without more thinking, in good part

Time's gentle admonition;
Who did so sweetly death's sad taste convey,
Making my mind to smell my fatal day,
      Yet sugaring the suspicion.

Farewell, dear flowers; sweetly your time ye spent,
Fit, while ye lived, for smell or ornament,
      And after death for cures.
I follow straight, without complaints or grief,
Since, if my scent be good, I care not if
      It be as short as yours.   *G. Herbert.*

The Temple, 1633.

LOVE

Love bade me welcome: yet my soul drew back,
      Guilty of dust and sin.
But quick-eyed Love, observing me grow slack
      From my first entrance in,
Drew nearer to me, sweetly questioning,
      If I lacked any thing.

'A guest,' I answered, 'worthy to be here.'
      Love said, 'You shall be he.'
'I, the unkind, ungrateful?   Ah! my dear,
      I cannot look on thee.'
Love took my hand, and smiling did reply,
      'Who made the eyes but I?'

'Truth, Lord! but I have marred them: let my shame
      Go where it doth deserve.'
'And know you not,' says Love, 'who bore the blame?'
      'My dear, then I will serve.'
'You must sit down,' says Love, 'and taste my meat.'
      So I did sit and eat.

Ibid.
                  G. Herbert.

THE COLLAR

I struck the board, and cried, No more;
   I will abroad.
What! shall I ever sigh and pine?
My lines and life are free; free as the road,
Loose as the wind, as large as store.
  Shall I be still in suit?
Have I no harvest but a thorn
To let me blood, and not restore
What I have lost with cordial fruit?
    Sure there was wine
Before my sighs did dry it: there was corn
  Before my tears did drown it.
Is the year only lost to me?
  Have I no bays to crown it?
No flowers, no garlands gay?   All blasted?
    All wasted?
Not so, my heart; but there is fruit,
    And thou hast hands.
Recover all thy sigh-blown age
On double pleasures: leave thy cold dispute
Of what is fit and not; forsake thy cage,
    Thy rope of sands,
Which petty thoughts have made, and made to thee
Good cable, to enforce and draw
    And be thy law,
While thou didst wink and wouldst not see.
    Away; take heed:
    I will abroad.
Call in thy death's head there: tie up thy fears.
   He that forbears
  To suit and serve his need,
    Deserves his load.

But as I raved and grew more fierce and wild
        At every word,
Methought I heard one calling, 'Child':
And I replied, 'My Lord.'   *G. Herbert.*

The Temple, 1633.

THE WORLD

Love built a stately house; where Fortune came,
And, spinning fancies, she was heard to say
That her fine cobwebs did support the frame,
Whereas they were supported by the same;
But Wisdom quickly swept them all away.

Then Pleasure came, who, liking not the fashion,
Began to make balcònies, terraces,
Till she had weakened all by alteration;
But reverend laws, and many a proclamation
Reforméd all at length with menaces.

Then entered Sin, and with that sycamore
Whose leaves first sheltered man from drought and dew,
Working and winding slily evermore,
The inward walls and sommers cleft and tore;
But Grace shored these, and cut that as it grew.

Then Sin combined with Death in a firm band,
To raze the building to the very floor;
Which they effected, none could them withstand:
But Love and Grace took Glory by the hand,
And built a braver palace than before.   *G. Herbert.*

Ibid.

sommers] main beams.

VIRTUE

Sweet day, so cool, so calm, so bright,
The bridal of the earth and sky,
The dew shall weep thy fall to-night,
        For thou must die.

Sweet rose, whose hue, angry and brave,
Bids the rash gazer wipe his eye,
Thy root is ever in its grave,
        And thou must die.

Sweet spring, full of sweet days and roses,
A box where sweets compacted lie,
My music shows ye have your closes,
        And all must die.

Only a sweet and virtuous soul,
Like seasoned timber, never gives;
But as usual though the whole world turn to coal,
        Then chiefly lives.   *G. Herbert.*

The Temple, * 1633.

TIME

Meeting with Time, 'Slack thing,' said I,
'Thy scythe is dull; whet it for shame.'
'No marvel, sir,' he did reply,
'If it at length deserve some blame;
    But where one man would have me grind it,
    Twenty for one too sharp do find it.'

'Perhaps some such of old did pass,
Who above all things loved this life;
To whom thy scythe a hatchet was,
Which now is but a pruning knife.

Christ's coming hath made man thy debtor,
Since by thy cutting he grows better.

'And in his blessing thou art blessed:
For where thou only wert before
An executioner at best,
Thou art a gardener now; and more,
    An usher to convey our souls
    Beyond the utmost stars and poles.

'And this is that makes life so long,
While it detains us from our God.
Ev'n pleasures here increase the wrong,
And length of days lengthens the rod.
    Who wants the place where God doth dwell,
    Partakes already half of hell.

'Of what strange length must that needs be,
Which ev'n eternity excludes!'
Thus far Time heard me patiently,
Then chafing said, 'This man deludes;
    What do I here before his door?
    He doth not crave less time, but more.'

*Ibid.**   G. Herbert.

THE PULLEY

When God at first made man,
Having a glass of blessings standing by;
'Let us,' said he, 'pour on him all we can:
Let the world's riches, which dispersëd lie,
        Contract into a span.'

        So strength first made a way;
Then beauty flowed, then wisdom, honour, pleasure:

When almost all was out, God made a stay,
Perceiving that alone of all his treasure
    Rest in the bottom lay.

    'For if I should,' said he,
'Bestow this jewel also on my creature,
He would adore my gifts instead of me,
And rest in Nature, not the God of Nature:
    So both should losers be.

    'Yet let him keep the rest,
But keep them with repining restlessness:
Let him be rich and weary, that at least
If goodness lead him not, yet weariness
    May toss him to my breast.'   *G. Herbert.*

The Temple, 1633.

THE TEMPER

How should I praise thee, Lord! how should my rhymes
    Gladly engrave thy love in steel,
    If what my soul doth feel sometimes,
        My soul might ever feel!

Although there were some forty heavens, or more,
    Sometimes I peer above them all;
    Sometimes I hardly reach a score;
        Sometimes to hell I fall.

O rack me not to such a vast extent;
    Those distances belong to thee:
    The world 's too little for thy tent,
        A grave too big for me.

Wilt thou mete arms with man, that thou dost stretch
    A crumb of dust from heaven to hell?
    Will great God measure with a wretch?
        Shall he thy stature spell?

O let me, when thy roof my soul hath hid,
    O let me roost and nestle there;
    Then of a sinner thou art rid,
        And I of hope and fear.

Yet, take thy way; for sure thy way is best:
    Stretch or contract me, thy poor debtor;
    This is but tuning of my breast,
        To make the music better.

Whether I fly with angels, fall with dust,
    Thy hands made both, and I am there:
    Thy power and love, my love and trust,
        Make one place everywhere.   *G. Herbert.*

Ibid.

DEATH

Death, thou wast once an uncouth hideous thing,
    Nothing but bones,
    The sad effect of sadder groans:
Thy mouth was open, but thou couldst not sing.

For we considered thee as at some six
    Or ten years hence,
    After the loss of life and sense,
Flesh being turned to dust, and bones to sticks.

We looked on this side of thee, shooting short;
        Where we did find
    The shells of fledge souls left behind,
Dry dust, which sheds no tears, but may extort.

But since our Saviour's death did put some blood
        Into thy face,
    Thou art grown fair and full of grace,
Much in request, much sought for, as a good.

For we do now behold thee gay and glad,
        As at dooms-day,
    When souls shall wear their new array,
And all thy bones with beauty shall be clad.

Therefore we can go die as sleep, and trust
        Half that we have
    Unto an honest faithful grave;
Making our pillows either down, or dust.   *G. Herbert.*

The Temple, 1633.

LINES ON HIS COMPANIONS WHO DIED IN THE NORTHERN SEAS

I were unkind unless that I did shed,
Before I part, some tears upon our dead:
And when my eyes be dry, I will not cease
In heart to pray their bones may rest in peace:
Their better parts (good souls) I know were given
With an intent they should return to heaven.
Their lives they spent, to the last drop of blood,
Seeking God's glory and their country's good;
And as a valiant soldier rather dies

Than yields his courage to his enemies;
And stops their way with his hewed flesh, when death
Hath quite deprived him of his strength and breath;
So have they spent themselves; and here they lie,
A famous mark of our discovery.
We that survive, perchance may end our days
In some employment meriting no praise,
And in a dunghill rot; when no man names
The memory of us, but to our shames.
They have outlived this fear, and their brave ends
Will ever be an honour to their friends.
Why drop ye so, mine eyes? Nay, rather pour
My sad departure in a solemn shower.
The winter's cold, that lately froze our blood,
Now were it so extreme, might do this good,
As make these tears bright pearls, which I would lay
Tombed safely with you, till doom's fatal day.
That in this solitary place, where none
Will ever come to breathe a sigh or groan,
Some remnant might be extant of the true
And faithful love I ever tendered you.
Oh! rest in peace, dear friends, and let it be
No pride to say, the sometime part of me.
What pain and anguish doth afflict the head,
The heart and stomach, when the limbs are dead!
So grieved, I kiss your graves, and vow to die
A foster-father to your memory.   *James.*

The Strange and Dangerous Voyage . . . 1633.*

O'ER THE SMOOTH ENAMELLED GREEN

O'er the smooth enamelled green,
Where no print of step hath been,

Follow me, as I sing
And touch the warbled string:
Under the shady roof
Of branching elm star-proof
Follow me:
I will bring you where she sits
Clad in splendour as befits
Her deity.
Such a rural queen
All Arcadia hath not seen.   *Milton.*

Arcades, in *Poems,* 1645. (Text 1673. Performed 1633 ?)*

NYMPHS AND SHEPHERDS, DANCE NO MORE

Nymphs and shepherds, dance no more
By sandy Ladon's lilied banks;
On old Lycaeus or Cyllene hoar,
Trip no more in twilight ranks;
Though Erymanth your loss deplore,
A better soil shall give ye thanks.
From the stony Maenalus
Bring your flocks and live with us;
Here ye shall have greater grace,
To serve the Lady of this place.
Though Syrinx your Pan's mistress were,
Yet Syrinx well might wait on her.
Such a rural queen
All Arcadia hath not seen.   *Milton.*

Ibid.

SONG

What a dainty life the milkmaid leads!
When over the flowery meads

She dabbles in the dew,
And sings to her cow;
And feels not the pain
Of love or disdain:
She sleeps in the night though she toils
    in the day,
And merrily passeth her time away.   *Nabbes.*

Tottenham Court, 1638. (Acted 1633.)*

THE RELIEF ON EASTER EVE

Like an hart, the live-long day
That in thorns and thickets lay,
Rouse thee, soul, thy flesh forsake,
Get to rèlief from thy brake;
Shuddering I would have thee part,
And at every motion start.
Look behind thee still to see
If thy frailties follow thee.
Deep in silence of the night
Take a sweet and stol'n delight;
Graze on clover by this calm
Precious spring of bleeding balm:
Thou rememberest how it ran
From his side, that 's God and man.
Taste the pleasures of this stream,
Thou wilt think thy flesh a dream.
Nightly this repast go take,
Get to rèlief from thy brake.   *Pestel.*

Sermons and Devotions, 1659. (Poem written before 1634?)*

rèlief] term used for a hart seeking food, or feeding.   Get to] N.A. (*bis*);
Got to, 1659.   part] depart.

AN ODE TO MASTER ANTHONY STAFFORD,
TO HASTEN HIM INTO THE COUNTRY

Come, spur away!
I have no patience for a longer stay;
                But must go down,
And leave the chargeable noise of this great town.
            I will the country see;
            Where old simplicity,
                Though hid in grey,
                Doth look more gay
Than foppery in plush and scarlet clad.
            Farewell, you city-wits that are
                Almost at civil war!
'Tis time that I grow wise, when all the world grows mad.

            More of my days
I will not spend to gain an idiot's praise;
                Or to make sport
For some slight Puisne of the Inns of Court.
            Then, worthy Stafford, say,
            How shall we spend the day?
                With what delights
                Shorten the nights?
When from this tumult we are got secure,
            Where mirth with all her freedom goes,
                Yet shall no finger lose;
Where every word is thought, and every thought is pure.

            There from the tree
We 'll cherries pluck; and pick the strawberry;
                And every day
Go see the wholesome country girls make hay,

        Whose brown hath lovelier grace
         Than any painted face
            That I do know
            Hyde Park can show.
Where I had rather gain a kiss, than meet
     (Though some of them in greater state
         Might court my love with plate)
The beauties of the Cheap, and wives of Lombard Street.

        But think upon
Some other pleasures; these to me are none.
         Why do I prate
Of women, that are things against my fate?
       I never mean to wed
        That torture to my bed:
          My Muse is she
          My Love shall be.
Let clowns get wealth, and heirs; when I am gone,
     And the great bugbear, grisly Death,
        Shall take this idle breath,
If I a poem leave, that poem is my son.

        Of this, no more!
We 'll rather taste the bright Pomona's store.
        No fruit shall 'scape
Our palates, from the damson to the grape.
       Then, full, we 'll seek a shade,
        And hear what music 's made:
         How Philomel
         Her tale doth tell;
And how the other birds do fill the quire;
     The thrush and blackbird lend their throats,
        Warbling melodious notes.
We will all sports enjoy, which others but desire:

Ours is the sky,
Where, at what fowl we please, our hawk shall fly;
Nor will we spare
To hunt the crafty fox, or timorous hare;
But let our hounds run loose
In any ground they 'll choose;
The buck shall fall,
The stag, and all.
Our pleasures must from their own warrants be,
For, to my Muse, if not to me,
I 'm sure all game is free;
Heaven, earth, are all but parts of her great royalty.

And when we mean
To taste of Bacchus' blessings now and then,
And drink by stealth
A cup or two to noble Barkley's health:
I 'll take my pipe and try
The Phrygian melody,
Which he that hears,
Lets through his ears
A madness to distemper all the brain.
Then I another pipe will take
And Doric music make,
To civilize with graver notes our wits again.   *Randolph.*

Poems, 1638. (Poem written before 1634 ?)*

UPON HIS PICTURE

When age hath made me what I am not now;
And every wrinkle tells me where the plough
Of time hath furrowed; when an ice shall flow
Through every vein, and all my head wear snow:

When death displays his coldness in my cheek;
And I myself in my own picture seek,
Not finding what I am, but what I was,
In doubt which to believe, this, or my glass:
Yet though I alter, this remains the same
As it was drawn, retains the primitive frame
And first complexion; here will still be seen
Blood on the cheek, and down upon the chin:
Here the smooth brow will stay, the lively eye,
The ruddy lip, and hair of youthful dye.
Behold what frailty we in man may see,
Whose shadow is less given to change than he!

Ibid.   *Randolph.*

REQUIEM

Matilda, now go take thy bed
In the dark dwellings of the dead;

And rise in the great waking day,
Sweet as incense, fresh as May.

Rest thou, chaste soul, fixed in thy proper sphere,
Amongst Heaven's fair ones; all are fair ones there.

Rest there, chaste soul, whilst we here troubled say,
'Time gives us griefs, Death takes our joys away.'

Davenport.

King John and Matilda, 1655. (Written before 1634?)*

TO ROSES IN THE BOSOM OF CASTARA

Ye blushing virgins happy are
In the chaste nunnery of her breasts:

For he 'd profane so chaste a fair,
   Whoe'er should call them Cupid's nests.

Transplanted thus, how bright ye grow,
   How rich a perfume do ye yield!
In some close garden, cowslips so
   Are sweeter than i' the open field.

In those white cloisters live secure
   From the rude blasts of wanton breath,
Each hour more innocent and pure,
   Till you shall wither into death.

Then that which, living, gave you room,
   Your glorious sepulchre shall be:
There wants no marble for a tomb,
   Whose breast hath marble been to me.

Castara, 1634.   *Habington.*

UPON CASTARA'S DEPARTURE

Vows are vain.   No suppliant breath
Stays the speed of swift-heeled death.
Life with her is gone, and I
Learn but a new way to die.
See the flowers condole, and all
Wither in my funeral.
The bright lily, as if day
Parted with her, fades away.
Violets hang their heads and lose
All their beauty.   That the rose
A sad part in sorrow bears,
Witness all those dewy tears,

Parted] Departed.

Which as pearl, or diamond like,
Swell upon her blushing cheek.
All things mourn, but oh, behold
How the withered marigold
Closeth up now she is gone,
Judging her the setting sun!   *Habington.*

Ibid.

HENCE WITH PASSION, SIGHS AND TEARS

Hence with passion, sighs and tears,
Disasters, sorrows, cares and fears!
See, my Love, my Love, appears,
   That thought himself exiled!
Whence might all these loud joys grow,
Whence might mirth and banquets flow,
But that he 's come, he 's come, I know?
   Fair Fortune, thou hast smiled.

Give to these blind windows eyes,
Daze the stars and mock the skies,
And let us two, us two, devise
   To lavish our best treasures;
Crown our wishes with content,
Meet our souls in sweet consent,
And let this night, this night, be spent
   In all abundant pleasures.   *Heywood.*

A Maidenhead well lost, 1634.*

SWEET ECHO, SWEETEST NYMPH

Sweet Echo, sweetest nymph that liv'st unseen
Within thy airy shell

By slow Meander's margent green,
And in the violet-embroidered vale
Where the love-lorn nightingale
Nightly to thee her sad song mourneth well;
Canst thou not tell me of a gentle pair
That likest thy Narcissus are?
Oh, if thou have
Hid them in some flowery cave,
Tell me but where,
Sweet queen of parley, daughter of the sphere!
So may'st thou be translated to the skies,
And give resounding grace to all heaven's harmonies.

Milton.

A Masque, [*Comus,*] 1637. (Text 1673. Performed 1634.)*

SABRINA FAIR

Sabrina fair,
Listen where thou art sitting
Under the glassy, cool, translucent wave,
In twisted braids of lilies knitting
The loose train of thy amber-dropping hair;
Listen for dear honour's sake,
Goddess of the silver lake,
Listen and save!

Listen and appear to us,
In name of great Oceanus,
By the earth-shaking Neptune's mace,
And Tethys' grave majestic pace;
By hoary Nereus' wrinkled look,
And the Carpathian wizard's hook;
By scaly Triton's winding shell,
And old soothsaying Glaucus' spell;

By Leucothea's lovely hands,
And her son that rules the strands;
By Thetis' tinsel-slippered feet,
And the songs of Sirens sweet;
By dead Parthenope's dear tomb,
And fair Ligea's golden comb,
Wherewith she sits on diamond rocks
Sleeking her soft alluring locks;
By all the nymphs that nightly dance
Upon thy streams with wily glance,—
Rise, rise, and heave thy rosy head
From thy coral-paven bed,
And bridle in thy headlong wave,
Till thou our summons answered have.
                    Listen and save!

Ibid.   *Milton.*

WISHES

To his (supposed) Mistress

Whoe'er she be
That not impossible she
That shall command my heart and me;

Where'er she lie,
Locked up from mortal eye,
In shady leaves of destiny;

Till that ripe birth
Of studied fate stand forth
And teach her fair steps tread our earth;

paven] 1637;   pav'n, 1673.

Till that divine
Idea take a shrine
Of crystal flesh, through which to shine;

Meet you her, my wishes,
Bespeak her to my blisses,
And be ye called my absent kisses.

I wish her beauty,
That owes not all its duty
To gaudy tire, or glistering shoo-ty;

Something more than
Taffeta or tissue can,
Or rampant feather, or rich fan;

More than the spoil
Of shop, or silkworm's toil,
Or a bought blush, or a set smile;

A face that 's best
By its own beauty dressed,
And can alone command the rest;

A face made up
Out of no other shop
Than what Nature's white hand sets ope;

A cheek where youth
And blood, with pen of truth
Write what the reader sweetly ru'th;

shoo-ty] shoe-tie; cf. shooties, p. 259.

A cheek where grows
More than a morning rose,
Which to no box its being owes;

Lips where all day
A lover's kiss may play,
Yet carry nothing thence away;

Looks that oppress
Their richest tires, but dress
And clothe their simplest nakedness;

Eyes that displace
The neighbour diamond and outface
That sun-shine by their own sweet grace;

Tresses that wear
Jewels, but to declare
How much themselves more precious are,

Whose native ray
Can tame the wanton day
Of gems that in their bright shades play;

Each ruby there
Or pearl that dares appear,
Be its own blush, be its own tear;

A well-tamed heart,
For whose more noble smart
Love may be long choosing a dart;

Eyes that bestow
Full quivers on Love's bow,
Yet pay less arrows than they owe;

Smiles that can warm
The blood, yet teach a charm
That chastity shall take no harm;

Blushes that bin
The burnish of no sin,
Nor flames of aught too hot within;

Joys that confess
Virtue their mistress,
And have no other head to dress;

Fears fond and slight
As the coy bride's, when night
First does the longing lover right;

Tears quickly fled
And vain, as those are shed
For a dying maidenhead;

Days that need borrow
No part of their good morrow
From a fore-spent night of sorrow;

Days that, in spite
Of darkness, by the light
Of a clear mind are day all night;

Nights, sweet as they,
Made short by lovers' play,
Yet long by the absence of the day;

Life that dares send
A challenge to his end,
And when it comes say, 'Welcome, friend!'

Sydnaean showers
Of sweet discourse, whose powers
Can crown old winter's head with flowers;

Soft silken hours,
Open suns, shady bowers;
'Bove all, nothing within that lours;

Whate'er delight
Can make day's forehead bright
Or give down to the wings of night.

In her whole frame
Have Nature all the name,
Art and ornament the shame.

Her flattery,
Picture and poesy;
Her counsel her own virtue be.

I wish her store
Of worth may leave her poor
Of wishes; and I wish——no more.

Now, if Time knows
That her whose radiant brows
Weave them a garland of my vows,

Her whose just bays
My future hopes can raise,
A trophy to her present praise;

Her that dares be
What these lines wish to see:
I seek no further, it is she.

'Tis she: and here
Lo! I unclothe and clear
My wishes' cloudy character.

May she enjoy it
Whose merit dares apply it
But modesty dares still deny it.

Such worth as this is
Shall fix my flying wishes,
And determine them to kisses.

Let her full glory,
My fancies! fly before ye;
Be ye my fictions, but her story.   *Crashaw.*

The Delights of the Muses, 1646; and B.M. Harl. MS. 6917. (Poem written
before 1635.) *

AN EPITAPH UPON A YOUNG MARRIED COUPLE

DEAD AND BURIED TOGETHER

To these, whom Death again did wed,
This grave 's their second marriage-bed;
For though the hand of Fate could force
'Twixt soul and body a divorce,
It could not sunder man and wife,
Because they both lived but one life.
Peace, good Reader, do not weep.
Peace, the lovers are asleep.
They, sweet turtles, folded lie

Because they both lived] 1646; 'Cause they both lived, 1648 and 1652.

In the last knot Love could tie.
And though they lie as they were dead,
Their pillow stone, their sheets of lead,
(Pillow hard, and sheets not warm)
Love made the bed; they 'll take no harm.
Let them sleep: let them sleep on,
Till this stormy night be gone,
Till the eternal morrow dawn;
Then the curtains will be drawn
And they wake into a light,
Whose day shall never die in night.   *Crashaw.*

Carmen Deo Nostro, 1652. (Poem printed 1646; written before 1635.)*

SONG

O thou that sleep'st like pig in straw,
  Thou lady dear, arise!
Open, to keep the sun in awe,
  Thy pretty pinking eyes:
And, having stretched each leg and arm,
  Put on your clean white smock,
And then, I pray, to keep you warm,
  A petticoat on dock.

Arise, arise! Why should you sleep
  When you have slept enough?
Long since, French boys cried 'Chimney-sweep,'
  And damsels 'Kitchen-stuff.'
The shops were opened long before,
  And youngest prentice goes
To lay at 's mistress' chamber-door
  His master's shining shoes.

Arise, arise!   Your breakfast stays—
   Good water-gruel warm,
Or sugar-sops, which Galen says
   With mace will do no harm.
Arise, arise!   When you are up
   You 'll find more to your cost—
For morning's-draught in caudle-cup,
   Good nut-brown ale and toast.   *Davenant.*

News from Plymouth, in *The Works,* 1673. (Licensed 1635.)*

COME, LOVERS, BRING YOUR CARES

Come, lovers, bring your cares,
Bring sigh-perfumëd sweets,
Bedew the grave with tears,
Where death and virtue meets:
Sigh for the hapless hour
That knit two hearts in one,
And only gave love power
To die when 'twas begun.   *Jones.*

Adrasta, 1635.

SONG

Beauty no more the subject be
Of wanton art to flatter thee;
Or in dull figures call thee spring,
Lily, or rose, or other thing:
All which beneath thee are, and grow
Into contempt when thou dost show
The unmatched glory of thy brow.
Behold a sphere of virgins move,

None 'mongst them less than queen of love;
And yet their queen so far excells,
Beauty and she are only parallels.   *Nabbes.*

Hannibal and Scipio, 1637. (Acted 1635.)

SAILORS FOR MY MONEY

Countrymen of England, who live at home with ease,
And little think what dangers are incident o' the seas:
Give ear unto the sailor who unto you will show
  His case, his case: Howe'er the wind doth blow.

He that is a sailor must have a valiant heart,
For when he is upon the sea, he is not like to start;
But must with noble courage all dangers undergo:
  Resolve, resolve: Howe'er the wind doth blow.

Our calling is laborious and subject to much care,
But we must still contented be, with what falls to our share.
We must not be faint-hearted, come tempest, rain or snow,
  Nor shrink, nor shrink: Howe'er the wind doth blow.

Sometimes on Neptune's bosom our ship is tossed with waves,
And every minute we expect the sea must be our graves.
Sometimes on high she mounteth, then falls again as low,
  With waves, with waves: When stormy winds do blow.

Then with unfeignëd prayers, as Christian duty binds,
We turn unto the Lord of hosts with all our hearts and minds;
To him we flee for succour, for he, we surely know,
  Can save, can save: Howe'er the wind doth blow.

care] J. W. Ebsworth, 1889; woe, 1635.

Then he who breaks the rage, the rough and blusterous seas,
When his disciples were afraid, will straight the storms ap-
    pease,
And give us cause to thank, on bended knees full low,
    Who saves, who saves: Howe'er the wind doth blow.

Our enemies approaching, when we on sea espy,
We must resolve incontinent to fight, although we die;
With noble resolution we must oppose our foe,
    In fight, in fight: Howe'er the wind doth blow.

And when by God's assistance, our foes are put to the foil,
To animate our courages, we all have share o' the spoil.
Our foes into the ocean we back to back do throw,
    To sink, or swim: Howe'er the wind doth blow.   *Parker.*

Pepys 2505, p. 420. (Poem written c. 1635.)*

SONG

Oh, the fickle state of lovers!
A heart perplexed with hopes and fears
To-day a world of joy discovers,
And to-morrow 's drowned in tears:
    A lover's state 's like April's weather,
    Rain and sunshine both together.

If his mistress do but smile,
A heaven of joy is in his heart;
If her brow but frown a while,
Hell can find no greater smart:
    In a lover's breast doth dwell
    Very heaven, or very hell.   *Quarles.*

H. Lawes' *Airs and Dialogues, I.,* 1653. (Poem written c. 1635 ?)*

WHY DOST THOU SHADE THY LOVELY FACE?

Why dost thou shade thy lovely face? Oh, why
Does that eclipsing hand so long deny
The sun-shine of thy soul-enlivening eye?

Without that light, what light remains in me?
Thou art my life, my way, my light; in thee
I live, I move, and by thy beams I see.

Thou art my life; if thou but turn away
My life 's a thousand deaths: thou art my way;
Without thee, Lord, I travel not, but stray.

My light thou art; without thy glorious sight
Mine eyes are darkened with perpetual night.
My God, thou art my way, my life, my light.

Thou art my way; I wander if thou fly:
Thou art my light; if hid, how blind am I!
Thou art my life; if thou withdraw, I die.

Mine eyes are blind and dark, I cannot see;
To whom or whither should my darkness flee,
But to the light? and who 's that light but thee?

My path is lost, my wandering steps do stray;
I cannot safely go, nor safely stay;
Whom should I seek but thee, my path, my way?

Oh, I am dead: to whom shall I, poor I,
Repair? to whom shall my sad ashes fly,
But life? and where is life but in thine eye?

And yet thou turn'st away thy face, and fly'st me;
And yet I sue for grace, and thou deny'st me;
Speak, art thou angry, Lord, or only try'st me?

Unscreen those heavenly lamps, or tell me why
Thou shad'st thy face; perhaps thou think'st no eye
Can view those flames, and not drop down and die.

If that be all, shine forth, and draw thee nigher;
Let me behold and die, for my desire
Is phoenix-like to perish in that fire.

Death-conquered Laz'rus was redeemed by thee;
If I am dead, Lord, set death's prisoner free;
Am I more spent, or stink I worse than he?

If my puffed life be out, give leave to tine
My shameless snuff at that bright lamp of thine;
Oh, what 's thy light the less for lighting mine?

If I have lost my path, great Shepherd, say,
Shall I still wander in a doubtful way?
Lord, shall a lamb of Israel's sheep-fold stray?

Thou art the pilgrim's path, the blind man's eye,
The dead man's life; on thee my hopes rely;
If thou remove, I err, I grope, I die.

Disclose thy sun-beams; close thy wings, and stay;
See, see how I am blind, and dead, and stray,
O thou that art my light, my life, my way.

Emblems, 1635. (Text 1643.)*   *Quarles.*

tine] kindle.

HYMEN

Hymen, god of marriage-bed,
Be thou ever honourëd:
Thou, whose torch's purer light
Death's sad tapers did affright,
And instead of funeral fires
Kindled lovers' chaste desires:
    May their love
    Ever prove
True and constant; let not age
Know their youthful heat to assuage.

Maids, prepare the genial bed:
Then come, night, and hide that red
Which her cheeks, his heart does burn,
Till the envious day return,
And the lusty bridegroom say,
'I have chased her fears away,
    And instead
    Of virginhead,
Given her a greater good,
Perfection and womanhood.'   *Rutter.*

The Shepherd's Holiday, 1635.

THE MARIGOLD

When with a serious musing I behold
The grateful and obsequious marigold,
How duly, every morning, she displays
Her open breast, when Titan spreads his rays;
How she observes him in his daily walk,
Still bending towards him her tender stalk;
How, when he down declines, she droops and mourns,

Bedewed, as 'twere, with tears, till he returns;
And how she veils her flowers when he is gone,
As if she scornëd to be lookëd on
By an inferior eye; or did contemn
To wait upon a meaner light than him:
When this I meditate, methinks the flowers
Have spirits far more generous than ours,
And give us fair examples, to despise
The servile fawnings and idolatries
Wherewith we court these earthly things below,
Which merit not the service we bestow.
    But, O my God! though grovelling I appear
Upon the ground, and have a rooting here
Which hales me downward, yet in my desire
To that which is above me I aspire;
And all my best affections I profess
To him that is the Sun of Righteousness.
Oh! keep the morning of his incarnation,
The burning noontide of his bitter passion,
The night of his descending, and the height
Of his ascension, ever in my sight:
That, imitating him in what I may,
I never follow an inferior way.   *Wither.*

A Collection of Emblems, 1635.*

THE GARLAND OF THE BLESSED VIRGIN MARIE

Here are five letters in this blessëd name,
Which, changed, a five-fold mystery design,
The M the Myrtle, A the Almonds claim,
R Rose, I Ivy, E sweet Eglantine.

These form thy garland, whereof Myrtle green,
The gladdest ground to all the numbered five,

Is so implexëd and laid in between,
As love here studied to keep grace alive.

The second string is the sweet Almond bloom
Ymounted high upon Selinis crest:
As it, alone (and only it) had room,
To knit thy crown, and glorify the rest.

The third is from the garden, called the Rose,
The eye of flowers, worthy for his scent
To top the fairest lily now, that grows
With wonder on the thorny regiment.

The fourth is humble Ivy, intersert,
But lowly laid, as on the earth asleep,
Preservëd in her antique bed of vert,
No faith 's more firm or flat than where 't doth creep.

But that, which sums all, is the Eglantine
Which of the field is cleped the sweetest brier,
Inflamed with ardour to that mystic shine
In Moses' bush, unwasted in the fire.

Thus love, and hope, and burning charity,
(Divinest graces) are so intermixed
With odorous sweets and soft humility,
As if they adored the head, whereon they 're fixed.

A. Stafford's *The Female Glory*, 1635.   *B. I.*

TO CHLOE, WHO WISHED HERSELF YOUNG
ENOUGH FOR ME

Chloe, why wish you that your years
   Would backwards run, till they meet mine,

they 're] th' are, 1635.

That perfect likeness, which endears
  Things unto things, might us combine?
Our ages so in date agree,
That twins do differ more than we.

There are two births: the one, when light
  First strikes the new awakened sense;
The other, when two souls unite,
  And we must count our life from thence:
When you loved me, and I loved you,
Then both of us were born anew.

Love then to us did new souls give,
  And in those souls did plant new powers;
Since when another life we live,
  The breath we breathe is his, not ours;
Love makes those young, whom age doth chill,
And whom he finds young, keeps young still.

Love, like that angel that shall call
  Our bodies from the silent grave,
Unto one age doth raise us all,
  None too much, none too little, have;
Nay, that the difference may be none,
He makes two, not alike, but one.

And now since you and I are such,
  Tell me what 's yours, and what is mine?
Our eyes, our ears, our taste, smell, touch,
  Do, like our souls, in one combine;
So by this, I as well may be
Too old for you, as you for me.   *Cartwright.*

Poems, in *Comedies*, etc., 1651. (Poem written before 1636 ?)*

A VALEDICTION

Bid me not go where neither suns nor showers
        Do make or cherish flowers;
Where discontented things in sadness lie,
        And Nature grieves as I;
    When I am parted from those eyes,
    From which my better day doth rise,
        Though some propitious power
        Should plant me in a bower,
Where amongst happy lovers I might see
        How showers and sun-beams bring
        One everlasting spring,
Nor would those fall, nor these shine forth to me:
    Nature herself to him is lost,
    Who loseth her he honours most.
Then, fairest, to my parting view display
        Your graces all in one full day;
Whose blessèd shapes I 'll snatch and keep, till when
        I do return and view again:
So, by this art, fancy shall fortune cross,
And lovers live by thinking on their loss.

Ibid.   *Cartwright.*

A GOOD EATING SONG

Then our music is in prime,
When our teeth keep triple time;
    Hungry notes are fit for knells:
        May lankness be
        No quest to me.
    The bag-pipe sounds when that it swells.
                May lankness, &c.

A mooting-night brings wholesome smiles,
When John-a-Nokes and John-a-Stiles
    Do grease the lawyer's satin.
        A reading day
        Frights French away,
    The benchers dare speak Latin.
                                        A reading, &c.

He that 's full doth verse compose;
Hunger deals in sullen prose:
    Take notice and discard her.
        The empty spit
        Ne'er cherished wit;
    Minerva loves the larder.
                                        The empty spit, &c.

First to break fast, then to dine,
Is to conquer Bellarmine:
    Distinctions then are budding.
        Old Sutcliff's wit
        Did never hit,
    But after his bag-pudding.
                                        Old Sutcliff's wit, &c.
                                                            Cartwright.

The Ordinary, in *Comedies,* etc., 1651. (Written before 1636.)*

SEAL UP HER EYES, O SLEEP

Seal up her eyes, O sleep, but flow
Mild as her manners, to and fro;
Slide soft into her, that yet she
May receive no wound from thee.
And ye present her thoughts, O dreams,
With hushing winds and purling streams,

Whiles hovering silence sits without,
Careful to keep disturbance out.
Thus seize her, sleep, thus her again resign;
So what was Heaven's gift we 'll reckon thine.

Cartwright.

The Siege, in *Comedies,* etc., 1651. (Written before 1636 ?)*

DRINKING SONG

Now, now the sun is fled
Down into Tethys' bed,
Ceasing his solemn course awhile. What then?
'Tis not to sleep, but be
Merry all night, as we:
Gods can be mad sometimes as well as men.
*Then laugh we, and quaff we, until our rich noses
Grow red and contest with our chaplets of roses.*

If he be fled, whence may
We have a second day,
That shall not set till we command? Here see
A day that does arise
Like his, but with more eyes,
And warms us with a better fire than he.
*Then laugh we, and quaff we, until our rich noses
Grow red and contest with our chaplets of roses.*

Thus then we chase the night
With these true floods of light,
This Lesbian wine, which with its sparkling streams,
Darting diviner graces,
Casts glories round our faces,
And dulls the tapers with majestic beams.

> *Then laugh we, and quaff we, until our rich noses*
> *Grow red and contest with our chaplets of roses.*
>
> Cartwright.

The Royal Slave, 1639. (Acted 1636; written earlier?)*

TO HIS MISTRESS

Tyrian dye why do you wear,
You whose cheeks best scarlet are?
  Why do you fondly pin
  Pure linens o'er your skin
  (Your skin that 's whiter far),
Casting a dusky cloud before a star?

Why bears your neck a golden chain?
Did Nature make your hair in vain
  Of gold most pure and fine?
  With gems why do you shine?
  They, neighbours to your eyes,
Show but like Phosphor when the sun doth rise.

I would have all my mistress' parts
Owe more to Nature than to arts;
  I would not woo the dress,
  Or one whose nights give less
  Contentment than the day;
She 's fair whose beauty only makes her gay.

For 'tis not buildings make a court,
Or pomp, but 'tis the King's resort:
  If Jupiter down pour
  Himself, and in a shower
  Hide such bright majesty,
Less than a golden one it cannot be.

Cowley.

Sylva, 1636.

SONG

My limbs I will fling
Out of joint and sing,
And dancing will shake my hair:
Not bow at each beck,
Nor break my neck
With sorrow and deep despair.

Such a chirping din,
With mirth within,
And a head not needing a clout,
Is much better far
Than a careful chair
And a wreath of thorns without.   *Strode.*

The Floating Island, 1655. (Acted 1636.)*

LOVE AND DEATH

Though I am young and cannot tell
Either what Death or Love is well,
Yet I have heard they both bear darts,
And both do aim at human hearts:
And then again, I have been told,
Love wounds with heat, as Death with cold;
So that I fear they do but bring
Extremes to touch, and mean one thing.
As in a ruin we it call
One thing to be blown up, or fall;
Or to our end like way may have
By a flash of lightning, or a wave:
So Love's inflaméd shaft or brand,
May kill as soon as Death's cold hand;

> Except Love's fires the virtue have
> To fright the frost out of the grave.   *Jonson.*

The Sad Shepherd, in *The Works,* 1640. (Poem written before 1637.)*

Milton's *Lycidas* (first printed in *Obsequies to the Memory of Mr. Edward King,* 1638) was written 1637.

NIGHT'S SONG

In wet and cloudy mists I slowly rise,
    As with mine own dull weight oppressed,
To close with sleep the jealous lovers' eyes,
    And give forsaken virgins rest.

The adventurous merchant and the mariner,
    Whom storms all day vex in the deep,
Begin to trust the winds when I appear,
    And lose their dangers in their sleep.

The studious, that consume their brains and sight
    In search where doubtful knowledge lies,
Grow weary of their fruitless use of light,
    And wish my shades to ease their eyes.

The ambitious toiling statesman, that prepares
    Great mischiefs ere the day begins,
Not measures day by hours, but by his cares;
    And night must intermit his sins.

Then why, when my slow chariot used to climb,
    Did old mistaking sages weep,
As if my empire did usurp their time,
    And hours were lost when spent in sleep?

> I come to ease their labours, and prevent
> That weariness which would destroy:
> The profit of their toils are still mis-spent
> Till rest enables to enjoy.   *Davenant* (?)

Luminalia, 1637.*

EPITAPH

> In this marble, buried lies
> Beauty may enrich the skies,
> And add light to Phoebus' eyes:
>
> Sweeter than Aurora's air
> When she paints the lilies fair,
> And gilds cowslips with her hair:
>
> Chaster than the virgin spring,
> Ere her blossoms she doth bring,
> Or cause Philomel to sing.
>
> If such goodness live 'mongst men,
> Bring me to it, I know then
> She is come from heaven again;
>
> But if not, ye standers-by,
> Cherish me, and say that I
> Am the next designed to die.   *Jordan.*

Poetical Varieties, 1637.*

WHY SO PALE AND WAN, FOND LOVER

> Why so pale and wan, fond lover?
> Prithee why so pale?
> Will, when looking well can't move her,
> Looking ill prevail?
> Prithee why so pale?

Why so dull and mute, young sinner?
        Prithee why so mute?
Will, when speaking well can't win her,
        Saying nothing do 't?
        Prithee why so mute?

Quit, quit, for shame; this will not move,
        This cannot take her;
If of herself she will not love,
        Nothing can make her:
        The devil take her!   *Suckling.*

Aglaura, 1638. (Acted 1637 ?) *

THE TINKER AND THE MONKS

Drink full ones, tinker, methinks the monks are dry,
Drink healths, mine host, the monks do fear a thirst.
Are the monks thirsty? the monks will quickly try
If they or the tinker want a pillow first.
    Else will we jig and hay unto the black pot's sound,
    Till, to that music, the house shall dance the round.

Then fill a dozen, hostess, we 'll have a merry cup,
And make the tinker forfeit his budget and his brass.
'Faith!' says the tinker, 'I 'll make your monkships sup
Till ye sing requiems in reading of the mass.'
    Then fill a gallon, hostess, we 'll health it all about,
    Till all complain o' th' headache, the falling, or the gout.

Come on, dropping shavelings, let 's see you count your beads,
I am half afraid you 'll stutter in the mass.
Gramercy, lovely pots, and nimble Ganymedes,
That brought more water than what holy was.

Well, saucy tinker, well, pray finger you your brass,
And let the monks alone, 'lone, they 'll finger well the mass.

Le hore di recreatione, 1637.   *Whiting.*

WHERE DID YOU BORROW THAT LAST SIGH?

Where did you borrow that last sigh,
    And that relenting groan?
For those that sigh, and not for love,
    Usurp what 's not their own.
Love's arrows sooner armour pierce
    Than your soft snowy skin;
Your eyes can only teach us love,
    But cannot take it in.   *Berkley.*

The Lost Lady, 1639. (Acted 1638.)*

SPORT

The merry waves dance up and down, and play,
    Sport is granted to the sea;
Birds are the quiristers of the empty air,
    Sport is never wanting there;
The ground doth smile at the spring's flowery birth,
    Sport is granted to the earth;
The fire its cheering flame on high doth rear,
    Sport is never wanting there.
If all the elements, the earth, the sea,
    Air, and fire, so merry be,
Why is man's mirth so seldom and so small,
    Who is compounded of them all?

Love's Riddle, 1638.   *Cowley.*

TO THE QUEEN,
ENTERTAINED AT NIGHT BY THE COUNTESS OF ANGLESEY

Fair as unshaded light, or as the day
In its first birth, when all the year was May;
Sweet as the altar's smoke, or as the new
Unfolded bud, swelled by the early dew;
Smooth as the face of waters first appeared,
Ere tides began to strive or winds were heard;
Kind as the willing saints, and calmer far
Than in their sleeps forgiven hermits are:
You, that are more than our discreeter fear
Dares praise with such dull art, what make you here?
Here, where the summer is so little seen
That leaves (her cheapest wealth) scarce reach at green;
You come, as if the silver planet were
Misled a while from her much injured sphere,
And to ease the travails of her beams to-night,
In this small lanthorn would contract her light.   *Davenant.*

Madagascar, 1638.*

ON A MISTRESS OF WHOSE AFFECTIONS HE WAS DOUBTFUL

What though with figures I should raise
Above all height my mistress' praise:
Calling her cheek a blushing rose,
The fairest June did e'er disclose;
Her forehead lilies, and her eyes
The luminaries of the skies;
That on her lips ambrosia grows,

dull art] 1638;   full art, 1648 and 1673.

And from her kisses nectar flows?
Too great hyperboles; unless
She loves me she is none of these.
But if her heart and her desires
Do answer mine with equal fires,
These attributes are then too poor:
She is all these, and ten times more.   *Nabbes.*

The Spring's Glory, 1638.

A DESCRIPTION OF THE SPRING

And now all Nature seemed in love:
The lusty sap began to move;
New juice did stir the embracing vines,
And birds had drawn their valentines;
The jealous trout, that low did lie,
Rose at a well-dissembled fly;
There stood my friend, with patient skill
Attending of his trembling quill.
Already were the eaves possessed
With the swift pilgrims' daubëd nest;
The groves already did rejoice
In Philomel's triumphing voice.
The showers were short, the weather mild,
The morning fresh, the evening smiled.
Joan takes her neat-rubbed pail, and now
She trips to milk the sand-red cow;
Where, for some sturdy football swain,
Joan strokes a sillabub or twain.
The fields and gardens were beset
With tulip, crocus, violet;

And now all] 1651;   This day Dame, 1653.   New] 1651;   Fresh, 1653.
tulip] 1651;   tulips, 1653.

And now, though late, the modest rose
Did more than half a blush disclose.
Thus all looked gay, all full of cheer,
To welcome the new-liveried year.   *Wotton.*

Reliquiae Wottonianae, 1651. (And in *The Complete Angler,* 1653. Poem
written c. 1638.) *

ASK ME NO MORE

Ask me no more where Jove bestows,
When June is past, the fading rose;
For in your beauties, orient deep,
These flowers, as in their causes, sleep.

Ask me no more whither do stray
The golden atoms of the day;
For in pure love heaven did prepare
Those powders to enrich your hair.

Ask me no more whither doth haste
The nightingale, when May is past;
For in your sweet dividing throat
She winters, and keeps warm her note.

Ask me no more where those stars light,
That downwards fall in dead of night;
For in your eyes they sit, and there
Fixëd become, as in their sphere.

Ask me no more if east or west
The phoenix builds her spicy nest;

looked gay, all] 1651; looks gay, and, 1653.

For unto you at last she flies,
And in your fragrant bosom dies.   *Carew.*

Poems, 1640. (Written before 1639.)*

MEDIOCRITY IN LOVE REJECTED

Give me more love, or more disdain;
    The torrid or the frozen zone
Bring equal ease unto my pain;
    The temperate affords me none:
Either extreme, of love or hate,
Is sweeter than a calm estate.

Give me a storm; if it be love,
    Like Danae in that golden shower,
I 'll swim in pleasure; if it prove
    Disdain, that torrent will devour
My vulture hopes; and he 's possessed
Of heaven, that 's but from hell released.
Then crown my joys, or cure my pain;
Give me more love, or more disdain.   *Carew.*

Ibid.*

TO MY INCONSTANT MISTRESS

When thou, poor excommunicate
    From all the joys of love, shalt see
The full reward, and glorious fate,
    Which my strong faith shall purchase me,
    Then curse thine own inconstancy.

A fairer hand than thine shall cure
    That heart, which thy false oaths did wound;

I 'll swim] Mod. eds.;   I swim, 1640, 1642, and 1651.

And to my soul, a soul more pure
    Than thine, shall by Love's hand be bound,
    And both with equal glory crowned.

Then shalt thou weep, entreat, complain
    To Love, as I did once to thee;
When all thy tears shall be as vain
    As mine were then, for thou shalt be
    Damned for thy false apostasy.   *Carew.*

Poems, 1640. (Written before 1639.)*

CELIA SINGING

You that think Love can convey
    No other way
But through the eyes, into the heart,
    His fatal dart,
Close up those casements, and but hear
    This siren sing;
    And on the wing
Of her sweet voice, it shall appear
That Love can enter at the ear.

Then unveil your eyes; behold
    The curious mould
Where that voice dwells, and as we know,
    When the cocks crow,
And Sol is mounted on his way,
    We freely may
    Gaze on the day;
So may you, when the music 's done,
Awake, and see the rising sun.   *Carew.*

Ibid.*

PERSUASIONS TO ENJOY

If the quick spirits in your eye
Now languish, and anon must die;
If every sweet and every grace
Must fly from that forsaken face;
  Then, Celia, let us reap our joys
  Ere time such goodly fruit destroys.

Or, if that golden fleece must grow
For ever free from aged snow;
If those bright suns must know no shade,
Nor your fresh beauties ever fade;
Then fear not, Celia, to bestow
What, still being gathered, still must grow.
  Thus, either Time his sickle brings
  In vain, or else in vain his wings.   *Carew.*

*Ibid.**

EPITAPH ON THE LADY MARY VILLIERS

The Lady Mary Villiers lies
Under this stone: with weeping eyes
The parents that first gave her birth,
And their sad friends, laid her in earth.
If any of them, reader, were
Known unto thee, shed a tear;
Or if thyself possess a gem,
As dear to thee as this to them,
Though a stranger to this place,
Bewail in theirs thine own hard case;
For thou perhaps at thy return
May'st find thy darling in an urn.   *Carew.*

Ibid.

TO A LADY THAT DESIRED I WOULD LOVE HER

Now you have freely given me leave to love,
What will you do?
Shall I your mirth or passion move
When I begin to woo?
Will you torment, or scorn, or love me too?

Each petty beauty can disdain, and I,
Spite of your hate,
Without your leave can see, and die.
Dispense a nobler fate!
'Tis easy to destroy; you may create.

Then give me leave to love, and love me too:
Not with design
To raise, as Love's curst rebels do,
When puling poets whine,
Fame to their beauty, from their blubbered eyne.

Grief is a puddle, and reflects not clear
Your beauties' rays;
Joys are pure streams; your eyes appear
Sullen in sadder lays;
In cheerful numbers they shine bright with praise;

Which shall not mention, to express you fair,
Wounds, flames, and darts,
Storms in your brow, nets in your hair,
Suborning all your parts,
Or to betray, or torture captive hearts.

I 'll make your eyes like morning suns appear,
As mild and fair;

Your brow as crystal smooth and clear;
  And your dishevelled hair
Shall flow like a calm region of the air.

Rich Nature's store, which is the poet's treasure,
  I 'll spend to dress
Your beauties, if your mine of pleasure
  In equal thankfulness
You but unlock, so we each other bless.   *Carew.**

Poems, 1640. (Written before 1639.)

BOLDNESS IN LOVE

Mark how the bashful morn in vain
  Courts the amorous marigold
With sighing blasts and weeping rain,
  Yet she refuses to unfold;
But when the planet of the day
Approacheth with his powerful ray,
Then she spreads, then she receives
His warmer beams into her virgin leaves.

So shalt thou thrive in love, fond boy:
  If thy tears and sighs discover
Thy grief, thou never shalt enjoy
  The just reward of a bold lover;
But when with moving accents thou
Shalt constant faith and service vow,
Thy Celia shall receive those charms
With open ears, and with unfolded arms.   *Carew.*

*Ibid.**

THE WINTER STORMS

Blow, blow!   The winds are so hoarse they cannot blow.
Cold, cold!   Our tears freeze to hail, our spittle to snow.
  The waves are all up, they swell as they run:
        Let them rise and rise
        As high as the skies,
  And higher to wash the face of the sun.

Port, port!   The pilot is blind!   Port at the helm!
Yare, yare!   For one foot of shore take a whole realm.
  A-lee, or we sink!   Does no man know how to wind her?
        Less noise, and more room!
        We sail in a drum,
  Our sails are but rags, which lightning turns to tinder.

Aloof, aloof!   Hey, how those carracks and ships
Fall foul and are tumbled and driven like chips!
  Our boatsen, alas, a silly weak gristle,
        For fear to catch cold
        Lies down in the hold,
  We all hear his sighs, but few hear his whistle.

The Works, 1673. (Poem written before 1639?)*   *Davenant.*

TO HIS MISTRESS CONFINED

Think not, my Phoebe, 'cause a cloud
Doth now thy heavenly beauty shroud,
    My wandering eye
Can stoop to common beauties of the sky.
    Be thou but kind, and this eclipse
    Shall neither hinder eyes nor lips;
    For we will meet
Within our hearts, and kiss, when none shall see 't.

Nor canst thou in thy prison be
Without some loving signs of me:
        When thou dost spy
A sunbeam peep into thy room, 'tis I,
        For I am hid within that flame,
        And thus unto thy chamber came
            To let thee see
In what a martyrdom I burn for thee.

There 's no sad picture that doth dwell
Upon thy arras wall, but well
            Resembles me.
No matter though our years do not agree,
        Love can make old, as well as time,
        And he that doth but twenty climb,
            If he will prove
As true as I, shows fourscore years in love.

J. Shirley's *Poems &c*, 1646.   *Pick, Carew,* or *Shirley.*
(Variant written before 1639; printed 1639.)*

UNCLOSE THOSE EYELIDS

Unclose those eyelids, and out-shine
    The brightness of the breaking day;
The light they cover is divine,
    Why should it fade so soon away?
Stars vanish so and day appears,
The sun 's so drowned i' the morning's tears.

Oh! let not sadness cloud this beauty,
    Which if you lose, you 'll ne'er recover;
It is not love's, but sorrow's duty
    To die so soon for a dead lover.

Banish, oh! banish grief, and then
Our joys will bring our hopes again.   *Glapthorne.*

Poems, 1639.

HOLLO, MY FANCY!

In a melancholy fancy,
Out of myself,
Thorough the welkin dance I,
All the world surveying,
No where staying,
Like unto the fiery elf;
Over the tops of highest mountains skipping,
Over the plains, the woods, the valleys, tripping,
Over the seas without oar of shipping,
Hollo, my fancy! whither wilt thou go?

Amidst the cloudy vapours
Fain would I see
What are those burning tapers
Which benight us
And affright us,
And what the meteors be.
Fain would I know what is the roaring thunder,
And the bright lightning which cleaves the clouds in
sunder;
And what the comets are at which men gaze and
wonder;
Hollo, my fancy! whither wilt thou go?

Look but down below me
Where you may be bold,
Where none can see or know me,
All the world of gadding,
Running, of madding,
None can their stations hold:

One he sits drooping all in a dumpish passion,
Another he is for mirth and recreation,
The third he hangs his head because he 's out of
          fashion;
     Hollo, my fancy! whither wilt thou go?

          See, see, see what a bustling!
          Now I descry
          One another justling,
          How they are turmoiling,
          One another foiling,
          And how I passed them by!
He that 's above, him that 's below despiseth;
He that 's below doth envy him that riseth;
Every man his plot and counter-plot deviseth;
     Hollo, my fancy! whither wilt thou go?

          Ships, ships, ships, I descry now,
          Crossing on the main;
          I 'll go too and try now
          What they are projecting
          And protecting,
          And when they turn again:
One he 's to keep his country from invading;
Another he is for merchandise and trading;
The other lies at home like summer's cattle shading;
     Hollo, my fancy! whither wilt thou go?

          Hollo, my fancy, hollo!
          I pray thee come unto me,
          I can no longer follow;
          I pray thee come and try me,

try me] Ballad;   MS. omits 'me.'

Do not fly me,
Sith it will no better be;
Come, come away! leave off thy lofty soaring;
Come stay at home, and on this book be poring;
For he that gads abroad he hath the less in storing.
Welcome, my fancy! welcome home to me!   *Anon.*

B.M. Add. MS. 27879. (Variant, Douce Ballads 269. Poem written c. 1639?)*

ON HIS MISTRESS CROSSING THE SEA

Farewell, fair saint! let not the seas and wind
Swell like the eyes and hearts you leave behind;
But, smooth and gentle as the looks you bear,
Smile in your face and whisper in your ear.
May no bold billow venture to arise
That it may nearer gaze upon your eyes,
Lest wind and waves enamoured of your form
Should crowd and throng themselves into a storm.
But if it be your fate, vast seas! to love,
Of my becalmëd breast learn how to move:
Move then, but in a gentle lover's pace,
No wrinkle nor no furrow in your face.
And you, fierce winds! see that you tell your tale
In such a breath as may but fill her sail.
So whilst you court her each your several way
You may her safely to her port convey,
And lose her by the noblest way of wooing,
Whilst both contribute to your own undoing.   *T. Cary.*

R. Fanshawe's *Il Pastor Fido*, 1647. (Poem written before 1640.)*

TO MY SOUL IN ITS BLINDNESS

How is 't, my Soul, that thou giv'st eyes their sight
To view their objects, yet hast none

To see thine own?
Earth's, air's, heaven's beauties they discern: their light
    Fair flowers admires, their several dresses,
        Their golden tresses;
The lily, rose, the various tulip, scorning
The pride of princes in their choice adorning.

They joy to view the aïr's painted nations:
    The peacock's train which the head outvies
        With fairer eyes,
And emulates the heavenly constellations:
    The ostrich whose fair plume embraves
        Kings, captains, slaves;
The halcyons whose Triton-bills appease
Curled waves, and with their eggs lay stormy seas.

Pilots' fixed eyes observe the arctic Bear
    With all her unwashed starry trains
        In heavenly plains;
Night-travellers behold the moon to steer
    Her ship, sailing, while Eol raves,
        Through cloudy waves;
Our less world's suns with pleasure view the light
Which gives all beauties beauty, them their sight.

Thou that giv'st sight to clay, to blackness light,
    How art so dull, so dim in duty
        To view his beauty
Who quickens every life, lights every light?
    His height those eagles' eyes surpasses:
        Thou wants thy glasses:
Take up that pèrspective and view those streams
Of light, and fill thy waning orb with beams.

Then see the flowers clad in his liveries,
    And from his cheek and lovely face
       Steal all their grace:
See fowls from him borrow their braveries,
    And all their feather-painted dresses
       From his fair tresses:
See stars, and moon, the sun and all perfection
Beg light and life from his bright eyes' reflection.

Look on his lips: heaven's gate there open lies,
    Thence that grace-breathing Spirit blows,
       Thence honey flows.
Look on his hands: the world's full treasuries.
    Fix all thy looks his heart upon:
       Love's highest throne.
And, when thy sight that radiant beauty blears
And dazzles thy weak eyes, see with thine ears.

A Father's Testament, 1670. (Written before 1640 ?)*   *P. Fletcher.*

SONG

Blow there, sweet Zephyrus! where thou shalt find
A breath more aromatic than thy wind,
When through the Arabian coast perfumed it flies
By spicy flames in which the phoenix dies.
Blow there, and add unto thy sweetness store,
Such as, when she is not, shall be no more.

Cavern it up, and keep that sovereign breath
To purify the air in time of death.
Blow there, and in soft language spoken low,
Thou gentle air, in secret make her know
How, like the phoenix, I do sacrifice
My heart to her, inflamèd by her eyes.   *Anon.*

B.M. Eg. MS. 2013. (Poem written before 1640 ?)*

STAY, STAY, OLD TIME

Stay, stay, old Time! repose thy restless wings:
Pity thyself, though thou obdurate be,
And wilfully wear'st out all other things.
Stay, and behold a face, which, but to see,
Will make thee shake off half a world of days,
And wearied pinions feather with new plumes.
Lay down thy sandy glass, that never stays,
And cruel crooked scythe, that all consumes,
To gaze on her more lovely than Apollo.
Renew thyself: continue still her youth:
Oh, stay with her (and him no longer follow)
That is as beauteous as thy darling Truth!   *Anon.*

Ibid.

GRIEVE NOT, DEAR LOVE

Grieve not, dear Love, although we often part;
    But know that Nature gently doth us sever,
Thereby to train us up with tender art,
    To brook the day when we must part for ever.

For Nature, doubting we should be surprised
    By that sad day, whose dread doth chiefly fear us,
Doth keep us daily schooled and exercised,
    Lest that the fright thereof should overbear us.
                                J. Digby, Earl of Bristol.

B.M. Add. MS. 25707, [c. 1640]. (Printed in H. Lawes' *Airs and Dialogues, I.,*
1653.)

NOX NOCTI INDICAT SCIENTIAM

When I survey the bright
    Celestial sphere;

So rich with jewels hung, that night
Doth like an Ethiop bride appear;

My soul her wings doth spread
      And heaven-ward flies,
The Almighty's mysteries to read
In the large volumes of the skies.

For the bright firmament
      Shoots forth no flame
So silent, but is eloquent
In speaking the Creator's name.

No unregarded star
      Contracts its light
Into so small a character,
Removed far from our human sight,

But if we steadfast look
      We shall discern
In it, as in some holy book,
How man may heavenly knowledge learn.

It tells the conqueror,
      That far-stretched power,
Which his proud dangers traffic for,
Is but the triumph of an hour;

That from the farthest north,
      Some nation may,
Yet undiscovered, issue forth,
And o'er his new-got conquest sway:

Some nation yet shut in
      With hills of ice

May be let out to scourge his sin
Till they shall equal him in vice.

And then they likewise shall
      Their ruin have;
For as yourselves your empires fall,
And every kingdom hath a grave.

Thus those celestial fires,
      Though seeming mute,
The fallacy of our desires
And all the pride of life confute:

For they have watched since first
      The world had birth;
And found sin in itself accurst,
And nothing permanent on earth.   *Habington.*

*Castara, 1640.**

OF DEATH

Noblest bodies are but gilded clay:
      Put away
   But the precious shining rind,
The inmost rottenness remains behind.
Kings, on earth though gods they be,
Yet in death are vile as we;
He, a thousands' king before,
Now is vassal unto more.
Vermin now insulting lie,
And dig for diamonds in each eye:
Whilst the sceptre-bearing hand
Cannot their inroads withstand.
Here doth one in odours wade
By the regal unction made,

While another dares to gnaw
On that tongue, his people's law.
Fools! ah, fools are we, who so contrive,
And do strive,
In each gaudy ornament,
Who shall his corpse in the best dish present.

Harding.

Sicily and Naples, 1640.

SONG

Was it a form, a gait, a grace,
Was it their sweetness merely?
Was it the heaven of a bright face,
That made me love so dearly?

Was it a skin of silk and snow,
That soul and senses wounded?
Was 't any of these, or all of these,
Whereon my faith was founded?

Ah, no! 'twas a far deeper part
Than all the rest that won me:
'Twas a fair-clothed but feigning heart
I loved, and has undone me.   *H. Reynolds.*

H. Lawes' *Airs and Dialogues, II.,* 1655. (And c. 1640, in B.M. Add. MS. 25707.)

10

You virgins, that did late despair
To keep your wealth from cruel men,
Tie up in silk your careless hair:
Soft peace is come again.

Now lovers' eyes may gently shoot
  A flame that will not kill;
The drum was angry, but the lute
  Shall whisper what you will.

Sing Io, Io! for his sake
  Who hath restored your drooping heads;
With choice of sweetest flowers make
  A garden where he treads;

Whilst we whole groves of laurel bring,
  A petty triumph to his brow,
Who is the master of our spring
  And all the bloom we owe.   *Shirley.*

The Imposture, 1652. (Licensed 1640. Song printed 1646.) *

SHE'S PRETTY TO WALK WITH

She 's pretty to walk with:
  And witty to talk with:
And pleasant too to think on.
  But the best use of all
  Is, her health is a stale,
And helps us to make us drink on.   *Suckling.*

The Discontented Colonel, [1640 ?]. (Text from *Fragmenta Aurea,* 1646.) *

TO PHILOMEL

Leave, Philomel, to make thy moan!
'Tis I have cause to grieve alone:

will not] Mod. eds.; wo' not, 1646 and 1652.   we owe.] we own.
a stale] a pretext, *i.e.* for drinking.

Thy woes had periods, mine must be
Invaded with fresh cruelty.
The joys I have are such as may
Make the green spring a winter's day;
Or such as, when desired, do take
A course to kill.   For pity sake,
Cease then thy noise of woe, unless
Thou 'lt grieve for my unhappiness.   *Tatham.*

The Fancies Theatre, 1640.

FATUM SUPREMUM

All buildings are but monuments of death,
     All clothes but winding sheets for our last knell,
All dainty fattings for the worms beneath,
     All curious music but our passing bell:
Thus death is nobly waited on, for why
All that we have is but death's livery.   *Anon.*

Wit's Recreations, 1640.*

THE SYMPATHY

If at this time I am derided,
     And you please to laugh at me,
Know I am not unprovided
     Every way to answer thee,
     Love or hate, whate'er it be.

Never twins so nearly met
     As thou and I in our affection:
When thou weep'st my eyes are wet,

for why] because.

That thou lik'st is my election,
I am in the same subjection.

In one centre we are both,
 Both our lives the same way tending:
Do thou refuse, and I shall loathe,
 As thy eyes, so mine are bending,
 Either storm or calm portending.

I am careless if despisèd,
 For I can contemn again;
How can I be then surprisèd
 Or with sorrow, or with pain,
 When I can both love and disdain?   *Anon.*

Choice Drollery, 1656. (And c. 1640, in B.M. Add. 25707.) *

ON A LADY SLEEPING

Calmly as the morning's soft tears shed
Upon some rose or violet bed,
May your slumbers fall upon you,
All your thoughts sit easy on you,
Gently rocking heart and eyes
With their tuneful lullabies,
While I, till the early morrow light
Shall with your dreams have chased the night,
Like the sick flower, which when to bed
The sun is gone hangs the faint head
As every other warmth despising,
Will lie and wait your eyelids' fair uprising.   *Anon.*

J. Wilson's Autograph MS., Bodley MS. Mus. b. 1. (And c. 1640, in B.M.
Add. MS. 25707.) *

I, till] N.A.; I tell, Bod. MS.; still B.M. MS.   chased] Bod. MS.;
charmed, B.M. MS.

BELIEVE NOT HIM

Believe not him whom love hath left so wise
    As to have power his own tale to tell;
For children's griefs do yield the loudest cries,
    And cold desires may be expressëd well.
In well-told love most often falsehood lies,
But pity him that only sighs and dies.   *Anon.*

B.M. Stowe MS. 962, [c. 1640]. (Poem printed 1661.)*

THE CHOICE

What care I though she be fair—
    Hair, snow-like hand, or sun-like eye—
If in that beauty I not share?
    Were she deformëd, what care I?

What care I though she be foul—
    Hair, swarthy hand, or sun-burnt eye—
So long as I enjoy her soul?
    Let her be so, why what care I?

Dim sight is cozened with a gloss
    Of gaudy gown, or humorous hair;
Such gold in melting leaves more dross
    Than some unpolished pieces share.

Be she fair, or foul, or either,
Or made up of both together,
Be her heart mine, hair, hand, or eye
Be what it will, why what care I?   *Beedome.*

Poems, Divine and Humane, 1641. (Written before 1641.)*

gloss] 1653; glasse, 1641.   leaves] 1653; leave, 1641.   pieces] N.A.;
prices, 1641 and 1653.

SONG OF THE BEGGARS

From hunger and cold who lives more free,
Or who more richly clad than we?
Our bellies are full, our flesh is warm,
And against pride our rags are a charm.
Enough is our feast, and for to-morrow
Let rich men care; we feel no sorrow:
    No sorrow, no sorrow, no sorrow, no sorrow,
    Let rich men care, we feel no sorrow.

Each city, each town, and every village
Affords us either an alms or pillage.
And if the weather be cold or raw,
Then in a barn we tumble in straw;
If warm and fair, by yea-cock and nay-cock
The fields will afford us a hedge or a hay-cock:
    A hay-cock, a hay-cock, a hay-cock, a hay-cock,
    The fields will afford us a hedge or a hay-cock.

A Jovial Crew, 1652. (Acted 1641.)*   R. Brome.

A BALLAD UPON A WEDDING

I tell thee, Dick, where I have been,
Where I the rarest things have seen,
    Oh, things without compare!
Such sights again can not be found
In any place on English ground,
    Be it at wake or fair.

At Charing Cross, hard by the way
Where we, thou know'st, do sell our hay,
    There is a house with stairs;
And there did I see coming down
Such folk as are not in our town,
    Vorty at least, in pairs.

Amongst the rest, one pestilent fine
(His beard no bigger though than thine,)
   Walked on before the rest:
Our landlord looks like nothing to him;
The King (God bless him!) 'twould undo him
   Should he go still so dressed.

At course-a-park, without all doubt,
He should have first been taken out
   By all the maids i' the town,
Though lusty Roger there had been,
Or little George upon the Green,
   Or Vincent of the Crown.

But wot you what? the youth was going
To make an end of all his wooing;
   The parson for him stayed:
Yet by his leave, for all his haste,
He did not so much wish all past,
   Perchance, as did the maid.

The maid—and thereby hangs a tale,
For such a maid no Whitson-ale
   Could ever yet produce:
No grape that 's kindly ripe could be
So round, so plump, so soft as she,
   Nor half so full of juice.

Her finger was so small, the ring
Would not stay on which he did bring,
   It was too wide a peck;
And to say truth (for out it must)

---

course-a-park] a country game.   Whitson-ale] Whitsun festival.

It looked like the great collar, just,
    About our young colt's neck.

Her feet beneath her petticoat
Like little mice stole in and out,
    As if they feared the light;
But, Dick! she dances such a way,
No sun upon an Easter day
    Is half so fine a sight.

He would have kissed her once or twice,
But she would not, she was so nice,
    She would not do 't in sight;
And then she looked as who should say
I will do what I list to-day,
    And you shall do 't at night.

Her cheeks so rare a white was on,
No daisy makes comparison,
    (Who sees them is undone,)
For streaks of red were mingled there
Such as are on a Katherine pear,
    The side that 's next the sun.

Her lips were red, and one was thin
Compared to that was next her chin—
    Some bee had stung it newly:
But, Dick, her eyes so guard her face,
I durst no more upon them gaze
    Than on the sun in July.

Her mouth so small, when she does speak,
Thou'dst swear her teeth her words did break,

---

was so nice] Mod. eds.;   was nice, 1646, 1648, and 1658.

That they might passage get;
But she so handled still the matter,
They came as good as ours, or better,
  And are not spent a whit.

If wishing should be any sin
The parson himself had guilty bin,
  She looked that day so purely;
And did the youth so oft the feat
At night, as some did in conceit,
  It would have spoiled him, surely.

Passion o' me! how I run on!
There 's that that would be thought upon,
  I trow, besides the bride:
The business of the kitchen 's great,
For it is fit that men should eat;
  Nor was it there denied.

Just in the nick the cook knocked thrice,
And all the waiters in a trice
  His summons did obey;
Each serving-man with dish in hand
Marched boldly up, like our trained band,
  Presented, and away.

When all the meat was on the table
What man of knife, or teeth, was able
  To stay to be intreated?
And this the very reason was
Before the parson could say grace
  The company was seated.

Passion o' me] Mod. eds.;   Passion oh me, 1646, 1648, and 1658.

Now hats fly off, and youths carouse;
Healths first go round, and then the house,
   The bride's came thick and thick;
And when 'twas named another's health,
Perhaps he made it hers by stealth:
   (And who could help it? Dick!)

O' the sudden up they rise and dance;
Then sit again, and sigh, and glance;
   Then dance again and kiss:
Thus several ways the time did pass,
Whilst every woman wished her place,
   And every man wished his.

By this time all were stol'n aside
To counsel and undress the bride,
   But that he must not know:
But yet 'twas thought he guessed her mind,
And did not mean to stay behind
   Above an hour or so.

When in he came, Dick, there she lay
Like new-fall'n snow melting away,
   ('Twas time, I trow, to part,)
Kisses were now the only stay,
Which soon she gave, as who would say
   God b'w'ye! with all my heart.

But just as heavens would have to cross it
In came the bridesmaids with the posset:
   The bridegroom ate in spite;

God b'w'ye] God B'w'y', 1648;   Good Boy, 1646 and 1658.

For had he left the women to 't,
It would have cost two hours to do 't,
 Which were too much that night.

At length the candle 's out, and now
All that they had not done they do:
 What that is, who can tell?
But I believe it was no more
Than thou and I have done before
 With Bridget and with Nell.   *Suckling.*

Fragmenta Aurea, 1648. (Poem written 1641.)*

IF ALL THE WORLD WERE PAPER

If all the world were paper,
 And all the sea were ink,
And all the trees were bread and cheese,
 How should we do for drink?

If all the world were sand-o,
 Oh, then what should we lack-o?
If, as they say, there were no clay,
 How should we take tobacco?

If all our vessels ran-a,
 If none but had a crack-a;
If Spanish apes ate all the grapes,
 How should we do for sack-a?

If friars had no bald pates,
 Nor nuns had no dark cloisters;
If all the seas were beans and peas,
 How should we do for oysters?

If there had been no projects,
    Nor none that did great wrongs;
If fiddlers shall turn players all,
    How should we do for songs?

If all things were eternal,
    And nothing their end bringing;
If this should be, then how should we
    Here make an end of singing?   *Anon.*

Wit's Recreations, 1641.*

AN INCOMPARABLE KISS

Give me a kiss from those sweet lips of thine
And make it double by enjoining mine,
Another yet, nay yet and yet another,
And let the first kiss be the second's brother.
Give me a thousand kisses and yet more;
And then repeat those that have gone before;
Let us begin while daylight springs in heaven,
And kiss till night descends into the even,
And when that modest secretary, night,
Discolours all but thy heaven beaming bright,
We will begin revels of hidden love
In that sweet orb where silent pleasures move.
In high new strains, unspeakable delight,
We 'll vent the dull hours of the silent night:
Were the bright day no more to visit us,
Oh, then for ever would I hold thee thus,
Naked, enchained, empty of idle fear,
As the first lovers in the garden were.
I 'll die betwixt thy breasts that are so white,

enjoining] 1650;   enjoying, 1641 and 1645.

For, to die there, would do a man delight.
Embrace me still, for time runs on before,
And being dead we shall embrace no more.
Let us kiss faster than the hours do fly,
Long live each kiss and never know to die.
Yet, if that fade and fly away too fast,
Impress another and renew the last;
Let us vie kisses, till our eyelids cover,
And if I sleep, count me an idle lover;
Admit I sleep, I 'll still pursue the theme,
And eagerly I 'll kiss thee in a dream.
Oh! give me way: grant love to me thy friend!
Did hundred thousand suitors all contend
For thy virginity, there 's none shall woo
With heart so firm as mine; none better do
Than I with your sweet sweetness; if you doubt,
Pierce with your eyes my heart, or pluck it out.

Wit's Recreations, 1641.*   *Anon.*

THAT NONE BEGUILËD BE

That none beguilëd be by Time's quick flowing,
Lovers have in their hearts a clock still going;
            For though Time be nimble, his motions
                        Are quicker,
                        And thicker,
            Where Love hath his notions.

Hope is the mainspring, on which moves desire,
And these do the less wheels, fear, joy, inspire,
            The balance is thought, evermore
                        Clicking,

Pierce with your] 1645;   Pierce your, 1641.

And striking,
And ne'er giving o'er.

Occasion 's the hand, which still 's moving round,
Till by it the critical hour may be found;
And when that falls out, it will strike
Kisses,
Strange blisses,
And what you best like.   *Suckling.*

Fragmenta Aurea, 1646. (Written before 1642.)

OF THEE, KIND BOY

Of thee, kind boy, I ask no red and white
To make up my delight,
No odd becoming graces,
Black eyes, or little know-not-whats in faces;
Make me but mad enough, give me good store
Of love for her I court,
I ask no more;
'Tis love in love that makes the sport.

There 's no such thing as that we beauty call,
It is mere cozenage all;
For though some, long ago,
Liked certain colours mingled so and so,
That doth not tie me now from choosing new:
If I a fancy take
To black and blue,
That fancy doth it beauty make.

'Tis not the meat, but 'tis the appetite
Makes eating a delight;
And if I like one dish

More than another, that a pheasant is:
What in our watches, that in us is found;
So to the height and nick
We up be wound,
No matter by what hand or trick.   *Suckling.*

Fragmenta Aurea, 1646. (Written before 1642.)*

I PRITHEE SEND ME BACK MY HEART

I prithee send me back my heart,
Since I can not have thine:
For if from yours you will not part,
Why then shouldst thou have mine?

Yet now I think on 't, let it lie;
To find it, were in vain:
For th' hast a thief in either eye
Would steal it back again.

Why should two hearts in one breast lie,
And yet not lodge together?
O Love, where is thy sympathy,
If thus our breasts thou sever?

But love is such a mystery
I cannot find it out:
For when I think I 'm best resolved,
I then am in most doubt.

Then farewell care, and farewell woe,
I will no longer pine:
For I 'll believe I have her heart,
As much as she has mine.   *Suckling (?)*

The Last Remains, 1659. (Written before 1642.)*

SONG

Out upon it, I have loved
   Three whole days together;
And am like to love three more,
   If it prove fair weather.

Time shall moult away his wings
   Ere he shall discover
In the whole wide world again
   Such a constant lover.

But the spite on 't is, no praise
   Is due at all to me:
Love with me had made no stays,
   Had it any been but she.

Had it any been but she,
   And that very face,
There had been at least ere this
   A dozen dozen in her place.   *Suckling.*

*Ibid.**

AN ANSWER
(To the foregoing)

Say, but did you love so long?
   In troth, I needs must blame you:
Passion did your judgement wrong,
   Or want of reason shame you.

Truth, Time's fair and witty daughter,
   Shortly shall discover,

You 're a subject fit for laughter,
  And more fool than lover.

But I grant you merit praise
  For your constant folly:
Since you doted three whole days,
  Were you not melancholy?

She, to whom you proved so true,
  And that very very face,
Puts each minute such as you
  A dozen dozen to disgrace.   *Matthews.*

The Last Remains of Sir John Suckling, 1659. (Poem written before 1642 ?) *

A COLLOQUY WITH GOD

The night is come, like to the day;
Depart not thou, great God, away.
Let not my sins, black as the night,
Eclipse the lustre of thy light.
Keep still in my horizon; for to me
The sun makes not the day, but thee.
Thou whose nature cannot sleep,
On my temples sentry keep;
Guard me 'gainst those watchful foes,
Whose eyes are open while mine close;
Let no dreams my head infest,
But such as Jacob's temples blessed.
While I do rest, my soul advance;
Make my sleep a holy trance,
That I may, my rest being wrought,
Awake into some holy thought;

You 're] Y' are, 1659.

And with as active vigour run
My course as doth the nimble sun.
Sleep is a death; oh! make me try,
By sleeping, what it is to die:
And as gently lay my head
On my grave, as now my bed.
Howe'er I rest, great God, let me
Awake again at last with thee.
And thus assured, behold I lie
Securely, or to wake or die.
These are my drowsy days; in vain
I do now wake to sleep again:
Oh! come that hour, when I shall never
Sleep again, but wake for ever.

Sir Thomas Browne.

Religio Medici, 1643. (Spurious edition printed 1642.)*

SOMNUS

Somnus, the humble god that dwells
In cottages and smoky cells,
Hates gilded roofs and beds of down;
And, though he fears no prince's frown,
Flies from the circle of a crown.

Come, I say, thou powerful god,
And thy leaden charming rod,
Dipped in the Lethean lake,
O'er his wakeful temples shake,
Lest he should sleep, and never wake.

Nature, alas, why art thou so
Obligèd to thy greatest foe?
Sleep, that is thy best repast,

Yet of death it bears a taste,
And both are the same thing at last.   *Denham.*

The Sophy, 1642.*

TO CYNTHIA, ON CONCEALMENT OF HER BEAUTY

Do not conceal thy radiant eyes,
The star-light of serenest skies;
Lest, wanting of their heavenly light,
They turn to Chaos' endless night.

Do not conceal those tresses fair,
The silken snares of thy curled hair;
Lest, finding neither gold nor ore,
The curious silk-worm work no more.

Do not conceal those breasts of thine,
More snow-white than the Apennine;
Lest, if there be like cold or frost,
The lily be for ever lost.

Do not conceal that fragrant scent
Thy breath, which to all flowers hath lent
Perfumes; lest, it being suppressed,
No spices grow in all the East.

Do not conceal thy heavenly voice,
Which makes the hearts of gods rejoice;
Lest, music hearing no such thing,
The nightingale forget to sing.

Do not conceal, nor yet eclipse
Thy pearly teeth with coral lips;
Lest that the seas cease to bring forth
Gems, which from thee have all their worth.

Do not conceal no beauty, grace,
That 's either in thy mind or face;
Lest virtue, overcome by vice,
Make men believe no Paradise.   *Kynaston.*

Cynthiades, in *Leoline and Sydanis,* 1642.

TO CYNTHIA, ON HER CHANGING

Dear Cynthia, though thou bear'st the name
    Of the pale queen of night,
Who changing yet is still the same,
    Renewing still her light:
Who monthly doth herself conceal,
    And her bright face doth hide,
That she may to Endymion steal,
    And kiss him unespied:

Do not thou so, not being sure,
    When this thy beauty 's gone,
Thou such another canst procure
    And wear it as thine own;
For the by-sliding silent hours,
    Conspirators with grief,
May crop thy beauty's lovely flowers,
    Time being a sly thief:

Which with his wings will fly away
    And will return no more;
As having got so rich a prey,
    Nature can not restore.
Reserve thou then and do not waste
    That beauty which is thine,
Cherish those glories which thou hast,
    Let not grief make thee pine.

Think that the lily we behold,
    Or Jùly-flower may
Flourish, although the mother mould
    That bred them be away:
There is no cause, nor yet no sense,
    That dainty fruits should not,
Though the tree die, and wither, whence
    The apricots were got.   *Kynaston.*

Cynthiades, in *Leoline and Sydanis,* 1642.

OR LOVE ME LESS OR LOVE ME MORE

Or love me less or love me more,
    And play not with my liberty,
Either take all, or all restore,
    Bind me at least or set me free;
Let me some nobler torture find
Than of a doubtful wavering mind;
Take all my peace; but you betray
Mine honour too this cruel way.

'Tis true that I have nursed before
    That hope of which I now complain,
And having little, sought no more,
    Fearing to meet with your disdain:
The sparks of favour you did give
I gently blow to make them live:
And yet have gained by all this care
No rest in hope, nor in despair.

I see you wear that pitying smile
    Which you have still vouchsafed my smart,
Content thus cheaply to beguile

And entertain an harmless heart:
But I no longer can give way
To hope, which doth so little pay;
And yet I dare no freedom owe
Whilst you are kind, though but in show.

Then give me more or give me less,
    Do not disdain a mutual sense,
Or your unpitying beauties dress
    In their own free indifference.
But show not a severer eye
Sooner to give me liberty,
For I shall love the very scorn
Which for my sake you do put on.   *Godolphin.*

Bodley MS. Malone 13. (Poem written before 1643.)

TO CHLORIS

Chloris, it is not thy disdain
    Can ever cover with despair,
    Or in cold ashes hide that care
Which I have fed with so long pain:
I may perhaps mine eyes refrain,
And fruitless words no more impart,
But yet still serve, still serve thee in my heart.

What though I spend my hapless days
    In finding entertainments out,
    Careless of what I go about,
Or seek my peace in skilful ways,
Applying to my eyes new rays
Of beauty, and another flame
Unto my heart, my heart is still the same.

'Tis true that I could love no face
    Inhabited by cold disdain,
    Taking delight in others' pain.
Thy looks are full of native grace;
Since then by chance scorn there hath place
'Tis to be hoped I may remove
This scorn one day, one day by endless love.

Godolphin.

Bodley MS. Malone 13. (Poem written before 1643.)*

TO THE LADY MAY

Your smiles are not, as other women's be,
    Only the drawing of the mouth awry;
For breasts and cheeks and forehead we may see,
    Parts wanting motion, all stand smiling by:
Heaven hath no mouth, and yet is said to smile
                After your style:
No more hath earth, yet that smiles too,
                Just as you do.

No simpering lips nor looks can breed
Such smiles as from your face proceed:
The sun must lend his golden beams,
    Soft winds their breath, green trees their shade,
Sweet fields their flowers, clear springs their streams,
    Ere such another smile be made:
But these concurring, we may say
So smiles the spring and so smiles lovely May.

Townshend.

*Ibid.**

UPON KIND AND TRUE LOVE

'Tis not how witty, nor how free,
Nor yet how beautiful she be;

But how much kind and true to me.
Freedom and wit none can confine,
And beauty like the sun doth shine;
But kind and true are only mine.

Let others with attention sit
To listen and admire her wit;
That is a rock where I 'll not split.
Let others dote upon her eyes,
And burn their hearts for sacrifice;
Beauty 's a calm where danger lies.

But kind and true have been long tried,
A harbour where we may confide,
And safely there at anchor ride;
From change of winds there we are free,
And need not fear storm's tyranny,
Nor pirate, though a prince he be.

Townshend (?)

Choice Drollery, 1656. (And in B.M. Harl. MS. 3991. Poem written before 1643.) *

MY DEAR AND ONLY LOVE

My dear and only Love, I pray
This noble world of thee
Be governed by no other sway
But purest monarchy;
For if confusion have a part,
Which virtuous souls abhor,
And hold a synod in thy heart,
I 'll never love thee more.

A harbour] MS.;   And harbour, 1656.

Like Alexander I will reign,
    And I will reign alone:
My thoughts shall evermore disdain
    A rival on my throne.
He either fears his fate too much,
    Or his deserts are small,
That puts it not unto the touch
    To win or lose it all.

But I must rule and govern still,
    And always give the law,
And have each subject at my will,
    And all to stand in awe.
But 'gainst my battery, if I find
    Thou shunn'st the prize so sore
As that thou sett'st me up a blind,
    I 'll never love thee more.

Or in the empire of thy heart,
    Where I should solely be,
Another do pretend a part
    And dares to vie with me;
Or if committees thou erect,
    And go on such a score,
I 'll sing and laugh at thy neglect,
    And never love thee more.

But if thou wilt be constant then,
    And faithful of thy word,
I 'll make thee glorious by my pen
    And famous by my sword:
I 'll serve thee in such noble ways
    Was never heard before;

I 'll crown and deck thee all with bays,
And love thee evermore.   *Montrose.*

A Choice Collection of Comic and Serious Scots Poems, III., 1711. (Poem
written c. 1643.)*

THE CONTENTED LOVER

I 'll wish no more thou shouldst love me,
My joys are full in loving thee;
My heart 's too narrow to contain
My bliss, if thou shouldst love again.

Thy scorns may wound me, but my fate
Leads me to love, and thee to hate; ·
Yet must I love whilst I have breath,
For not to love were worse than death.

Then shall I sue for scorn or grace,
A lingering life or death embrace?
Since one of these I needs must try,
Love me but once and let me die.

Such mercy more thy fame shall raise
Than cruel life can yield thee praise;
It shall be counted, who so dies,
No murther but a sacrifice.   *Anon.*

B.M. Harl. MS. 6917. (Poem written before 1644.)*

TO THE VIRGINS, TO MAKE MUCH OF TIME

Gather ye rose-buds while ye may,
    Old Time is still a-flying:
And this same flower that smiles to-day,
    To-morrow will be dying.

The glorious lamp of heaven, the sun,
   The higher he 's a-getting,
The sooner will his race be run,
   And nearer he 's to setting.

That age is best which is the first,
   When youth and blood are warmer;
But being spent, the worse, and worst
   Times still succeed the former.

Then be not coy, but use your time;
   And while ye may, go marry:
For having lost but once your prime,
   You may for ever tarry.   *Herrick.*

Hesperides, 1648. (Poem written before 1645.)*

THE COMMENDATION OF MUSIC

When whispering strains, with creeping wind,
   Distil soft passion through the heart;
And when at every touch we find
   Our pulses beat and bear a part;
      When threads can make
      A heart-string shake,
      Philosophy
      Can not deny
Our souls consist of harmony.

When unto heavenly joys, we feign
   Whate'er the soul affecteth most,
Which only thus we can explain,
   By music of the heavenly host,
      Whose lays, methinks,

Make stars to shrink,
Philosophy
May judge thereby
Our souls consist of harmony.

Oh, lull me, lull me, charming air!
My senses rock with wonder sweet;
Like snow on wool thy fallings are,
Soft as a spirit's are thy feet;
Grief who need fear
That hath an ear?
Down let him lie
And slumbering die,
And change his soul for harmony.   *Strode.*

B.M. Harl. MS. 6917. (Poem written before 1645.)*

ON WESTWELL DOWNS

When Westwell Downs I 'gan to tread,
Where cleanly winds the green did sweep,
Methought a landscape there was spread,
Here a bush and there a sheep;
The pleated wrinkles on the face
Of wave-swoln earth did lend such grace,
As shadowings in imagery
Which both deceive and please the eye.

The sheep sometimes did tread a maze
By often winding in and in,
And sometimes round about they trace
Which milkmaids call a fairy ring.
Such semi-circles have they run,
Such lines across so trimly spun,

That shepherds learn, whene'er they please,
A new geometry with ease.

Here and there two hilly crests
Amidst them hug a pleasant green,
And these are like two swelling breasts
That close a tender fall between.
    Here could I read or sleep or pray
    From early morn till flight of day:
    But hark! a sheep's bell calls me up,
    Like Oxford college bells, to sup.   *Strode.*

B.M. Add. MSS. 30982, and 19268. (Poem written before 1645.)*

A CATCH

The Wisemen were but seven, ne'er more shall be for me;
The Muses were but nine, the Worthies three times three;
And three merry boys, and three merry boys, and three merry
    boys are we.

The Virtues they were seven, and three the greater be;
The Caesars they were twelve, and the fatal Sisters three;
And three merry girls, and three merry girls, and three merry
    girls are we.   *Anon.*

J. Playford's *A Musical Banquet,* 1651.* (Catch written before 1645.)

UPON BLACK EYES, AND BECOMING FROWNS

Black eyes, in your dark orbs doth lie
My ill or happy destiny:
If with clear looks you me behold,
You give me mines and mounts of gold;
If you dart forth disdainful rays,

To your own dye you turn my days.
  Black eyes, in your dark orbs by changes dwell
  My bane or bliss, my paradise or hell.

That lamp, which all the stars doth blind,
Yields to your lustre in some kind,
Though you do wear to make you bright
No other dress but that of night;
He glitters only in the day,
You in the dark your beams display.
  Black eyes, in your two orbs, &c.

The cunning thief that lurks for prize,
At some dark corner watching lies:
So that heart-robbing god doth stand
In your black lobbies, shaft in hand,
To rifle me of what I hold
More precious far than Indian gold.
  Black eyes, in your dark orbs, &c.

O powerful negromantic eyes!
Who in your circles strictly pries,
Will find that Cupid with his dart
In you doth practise the black art:
And, by the enchantment I 'm possessed,
Tries his conclusions in my breast.
  Black eyes, in your dark orbs, &c.

Look on me, though in frowning wise;
Some kind of frowns become black eyes,
As pointed diamonds, being set,
Cast greater lustre out of jet.
Those pieces we esteem most rare,
Which in night-shadows postured are:

Darkness in churches congregates the sight,
Devotion strays in glaring light.
  Black eyes, in your dark orbs by changes dwell
  My bane or bliss, my paradise or hell.   *Howell.*

Epistolae Ho-Elianae, 1645.*

A CAVALIER'S LULLABY FOR HIS MISTRESS

Sweet! sleep; lie still, my dear!
          Dangers be strangers
For ever, unto thy eye or ear;
No sounds, or woe for wounds
          Number thy slumbers,
Or dare to approach within thy bounds;
    But such songs as seraphs sing,
          Which move by love
          Unto their King:
That thy sight, touch, taste, or smells
          May say, all joy
          In hearing dwells.

And when thou wakest again,
          Fortune importune
Thy senses to see us happy men:
That we may so agree,
          Dangers of strangers
May never destroy our unity:
    So shall peace ascend her throne,
          For than each man
          May claim his own.
    We like raging seas will run,

For than] For then.

That meet and fight,
Then flow in one.   *Jordan.*

Divinity & Morality in Robes of Poetry, [n.d]. (Poem written 1645.)*

THE SECRET
(*Written at the time of the Civil War*)

Hark, Celia, hark! but lay thou close thine ear;
    There 's for it a concerning reason:
For I 've a secret now to tell my dear,
    And 'tis no less than treason.

Let silly worldlings of their causes prate
    From whence our civil rage begins;
Let wise men talk of errors in our state,
    And churchmen of our sins;

Let others blame the stars' malignancy,
    Others the people's peevish call;
But, dearest, speak not of 't, for thou and I
    Are authors of it all:

We have all love engrossed; in us alone
    All kindness extant doth abide:
Nor have we left the land enough t' atone
    One pair of hearts beside.

When close as men in famines viands do,
    Let us our loves in secret lay:
Such useful treasure should the world but know,
    Alas, they 'd take 't away.

---

viands do] *i.e.* do[lay] viands (see next line).

No, Celia, no; our love's transcendent worth
  No force, no injury, can fear;
Then let it stream with all its glory forth,
  And like itself appear:

That when great Charles shall clear our troubled air,
  And crown our orb with peaceful hours,
The nation all may unto us repair,
  And light their loves at ours.   *Anon.*

J. Wilson's Autograph MS.; Bodley MS. Mus. b. 1. (Poem written c. 1645.)*

LOVE'S MATRIMONY

There is no happy life
But in a wife;
The comforts are so sweet
When they do meet:
'Tis plenty, peace, a calm
Like dropping balm:
Love's weather is so fair,
Perfumèd air,
Each word such pleasure brings
Like soft-touched strings;
Love's passion moves the heart
On either part.
Such harmony together,
So pleased in either,
No discords, concords still,
Sealed with one will.
By love, God man made one,
Yet not alone:

Like stamps of king and queen
It may be seen,
Two figures but one coin;
So they do join,
Only they not embrace,
We face to face.   *Duke of Newcastle.*

The Fancies. B.M. Add. MS. 32497. (Written c. 1645?)*

THE HEAVEN'S MOULD

So straight, so slender, and so tall,
But that 's not all:
A face out of the common road
With smiles so strowed
To grace that feature and that form
Without a storm:
You heaven's mould sent down so fresh and new,
None can be handsome that 's not thought like you.

So beautiful you are, so fair,
Transparent air
Doth sully and doth stain your skin;
It is so thin
The gentlest blush no where can hide,
So soon 'tis spied;
And your each curlèd hair those locks doth grace
Like pencilled shadows for your lovely face.
                                           Duke of Newcastle.

*Ibid.**

THE MAIDEN GOWN

Your milk-white maiden gown
Sets off your curlèd brown,

Those shadowed hairs doth grace
The beauty of your face;
Your innocent and virgin dye
Says only virtue there doth lie.

Your yellow-golden dress
Jealousy did express;
The tincture gave to thee,
So when you look of me
Thought me so too, then if you please
'Tis love's jaundice that 's a disease.

Your sable robe divine
Sets off the sacred shrine,
And shows the saint that 's thee
Still worshipped for to be:
Thus heaven only sent you down
By various shapes virtue to crown.

Duke of Newcastle.

The Fancies, [c. 1645]. B.M. Add. MS. 32497.*

LOVE'S VISION

Dear, let us two each other spy:
How curious! in each other's eye
We 're drawn to life, and thus we see
Ourselves at once, both thee and me,
Distinctly two, yet not alone,
Incorporated, that 's but one.

My picture in your eyes you bear;
I yours, as much as mine you wear.
'Tis not our spreties can not pass,

spreties] spirits.

Or shining makes a looking glass,
Nor picture, really we lie
Contracted each in other's eye.

When that our milk-white purer lawn,
Our eyelid curtains, when they 're drawn,
Soft sleep, made with sweet vapours' rain,
To cool us shrinks into each brain,
Rejoicing with love's running streams,
Which grosser lovers calls but dreams.

Because we two must never part
We move down to each other's heart,
And there, all passions turned to joy,
Our loving hearts feels no annoy
Delated, lest our souls outskips
With joy, kiss quickly! stop our lips!

Duke of Newcastle.

Ibid.

GO, LOVELY ROSE

Go, lovely rose,
Tell her that wastes her time and me,
    That now she knows,
When I resemble her to thee,
How sweet and fair she seems to be.

    Tell her that 's young
And shuns to have her graces spied,
    That hadst thou sprung
In deserts where no men abide,
Thou must have uncommended died.

delated] transferred.

Small is the worth
Of beauty from the light retired:
Bid her come forth,
Suffer herself to be desired,
And not blush so to be admired.

Then die, that she
The common fate of all things rare
May read in thee,
How small a part of time they share
That are so wondrous sweet and fair.   *Waller.*

Poems, &c., 1645.*

ON A GIRDLE

That which her slender waist confined
Shall now my joyful temples bind;
No monarch but would give his crown
His arms might do what this has done.

It was my heaven's extremest sphere,
The pale which held that lovely dear;
My joy, my grief, my hope, my love,
Did all within this circle move.

A narrow compass, and yet there
Dwelt all that 's good, and all that 's fair:
Give me but what this ribbon bound,
Take all the rest the sun goes round.   *Waller.*

Ibid. (Text 1686.)

TO A LADY SINGING A SONG OF HIS OWN
COMPOSING

Chloris, yourself you so excel,
When you vouchsafe to breathe my thought,

That like a spirit with this spell
   Of my own teaching I am caught.

That eagle's fate and mine are one,
   Which, on the shaft that made him die,
Espied a feather of his own,
   Wherewith he wont to soar so high.

Had Echo, with so sweet a grace,
   Narcissus' loud complaints returned,
Not for reflection of his face,
   But of his voice, the boy had burned.   *Waller.*

*Ibid.**

CHLORIS AND HYLAS

(Made to a Saraband)

CHLORIS

Hylas, O Hylas! why sit we mute,
Now that each bird saluteth the spring?
Wind up the slackened strings of thy lute,
Never canst thou want matter to sing:
   For love thy breast does fill with such a fire,
   That whatsoe'er is fair moves thy desire.

HYLAS

Sweetest, you know, the sweetest of things
Of various flowers the bees do compose;
Yet no particular taste it brings
Of violet, woodbine, pink, or rose:
   So love the result is of all the graces
   Which flow from a thousand several faces.

CHLORIS

Hylas, the birds which chant in this grove,
Could we but know the language they use,

They would instruct us better in love,
And reprehend thy inconstant Muse;
    For love their breasts does fill with such a fire,
    That what they once do choose, bounds their desire.

HYLAS

Chloris, this change the birds do approve,
Which the warm season hither does bring;
Time from yourself does further remove
You, than the winter from the gay spring;
    She that like lightning shined while her face lasted,
    The oak now resembles which lightning hath blasted.

Waller.

Poems &c., 1645. (Text 1686.)

TO A VERY YOUNG LADY

Why came I so untimely forth
    Into a world which, wanting thee,
Could entertain us with no worth
    Or shadow of felicity,
That time should me so far remove
From that which I was born to love?

Yet, fairest blossom, do not slight
    That age which you may know so soon:
The rosy morn resigns her light
    And milder glory to the noon:
And then what wonders shall you do
Whose dawning beauty warms us so?

Hope waits upon the flowery prime;
    And summer, though it be less gay,

Yet is not looked on as a time
    Of declination or decay:
For with a full hand that does bring
All that was promised by the spring.

Waller.

Ibid.

SIGHS

All night I muse, all day I cry,
            Ay me!
Yet still I wish, though still deny,
            Ay me!
I sigh, I mourn, and say that still
I only live my joys to kill,
            Ay me!

I feed the pain that on me feeds,
            Ay me!
My wound I stop not, though it bleeds,
            Ay me!
Heart, be content, it must be so,
For springs were made to overflow,
            Ay me!

Then sigh and weep, and mourn thy fill,
            Ay me!
Seek no redress, but languish still,
            Ay me!
Their griefs more willing they endure
That know when they are past recure,
            Ay me!

Anon.

Wit's Recreations, 1645.

A HYMN TO THE NAME AND HONOUR OF THE
ADMIRABLE SAINT TERESA

Love, thou art absolute sole lord
Of life and death.   To prove the word
We 'll now appeal to none of all
Those thy old soldiers, great and tall,
Ripe men of martyrdom, that could reach down
With strong arms their triumphant crown;
Such as could with lusty breath,
Speak loud into the face of Death
Their great Lord's glorious name, to none
Of those whose spacious bosoms spread a throne
For Love at large to fill; spare blood and sweat:
And see him take a private seat,
Making his mansion in the mild
And milky soul of a soft child.

Scarce has she learnt to lisp the name
Of martyr; yet she thinks it shame
Life should so long play with that breath
Which spent can buy so brave a death.
She never undertook to know
What Death with Love should have to do;
Nor has she e'er yet understood
Why to show love, she should shed blood,
Yet though she cannot tell you why,
She can love, and she can die.

Scarce has she blood enough to make
A guilty sword blush for her sake;
Yet has she a heart dares hope to prove
How much less strong is Death than Love.

Be Love but there; let poor six years
Be posed with the maturest fears
Man trembles at, you straight shall find

Love knows no nonage, nor the mind;
'Tis love, not years or limbs, that can
Make the martyr, or the man.
   Love touched her heart, and lo, it beats
High, and burns with such brave heats,
Such thirsts to die, as dares drink up
A thousand cold deaths in one cup.
Good reason; for she breathes all fire;
Her weak breast heaves with strong desire
Of what she may, with fruitless wishes,
Seek for amongst her mother's kisses.
   Since 'tis not to be had at home
She 'll travel to a martyrdom.
No home for her, confesses she,
But where she may a martyr be.
   She 'll to the Moors; and trade with them
For this unvalued diadem:
She 'll offer them her dearest breath,
With Christ's name in 't, in change for death:
She 'll bargain with them, and will give
Them God; teach them how to live
In him: or, if they this deny,
For him she 'll teach them how to die.
So shall she leave amongst them sown
Her Lord's blood; or at least her own.
   Farewell then, all the world, adieu!
Teresa is no more for you.
Farewell, all pleasures, sports, and joys,
Never till now esteeméd toys:
Farewell, whatever dear may be,

---

weak breast] 1646, 1648, and 1670;   what breast, 1652.   No home for her]
1646 and 1670;   No home for hers, 1648 and 1652.   Farewell, whatever
dear may be,] 1646, 1648, and 1670;   line omitted, 1652.

Mother's arms, or father's knee:
Farewell house, and farewell home!
She 's for the Moors, and martyrdom.
    Sweet, not so fast! lo, thy fair Spouse,
Whom thou seek'st with so swift vows,
Calls thee back, and bids thee come
To embrace a milder martyrdom.
    Blest powers forbid, thy tender life
Should bleed upon a barbarous knife:
Or some base hand have power to rase
Thy breast's chaste cabinet, and uncase
A soul kept there so sweet: Oh no,
Wise Heaven will never have it so.
Thou art Love's victim; and must die
A death more mystical and high:
Into Love's arms thou shalt let fall
A still-surviving funeral.
His is the dart must make the death
Whose stroke shall taste thy hallowed breath:
A dart thrice dipped in that rich flame
Which writes thy Spouse's radiant name
Upon the roof of heaven, where aye
It shines; and with a sovereign ray
Beats bright upon the burning faces
Of souls which in that name's sweet graces
Find everlasting smiles: so rare,
So spiritual, pure, and fair
Must be the immortal instrument
Upon whose choice point shall be sent
A life so loved: and that there be
Fit executioners for thee,
The fairest and first-born sons of fire,

The fairest] 1646 and 1670; The fair'st, 1648 and 1652.

Blest seraphim, shall leave their quire,
And turn Love's soldiers, upon thee
To exercise their archery.
   Oh! how oft shalt thou complain
Of a sweet and subtle pain:
Of intolerable joys;
Of a death, in which who dies
Loves his death, and dies again,
And would for ever so be slain;
And lives, and dies; and knows not why
To live, but that he thus may never leave to die.
   How kindly will thy gentle heart
Kiss the sweetly-killing dart,
And close in his embraces keep
Those delicious wounds, that weep
Balsam to heal themselves with; thus
When these thy deaths, so numerous,
Shall all at last die into one,
And melt thy soul's sweet mansïon;
Like a soft lump of incense, hasted
By too hot a fire, and wasted
Into perfuming clouds, so fast
Shalt thou exhale to Heaven at last
In a resolving sigh, and then
Oh, what? Ask not the tongues of men;
Angels cannot tell; suffice
Thyself shalt feel thine own full joys,
And hold them fast for ever there.
So soon as thou shalt first appear,
The moon of maiden stars, thy white
Mistress, attended by such bright
Souls as thy shining self, shall come,

as thou shalt first] 1646, 1648, and 1670;   as you first, 1652.

And in her first ranks make thee room;
Where 'mongst her snowy family
Immortal welcomes wait for thee.
　O what delight, when revealed Life shall stand,
And teach thy lips heaven with his hand;
On which thou now may'st to thy wishes
Heap up thy consecrated kisses.
What joys shall seize thy soul, when she,
Bending her blessèd eyes on thee,
Those second smiles of Heaven, shall dart
Her mild rays through thy melting heart.
　Angels, thy old friends, there shall greet thee,
Glad at their own home now to meet thee.
　All thy good works which went before,
And waited for thee at the door,
Shall own thee there; and all in one
Weave a constellation
Of crowns, with which the King thy Spouse
Shall build up thy triumphant brows.
　All thy old woes shall now smile on thee,
And thy pains sit bright upon thee,
All thy sorrows here shall shine,
All thy sufferings be divine:
Tears shall take comfort, and turn gems,
And wrongs repent to diadems.
Ev'n thy deaths shall live; and new
Dress the soul, that erst they slew.
Thy wounds shall blush to such bright scars
As keep account of the Lamb's wars.
　Those rare works where thou shalt leave writ
Love's noble history, with wit

All thy sorrows here shall shine,] 1646, 1648, and 1670;   omitted, 1652.
thy deaths] 1646, 1648, and 1670;   thy death, 1652.

Taught thee by none but him, while here
They feed our souls, shall clothe thine there.
Each heavenly word, by whose hid flame
Our hard hearts shall strike fire, the same
Shall flourish on thy brows, and be
Both fire to us and flame to thee;
Whose light shall live bright in thy face
By glory, in our hearts by grace.
    Thou shalt look round about, and see
Thousands of crowned souls throng to be
Themselvse thy crown: sons of thy vows,
The virgin-births with which thy sovereign Spouse
Made fruitful thy fair soul.   Go now
And with them all about thee, bow
To him.   Put on, (he 'll say,) put on,
My rosy Love, that thy rich zone
Sparkling with the sacred flames
Of thousand souls, whose happy names
Heaven keep upon thy score: thy bright
Life brought them first to kiss the light
That kindled them to stars; and so
Thou with the Lamb, thy Lord, shalt go,
And wheresoe'er he sets his white
Steps, walk with him those ways of light,
Which who in death would live to see,
Must learn in life to die like thee.   *Crashaw.*

Carmen Deo Nostro, 1652. (First printed, *Steps to the Temple*, 1646; but
written earlier.)

THE CALL

Romira, stay,
And run not thus like a young roe away;
No enemy

Pursues thee, foolish girl, 'tis only I;
           I 'll keep off harms,
If thou 'll be pleased to garrison mine arms.
           What! dost thou fear
I 'll turn a traitor?   May these roses here
           To paleness shred,
And lilies stand disguisëd in new red,
           If that I lay
A snare, wherein thou wouldst not gladly stay.
           See, see, the sun
Does slowly to his azure lodging run;
           Come, sit but here,
And presently he 'll quit our hemisphere:
           So still among
Lovers, time is too short or else too long.
           Here will we spin
Legends for them that have love-martyrs been:
           Here on this plain
We 'll talk Narcissus to a flower again.
           Come here, and choose
On which of these proud plats thou would repose;
           Here may'st thou shame
The rusty violets, with the crimson flame
           Of either cheek,
And primroses white as thy fingers seek:
           Nay, thou may'st prove
That man's most noble passion is to love.   *Hall.*

Poems, 1646.*

THE MORNING STAR

Still herald of the morn, whose ray,
Being page and usher to the day,

Doth mourn behind the sun, before him play;
   Who sets a golden signal, ere
   The bat retire, the lark appear,
The early cocks cry comfort, screech-owls fear;

   Who wink'st while lovers plight their troth,
   Then falls asleep, while they are loth
To part without a more engaging oath,—
   Steal in a message to the eyes
   Of Julia, tell her that she lies
Too long, thy lord the sun will quickly rise.

   Yet is it midnight still with me,
   Nay worse, unless that kinder she
Smile day, and in my zenith seated be.
   But if she will obliquely run,
   I needs a calenture must shun,
And like an Ethiopian hate my sun.   *Hall.*

Ibid.

A PASTORAL HYMN

Happy choristers of air,
Who by your nimble flight draw near
   His throne, whose wondrous story,
   And unconfinèd glory
Your notes still carol, whom your sound
And whom your plumy pipes rebound.

Yet do the lazy snails no less
The greatness of our Lord confess,
   And those whom weight hath chained,
   And to the earth restrained,

Their ruder voices do as well,
Yea, and the speechless fishes tell.

Great Lord, from whom each tree receives,
Then pays again, as rent, his leaves;
   Thou dost in purple set
   The rose and violet,
And giv'st the sickly lily white;
Yet in them all thy name dost write.   *Hall.*

Poems, &c., 1646.

COCK-THROWING

Cock a doodle do! 'tis the bravest game,
Take a cock from his dame,
And bind him to a stake:
How he struts! how he throws!
How he swaggers! how he crows!
As if the day newly brake.
How his mistress cackles
Thus to find him in shackles
And tied to a pack-thread garter!
Oh, the bears and the bulls
Are but corpulent gulls
To the valiant Shrovetide martyr!   *Lluellyn.*

Men-Miracles, 1646.*

UPON HIS MISTRESS DANCING

I stood and saw my mistress dance,
   Silent, and with so fixed an eye,
Some might suppose me in a trance.
   But being askèd, why?
By one that knew I was in love,

I could not but impart
My wonder, to behold her move
So nimbly with a marble heart.   *Shirley.*
Poems, &c., 1646.

MR. LE STRANGE HIS VERSES IN THE PRISON
AT LINN

Beat on, proud billows; Boreas blow;
    Swell, curlëd waves, high as Jove's roof;
Your incivility shall know
    That innocence is tempest-proof:
Though surly Nereus roar, my thoughts are calm;
Then strike, affliction, for thy wounds are balm.

That which the world miscalls a jail,
    A private closet is to me,
Whilst a good conscience is my bail,
    And innocence my liberty:
Locks, bars, walls, loneliness, together met,
Make me no prisoner, but an anchoret.

I, while I wished to be retired,
    Into this private room was turned,
As if their wisdoms had conspired
    A salamander should be burned;
Or like those sophies that would drown a fish,
I am constrained to suffer what I wish.

So he, that struck at Jason's life
    Thinking to make his purpose sure,
By a malicious friendly knife
    Did only wound him to a cure:

Malice, I see, wants wit, for what it meant,
Mischief, oft times proves favour in the event.

These manacles upon mine arm
   I as my sweetheart's favours wear;
And then to keep mine ankles warm
   I have some iron shackles there.
Contentment cannot smart, stoics we see
Make torments easy by their apathy.

Here sin for want of food doth starve
   Where tempting objects are not seen;
And these strong walls do only serve
   To keep vice out, and keep me in:
Malice of late grows charitable sure,
I 'm not committed, but I 'm kept secure.

When once my Prince affliction hath,
   Prosperity doth treason seem;
And then to smooth so rough a path
   I can learn patience e'en from him:
Now not to suffer shows no loyal heart,
When kings want ease, subjects must learn to smart.

What though I cannot see my King
   Either in his person or his coin;
Yet contemplation is a thing
   Will render what I have not, mine:
My King from me what adamant can part
Whom I do wear engraven in my heart.

My soul 's as free as the ambient air,
   Although my baser part 's immured,
While loyal thoughts do still repair

To accompany my solitude:
And though rebellion do my body bind,
My King can only captivate my mind.

Have you beheld the nightingale,
    A pilgrim turned into a cage,
How still she tells her wonted tale
    In this her private hermitage?
E'en there her chanting melody doth prove
That all her bars are trees, her cage a grove.

I am the bird whom they combine
    Thus to deprive of liberty;
And though they do my corpse confine,
    Yet, maugre hate, my soul is free:
And though immured, yet here I 'll chirp and sing,
Disgrace to rebels, glory to my King.   *L'Estrange.*

B.M. Harl. MS. 3511, [c. 1650]. (Poem printed 1656; written before 1647 ?) *

MARK ANTONY

When as the nightingale chanted her vespers,
And the wild forester couched on the ground,
Venus invited me in the evening whispers
Unto a fragrant field with roses crowned,
        Where she before had sent
        My wishes' complement,
        Unto my heart's content
        Played with me on the green.
            Never Mark Antony
            Dallied more wantonly
            With the fair Egyptian Queen.

First on her cherry cheeks I mine eyes feasted,
Thence fear of surfeiting made me retire;
Next on her warmer lips, which when I tasted,
My duller spirits made active as fire.
>   Then we began to dart,
>   Each at another's heart,
>   Arrows that knew no smart,
>   Sweet lips and smiles between
>   Never Mark Antony, &c.

Wanting a glass to plait her amber tresses
Which like a bracelet rich deckéd mine arm,
Gaudier than Juno wears when as she graces
Jove with embraces more stately than warm;
>   Then did she peep in mine
>   Eyes' humour crystalline;
>   I in her eyes was seen
>   As if we one had been.
>   Never Mark Antony, &c.

Mystical grammar of amorous glances;
Feeling of pulses, the physic of love;
Rhetorical courtings and musical dances;
Numb'ring of kisses arithmetic prove;
>   Eyes like astronomy;
>   Straight-limbed geometry;
>   In her art's ingeny
>   Our wits were sharp and keen.
>   Never Mark Antony

---

warmer lips] 1653 and 1677; warmer, 1657; warm lips, 1647.   made
active] 1647; made me active, 1657.   art's] 1677 and MSS.; heart's, 1657.
wits were] 1677; wits are, 1657.

Dallied more wantonly
With the fair Egyptian Queen.   *Cleveland.*

The Character of a London Diurnal, 1647. (Text from *Poems,* 1657.)*

MY DIET

Now, by my love—the greatest oath that is—
    None loves you half so well as I:
    I do not ask your love for this;
But, for heaven's sake, believe me, or I die.
    No servant e'er but did deserve
His master should believe that he does serve;
And I 'll ask no more wages, though I sterve.

'Tis no luxurious diet this, and sure
    I shall not by 't too lusty prove;
    Yet shall it willingly endure,
If 't can but keep together life and love.
    Being your prisoner and your slave,
I do not feasts and banquets look to have,
A little bread and water 's all I crave.

On a sigh of pity I a year can live,
    One tear will keep me twenty at least,
    Fifty a gentle look will give;
An hundred years on one kind word I 'll feast,
    A thousand more will added be
If you an inclination have for me;
And all beyond is vast eternity.   *Cowley.*

The Mistress, 1647. (Text 1656.)*

THE THIEF

Thou robb'st my days of business and delights,
    Of sleep thou robb'st my nights;

Ah, lovely thief, what wilt thou do?
What? rob me of Heaven too?
Thou even my prayers dost steal from me:
And I, with wild idolatry,
Begin, to God, and end them all, to thee.

Is it a sin to love, that it should thus
Like an ill conscience torture us?
Whate'er I do, where'er I go
(None guiltless e'er was haunted so)
Still, still, methinks, thy face I view,
And still thy shape does me pursue,
As if, not you me, but I had murthered you.

From books I strive some remedy to take,
But thy name all the letters make:
Whate'er 'tis writ, I find that there,
Like points and commas every where.
Me blessed for this let no man hold;
For I, as Midas did of old,
Perish by turning every thing to gold.

What do I seek, alas, or why do I
Attempt in vain from thee to fly?
For, making thee my deity,
I gave thee then ubiquity.
My pains resemble hell in this:
The divine presence there too is,
But to torment men, not to give them bliss.

                                                        Cowley.

The Mistress, 1647. (Text 1656.)*

Stz. 1, l. 5,] 1656; Even in my prayers thou hauntest me, 1647.

ALL-OVER LOVE

'Tis well, 'tis well with them, say I,
Whose short-lived passions with themselves can die:
For none can be unhappy, who
'Midst all his ills a time does know
(Though ne'er so long) when he shall not be so.

Whatever parts of me remain,
Those parts will still the love of thee retain;
For 'twas not only in my heart,
But, like a god, by powerful art
'Twas all in all, and all in every part.

My affection no more perish can
Than the first matter that compounds a man.
Hereafter if one dust of me
Mixed with another's substance be,
'Twill leaven that whole lump with love of thee.

Let Nature, if she please, disperse
My atoms over all the universe,
At the last they easily shall
Themselves know, and together call;
For thy love, like a mark, is stamped on all.   *Cowley.*

*Ibid.**

THE WISH

Well then; I now do plainly see
This busy world and I shall ne'er agree.
The very honey of all earthly joy
Does, of all meats, the soonest cloy;

And they, methinks, deserve my pity
Who for it can endure the stings,
The crowd, and buzz, and murmurings
    Of this great hive, the city.

And yet, ere I descend to the grave,
May I a small house and large garden have;
And a few friends, and many books, both true,
Both wise, and both delightful too!
    And since love ne'er will from me flee,
A mistress moderately fair,
And good as guardian angels are,
    Only beloved, and loving me!

O fountains! when in you shall I
Myself eased of unpeaceful thoughts espy?
O fields! O woods! when, when shall I be made
The happy tenant of your shade?
    Here 's the spring-head of pleasure's flood;
Here 's wealthy Nature's treasury,
Where all the riches lie that she
    Has coined and stamped for good.

Pride and ambition here
Only in far-fetched metaphors appear;
Here nought but winds can hurtful murmurs scatter,
And nought but echo flatter.
    The gods, when they descended, hither
From heaven did always choose their way;
And therefore we may boldly say
    That 'tis the way too thither.

Stz. 3, l. 6,] 1647; line omitted, 1656 and 1668.

How happy here should I
And one dear she live, and embracing die!
She who is all the world, and can exclude
In deserts solitude.
    I should have then this only fear;
Lest men, when they my pleasures see,
Should hither throng to live like me,
    And so make a city here.   *Cowley.*

The Mistress, 1647. (Text 1656.)

A ROSE

Blown in the morning, thou shalt fade ere noon:
What boots a life which in such haste forsakes thee?
Thou 'rt wondrous frolic, being to die so soon;
And passing proud a little colour makes thee.
If thee thy brittle beauty so deceives,
Know then the thing that swells thee is thy bane;
For the same beauty doth, in bloody leaves,
The sentence of thy early death contain.
Some clown's coarse lungs will poison thy sweet flower,
If by the careless plough thou shalt be torn;
And many Herods lie in wait each hour
To murder thee as soon as thou art born;
    Nay, force thy bud to blow; their tyrant breath
    Anticipating life, to hasten death.   *Fanshawe.*

Il Pastor Fido, 1647.

OF TIME

Let us use time whilst we may;
Snatch those joys that haste away!

Thou 'rt] Th' art, 1647.   use time] 1677; use it, 1647.

Earth her winter coat may cast,
And renew her beauties past;
But, our winter come, in vain
We solicit spring again:
And when our furrows snow shall cover,
Love may return, but never lover.   *Fanshawe.*

Il Pastor Fido, 1647.*

HIS LITANY, TO THE HOLY SPIRIT

In the hour of my distress,
When temptations me oppress,
And when I my sins confess,
    Sweet Spirit, comfort me!

When I lie within my bed,
Sick in heart and sick in head,
And with doubts discomforted,
    Sweet Spirit, comfort me!

When the house doth sigh and weep,
And the world is drowned in sleep,
Yet mine eyes the watch do keep,
    Sweet Spirit, comfort me!.

When the artless doctor sees
No one hope, but of his fees,
And his skill runs on the lees,
    Sweet Spirit, comfort me!

When his potion and his pill,
His, or none or little, skill,

---

beauties] 1677;   beauty, 1647.

Meet for nothing, but to kill,
     Sweet Spirit, comfort me!

When the passing bell doth toll,
And the Furies in a shoal
Come to fright a parting soul,
     Sweet Spirit, comfort me!

When the tapers now burn blue,
And the comforters are few,
And that number more than true,
     Sweet Spirit, comfort me!

When the priest his last hath prayed,
And I nod to what is said,
'Cause my speech is now decayed,
     Sweet Spirit, comfort me!

When, God knows, I 'm tossed about,
Either with despair or doubt;
Yet before the glass be out,
     Sweet Spirit, comfort me!

When the tempter me pursu'th
With the sins of all my youth,
And half damns me with untruth,
     Sweet Spirit, comfort me!

When the flames and hellish cries
Fright mine ears, and fright mine eyes,
And all terrors me surprise,
     Sweet Spirit, comfort me!

When the judgement is revealed,
And that opened which was sealed,
When to thee I have appealed,
      Sweet Spirit, comfort me!   *Herrick.*

His Noble Numbers, 1647. (Published with *Hesperides,* 1648.)*

THE WHITE ISLAND: OR PLACE OF THE BLEST

In this world (the Isle of Dreams)
While we sit by sorrow's streams,
Tears and terrors are our themes
      Reciting:

But when once from hence we fly,
More and more approaching nigh
Unto young Eternity
      Uniting:

In that whiter Island, where
Things are evermore sincere;
Candour here, and lustre there
      Delighting:

There no monstrous fancies shall
Out of hell an horror call,
To create (or cause at all)
      Affrighting.

There in calm and cooling sleep
We our eyes shall never steep;
But eternal watch shall keep,
      Attending

Pleasures, such as shall pursue
Me immortalized, and you;
And fresh joys, as never too
                    Have ending.   *Herrick.*

Ibid.

ETERNITY

O years, and age, farewell!
      Behold I go
      Where I do know
Infinity to dwell.

And these mine eyes shall see
      All times, how they
      Are lost i' the sea
Of vast Eternity,

Where never moon shall sway
      The stars; but she,
      And night, shall be
Drowned in one endless day.   *Herrick.*

Ibid.

THE PHILOSOPHER'S DEVOTION

Sing aloud, his praise rehearse,
Who hath made the universe.
He the boundless heavens has spread,
All the vital orbs has kned;

---

kned] moulded, formed.

He that on Olympus high
Tends his flocks with watchful eye,
And this eye has multiplied
'Midst each flock for to reside:
Thus as round about they stray,
Toucheth each with out-stretched ray;
Nimble they hold on their way,
Shaping out their night and day.
Summer, winter, autumn, spring,
Their inclinëd axes bring.
Never slack they; none respires,
Dancing round their central fires.
    In due order as they move,
Echoes sweet be gently drove
Thorough heaven's vast hollowness,
Which unto all corners press:
Music that the heart of Jove
Moves to joy and sportful love;
Fills the listening sailors' ears
Riding on the wandering spheres.
Neither speech nor language is
Where their voice is not transmiss.
    God is good, is wise, is strong,
Witness all the creature-throng,
Is confessed by every tongue:
All things back from whence they sprung,
As the thankful rivers pay
What they borrowed of the sea.
    Now myself I do resign;
Take me whole, I all am thine.
Save me, God! from self-desire,

respires] has respite.   transmiss] transmitted.

Death's pit, dark hell's raging fire,
Envy, hatred, vengeance, ire,
Let not lust my soul bemire.
   Quit from these, thy praise I 'll sing,
Loudly sweep the trembling string.
Bear a part, O wisdom's sons!
Freed from vain religïons.
Lo! from far I you salute,
Sweetly warbling on my lute,
Indie, Egypt, Araby,
Asia, Greece, and Tartary,
Carmel-tracts and Lebanon,
With the Mountains of the Moon
From whence muddy Nile doth run,
Or where ever else you won;
Breathing in one vital air,
One we are, though distant far.
   Rise at once; let 's sacrifice,
Odours sweet perfume the skies.
See how heavenly lightning fires
Hearts inflamed with high aspires!
All the substance of our souls
Up in clouds of incense rolls;
Leave we nothing to ourselves
Save a voice, what need we else?
Or an hand to wear and tire
On the thankful lute or lyre.
   Sing aloud, his praise rehearse,
Who hath made the universe.

More.

Philosophical Poems, 1647.

won] dwell.

THE RELAPSE

O turn away those cruel eyes,
    The stars of my undoing;
Or death in such a bright disguise
    May tempt a second wooing.

Punish their blindly impious pride,
    Who dare contemn thy glory;
It was my fall that deified
    Thy name, and sealed thy story.

Yet no new sufferings can prepare
    A higher praise to crown thee;
Though my first death proclaim thee fair,
    My second will unthrone thee.

Lovers will doubt thou canst entice
    No other for thy fuel,
And if thou burn one victim twice,
    Both think thee poor and cruel.   *Stanley.*

Poems and Translations, 1647. (Text 1651.)*

EXPECTATION

Chide, chide no more away
The fleeting daughters of the day,
Nor with impatient thoughts outrun
        The lazy sun,
Or think the hours do move too slow;
        Delay is kind,
    And we too soon shall find
That which we seek, yet fear to know.

The mystic dark decrees
Unfold not of the Destinies,
Nor boldly seek to antedate
The laws of Fate,
Thy anxious search awhile forbear,
Suppress thy haste,
And know that time at last
Will crown thy hope, or fix thy fear.   *Stanley.*

Ibid. (Poem not reprinted 1651.)

THE EXEQUIES

Draw near,
You lovers that complain
Of fortune or disdain,
And to my ashes lend a tear:
Melt the hard marble with your groans,
And soften the relentless stones,
Whose cold embraces the sad subject hide
Of all love's cruelties, and beauty's pride.

No verse,
No epicedium bring,
Nor peaceful requiem sing,
To charm the terrors of my hearse;
No profane numbers must flow near
The sacred silence that dwells here.
Vast griefs are dumb; softly, oh! softly mourn,
Lest you disturb the peace attends my urn.

Yet strew
Upon my dismal grave

Such offerings as you have—
Forsaken cypress and sad yew;
For kinder flowers can take no birth
Or growth from such unhappy earth.
Weep only o'er my dust, and say, 'Here lies
To love and fate an equal sacrifice.'

Stanley.

Poems and Translations, 1647. (Text 1651.)

THE GUEST

Yet if his majesty, our sovereign lord,
Should of his own accord
Friendly himself invite,
And say 'I 'll be your guest to-morrow night,'
How should we stir ourselves, call and command
All hands to work! 'Let no man idle stand.
Set me fine Spanish tables in the hall,
See they be fitted all;
Let there be room to eat,
And order taken that there want no meat.
See every sconce and candlestick made bright,
That without tapers they may give a light.
Look to the presence: are the carpets spread,
The dazie o'er the head,
The cushions in the chairs,
And all the candles lighted on the stairs?
Perfume the chambers, and in any case
Let each man give attendance in his place.'
Thus if the king were coming would we do;
And 'twere good reason too:
For 'tis a duteous thing

dazie] daïs.

To show all honour to an earthly king;
And, after all our travail and our cost,
So he be pleased, to think no labour lost.
But at the coming of the King of heaven
All 's set at six and seven:
We wallow in our sin;
Christ cannot find a chamber in the inn.
We entertain him always like a stranger,
And, as at first, still lodge him in the manger.

Anon.

Christ Church MS. 736–8. (Poem written before 1648.)*

THE THIEF

'Say, bold but blessëd thief,
That in a trice
Slipped into paradise,
And in plain day
Stol'st heaven away,
What trick couldst thou invent
To compass thy intent?
What arms?
What charms?'
'Love and belief.'

'Say, bold but blessëd thief,
How couldst thou read
A crown upon that head?
What text, what gloss,
A kingdom and a cross?
How couldst thou come to spy
God in a man to die?
What light?

What sight?'
'The sight of grief—

'I sight to God his pain;
And by that sight
I saw the light;
Thus did my grief
Beget relief.
And take this rule from me,
Pity thou him he 'll pity thee.
Use this,
Ne'er miss,
Heaven may be stol'n again.'   *Anon.*

Christ Church MS. 736–8. (Poem written before 1648.)*

SONG

Sweet, yet cruel unkind is she
To creep into my heart and murder me.
Yet those bright beams from her eyes
Dims Apollo at his rise;
And all those purer graces,
All in their several places,
Begets a glory doth surprise
All hearts, all eyes,
For only she
Gives life eternity;
And when her presence deigns but to appear
Never wish greater bliss than shines from her bright sphere:
Her absence wounds, strikes dead all hearts with fear.
                                                Anon.

Ibid.

I sight] *i.e.* I sighed;   old past tense, probable play on words.

THE FLAMING HEART

Upon the book and picture of the seraphical Saint Teresa,
as she is usually expressed with a seraphim beside her

Well-meaning readers! you that come as friends,
And catch the precious name this piece pretends;
Make not too much haste to admire
That fair-cheeked fallacy of fire.
That is a seraphim, they say,
And this the great Teresia.
Readers, be ruled by me; and make
Here a well-placed and wise mistake;
You must transpose the picture quite,
And spell it wrong to read it right;
Read him for her, and her for him,
And call the saint the seraphim.
　　Painter, what didst thou understand
To put her dart into his hand?
See, even the years and size of him
Shows this the mother seraphim.
This is the mistress flame; and duteous he
Her happy fire-works, here, comes down to see.
O most poor-spirited of men!
Had thy cold pencil kissed her pen,
Thou couldst not so unkindly err
To show us this faint shade for her.
Why, man, this speaks pure mortal frame;
And mocks with female frost Love's manly flame.
One would suspect thou meant'st to paint
Some weak, inferior, woman-saint.
But had thy pale-faced purple took

to paint] 1648;   to print, 1652 and 1670.

Fire from the burning cheeks of that bright book,
Thou wouldst on her have heaped up all
That could be formed seraphical;
Whate'er this youth of fire wears fair,
Rosy fingers, radiant hair,
Glowing cheeks, and glistering wings,
All those fair and flagrant things,
But before all, that fiery dart
Had filled the hand of this great heart.

　　Do then, as equal right requires;
Since his the blushes be, and hers the fires.
Resume and rectify thy rude design;
Undress thy seraphim into mine;
Redeem this injury of thy art,
Give him the veil, give her the dart.

　　Give him the veil, that he may cover
The red cheeks of a rivalled lover;
Ashamed that our world now can show
Nests of new seraphims here below.

　　Give her the dart, for it is she,
Fair youth, shoots both thy shaft and thee;
Say, all ye wise and well-pierced hearts
That live and die amidst her darts,
What is 't your tasteful spirits do prove
In that rare life of her, and Love?
Say, and bear witness.　Sends she not
A seraphim at every shot?
What magazines of immortal arms there shine!
Heaven's great artillery in each love-spun line.
Give then the dart to her who gives the flame;
Give him the veil, who gives the shame.

---

formed] 1648;　found, 1652 and 1670.　　glowing cheeks] 1648;　glowing
cheek, 1652 and 1670.　　flagrant] burning, glowing.

But if it be the frequent fate
Of worst faults to be fortunate;
If all 's prescription; and proud wrong
Harkens not to an humble song;
For all the gallantry of him,
Give me the suffering seraphim.
His be the bravery of all those bright things,
The glowing cheeks, the glistering wings;
The rosy hand, the radiant dart;
Leave her alone the flaming heart.

Leave her that; and thou shalt leave her
Not one loose shaft, but Love's whole quiver;
For in Love's field was never found
A nobler weapon than a wound.
Love's passives are his activ'st part:
The wounded is the wounding heart.
O heart! the equal poise of Love's both parts,
Big alike with wound and darts,
Live in these conquering leaves; live all the same;
And walk through all tongues one triumphant flame.
Live here, great heart; and love, and die, and kill;
And bleed, and wound; and yield and conquer still.
Let this immortal life where'er it comes
Walk in a crowd of loves and martyrdoms.
Let mystic deaths wait on 't; and wise souls be
The love-slain witnesses of this life of thee.

O sweet incendiary! show here thy art,
Upon this carcass of a hard cold heart:
Let all thy scattered shafts of light that play
Among the leaves of thy large books of day,
Combined against this breast at once break in
And take away from me myself and sin;
This gracious robbery shall thy bounty be,

And my best fortunes such fair spoils of me.
O thou undaunted daughter of desires!
By all thy dower of lights and fires;
By all the eagle in thee, all the dove;
By all thy lives and deaths of love;
By thy large draughts of intellectual day,
And by thy thirsts of love more large than they;
By all thy brim-filled bowls of fierce desire,
By thy last morning's draught of liquid fire;
By the full kingdom of that final kiss
That seized thy parting soul, and sealed thee his;
By all the heavens thou hast in him,
Fair sister of the seraphim!
By all of him we have in thee;
Leave nothing of myself in me.
Let me so read thy life, that I
Unto all life of mine may die.   *Crashaw.*

Carmen Deo Nostro, 1652. (First printed, *Steps to the Temple*, 1648, but with the last 24 lines omitted.)

TO BLOSSOMS

Fair pledges of a fruitful tree,
　　Why do ye fall so fast?
　　Your date is not so past,
But you may stay yet here awhile
　　To blush and gently smile,
　　　　And go at last.

What, were ye born to be
　　An hour or half's delight,
　　And so to bid good-night?
'Twas pity Nature brought ye forth

Merely to show your worth,
And lose you quite.

But you are lovely leaves, where we
May read how soon things have
Their end, though ne'er so brave:
And after they have shown their pride
Like you, awhile: they glide
Into the grave.   *Herrick.*

Hesperides, 1648.

TO DAFFODILS

Fair daffodils, we weep to see
You haste away so soon:
As yet the early-rising sun
Has not attained his noon.
Stay, stay,
Until the hasting day
Has run
But to the even-song;
And, having prayed together, we
Will go with you along.

We have short time to stay, as you,
We have as short a spring;
As quick a growth to meet decay
As you, or any thing.
We die,
As your hours do, and dry
Away
Like to the summer's rain;
Or as the pearls of morning's dew
Ne'er to be found again.   *Herrick.*

Ibid.

TO PRIMROSES
FILLED WITH MORNING-DEW

Why do ye weep, sweet babes? can tears
        Speak grief in you,
        Who were but born
        Just as the modest morn
    Teemed her refreshing dew?
Alas, you have not known that shower,
        That mars a flower;
        Nor felt the unkind
        Breath of a blasting wind;
    Nor are ye worn with years;
        Or warped, as we,
        Who think it strange to see
Such pretty flowers, like to orphans young,
To speak by tears, before ye have a tongue.

Speak, whimpering younglings, and make known
        The reason, why
        Ye droop, and weep;
        Is it for want of sleep?
    Or childish lullaby?
Or that ye have not seen as yet
        The violet?
        Or brought a kiss
        From that sweet-heart, to this?
    No, no, this sorrow shown
        By your tears shed,
        Would have this lecture read,
That things of greatest, so of meanest worth,
Conceived with grief are, and with tears brought forth.

Herrick.

Hesperides, 1648.

TO MEADOWS

Ye have been fresh and green,
   Ye have been filled with flowers:
And ye the walks have been
   Where maids have spent their hours.

You have beheld, how they
   With wicker arks did come
To kiss, and bear away
   The richer cowslips home.

You 've heard them sweetly sing,
   And seen them in a round:
Each virgin, like a spring,
   With honey-suckles crowned.

But now we see none here,
   Whose silvery feet did tread,
And with dishevelled hair,
   Adorned this smoother mead.

Like unthrifts, having spent
   Your stock, and needy grown,
You 're left here to lament
   Your poor estates, alone.   *Herrick.*

Ibid.

TO ANTHEA, WHO MAY COMMAND HIM ANY THING

Bid me to live, and I will live
   Thy Protestant to be:

You 've, You 're] Y 'ave, Y 'are, 1648.

Or bid me love, and I will give
    A loving heart to thee.

A heart as soft, a heart as kind,
    A heart as sound and free
As in the whole world thou canst find,
    That heart I 'll give to thee.

Bid that heart stay, and it will stay,
    To honour thy decree:
Or bid it languish quite away,
    And 't shall do so for thee.

Bid me to weep, and I will weep
    While I have eyes to see:
And having none, yet I will keep
    A heart to weep for thee.

Bid me despair, and I 'll despair,
    Under that cypress tree:
Or bid me die, and I will dare
    E'en death, to die for thee.

Thou art my life, my love, my heart,
    The very eyes of me,
And hast command of every part,
    To live and die for thee.   *Herrick.*

Hesperides, 1648.*

THE NIGHT-PIECE, TO JULIA

Her eyes the glow-worm lend thee,
The shooting stars attend thee;
    And the elves also,

                    Whose little eyes glow
                    Like the sparks of fire, befriend thee.

                    No will-o'-the-wisp mislight thee;
                    Nor snake or slow-worm bite thee:
                            But on, on thy way
                            Not making a stay,
                    Since ghost there 's none to affright thee.

                    Let not the dark thee cumber;
                    What though the moon does slumber?
                            The stars of the night
                            Will lend thee their light,

                    Like tapers clear without number.
                    Then, Julia, let me woo thee,
                    Thus, thus to come unto me:
                            And when I shall meet
                            Thy silvery feet,
                    My soul I 'll pour into thee.   *Herrick.*
*Ibid.**

UPON JULIA'S VOICE

So smooth, so sweet, so silvery is thy voice,
As, could they hear, the damned would make no noise,
But listen to thee, walking in thy chamber,
Melting melodious words to lutes of amber.   *Herrick.*
Ibid.

DELIGHT IN DISORDER

            A sweet disorder in the dress
            Kindles in clothes a wantonness:

A lawn about the shoulders thrown
Into a fine distractïon;
An erring lace, which here and there
Enthralls the crimson stomacher;
A cuff neglectful, and thereby
Ribbons to flow confusedly;
A winning wave, deserving note,
In the tempestuous petticoat;
A careless shoe-string, in whose tie
I see a wild civility,——
Do more bewitch me, than when art
Is too precise in every part.   *Herrick.*

Hesperides, 1648.

THE MAD MAID'S SONG

Good morrow to the day so fair;
    Good morning, sir, to you:
Good morrow to mine own torn hair
    Bedabbled with the dew.

Good morning to this primrose too;
    Good morrow to each maid,
That will with flowers the tomb bestrew,
    Wherein my Love is laid.

Ah! woe is me, woe, woe is me;
    Alack and well-a-day!
For pity, sir, find out that bee,
    Which bore my Love away.

I 'll seek him in your bonnet brave;
    I 'll seek him in your eyes;

Nay, now I think they 've made his grave
  I' the bed of strawberries.

I 'll seek him there; I know, ere this,
  The cold, cold earth doth shake him;
But I will go, or send a kiss
  By you, sir, to awake him.

Pray hurt him not; though he be dead,
  He knows well who do love him,
And who with green-turfs rear his head,
  And who do rudely move him.

He 's soft and tender, pray take heed,
  With bands of cowslips bind him;
And bring him home; but 'tis decreed,
  That I shall never find him.   *Herrick.*

*Ibid.**

TO MUSIC, TO BECALM HIS FEVER

Charm me asleep, and melt me so
  With thy delicious numbers,
That being ravished, hence I go
  Away in easy slumbers.
    Ease my sick head,
    And make my bed,
Thou power that canst sever
    From me this ill;
    And quickly still,
Though thou not kill
    My fever.

they 've] th 'ave, 1648.

Thou sweetly canst convert the same
   From a consuming fire,
Into a gentle-licking flame,
   And make it thus expire.
      Then make me weep
      My pains asleep,
And give me such reposes,
      That I, poor I,
      May think, thereby,
     I live and die
        'Mongst roses.

Fall on me like a silent dew,
   Or like those maiden showers,
Which, by the peep of day, do strew
   A baptism o'er the flowers.
      Melt, melt my pains,
      With thy soft strains;
That having ease me given,
      With full delight
      I leave this light,
     And take my flight
        For Heaven.   *Herrick.*

Hesperides, 1648.

HIS POETRY, HIS PILLAR

Only a little more
   I have to write,
   Then I 'll give o'er,
And bid the world good-night.

'Tis but a flying minute,
   That I must stay,

Or linger in it;
And then I must away.

O Time that cutt'st down all!
And scarce leav'st here
Memorial
Of any men that were:

How many lie forgot
In vaults beneath,
And piece-meal rot
Without a fame in death!

Behold this living stone,
I rear for me,
Ne'er to be thrown
Down, envious Time, by thee.

Pillars let some set up,
If so they please,
Here is my hope,
And my Pyramides.   *Herrick.*

Ibid.

TIME

Time is a feathered thing,
And, whilst I praise
The sparklings of thy looks and call them rays,
Takes wing,
Leaving behind him as he flies
An unperceivèd dimness in thine eyes.

His minutes whilst they 're told
Do make us old;
And every sand of his fleet glass,
Increasing age as it doth pass,
Insensibly sows wrinkles there
Where flowers and roses do appear.
Whilst we do speak, our fire
Doth into ice expire;
Flames turn to frost,
And ere we can
Know how our crow turns swan,
Or how a silver snow
Springs there where jet did grow,
Our fading spring is in dull winter lost.

Since, then, the night hath hurled
Darkness, love's shade,
Over its enemy the day, and made
The world
Just such a blind and shapeless thing
As 'twas before light did from darkness spring,
Let us employ its treasure
And make shade pleasure;
Let 's number out the hours by blisses,
And count the minutes by our kisses;
Let the heavens new motions feel
And by our embraces wheel.
And, whilst we try the way
By which love doth convey
Soul into soul,
And mingling so
Makes them such raptures know

they 're] th' are, 1648.

As makes them entrancëd lie
In mutual ecstasy,
Let the harmonious spheres in music roll.   *Mayne.*

The Amorous War, 1648.*

IN PRAISE OF FIDELIA

Get thee a ship well rigged and tight,
With ordnance store, and manned for fight,
Snug in her timbers' mould for the seas,
Yet large in hold for merchandies;
Spread forth her cloth, and anchors weigh,
And let her on the curled waves play
Till, Fortune-towed, she chance to meet
The Hesperian home-bound western fleet;
Then let her board 'em, and for price
Take gold-ore, sugar-canes, and spice,—
     Yet when all these sh' hath brought ashore,
     In my Fidelia I 'll find more.   *Westmorland.*

Otia Sacra, 1648.

ON MORPHEUS

Great son of night! come from thine ebon cell,
Where softest slumbers do delight to dwell;
With wreaths of poppy bound about thy head,
Make haste, and bring my troubled thoughts to bed.
Some sweet illusion, gentle Sleep! devise,
To draw the fringëd curtains of mine eyes
Before I am aware; my restless mind
Implores thine aid; in silken cordage bind

my troubled] 1688;   thy troubled, MS.

My scattered senses with all mighty hand,
And charm them gently with thy silver wand.   *Anon.*

B.M. Add. MS. 22118. (Written before 1649. Poem printed 1688.)*

ON A ROSEBUD SENT TO HER LOVER

The tender bud within herself doth close
With secret sweetness till it prove a rose;
And then as fit for profit as for pleasure
Yields sweet content to him that gains the treasure:
    So she that sent this, yet a bud unblown,
      In time may prove a rose, and be your own.   *Anon.*

B.M. Add. MS. 22118. (Written before 1649.)*

TO ELIZA, UPON MAY DAY MORNING, 1649

See, Fairest! virgins gather dew;
  Winged heralds blaze on every bough
May 's come: if you say so, 'tis true.
For thus your power 's 'bove his that seasons sway,
He brings the month, but you must make it May.
     Arise, arise,
     Bright eyes,
   And silver over beauty's skies:
  You set, noon 's night; you up, each day
     Turns jolly May.

Now Venus hatches her young doves,
This fruitful month 's proper for loves,
Though April says like her it moves
Full of sad change; but you may chase away
All showers with smiles, and make all our days May.
    Arise, arise, &c.

All but you love, (though all love you),
The birds their song each morn renew,
Even earth has donned her gaudy hue.
Since all things else are blithe, let your kind ray
Do more than Sol's, and make in me too May.
                Arise, arise, &c.

May this month last; when bald Time shall
Climb your fair hill of youth, may all
His steps be slipp'ry, and he back fall
To beauty's spring, that your cheek may alway
That lustre wear that now adorneth May.
                Arise, arise,
                Bright eyes,
        And silver over beauty's skies:
        You set, noon's night; you up, each day
                Turns jolly May.   *Baron.*

Pocula Castalia, 1650.

TO LUCASTA,
GOING BEYOND THE SEAS

If to be absent were to be
        Away from thee;
Or that when I am gone
        You or I were alone;
Then, my Lucasta, might I crave
Pity from blustering wind, or swallowing wave.

But I 'll not sigh one blast or gale
        To swell my sail,
Or pay a tear to swage
        The foaming blue god's rage;
For whether he will let me pass
Or no, I 'm still as happy as I was.

Though seas and land be 'twixt us both,
　　Our faith and troth,
　　Like separated souls,
　　All time and space controls:
Above the highest sphere we meet
Unseen, unknown, and greet as angels greet.

So then we do anticipate
　　Our after-fate,
　　And are alive i' the skies,
　　If thus our lips and eyes
Can speak like spirits unconfined
In Heaven, their earthy bodies left behind.

Lovelace.

Lucasta, 1649.

TO LUCASTA,
GOING TO THE WARS

Tell me not, Sweet, I am unkind
　　That from the nunnery
Of thy chaste breasts, and quiet mind,
　　To war and arms I fly.

True, a new mistress now I chase,
　　The first foe in the field;
And with a stronger faith embrace
　　A sword, a horse, a shield.

Yet this inconstancy is such
　　As you too shall adore;
I could not love thee, Dear, so much,
　　Loved I not honour more.　　　*Lovelace.*

Ibid.

be 'twixt] betwixt, 1649.

THE ROSE

Sweet, sèrene, sky-like flower,
Haste to adorn her bower,
   From thy long cloudy bed
   Shoot forth thy damask head.

New startled blush of Flora,
The grief of pale Aurora,
   Who will contest no more,
   Haste, haste to strow her floor.

Vermilion ball that 's given
From lip to lip in heaven,
   Love's couch's coverled,
   Haste, haste to make her bed.

Dear offspring of pleased Venus
And jolly plump Silenus,
   Haste, haste to deck the hair
   Of the only sweetly fair.

See! rosy is her bower,
Her floor is all this flower,
   Her bed a rosy nest
   By a bed of roses pressed.

But early as she dresses,
Why fly you her bright tresses?
   Ah! I have found I fear,
   Because her cheeks are near.   *Lovelace.*

Ibid.

GRATIANA DANCING AND SINGING

See! with what constant motïon,
Even and glorious as the sun,
   Gratiana steers that noble frame,
Soft as her breast, sweet as her voice
That gave each winding law and poise,
   And swifter than the wings of Fame.

She beat the happy pavëment
By such a star made firmament,
   Which now no more the roof envìes;
But swells up high, with Atlas even,
Bearing the brighter, nobler heaven,
   And, in her, all the deities.

Each step trod out a lover's thought
And the ambitious hopes he brought,
   Chained to her brave feet with such arts,
Such sweet command and gentle awe,
As, when she ceased, we sighing saw
   The floor lay paved with broken hearts.

So did she move; so did she sing,
Like the harmonious spheres that bring
   Unto their rounds their music's aid;
Which she performëd such a way
As all the enamoured world will say,
   'The Graces danced, and Apollo played.'

                               Lovelace.

Lucasta, 1649.

TO ALTHEA, FROM PRISON

When Love with unconfinëd wings
   Hovers within my gates,

And my divine Althea brings
    To whisper at the grates;
When I lie tangled in her hair
    And fettered to her eye,
The gods, that wanton in the air,
    Know no such liberty.

When flowing cups run swiftly round
    With no allaying Thames,
Our careless heads with roses bound,
    Our hearts with loyal flames;
When thirsty grief in wine we steep,
    When healths and draughts go free,
Fishes, that tipple in the deep,
    Know no such liberty.

When, like committed linnets, I
    With shriller throat shall sing
The sweetness, mercy, majesty
    And glories of my King;
When I shall voice aloud, how good
    He is, how great should be,
Enlargèd winds, that curl the flood,
    Know no such liberty.

Stone walls do not a prison make,
    Nor iron bars a cage;
Minds innocent and quiet take
    That for an hermitage:
If I have freedom in my love,
    And in my soul am free,
Angels alone, that soar above,
    Enjoy such liberty.

Ibid.   *Lovelace.*

THE GRASSHOPPER,

To my Noble Friend, Mr. Charles Cotton

O thou that swing'st upon the waving hair
    Of some well-fillëd oaten beard,
Drunk every night with a delicious tear
    Dropped thee from heaven, where now thou 'rt reared!

The joys of earth and air are thine entire,
    That with thy feet and wings dost hop and fly;
And when thy poppy works, thou dost retire
    To thy carved acorn-bed to lie.

Up with the day, the sun thou welcom'st then,
    Sport'st in the gilt plaits of his beams;
And all these merry days mak'st merry men,
    Thyself, and melancholy streams.

But ah, the sickle! golden ears are cropped,
    Ceres and Bacchus bid good-night;
Sharp frosty fingers all your flowers have topped,
    And what scythes spared, winds shave off quite.

Poor verdant fool! and now green ice! thy joys
    Large and as lasting as thy perch of grass,
Bid us lay in 'gainst winter, rain, and poise
    Their floods, with an o'erflowing glass.

Thou best of men and friends! we will create
    A genuine summer in each other's breast;
And spite of this cold time and frozen fate
    Thaw us a warm seat to our rest.

thou 'rt] th' art, 1649.   acorn-bed] acron-bed, 1649.   poise] equalise, match.

Our sacred hearths shall burn eternally
   As vestal flames; the north wind, he
Shall strike his frost-stretched wings, dissolve, and fly
   This Etna in epitome.

Dropping December shall come weeping in,
   Bewail the usurping of his reign;
But, when in showers of old Greek we begin,
   Shall cry, he hath his crown again!

Night, as clear Hesper shall our tapers whip
   From the light casements where we play,
And the dark hag from her black mantle strip,
   And stick there everlasting day.

Thus richer than untempted kings are we
   That, asking nothing, nothing need:
Though lord of all what seas embrace, yet he
   That wants himself, is poor indeed.

                                 Lovelace.

Lucasta, 1649.

TO HIS MISTRESS

That voice, that presence, or that face,
Each a more easy soul would take;
But resolution walled the place
Where mine resided, which could make
   Resistance against one, but all
   Have won my fort, o'erthrown the wall.

Enough, enough! pull from those eyes
The colours of defiance down,
And peaceful flag erect, where lies

Smiles that may cure the scars each frown
   Hath made; there can no honour grow
   By wounding of a yielded foe.

Each blow you strike hits yourself now,
For you will lose what you did win:
Kings, as their subjects lessen, grow
More weak: oh, let not then within
   Your beauty's white inn lodgëd be
   So black a guest as cruelty!

But with the conqueror still by
The captive may no laws be made:
No flower questions the gardener why
He planted it i' the sun, or shade:
   Nor must my love, your creature, know
   Why you that made it use it so.

The more I suffer, still the more
My truth's great miracle will show;
For whereas others' can before
The warmth of kindness only grow,
   The deathless love my breast doth nourish,
   Midst the cold blasts of scorn shall flourish.
T. Beaumont.

Bodley MS. Malone 18. (MS. written before 1650.)*

TO HIS MISTRESS,
SENDING HER THE ARCADIA

Go, happy book, and let my Candia see
   In thee the emblem of herself and me.

---

others'] *i.e.* others' love.

When she surveys thy story (thou shalt stand
Charmed in the whiter circle of her hand,
Rocked on the ivory cradle of her knee,
Her bright love-ruling stars bent over thee)
A Delphic fury in thy leaves shall swell
And all thy fictions turn to oracle.
For where thy quainter language draws each line
Of Beauty's map, and by a skill divine
Upon it does each native grace confer,
They will appear descriptïons of her.
And where thy amorous passions best discover
The rocky firmness of a constant lover,
They lively show those purer flames that rest
Still burning on the altar in my breast.
     So thou 'rt her glass where she herself may see,
     And in true lovers' parts remember me.

T. Beaumont.

Ibid.

HIS DESPAIR

Down, swelling thoughts, and do not press
     My too much yielding vein,
With whispering a happiness
     I never must obtain:
     You can tell me there 's a sun,
     But not help me pull it down;
And only show each several star,
But never seat me where they are.

Peace, then, and follow not this way,
     That but augments my care;
Or if you needs must speak, then say
     She 's not so heavenly fair;

So shall you allay my smarts
By darkening her angel parts,
And, making her a woman, spy
For me some possibility.

I am pursued by my desires,
And hunted out of breath;
Within me I retain those fires
That scorch me unto death:
Oh, whilst others strive to be
Versed in the art of memory,
I only wish I could profess
The dark art of forgetfulness.

Amidst the torments I have felt,
This hope doth with me stay,
That soon my violent thoughts will melt
My pains and me away:
For every hour I feel my share
Of love increase, but life impair,
So that in short time there will prove
Nothing left of me but my love.   *T. Beaumont.*

Bodley MS. Malone 18. (MS written before 1650.)*

WE MUST NOT PART

We must not part, as others do,
With sighs and tears, as we were two.
Though with these outward forms we part,
We keep each other in our heart.
What search hath found a being, where
I am not, if that thou be there?

True love hath wings, and can as soon
Survey the world, as sun or moon;
And everywhere our triumphs keep
Over absence, which makes others weep:
By which alone a power is given
To live on earth, as they in heaven.   *Anon.*

B.M. Eg. MS. 2013. (Poem printed 1658; written before 1650.)*

SONG

He or she that hopes to gain
Love's best sweets without some pain,
       Hopes in vain.
Cupid's livery no one wears
But must put on hopes and fears,
       Smiles and tears;
And, like to April weather,
Rain and shine both together,
       Both or neither.   *Anon.*

B.M. Harl. MS. 6917. (Poem written before 1650.)*

MONTROSS

Ask not why sorrow shades my brow,
   Nor why my sprightly looks decay:
Alas! what need I beauty now,
   Since he that loved it died to-day?

Can ye have ears, and yet not know
   Mirtillo, brave Mirtillo 's slain?
Can ye have eyes, and they not flow,
   Or hearts, that do not share my pain?

He 's gone! he 's gone! and I will go;
   For in my breast such wars I have,
And thoughts of him perplex me so
   That the whole world appears my grave.

But I 'll go to him, though he lie
   Wrapped in the cold, cold arms of death:
And under yon sad cypress tree
   I 'll mourn, I 'll mourn away my breath.

Cotton.

Poems, 1689. (Poem written 1650?)*

SONG

Tell me not I my time misspend,
   'Tis time lost to reprove me:
Pursue thou thine, I have my end,
   So Chloris only love me.

Tell me not others' flocks are full,
   Mine poor: let those despise me
That more abound in milk and wool,
   So Chloris only prize me.

Tire other easier ears with these
   Unappertaining stories:
He never feels the world's disease,
   That cares not for her glories.

For pity! thou that wiser art,
   Whose thoughts lie wide of mine,
Let me alone with mine own heart,
   And I 'll ne'er envy thine;

> Nor blame whoever blames my wit,
>   That seeks no higher prize
> Than, in unenvied shades, to sit
>   And sing of Chloris' eyes.

Eaton(?) or *P. King*(?)

B.M. Harl. MS. 6917, [c. 1650]. (Poem printed 1659.)*

ON CLARASTELLA, WALKING IN HER GARDEN

> See how Flora smiles to see
> This approaching deity!
> Where each herb looks young and green
> In presence of their coming queen.
> Ceres with all her fragrant store
> Could never boast so sweet a flower;
> While thus in triumph she doth go
> The greater goddess of the two.
> Here the violet bows to greet
> Her with homage to her feet;
> There the lily pales with white
> Got by her reflexèd light;
> Here a rose in crimson dye
> Blushes through her modesty;
> There a pansy hangs his head
> 'Bout to shrink into his bed,
> 'Cause so quickly she passed by,
> Not returning suddenly;
> Here the currants red and white
> In yon green bush at her sight
> Peep through their shady leaves, and cry,
> 'Come, eat me,' as she passes by;
> There a bed of camomil,
> When she presseth it, doth smell

More fragrant than the perfumed East
Or the phoenix' spicy nest;
Here the pinks in rows do throng
To guard her as she walks along;
There the flexive turnsole bends
Guided by the rays she sends
From her bright eyes, as if thence
It sucked life by influence;
Whilst she, the prime and chiefest flower
In all the garden, by her power
And only life-inspiring breath,
Like the warm sun, redeems from death
Their drooping heads, and bids them live,
To tell us she their sweets did give.   *Heath.*

Clarastella, 1650.

CLARASTELLA DISTRUSTING

You say you love me, nay, can swear it too;
But stay, sir, 'twill not do.
I know you keep your oaths
Just as you wear your clothes,
Whilst new and fresh in fashion;
But once grown old, you lay them by,
Forgot like words you speak in passion.
I 'll not believe you, I.   *Heath.*

*Ibid.**

THE EXCUSE

Your lovely fair did first invite
Me to that strange demand,

---

turnsole] heliotrope.*

Your wanton eye, big with delight,
　　Made me to understand
You pleasant as your looks, where every glance
Did raise and court my warm blood to advance.
　　Then blame not me for loving you,
　　Who if allowed would not do so?

Henceforth I 'll sit demure by you,
　　Nor speak when you would hear;
Just as I would your picture view,
　　Behold you and admire.
For if I speak, you prompt my tongue with love,
And 'cause I tell 't you, you unkind reprove.
　　Then blame not me for saying so,
　　Since 'twas your beauty bid me woo.　　*Heath.*

Ibid.

AN EPITAPH ON MISTRESS MARY PRIDEAUX

Happy grave, thou dost enshrine
That which makes thee a rich mine;
Yet remember, 'tis but loan,
And we look for back our own.
The very same, mark me, the same,
Thou shalt not cheat us with a lame,
Deformëd carcase;　this was fair,
Fresh as morning, soft as air;
Purer than other flesh as far
As other souls their bodies are:
And that thou may'st the better see
To find her out, two stars there be,
Eclipsëd now;　uncloud but those,
And they will point thee to the rose

That dyed each cheek, now pale and wan,
But will be, when she wakes again,
Fresher than ever; and howe'er
Her long sleep may alter her,
Her soul will know her body straight,
'Twas made so fit for 't, no deceit
Can suit another to it, none
Clothe it so neatly as its own.   *Morley* (?)

B.M. Harl. MS. 6917, [c. 1650]. (Poem printed 1655.)*

THE GARDEN'S QUEEN

Say, crimson rose and dainty daffodil,
      With violet blue,
Since you have seen the beauty of my saint,
      And eke her view,
Did not her sight (fair sight!) you lovely fill
      With sweet delight
Of goddess' grace and angel's sacred taint
      In fine, most bright?

Say, golden primrose, sanguine cowslip fair,
      With pink most fine,
Since you beheld the visage of my dear,
      And eyes divine,
Did not her globy front and glistering hair,
      With cheeks most sweet,
So gloriously like damask flowers appear,
      The gods to greet?

Say, snow-white lily, speckled gillyflower,
      With daisy gay,

---

taint] colour, hue.

Since you have viewed the queen of my desire
      In brave array,
Did not her ivory paps, fair Venus' bower,
      With heavenly glee,
Of Juno's grace, conjure you to require
      Her face to see?

Say rose, say daffodil, and violet blue,
      With primrose fair,
Since you have seen my nymph's sweet dainty face
      And gesture rare,
Did not (bright cowslip, bloomy pink) her view
      (White lily) shine
(Ah, gillyflowers and daisy!) with a grace
      Like stars divine?   *J. Reynolds.*

The Flower of Fidelity, 1650.

OF DEATH

Though here on earth men differ, in the grave
There 's no distinction; all alike they have.
Then must the conqueror with the captive spread
On one bare earth as in the common bed;
The all-commanding general hath no span
Of ground allowed, more than a common man;
Folly with wisdom hath an equal share,
The foul and fair to like dust changèd are;
This is, of all mortality, the end:
Thersites now with Nereus dares contend;
And with Achilles he hath equal place,
That living, durst not look him in the face.
The servant with his master, and the maid
Stretched by her mistress, both their heads are laid

Upon an equal pillow; subjects keep
Courts with kings equal, and as soft they sleep,
Lodging their heads upon a turf of grass,
As they on marble, or on figured brass.   *Sheppard.*

The Loves of Amandus and Sophronia, 1650.

SEEING A LADY

Oh, she is fair: fair as the eastern morn
When she is pleased the summer to adorn
With her spring's glory: sweet as——
Leave, begging Muse! thy praise gains no relief,
Since from her glory I derive my grief.   *Tatham.*

Ostella, 1650.

THE LAMP

'Tis dead night round about: horror doth creep
And move on with the shades; stars nod, and sleep,
And through the dark air spin a fiery thread
Such as doth gild the lazy glow-worm's bed.
    Yet burn'st thou here, a full day, while I spend
My rest in cares, and to the dark world lend
These flames, as thou dost thine to me; I watch
That hour, which must thy life and mine despatch;
But still thou dost outgo me, I can see
Met in thy flames all acts of piety:
Thy light is charity; thy heat is zeal;
And thy aspiring, active fires reveal
Devotion still on wing: then, thou dost weep
Still as thou burn'st, and the warm droppings creep
To measure out thy length, as if thou 'dst know

What stock, and how much time were left thee now;
Nor dost thou spend one tear in vain, for still
As thou dissolv'st to them, and they distil,
They 're stored up in the socket, where they lie,
When all is spent, thy last and sure supply:
And such is true repentance; every breath
We spend in sighs is treasure after death.
Only one point escapes thee; that thy oil
Is still out with thy flame, and so both fail;
But whensoe'er I 'm out, both shall be in,
And where thou mad'st an end, there I 'll begin.

Vaughan.

Silex Scintillans, 1650.

THE RETREAT

Happy those early days! when I
Shined in my angel-infancy.
Before I understood this place
Appointed for my second race,
Or taught my soul to fancy aught
But a white, celestial thought;
When yet I had not walked above
A mile or two from my first love,
And looking back, at that short space
Could see a glimpse of his bright face;
When on some gilded cloud or flower
My gazing soul would dwell an hour,
And in those weaker glories spy
Some shadows of eternity;
Before I taught my tongue to wound
My conscience with a sinful sound,
Or had the black art to dispense

A several sin to every sense,
But felt through all this fleshly dress
Bright shoots of everlastingness.
   Oh, how I long to travel back,
And tread again that ancient track!
That I might once more reach that plain,
Where first I left my glorious train;
From whence the enlightened spirit sees
That shady city of palm trees;
But ah! my soul with too much stay
Is drunk, and staggers in the way.
Some men a forward motion love,
But I by backward steps would move;
And when this dust falls to the urn,
In that state I came, return.   *Vaughan.*

Silex Scintillans, 1650.

PEACE

My soul, there is a country
  Far beyond the stars,
Where stands a wingèd sentry
  All skillful in the wars;
There, above noise and danger,
  Sweet peace sits crowned with smiles,
And one born in a manger
  Commands the beauteous files.
He is thy gracious friend,
  And (O my soul, awake!)
Did in pure love descend,
  To die here for thy sake.
If thou canst get but thither,
  There grows the flower of peace,

The rose that cannot wither,
  Thy fortress, and thy ease.
Leave then thy foolish ranges;
  For none can thee secure,
But one, who never changes,
  Thy God, thy life, thy cure.   *Vaughan.*

Ibid.

SINCE THOU ART GONE

Silence, and stealth of days! 'Tis now
      Since thou art gone,
Twelve hundred hours, and not a brow
      But clouds hang on.
As he that in some cave's thick damp,
      Locked from the light,
Fixeth a solitary lamp
      To brave the night,
And walking from his sun, when past
      That glimmering ray,
Cuts through the heavy mists in haste
      Back to his day;
So o'er fled minutes I retreat
      Unto that hour,
Which showed thee last, but did defeat
      Thy light and power;
I search, and rack my soul to see
      Those beams again,
But nothing but the snuff to me
      Appeareth plain;
That, dark and dead, sleeps in its known
      And common urn,
But those, fled to their Maker's throne,

There shine, and burn.
O could I track them! but souls must
Track one the other;
And now the spirit, not the dust,
Must be thy brother.
Yet I have one pearl, by whose light
All things I see;
And in the heart of earth and night
Find heaven, and thee.   *Vaughan.*

Silex Scintillans, 1650.*

I WALKED THE OTHER DAY, TO SPEND MY HOUR

I walked the other day, to spend my hour,
Into a field,
Where I sometimes had seen the soil to yield
A gallant flower;
But winter now had ruffled all the bower
And curious store
I knew there heretofore.

Yet I, whose search loved not to peep and peer
I' the face of things,
Thought with myself, there might be other springs
Besides this here,
Which, like cold friends, sees us but once a year;
And so the flower
Might have some other bower.

Then taking up what I could nearest spy,
I digged about
That place where I had seen him to grow out;
And by and by

I saw the warm recluse alone to lie,
  Where fresh and green
  He lived of us unseen.

Many a question intricate and rare
  Did I there strow;
But all I could extort was, that he now
  Did I there strow;
Such losses as befell him in this air,
  And would ere long
  Come forth most fair and young.

This past, I threw the clothes quite o'er his head,
  And, stung with fear
Of my own frailty, dropped down many a tear
  Upon his bed;
Then sighing whispered, 'Happy are the dead!
  What peace doth now
  Rock him asleep below!'

And yet, how few believe such doctrine springs
  From a poor root,
Which all the winter sleeps here under foot,
  And hath no wings
To raise it to the truth and light of things,
  But is still trod
  By every wandering clod!

O Thou, whose spirit did at first inflame
  And warm the dead,
And by a sacred incubation fed
  With life this frame,
Which once had neither being, form, nor name,

        Grant I may so
    Thy steps track here below,

That in these masques and shadows I may see
        Thy sacred way;
And by those hid ascents climb to that day
        Which breaks from thee,
Who art in all things, though invisibly;
        Show me thy peace,
    Thy mercy, love, and ease;

And from this care, where dreams and sorrows reign,
        Lead me above,
Where light, joy, leisure, and true comforts move
        Without all pain;
There, hid in thee, show me his life again,
        At whose dumb urn
    Thus all the year I mourn.   *Vaughan.*

Silex Scintillans, 1650.

             THE HUNTING OF THE GODS

    Songs of shepherds and rustical roundelays
        Formed of fancies and whistled on reeds,
    Songs to solace young nymphs upon holidays,
        Are too unworthy for wonderful deeds.
    Phoebus ingenious, or wingéd Cyllenius,
        His lofty genius may seem to declare
    In verse better coinéd and voice more refinéd
        How stars divinéd the hunting the hare.

    Stars enamoured with pastimes Olympical,
        Stars and planets that beautiful shone,

Would no longer that earthly men only shall
　Swim in pleasure, and they but look on.
Round about hornëd Lucina they swarmëd,
　And her informëd how minded they were,
Each god and goddess, to take human bodies
　As lords and ladies, to follow the hare.

Chaste Diana applauded the motion,
　And pale Proserpina, set in her place,
Lights the welkin and governs the ocean
　While she conducted her nephews in chase;
Who by her example, her father to trample,
　The old and ample earth, leave the air,
Neptune the water, the wine Liber Pater,
　And Mars the slaughter, to follow the hare.

Light god Cupid was horsed upon Pegasus
　Borrowed of Muses with kisses and prayers,
Strong Alcides upon cloudy Caucasus
　Mounts a centaur that proudly him bears;
Postilion of the sky, light-heelëd Mercury,
　Makes his courser fly, fleet as the air,
Yellow Apollo the kennel doth follow
　With whoop and hollo, after the hare.

Hymen ushers the ladies: Astraea
　The just, took hands with Minerva the bold,
Ceres the brown, with bright Cytherea,
　With Thetis the wanton, Bellona the old;
Shamefaced Aurora with subtle Pandora,
　And Maia with Flora, did company bear:
Juno was stated too high to be mated,
　But yet she hated not hunting the hare.

Drowned Narcissus, from his metamorphosis
    Roused by Echo, new manhood did take;
Snoring Somnus up-started in Cimmeris,
    That this thousand year was not awake,
To see club-footed old Mulciber booted,
    And Pan promoted on Chiron's mare;
Proud Faunus pouted, and Aeolus shouted,
    And Momus flouted, but followed the hare.

Deep Melampus and cunning Ichnobates,
    Nape and Tiger and Harper, the skies
Rend with roaring, whilst huntsman-like Hercules
    Winds the plentiful horn to their cries;
Till, with varieties to solace their pieties,
    The weary deities reposed them where
We shepherds were seated, and there we repeated
    What we conceited of their hunting the hare.

Young Amyntas supposed the gods came to breathe,
    After some battles, themselves on the ground;
Thyrsis thought the stars came to dwell here beneath,
    And that hereafter the world would go round.
Corydon agëd, with Phyllis engagëd,
    Was much enragëd with jealous despair;
But fury vaded, and he was persuaded
    When I thus applauded the hunting the hare.

Stars but shadows were, state but sorrow,
    Had they no motion, nor that no delight;
Joys are jovial, delight is the marrow
    Of life, and action the axle of might.
Pleasure depends upon no other friends,
    And yet freely lends to each virtue a share;

Only I measure the jewel of pleasure,
   Of pleasure the treasure is hunting the hare.

Three broad bowls to the Olympical Rector
   His Troy-born eagle he brings on his knee;
Jove to Phoebus carouses in nectar,
   And he to Hermes, and Hermes to me;
Wherewith infusëd, I piped and I musëd
   In songs unusëd this sport to declare:
And that the rouse of Jove round as his sphere may move—
   Health to all that love hunting the hare!   *Wasse.*

Westminster Drollery, II., 1672. (Poem written c. 1650 ?) *

CONSTANT AFFECTION

Set forty thousand on a row,
My love will make the greatest show;
   But I for my part have chosen one,
   And I 'll have my Love, or I 'll have none.

I bought my Love a pair of shoon
As black as jet, with shooties blue;
   She put them on, and away she 's flown,
   Yet I 'll have my Love, or I 'll have none.

Into some far country I 'll go,
And pine myself with care and woe,
   And sigh to think what I have done,
   Yet I 'll have my Love, or I 'll have none.

For who can love so true as I,
Who am more than sick, yet cannot die?

shooties] shoe-ties; *cf.* shoo-ty, p. 106.

My heart is broke, my delight is gone,
Yet I 'll have my Love, or I 'll have none.

And when my love she thus hath tried,
I 'm sure her self she 'll ne'er abide,
But find me out, and bring me home,
Then I 'll have my Love, or I 'll have none.

Anon.

Sportive Wit, 1656. (Poem written before 1651.)*

HYMN

Whilst I beheld the neck o' the dove,
I spied and read these words:
'This pretty dye
Which takes your eye,
Is not at all the bird's.
The dusky raven might
Have with these colours pleased your sight,
Had God but chose so to ordain above';
This label wore the dove.

Whilst I admired the nightingale,
These notes she warbled o'er:
'No melody
Indeed have I,
Admire me then no more:
God has it in his choice
To give the owl, or me, this voice;
'Tis he, 'tis he that makes me tell my tale';
This sang the nightingale.

I smelt and praised the fragrant rose,
Blushing, thus answered she:

'The praise you gave,
The scent I have,
Do not belong to me;
This harmless odour, none
But only God indeed does own;
To be his keepers, my poor leaves he chose';
And thus replied the rose.

I took the honey from the bee,
On the bag these words were seen:
'More sweet than this
Perchance nought is,
Yet gall it might have been:
If God it should so please,
He could still make it such with ease;
And as well gall to honey change can he';
This learnt I of the bee.

I touched and liked the down o' the swan;
But felt these words there writ:
'Bristles, thorns, here
I soon should bear,
Did God ordain but it;
If my down to thy touch
Seem soft and smooth, God made it such;
Give more, or take all this away, he can';
This was I taught by the swan.

All creatures, then, confess to God
That th' owe Him all, but I.
My senses find
True, what my mind
Would still, oft does, deny.
Hence, pride! out of my soul!

O'er it thou shalt no more control;
I 'll learn this lesson, and escape the rod:
I, too, have all from God.   *P. Carey.*

Trivial Poems and Triolets 1651. (Text 1820.)*

CRUCIFIXUS PRO NOBIS

CHRIST IN THE CRADLE

Look, how he shakes for cold!
How pale his lips are grown!
Wherein his limbs to fold
Yet mantle has he none.
His pretty feet and hands
(Of late more pure and white
Than is the snow
That pains them so)
Have lost their candour quite.
His lips are blue
(Where roses grew),
He 's frozen everywhere:
All th' heat he has
Joseph, alas,
Gives in a groan; or Mary in a tear.

CHRIST IN THE GARDEN

Look, how he glows for heat!
What flames come from his eyes!
'Tis blood that he does sweat,
Blood his bright forehead dyes:
See, see!   It trickles down:

---

candour] whiteness.

Look, how it showers amain!
Through every pore
His blood runs o'er,
And empty leaves each vein.
His very heart
Burns in each part;
A fire his breast doth sear:
For all this flame,
To cool the same
He only breathes a sigh, and weeps a tear.

CHRIST IN HIS PASSION

What bruises do I see!
What hideous stripes are those!
Could any cruel be
Enough, to give such blows?
Look, how they bind his arms
And vex his soul with scorns,
Upon his hair
They make him wear
A crown of piercing thorns.
Through hands and feet
Sharp nails they beat:
And now the cross they rear:
Many look on;
But only John
Stands by to sigh, Mary to shed a tear.

Why did he shake for cold?
Why did he glow for heat?
Dissolve that frost he could,
He could call back that sweat.
Those bruises, stripes, bonds, taunts,

Those thorns, which thou didst see,
Those nails, that cross,
His own life's loss,
Why, oh, why suffered he?
'Twas for thy sake.
Thou, thou didst make
Him all those torments bear:
If then his love
Do thy soul move,
Sigh out a groan, weep down a melting tear.

Trivial Poems and Triolets. 1651. (Text 1820.)

                                                    P. Carey.

CHAINS

'Tis true.   I am fettered,
But therein take pleasure:
My case is much bettered;
This chain is a treasure.
My prison delights me;
'Tis freedom that frights me;
I hate liberty:
I 'll not be lamented,
You 'd all be contented
To have such chains as I.

When, heretofore flying,
My loves oft I quitted,
I then was a-trying,
And now I am fitted.
I ne'er should have changëd
If she, whilst I rangëd,
Had first struck mine eye:
As soon as I met her,

Enchain me I let her:
Ye 'd all do as I.

Soft cords made of roses
Than mine would more gall me;
Her bright hair composes
Those bonds which enthrall me.
Now, when she has provëd
How much her I 've lovëd,
My hopes will soar high:
Perchance, to retain me
Her arms will enchain me;
Then who 'd not be I?   *P. Carey.*

Ibid.

TO PHOEBUS

SEEING A LADY BEFORE SUNRISE

Phoebus, lie still, and take thy rest
Securely on thy Tethys' breast,
Thou need'st not rise to gild the east:

For she is up whose wakings may
Give birth and measure to the day,
Although thou hide thyself away.

Phoebus, lie still, and keep the side
Warm of thy chaste and watery bride,
Thy useless glory laid aside:

For she is up whose beauty's might
Can change ev'n darkness into light,
When thou canst but succeed the night.

Phoebus, lie still, and shroud thy head
Within the covert of thy bed,
Or counterfeit that thou art dead:

For she is up, and I do find
Gazing on thee doth only blind
The outward eyes, but her the mind.

Yet, Phoebus, rise, and take thy chair
Once more, shaking dull vapours from thy hair;
But wink and look not on my fair:

For, if thou once her beauty view,
Ere night thou wilt thyself undo,
Nor have a home to go unto.

And were thy chariot empty, she
But too unfit a guide would be,
Having already scorchèd me:

For I'm afraid lest with desire
She once more set the world on fire,
Making all others Ethiops by her.   *Prestwich.*

Hippolytus . . . with divers other Poems, 1651.

AND SHE WASHED HIS FEET WITH HER TEARS, AND WIPED THEM WITH THE HAIRS OF HER HEAD

The proud Egyptian queen, her Roman guest,
(To express her love in height of state, and pleasure)
With pearl dissolved in gold, did feast,
            Both food, and treasure.

And now, dear Lord, thy lover, on the fair
And silver tables of thy feet, behold!
    Pearl in her tears, and in her hair
        Offers thee gold.   *Sherburne.*

Salmacis, etc., 1651.

WEEPING AND KISSING

A kiss I begged; but, smiling, she
    Denied it me:
When straight, her cheeks with tears o'erflown,
    Now kinder grown,
What smiling she 'd not let me have,
    She weeping gave.
Then you, whom scornful beauties awe,
    Hope yet relief;
For Love (who tears from smiles) can draw
    Pleasure from grief.   *Sherburne.*

Ibid.

THE VOW

    By my life I vow
    That my life art thou;
By my heart, and by my eyes:
    But thy faith denies
To my juster oath to incline,
For thou say'st I swear by thine.

    By this sigh I swear,
    By this falling tear,
By the undeservëd pains
    My grieved soul sustains:

Now thou may'st believe my moan,
These are too too much my own.

Salmacis, etc., 1651.*   *Sherburne.*

THE SWEET-MEAT

Thou gav'st me late to eat
A sweet without, but within, bitter meat:
As if thou wouldst have said, 'Here, taste in this
What Celia is.'

But if there ought to be
A likeness, dearest, 'twixt thy gift and thee,
Why first what 's sweet in thee should I not taste.
The bitter last?

                                             Sherburne.

Ibid.

THE GARDEN

The garden 's quit with me: as yesterday
I walked in that, to-day that walks in me;
Through all my memory
It sweetly wanders, and has found a way
To make me honestly possess
What still another's is.

Yet this gain's dainty sense doth gall my mind
With the remembrance of a bitter loss.
Alas, how odd and cross
Are earth's delights, in which the soul can find
No honey, but withal some sting
To check the pleasing thing!

For now I 'm haunted with the thought of that
Heaven-planted garden, where felicity
    Flourished on every tree.
Lost, lost it is; for at the guarded gate
   A flaming sword forbiddeth sin
    (That 's I,) to enter in.

O Paradise! when I was turnëd out,
Hadst thou but kept the serpent still within,
    My banishment had been
Less sad and dangerous: but round about
   This wide world runneth raging he
    To banish me from me.

I feel that through my soul he death hath shot:
And thou, alas, hast lockëd up life's tree.
    O miserable me!
What help were left, had Jesus' pity not
   Showed me another tree, which can
    Enliven dying man:

That tree, made fertile by his own dear blood,
And by his death with quickening virtue fraught.
    I now dread not the thought
Of barricado'd Eden, since as good
   A Paradise I planted see
    On open Calvary.   *Joseph Beaumont.*

Palmer MS., (Autograph). (Poem written 1652.)*

THE GENTLE CHECK

One half of me was up and dressed,
The other still in lazy rest;

For yet my prayers I had not said;
When I close at her matins heard
A dainty-tonguëd bird,
Who little thought how she did me upbraid.

But guilt caught hold of every note,
And through my breast the anthem shot;
My breast heard more than did my ear,
For now the tune grew sharp and chode
Me into thoughts of God,
To whom most due my earlier accents were.

How shall I blush enough to see
Poor birds prevent my praise to thee!
Dear Lord, my muse for pardon pants
And every tardy guilty tone
Doth languish to a groan:
Alas, to-day she sings not, but recants.

Forgive, forgive my lazy rhyme,
Which in its music keeps not time:
If thy sweet patience lets me borrow
Another morn of life, I give
My promise here to strive
Before the lark to be at heaven to-morrow.

Joseph Beaumont.

Palmer MS., (Autograph). (Poem written 1652.)*

TO HIS MUSE

Awake from slumbering lethargy! the gay
And circling charioteer of day,
In 's progress through the azure fields, sees, checks
our stay.

Arise! and, rising, emulate the rare
  Industrious spinsters, who with fair
Embroid'ries checker-work the chambers of the air.

Ascend! Sol does on hills his gold display,
  And, scattering sweets, does spice the day,
And shoots delight through Nature with each arrowed
    ray.

The opal-coloured dawns raise fancy high;
  Hymns ravish those who pulpits fly;
Convert dull lead to active gold by love-chemy.

As Nature's prime confectioner, the bee,
  By her flower-nibbling chemistry,
Turns *vert* to *or*: so, verse gross prose does rarefy.

                                        Benlowes.
Theophila, or Love's Sacrifice, 1652. (Canto I., Stzs. 63–67.)

SONNET

When I consider how my light is spent
Ere half my days, in this dark world and wide,
And that one talent which is death to hide
Lodged with me useless, though my soul more bent
To serve therewith my Maker, and present
My true account, lest he returning chide;
Doth God exact day-labour, light denied?
I fondly ask; but Patience, to prevent
That murmur, soon replies, God doth not need
Either man's work, or his own gifts: who best
Bear his mild yoke, they serve him best: his state

Is kingly; thousands at his bidding speed
And post o'er land and ocean without rest:
They also serve who only stand and wait.   *Milton.*

Poems, &c., upon Several Occasions, 1673. (Poem written 1652.)

SONG

Neither sighs, nor tears, nor mourning,
  Protestations, imprecations,
Moves her not, nor quench my burning;
  She so frigid, and so rigid,
That my love procures but scorning.

When I follow her she flies me,
  Swiftly running with more cunning
Than the hare or bird that spies me;
  Still disdaining my complaining,
And to hear my grief denies me.

Say alone, must it be so then?
  Shall she glory in my story,
And I unrevengëd go then?
  Prithee, Cupid, be not stupid,
Bend in my defence thy bow then.   *Anon.*

J. Playford's *Select Musical Airs and Dialogues,* 1652.*

AT PARTING

Fain would I, Chloris, whom my heart adores,
Longer awhile between thine arms remain,
But lo, the jealous morn her rosy doors,
To spite me, opes and brings the day again.

Farewell, farewell, Chloris, 'tis time I died:
The night departs, yet still my woes abide.

Hence! saucy fleering candle of the skies,
Let us alone, we have no need of thee:
Our nights are ever day where Chloris' eyes
Shine, that a pair of brighter tapers be.
　　Farewell, farewell, &c.

O night! whose sable veil was wont to be
More friend to lovers than the noisefull day:
Wherefore, oh, wherefore dost thou fly from me,
And carry with thee all my joys away?
　　Farewell, farewell, &c.　　　　　　*Anon.*

*Ibid.**

TELL ME, YOU WANDERING SPIRITS OF THE AIR

Tell me, you wandering spirits of the air,
Did you not see a nymph more bright, more fair
Than Beauty's darling, or of parts more sweet
Than stol'n content? If such a one you meet,
Wait on her hourly wheresoe'er she flies,
And cry, and cry, Amyntas for her absence dies.

Go search the valleys; pluck up every rose,
You 'll find a scent, a blush of her in those;
Fish, fish for pearl or coral, there you 'll see
How oriental all her colours be;
Go, call the echoes to your aid, and cry
Chloris! Chloris! for that 's her name for whom I die.

Amyntas] 1652 and 1653; Amyntor, 1659.

But stay a while, I have informed you ill,
Were she on earth, she had been with me still:
Go, fly to heaven, examine every sphere;
And try what star hath lately lighted there:
If any brighter than the sun you see,
Fall down, fall down and worship it, for that is she.

Anon.

J. Playford's *Select Musical Airs and Dialogues*, 1652.*

TO HIS COY MISTRESS

Had we but world enough, and time,
This coyness, Lady, were no crime.
We would sit down, and think which way
To walk, and pass our long love's day.
Thou by the Indian Ganges' side
Shouldst rubies find; I by the tide
Of Humber would complain.   I would
Love you ten years before the Flood;
And you should, if you please, refuse
Till the Conversion of the Jews.
My vegetable love should grow
Vaster than empires, and more slow.
An hundred years should go to praise
Thine eyes, and on thy forehead gaze;
Two hundred to adore each breast;
But thirty thousand to the rest:
An age, at least, to every part,
And the last age should show your heart.
For, Lady, you deserve this state;
Nor would I love at lower rate.
    But, at my back, I always hear
Time's wingèd chariot hurrying near:
And yonder, all before us lie

Deserts of vast eternity.
Thy beauty shall no more be found;
Nor, in thy marble vault, shall sound
My echoing song.   Then worms shall try
That long preserved virginity:
And your quaint honour turn to dust;
And into ashes all my lust.
The grave 's a fine and private place,
But none, I think, do there embrace.
     Now, therefore, while the youthful hue
Sits on thy skin like morning dew,
And while thy willing soul transpires
At every pore with instant fires,
Now let us sport us while we may;
And now, like amorous birds of prey,
Rather at once our time devour,
Than languish in his slow-chapt power.
Let us roll all our strength, and all
Our sweetness, up into one ball;
And tear our pleasures, with rough strife,
Thorough the iron gates of life.
     Thus, though we cannot make our sun
Stand still, yet we will make him run.   *Marvell.*

Miscellaneous Poems, 1681. (Poem written before 1653.)*

THE FAIR SINGER

To make a final conquest of all me,
    Love did compose so sweet an enemy,
In whom both beauties to my death agree,
    Joining themselves in fatal harmony:

---

dew] 1726;   glew, 1681.   slow-chapt] slow-jawed, slow-devouring.

That while she with her eyes my heart doth bind,
She with her voice might captivate my mind.

I could have fled from one but singly fair:
    My disentangled soul itself might save,
Breaking the curlèd trammels of her hair:
    But how should I avoid to be her slave,
Whose subtle art invisibly can wreathe
My fetters of the very air I breathe?

It had been easy fighting in some plain
    Where victory might hang in equal choice;
But all resistance against her is vain,
    Who has the advantage both of eyes and voice:
And all my forces needs must be undone,
She having gainèd both the wind and sun.   *Marvell.*

Miscellaneous Poems, 1681. (Poem written before 1653.)

THE MOWER TO THE GLOW-WORMS

Ye living lamps, by whose dear light
    The nightingale does sit so late,
And, studying all the summer night,
    Her matchless songs does meditate;

Ye country comets, that portend
    No war, nor prince's funeral,
Shining unto no higher end
    Than to presage the grasses' fall;

Ye glow-worms, whose officious flame
    To wandering mowers shows the way,

That in the night have lost their aim,
　　And after foolish fires do stray;

Your courteous lights in vain you waste,
　　Since Juliana here is come;
For she my mind hath so displaced
　　That I shall never find my home.　　　*Marvell.*
Ibid.

AMETAS AND THESTYLIS MAKING HAY-ROPES

AMETAS

Think'st thou that this love can stand
　　Whilst thou still dost say me nay?
Love unpaid does soon disband:
　　Love binds love, as hay binds hay.

THESTYLIS

Think'st thou that this rope would twine
　　If we both should turn one way?
Where both parties so combine
　　Neither love will twist, nor hay.

AMETAS

Thus you vain excuses find,
　　Which yourself and us delay:
And love ties a woman's mind
　　Looser than with ropes of hay.

THESTYLIS

What you cannot constant hope
　　Must be taken as you may.

AMETAS

Then let 's both lay by our rope,
And go and kiss within the hay.   *Marvell.*

Miscellaneous Poems, 1681. (Poem written before 1653.)

THE MOWER'S SONG

My mind was once the true survey
Of all these meadows fresh and gay,
And in the greenness of the grass
Did see its hopes as in a glass;
When Juliana came, and she,
What I do to the grass, does to my thoughts and me.

But these, while I with sorrow pine,
Grew more luxuriant still and fine,
That not one blade of grass you spied,
But had a flower on either side;
When Juliana came, and she,
What I do to the grass, does to my thoughts and me.

Unthankful meadows, could you so
A fellowship so true forgo,
And in your gaudy May-games meet,
While I lay trodden under feet?
When Juliana came, and she,
What I do to the grass, does to my thoughts and me.

But what you in compassion ought,
Shall now by my revenge be wrought;
And flowers, and grass, and I, and all,
Will in one common ruin fall;
For Juliana comes, and she,
What I do to the grass, does to my thoughts and me.

And thus, ye meadows, which have been
Companions of my thoughts more green,
Shall now the heraldry become
With which I shall adorn my tomb;
For Juliana comes, and she,
What I do to the grass, does to my thoughts and me.

Ibid.   *Marvell.*

THE GARDEN

How vainly men themselves amaze
To win the palm, the oak, or bays;
And their incessant labours see
Crowned from some single herb or tree,
Whose short and narrow-vergèd shade
Does prudently their toils upbraid;
While all the flowers and trees do close
To weave the garlands of repose.

Fair Quiet, have I found thee here,
And Innocence, thy sister dear!
Mistaken long, I sought you then
In busy companies of men.
Your sacred plants, if here below,
Only among the plants will grow:
Society is all but rude
To this delicious solitude.

No white nor red was ever seen
So amorous as this lovely green.
Fond lovers, cruel as their flame,

---

incessant] 1726; uncessant, 1681.   Stz. 1, l. 7] 1726; While all flowers
and all trees do close, 1681.

Cut in these trees their mistress' name:
Little, alas, they know or heed,
How far these beauties her exceed!
Fair trees! wheres'e'er your barks I wound,
No name shall but your own be found.

When we have run our passion's heat,
Love hither makes his best retreat.
The gods, that mortal beauty chase,
Still in a tree did end their race:
Apollo hunted Daphne so,
Only that she might laurel grow;
And Pan did after Syrinx speed,
Not as a nymph, but for a reed.

What wondrous life in this I lead!
Ripe apples drop about my head;
The luscious clusters of the vine
Upon my mouth do crush their wine;
The nectarine, and curious peach,
Into my hands themselves do reach;
Stumbling on melons, as I pass,
Ensnared with flowers, I fall on grass.

Meanwhile the mind, from pleasure less,
Withdraws into its happiness:
The mind, that ocean where each kind
Does straight its own resemblance find;
Yet it creates, transcending these,
Far other worlds, and other seas;
Annihilating all that 's made
To a green thought in a green shade.

Here at the fountain's sliding foot,
Or at some fruit-tree's mossy root,
Casting the body's vest aside,
My soul into the boughs does glide:
There like a bird it sits and sings,
Then whets, and combs its silver wings;
And, till prepared for longer flight,
Waves in its plumes the various light.

Such was that happy garden-state,
While man there walked without a mate:
After a place so pure and sweet,
What other help could yet be meet?
But 'twas beyond a mortal's share
To wander solitary there:
Two Paradises 'twere in one,
To live in Paradise alone.

How well the skilful gardener drew
Of flowers and herbs this dial new!
Where, from above, the milder sun
Does through a fragrant zodiac run;
And, as it works, the industrious bee
Computes its time as well as we.
How could such sweet and wholesome hours
Be reckoned but with herbs and flowers?   *Marvell.*

Miscellaneous Poems, 1681. (Poem written before 1653.)*

BERMUDAS

Where the remote Bermudas ride
In the ocean's bosom unespied,

From a small boat that rowed along
The listening winds received this song.
     'What should we do but sing his praise
That led us through the watery maze
Unto an isle so long unknown,
And yet far kinder than our own?
Where he the huge sea-monsters wracks,
That lift the deep upon their backs,
He lands us on a grassy stage,
Safe from the storms, and prelates' rage.
He gave us this eternal spring
Which here enamels every thing,
And sends the fowls to us in care
On daily visits through the air.
He hangs in shades the orange bright
Like golden lamps in a green night,
And does in the pomegranates close
Jewels more rich than Ormus shows.
He makes the figs our mouths to meet,
And throws the melons at our feet;
But apples plants of such a price,
No tree could ever bear them twice.
With cedars chosen by his hand
From Lebanon he stores the land;
And makes the hollow seas that roar
Proclaim the ambergris on shore.
He cast (of which we rather boast)
The Gospel's pearl upon our coast;
And in these rocks for us did frame
A temple where to sound his name.
O let our voice his praise exalt
Till it arrive at heaven's vault,
Which thence (perhaps) rebounding, may
Echo beyond the Mexique bay!'

Thus sung they, in the English boat,
An holy and a cheerful note:
And all the way, to guide their chime,
With falling oars they kept the time.   *Marvell.*

Miscellaneous Poems, 1681. (Poem written before 1653.)

AN EPITAPH UPON———

Enough: and leave the rest to fame!
'Tis to commend her, but to name.
Courtship which, living, she declined,
When dead, to offer were unkind.
Where never any could speak ill
Who would officious praises spill?
Nor can the truest wit or friend,
Without detracting, her commend.
To say she lived a virgin chaste
In this age loose and all unlaced;
Nor was, when vice is so allowed,
Of virtue or ashamed, or proud;
That her soul was on Heaven so bent,
No minute but it came and went;
That, ready her last debt to pay,
She summed her life up every day;
Modest as morn; as mid-day bright;
Gentle as evening; cool as night;
'Tis true: but all so weakly said;
'Twere more significant, *She's dead.*   *Marvell.*

Ibid.

THE DEFINITION OF LOVE

My love is of a birth as rare
   As 'tis for object strange and high:

It was begotten by Despair
   Upon Impossibility.

Magnanimous Despair alone
   Could show me so divine a thing,
Where feeble Hope could ne'er have flown
   But vainly flapped its tinsel wing.

And yet I quickly might arrive
   Where my extended soul is fixed;
But Fate does iron wedges drive,
   And always crowds itself betwixt.

For Fate with jealous eye doth see
   Two perfect loves; nor lets them close:
Their union would her ruin be
   And her tyrannic power depose.

And therefore her decrees of steel
   Us as the distant poles have placed,
(Though Love's whole world on us doth wheel)
   Not by themselves to be embraced:

Unless the giddy heaven fall,
   And earth some new convulsion tear,
And, us to join, the world should all
   Be cramped into a planisphere.

As lines, so loves oblique may well
   Themselves in every angle greet:
But ours, so truly parallel,
   Though infinite can never meet.

Therefore the love which us doth bind,
   But Fate so enviously debars,

Is the conjunction of the mind,
And opposition of the stars.   *Marvell.*

Miscellaneous Poems, 1681. (Poem written before 1653.)

INVOCATION OF SILENCE

Still-born Silence, thou that art
Floodgate of the deeper heart;
Offspring of a heavenly kind,
Frost o' the mouth and thaw o' the mind;
Secrecy's confident, and he
Who makes religion mystery;
Admiration's speaking'st tongue,—
Leave thy desert shades among
Reverend hermits' hallowed cells,
Where retired'st Devotion dwells:
With thy enthusiasms come,
Seize our tongues, and strike us dumb.   *Flecknoe.*

Miscellania, 1653.*

TO AMANDA WALKING IN THE GARDEN

And now what monarch would not gardener be,
My fair Amanda's stately gait to see?
How her feet tempt! how soft and light she treads,
Fearing to wake the flowers from their beds!
Yet from their sweet green pillows everywhere,
They start and gaze about to see my Fair.
Look at yon flower yonder, how it grows
Sensibly! how it opes its leaves and blows,
Puts its best Easter clothes on, neat and gay:

---

confident] confidant.

Amanda's presence makes it holiday!
Look how on tiptoe that fair lily stands
To look on thee, and court thy whiter hands
To gather it! I saw in yonder crowd—
That tulip bed of which Dame Flora 's proud—
A short dwarf flower did enlarge its stalk,
And shoot an inch to see Amanda walk.
Nay, look, my Fairest! look how fast they grow
Into a scaffold-method spring, as though,
Riding to Parliament, were to be seen
In pomp and state some royal amorous Queen!
The gravelled walks, though even as a die,
Lest some loose pebble should offensive lie,
Quilt themselves o'er with downy moss for thee;
The walls are hanged with blossomed tapestry
To hide their nakedness when looked upon;
The maiden fig tree puts Eve's apron on;
The broad-leaved sycamore, and every tree,
Shakes like the trembling asp, and bends to thee,
And each leaf proudly strives, with fresher air
To fan the curlëd tresses of thy hair.
Nay, and the bee, too, with his wealthy thigh,
Mistakes his hive, and to thy lips doth fly,
Willing to treasure up his honey there,
Where honey-combs so sweet and plenty are.
Look how that pretty modest columbine
Hangs down its head, to view those feet of thine!
See the fond motion of the strawberry
Creeping on th' earth, to go along with thee!
The lovely violet makes after too,
Unwilling yet, my dear, to part with you;
The knot-grass and the daisies catch thy toes,
To kiss my fair one's feet before she goes;

All court and wish me lay Amanda down,
And give my dear a new green-flowered gown.
    Come, let me kiss thee falling, kiss at rise,
    Thou in the garden, I in Paradise.   *Hookes.*

Amanda, 1653.

BEAUTY PARAMOUNT

Come, come, thou glorious object of my sight,
O my joy! my life! my only delight!
        May this glad minute be
        Blessed to eternity.

See how the glimmering tapers of the sky
Do gaze and wonder at our constancy;
        How they crowd to behold
        What our arms do infold!

How all do envy our felicities,
And grudge the triumphs of Selindra's eyes!
        How Cynthia seeks to shroud
        Her crescent in yon cloud!

Where sad night puts her sable mantle on,
Thy light mistaking, hasteth to be gone,
        Her gloomy shades give way,
        As at the approach of day;
And all the planets shrink, in doubt to be
Eclipsèd by a brighter deity.

                Look, oh, look! how the small
                    Lights do fall,
                    And adore
                    What before

The heavens have not shown,
Nor their god-heads known!

Such a faith, such a love
As may move
Mighty Jove
From above
To descend, and remain
Amongst mortals again.   *Killigrew.*

Selindra, 1665. (Poem printed 1653.)*

THE SOUL'S GARMENT

Great Nature clothes the soul, which is but thin,
With fleshly garments, which the Fates do spin;
And when these garments are grown old and bare,
With sickness torn, Death takes them off with care,
And folds them up in peace and quiet rest,
And lays them safe within an earthly chest:
Then scours them well and makes them sweet and clean,
Fit for the soul to wear those clothes again.

Poems and Fancies, 1653. (Text 1664.)   *Duchess of Newcastle.*

THE EXCELLENCY OF WINE

'Tis wine that inspires,
And quencheth love's fires;
Teaches fools how to rule a state:
Maids ne'er did approve it,
Because those that love it,
Despise and laugh at their hate.

And folds] 1653; Doth fold, 1664.

The drinkers of beer
Did ne'er yet appear
In matters of any weight:
'Tis he whose design
Is quickened by wine,
That raises things to their height.

We then should it prize,
For never black eyes
Made wounds which this could not heal:
Who then doth refuse
To drink of this juice,
Is a foe to the Common-weal.   *Orrery.*

H. Lawes' *Airs and Dialogues, I.,* 1653.*

SONG

Victorious men of earth, no more
Proclaim how wide your empires are;
Though you bind in every shore
And your triumphs reach as far
As night or day,
Yet you, proud monarchs! must obey
And mingle with forgotten ashes when
Death calls ye to the crowd of common men.

Devouring Famine, Plague, and War,
Each able to undo mankind,
Death's servile emissaries are;
Nor to these alone confined,
He hath at will
More quaint and subtle ways to kill:

A smile or kiss, as he will use the art,
Shall have the cunning skill to break a heart.

Cupid and Death, 1653.*   *Shirley.*

THE ANGLER'S SONG

Man's life is but vain, for 'tis subject to pain
    And sorrow, and short as a bubble;
'Tis a hodge-podge of business and money and care,
    And care and money and trouble.

But we 'll take no care when the weather proves fair,
    Nor will we vex now though it rain;
We 'll banish all sorrow, and sing till to-morrow,
    And angle and angle again.   *Anon.*

I. Walton's *The Complete Angler*, 1653.*

TO CELIA

When, Celia, I intend to flatter you,
And tell you lies to make you true,
            I swear
        There 's none so fair—
    And you believe it too.

Oft have I matched you with the rose, and said
No twins so like hath nature made:
            But 'tis
        Only in this—
    You prick my hand, and fade.

Oft have I said, there is no precious stone
But may be found in you alone;
            Though I

No stone espy—
Unless your heart be one.

When I praise your skin, I quote the wool
That silkworms from their entrails pull,
   And show
  That new-fall'n snow
 Is not more beautiful.

Yet grow not proud by such hyperboles:
Were you as excellent as these,
   Whilst I
  Before you lie—
 They might be had with ease.   *Anon.*

J. Playford's *Select Musical Airs and Dialogues*, 1653.*

A QUESTION

I ask thee, whence those ashes were
Which shrine themselves in plaits of hair?
Unknown to me; sure, each morn, dies
A phoenix for a sacrifice.

I ask, whence are those airs that fly
From birds in sweetest harmony?
Unknown to me; but sure the choice
Of accents echoed from her voice.

I ask thee, whence those active fires
Take light, which glide through burnished air?
Unknown to me; unless there flies
A flash of lightning from her eyes.

I ask thee, whence those ruddy blooms
Pierce on her cheeks on scarlet gowns?
Unknown to me; sure that which flies
From fading roses her cheek dyes.

I 'll ask thee of the lily, whence
It gained that type of innocence?
Unknown to me; sure Nature's deck
Was ravished from her snowy neck.   *Anon.*

The Card of Courtship, 1653. (Text 1658).*

AT THE FLORISTS' FEAST IN NORWICH

Song

Stay, oh, stay, ye wingëd hours!
      The winds that ransack east and west
Have breathed perfumes upon our flowers,
      More fragrant than the phoenix' nest:
            Then stay, oh, stay, sweet hours! that ye
            May witness that which Time ne'er see.

Stay a while, thou feathered scythe-man,
      And attend the queen of flowers;
Show thyself for once a blithe man,
      Come, dispense with a few hours:
            Else we ourselves will stay a while
            And make our pastime, Time beguile.

This day is deigned to Flora's use;
      If ye will revel too, to-night
We 'll press the grape, to lend ye juice

---

deigned] granted, given up.

Shall make a deluge of delight:
   And when ye can't hold up your heads,
   Our garden shall afford ye beds.   *Stevenson.*

Occasion's Offspring, 1654.

UPON A PASSING BELL

   Hark how the passing bell
   Rings out thy neighbour's knell,
   And thou for want of wit,
   Or grace, ne'er think'st on it,
     Because thou yet art well.

   Fool! in two days or three,
   The same may ring for thee;
   For Death's impartial dart
   Will surely hit thy heart;
     He will not take a fee.

   Since then he will not spare,
   See thou thyself prepare
   Against that dreadful day
   When thou shalt turn to clay,
     This bell bids thee beware.   *Washbourne.*

Divine Poems, 1654.

THE DYING LOVER

   Dear Love, let me this evening die!
     Oh, smile not to prevent it;
   Dead with my rivals let me lie,
     Or we shall both repent it.
   Frown quickly then, and break my heart,

That so my way of dying
May, though my life was full of smart,
    Be worth the world's envying.

Some, striving knowledge to refine,
    Consume themselves with thinking;
And some, who friendship seal in wine,
    Are kindly killed with drinking.
And some are wrecked on the Indian coast,
    Thither by gain invited;
Some are in smoke of battles lost,
    Whom drums, not lutes, delighted.

Alas, how poorly these depart,
    Their graves still unattended!
Who dies not of a broken heart
    Is not of death commended.
His memory is only sweet,
    All praise and pity moving,
Who kindly at his mistress' feet
    Does die with over-loving.

And now thou frown'st, and now I die,
    My corpse by lovers followed;
Which straight shall by dead lovers lie—
    That ground is only hallowed.
If priests are grieved I have a grave,
    My death not well approving,
The poets my estate shall have,
    To teach them the art of loving.

And now let lovers ring their bells
    For me, poor youth, departed,

Who kindly in his love excels
  By dying broken-hearted.
My grave with flowers let virgins strow,
  Which, if thy tears fall near them,
May so transcend in scent and show,
  As thou wilt shortly wear them.

Such flowers how much will florists prize,
  Which, on a lover growing,
Are watered with his mistress' eyes,
  With pity ever flowing.
A grave so decked will—though thou art
  Yet fearful to come nigh me—
Provoke thee straight to break thy heart,
  And lie down boldly by me.

Then everywhere all bells shall ring,
  All light to darkness turning;
While every choir shall sadly sing,
  And Nature's self wear mourning.
Yet we hereafter may be found,
  By destiny's right placing,
Making, like flowers, love under ground,
  Whose roots are still embracing.   *Davenant.*

The Works, 1673. (Variant printed 1655.)*

THE CRUEL MISTRESS

Tell me, O Love, why Celia, smooth
As seas when winds forbear to soothe
Their waves to wanton curls, than down
More soft, which doth the thistle crown,

---

soft] N.A.; swift, 1655.   (See note 296.)

Whiter than is the milky road
That leads to Jove's supreme abode,
Should harder far and rougher be
Than most obdurate rocks to me?
Sheds on my hopes as little day
As the pale moon's eclipsëd ray?
My heart would break, but that I hear
Love gently whisper in my ear,
    'Actions of women, by affection led,
    Must backward, like the sacred tongue, be read.'

                                                              Hammond.

Poems, 1655.*

HUSBANDRY

When I began my love to sow,
    Because with Venus' doves I ploughed,
Fool that I was, I did not know
    That frowns for furrows were allowed.

The broken heart, to make clods, torn
    By the sharp harrows of disdain,
Crumbled by pressing rolls of scorn,
    Gives issue to the springing grain.

Coyness shuts love into a stove;
    So frost-bound lands their own heat feed:
Neglect sits brooding upon love
    As pregnant snow on winter-seed.

The harvest is not till we two
    Shall into one contracted be;

Whiter] G. Saintsbury, 1906;   Whither, 1655.   the sacred tongue] Hebrew,
which is written from right to left.   rolls] rollers.

Love's crop alone doth richer grow,
    Decreasing to identity.

All other things not nourished are
    But by assimilatïon:
Love, in himself and diet spare,
    Grows fat by contradictïon.   *Hammond.*

*Ibid.**

SONNET

On the late Massacre in Piedmont

Avenge, O Lord! thy slaughtered saints, whose bones
Lie scattered on the Alpine mountains cold;
Ev'n them who kept thy truth so pure of old
When all our fathers worshipped stocks and stones,
Forget not: in thy book record their groans
Who were thy sheep, and in their ancient fold
Slain by the bloody Piedmontese, that rolled
Mother with infant down the rocks.   Their moans
The vales redoubled to the hills, and they
To Heaven.   Their martyred blood and ashes sow
O'er all the Italian fields, where still doth sway
The triple tyrant: that from these may grow
A hundred-fold, who, having learnt thy way,
Early may fly the Babylonian woe.   *Milton.*

Poems, &c., upon Several Occasions, 1673. (Massacre occurred 1655.)

THE PRAYER

My soul doth pant towards thee,
My God, source of eternal life.

Piedmont, Piedmontese] Piemont, Piemontese, 1673.

Flesh fights with me:
Oh, end the strife,
And part us, that in peace I may
Unclay
My wearied spirit, and take
My flight to thy eternal spring,
Where, for his sake
Who is my king,
I may wash all my tears away,
That day.

Thou conqueror of death,
Glorious triumpher o'er the grave,
Whose holy breath
Was spent to save
Lost mankind, make me to be styled
Thy child,
And take me when I die
And go unto my dust; my soul
Above the sky
With saints enrol,
That in thy arms, for ever, I
May lie.   *Taylor.*

The Golden Grove, 1655.

THEY ARE ALL GONE

They are all gone into the world of light,
And I alone sit lingering here;
Their very memory is fair and bright,
And my sad thoughts doth clear.

It glows and glitters in my cloudy breast,
Like stars upon some gloomy grove,

Or those faint beams in which this hill is dressed
    After the sun's remove.

I see them walking in an air of glory,
    Whose light doth trample on my days:
My days, which are at best but dull and hoary,
    Mere glimmering and decays.

O holy hope, and high humility!
    High as the heavens above!
These are your walks, and you have showed them me,
    To kindle my cold love.

Dear, beauteous death! the jewel of the just,
    Shining no where but in the dark;
What mysteries do lie beyond thy dust,
    Could man outlook that mark!

He that hath found some fledged bird's nest may know,
    At first sight, if the bird be flown;
But what fair well or grove he sings in now,
    That is to him unknown.

And yet, as angels in some brighter dreams
    Call to the soul when man doth sleep,
So some strange thoughts transcend our wonted themes,
    And into glory peep.

If a star were confined into a tomb,
    Her captive flames must needs burn there;
But when the hand that locked her up gives room,
    She 'll shine through all the sphere.

O Father of eternal life, and all
    Created glories under thee!
Resume thy spirit from this world of thrall
    Into true liberty.

Either disperse these mists, which blot and fill
    My pèrspective still as they pass,
Or else remove me hence unto that hill,
    Where I shall need no glass.   *Vaughan.*

Silex Scintillans, 1655.

THE NIGHT

    Through that pure virgin-shrine,
That sacred veil drawn o'er thy glorious noon
That men might look and live, as glow-worms shine
    And face the moon:
    Wise Nicodemus saw such light
    As made him know his God by night.

    Most blest believer he!
Who in that land of darkness and blind eyes
Thy long-expected healing wings could see
    When thou didst rise;
    And, what can never more be done,
    Did at midnight speak with the Sun!

    O who will tell me, where
He found thee at that dead and silent hour?
What hallowed solitary ground did bear
    So rare a flower,
    Within whose sacred leaves did lie
    The fulness of the Deity?

No mercy-seat of gold,
No dead and dusty cherub, nor carved stone,
But his own living works did my Lord hold
        And lodge alone;
        Where trees and herbs did watch and peep
        And wonder, while the Jews did sleep.

Dear night! this world's defeat;
The stop to busy fools; care's check and curb;
The day of spirits; my soul's calm retreat
        Which none disturb!
        Christ's progress, and his prayër-time;
        The hours to which high Heaven doth chime.

God's silent, searching flight:
When my Lord's head is filled with dew, and all
His locks are wet with the clear drops of night;
        His still, soft call;
        His knocking-time; the soul's dumb watch,
        When spirits their fair kindred catch.

Were all my loud, evil days
Calm and unhaunted as is thy dark tent,
Whose peace but by some angel's wing or voice
        Is seldom rent;
        Then I in heaven all the long year
        Would keep, and never wander here.

But living where the sun
Doth all things wake, and where all mix and tire
Themselves and others, I consent and run
        To every mire,

And by this world's ill-guiding light,
Err more than I can do by night.

There·is in God, some say,
A deep, but dazzling darkness; as men here
Say it is late and dusky, because they
See not all clear:
O for that night! where I in him
Might live invisible and dim.   *Vaughan.*

Silex Scintillans, 1655.

THE BIRD

Hither thou com'st: the busy wind all night
Blew through thy lodging, where thy own warm wing
Thy pillow was.   Many a sullen storm
(For which course man seems much the fitter born)
Rained on thy bed
And harmless head.

And now as fresh and cheerful as the light,
Thy little heart in early hymns doth sing
Unto that providence, whose unseen arm
Curbed them, and clothed thee well and warm.
All things that be, praise him: and had
Their lesson taught them, when first made.

So hills and valleys into singing break,
And though poor stones have neither speech nor tongue,
While active winds and streams both run and speak,
Yet stones are deep in admiration.

---

course] possibly coarse, sometimes so spelt.

Thus praise and prayër here beneath the sun
Make lesser mornings, when the great are done.

For each enclosëd spirit is a star
  Enlight'ning his own little sphere,
Whose light, though fetched and borrowëd from far,
  Both mornings makes and evenings there.

But as these birds of light make a land glad,
  Chirping their solemn matins on each tree:
  So in the shades of night some dark fowls be,
Whose heavy notes make all that hear them sad.

  The turtle then in palm-trees mourns,
   While owls and satyrs howl;
  The pleasant land to brimstone turns,
   And all her streams grow foul.

Brightness and mirth, and love and faith, all fly,
Till the day-spring breaks forth again from high.

           Vaughan.

Ibid.

THE LARK NOW LEAVES HIS WATERY NEST

 The lark now leaves his watery nest
  And climbing shakes his dewy wings.
 He takes this window for the east,
  And to implore your light he sings,
 Awake, awake! the morn will never rise
 Till she can dress her beauty at your eyes.

 The merchant bows unto the seaman's star,
  The ploughman from the sun his season takes;

But still the lover wonders what they are
　Who look for day before his mistress wakes.
Awake, awake! break through your veils of lawn;
　Then draw your curtains, and begin the dawn.

Davenant.

The Works, 1673. (Poem written before 1656.)*

AWAY, AWAY, VEX ME NO MORE

Away, away, vex me no more
　With thy too late complaining;
The treasure of thine eye grows poor,
　Nor avails their showery raining
To ripe my faith: oh, had thy youth
　But tasted my sad story,
I had not cast away my truth
　Nor hadst thou lost thy glory.

Away, away, hold thy disdain,
　Which erst thy brow did cover;
I am too cold now to complain,
　And you too late a lover
To catch my heart: oh, had thy fire
　Been equal good as cruel,
Then quenchless had been my desire,
　And thine ne'er wanted fuel.　　　　*Anon.*

J. Wilson's Autograph MS.; Bodley MS. Mus. b. 1, [Before 1656].*

SICKNESS, NOT SLEEP

She sleeps: peace crown thine eyes, sweet dreams in deep
Softest security thy senses steep.

Aye me! she groans; sadly, alas, oppressed
Lies the dear bosom gasping without rest.
Sickness, not sleep's numb hand, her eyes' faint ray
And those dead ashes of her cheek bewray,
Whose ominous hue, as bent to invert our years,
Like winter's snow on April buds appears:
So the vexed morn from her sere lover's bed
And cold embraces, with a look of lead
Pale and delightless rises; the autumn bower
So wanes; so falling droops the evening flower,
As life this fair declining lamp of light
(Her shine contracting) all o'erhaled in night.   *Anon.*

*Ibid.**

OF LOVE

Long annoys and short contentings,
Short rewards for long tormentings,
Vain desires and hopes deceiving,
Death that lives yet life bereaving,
Feignëd smiles and tears unfeignëd—
So lives he that 's with love painëd.

Count the flowers the meadows staining,
Count the bubbles in the raining,
Number all the stars adorning
Night, and dew-drops of the morning—
More by thousands are the cumber
Nightly breaks poor lovers' slumber.   *Anon.*

Ibid.

o'erhaled] covered, overwhelmed.   cumber] vexation, distress.

LET ME LAUGH

Let me laugh, while others grieve,
Sorrow never did relieve:
To be merry, laugh, and sing
Makes true content in every thing.
To myself I 'll be a friend,
Drench cares in wine, so let them end:
Oh! the soul that dares be merry
Never in his journey 's weary.   *Anon.*

J. Wilson's Autograph MS.; Bodley MS. Mus. b. 1, [Before 1656].

PITY AND LOVE

Pity of beauty in distress
    Should love in me constrain:
Beauty in you should find no less
    Than pity love again:
Your care my curse, your sighs my sorrows prove,
I love with pity, pity me with love.   *Anon.*

Ibid.

BE SHE FAIR AS LILIES BE

Be she fair as lilies be,
Lilies wither, so must she:
Be she youthful as the bud,
A frost one day will numb her blood.

Bear she high her wingèd thought,
Eagles' feathers come to nought:
Can she boast her eyes are bright,
Stars at last must lose their light.

Is she sweet and graceful borne,
Pride and age will breed her scorn:
She the soonest makes the best
Of nature's good that shows it least.   *Anon.*

Ibid.

THE BEE

Summer's nectar-gathering bee
On my mistress' lips did flee,
There he his honey labour left
And of sweets himself bereft;
But in her heart he fixed his sting,
Giving sweets with sorrowing.   *Anon.*

Ibid.

SONG

Fearless follow, thou sad soul,
Fair days are sweetest after foul;
Then follow boldly and here find
After pain thy peace of mind:
Sinful thoughts have bred thy woe
But thy grieved heart in time shalt know
Her long-lost joy, and thou shalt see
All comforts still attending thee.   *Anon.*

Ibid.

SONG

When I behold my mistress' face
Where beauty hath her dwelling-place,

And see those seeing stars her eyes
In whom love's fire for ever lies,
And hear her witty charming words
Her sweet tongue to mine ear affords,
Methinks he wants wit, ears and eyes,
Whom love makes not idolatrize.   *Anon.*

J. Wilson's *Cheerful Airs or Ballads*, 1660. (Poem written before 1656.)*

SONG

So have I seen a silver swan,
   As in a watery looking-glass,
Viewing her whiter form, and then
      Courting herself with lovely grace:
         As now she doth herself herself admire,
         Being at once the fuel and the fire.   *Anon.*

*Ibid.**

CHLORIS, FORBEAR A WHILE

Chloris, forbear a while, do not o'erjoy me;
Urge not another smile, lest it destroy me.
That beauty pleases most, and is best taking,
Which soon is won, soon lost, kind yet forsaking.
   I love a coming lady, faith! I do;
   But now and then I 'd have her scornful too.

O'ercloud those eyes of thine, bo-peep thy features;
Warm with an April shine, scorch not thy creatures:
Still to display thy ware, still to be fooling,
Argues how rude you are in Cupid's schooling.
   Disdain begets a suit, scorn draws us nigh:
   'Tis cause I would and cannot, makes me try.

Fairest, I 'd have thee wise: when gallants view thee
And court, do thou despise; fly, they 'll pursue thee.
Fasts move an appetite, make hunger greater;
Who 's stinted of delight falls to 't the better.
  Be kind and coy by turns, be calm and rough,
    And buckle now and then, and that 's enough.   *Bold.*

Poems, Lyric, Macaronic, Heroic, &c., 1664. (Variant in *Sportive Wit*,
1656.) *

THE SWALLOW

Foolish prater, what dost thou
So early at my window do
With thy tuneless serenade?
Well 't had been had Tereus made
Thee as dumb as Philomel;
There his knife had done but well.
In thy undiscovered nest
Thou dost all the winter rest,
And dreamest o'er thy summer joys
Free from the stormy season's noise:
Free from the ill thou 'st done to me:
Who disturbs, or seeks out thee?
Hadst thou all the charming notes
Of the wood's poetic throats,
All thy art could never pay
What thou 'st ta'en from me away:
Cruel bird, thou 'st ta'en away
A dream out of my arms to-day,
A dream that ne'er must equalled be
By all that waking eyes may see.
Thou this damage to repair,
Nothing half so sweet or fair,

> Nothing half so good canst bring,
> Though men say, thou bring'st the spring.

Cowley.

Anacreontiques, in *Poems*, 1656. (Text 1668.)*

AWAKE, AWAKE, MY LYRE!

> Awake, awake, my Lyre!
> And tell thy silent master's humble tale
>   In sounds that may prevail;
>   Sounds that gentle thoughts inspire:
>   Though so exalted she
>   And I so lowly be,
> Tell her, such different notes make all thy harmony.

>   Hark! how the strings awake:
> And, though the moving hand approach not near,
>   Themselves with awful fear
>   A kind of numerous trembling make.
>   Now all thy forces try;
>   Now all thy charms apply;
> Revenge upon her ear the conquests of her eye.

>   Weak Lyre! thy virtue sure
> Is useless here, since thou art only found
>   To cure, but not to wound,
>   And she to wound, but not to cure.
>   Too weak too wilt thou prove
>   My passion to remove;
> Physic to other ills, thou 'rt nourishment to love.

>   Sleep, sleep again, my Lyre!
> For thou canst never tell my humble tale

In sounds that will prevail,
Nor gentle thoughts in her inspire;
All thy vain mirth lay by,
Bid thy strings silent lie,
Sleep, sleep again, my Lyre, and let thy master die.

Cowley.

Davideis, in *Poems,* 1656.*

AN EPITAPH
ON HIS DECEASED FRIEND

Here lies the ruined cabinet
Of a rich soul more highly set:
The dross and refuse of a mind
Too glorious to be here confined.
Earth for a while bespake his stay,
Only to bait, and so away;
So that what here he doated on
Was merely accommodation.
Not that his active soul could be
At home but in eternity;
Yet, while he blessed us with the rays
Of his short-continued days,
Each minute had its weight of worth,
Each pregnant hour some star brought forth.
So, whiles he travelled here beneath,
He lived when others only breathe,
For not a sand of time slipped by
Without its action sweet as high.
  So good, so peaceable, so blest—
  Angels alone can speak the rest.   *R. Fletcher.*

Martial his Epigrams, etc., 1656.

SPRING

See, the spring her self discloses,
And the graces gather roses!
See, how the becalmëd seas
Now their swelling waves appease;
How the duck swims; how the crane
Comes from 's winter home again!
See, how Titan's cheerful ray
Chaseth the dark clouds away!
Now in their new robes of green
Are the ploughmen's labours seen;
Now the lusty teeming earth
Springs each hour with a new birth;
Now the olive blooms; the vine
Now doth with plump pendants shine;
And with leaves and blossoms now
Freshly burgeons every bough.   *Stanley.*

J. Gamble's *Airs and Dialogues*, 1656.

DRINKING SONG

How happy 's the prisoner that conquers his fate
   With silence, and ne'er on bad fortune complains,
But carelessly plays with his keys on the grate,
   And makes a sweet consort with them and his chains!
He drowns care with sack, while his thoughts are oppressed,
And makes his heart float like a cork in his breast.
     Then since we 're all slaves who islanders be,
     And our land 's a large prison enclosed with the sea,
     We will drink up the ocean and set ourselves free,
     For man is the world's epitome.

our land 's] 1656;   the world 's, 1660.

Let tyrants wear purple deep-dyed in the blood
  Of them they have slain, their sceptres to sway:
If our conscience be clear, and our title be good
  To the rags that hang on us, we 're richer than they:
We 'll drink down at night what we beg or can borrow,
And sleep without plotting for more the next morrow.
     Then since we 're all slaves, &c.

Come, drawer, and fill us a peck of Canary,
  One brimmer shall bid all our senses good-night.
When old Aristotle was frolic and merry,
  By the juice of the grape he turned Stagirite;
Copernicus once in a drunken fit found
By the course of his brains that the world turned round.
     Then since we 're all slaves, &c.

'Tis sack makes our faces like comets to shine,
  And gives beauty beyond a complexion mask;
Diogenes fell so in love with his wine
  That when 'twas all out he still lived in the cask,
And he so loved the scent of the wainscotted room
That dying he desirëd a tub for his tomb.
     Then since we 're all slaves who islanders be,
     And our land 's a large prison enclosed with the sea,
     We will drink up the ocean and set ourselves free,
     For man is the world's epitome.   Anon.

Cromwell's Conspiracy, 1660. (Earlier in *Choice Drollery*, 1656.)*

A CONTEST BETWEEN COURT AND COUNTRY

You courtiers scorn us country clowns,
  We country clowns do scorn the court;
We can be as merry upon the downs

As you are at midnight with all your sport.
  With a fadding, with a fadding.

You hawk, you hunt, you lie upon pallets,
  You eat, and drink, the Lord knows how;
We sit upon hillocks, and pick up our sallets,
  And sup up our sillabubs under a cow.

Your masques are made of knights and lords,
  And ladies that are fresh and gay;
We dance with such music as bag-pipes affords,
  And trick up our lasses as well as we may.

Your suits are made of silk and satin,
  And ours are made of good sheep's gray;
You mix your discourses with pieces of Latin,
  We speak our old English as well as we may.

Your rooms are hung with cloth of Arras,
  Our meadows are decked as fresh as may be,
And from this pastime you never shall bar us,
  Since Joan in the dark is as good as my lady.
   With a fadding, with a fadding.   *Anon.*

Oxford Drollery, 1671. (And in *Sportive Wit*, 1656.)*

OF A MISTRESS

I love a lass as fair as e'er was seen,
  Yet have I never seen if she be fair:
Grandees her suitors have and servants been,
  And they that woo her now great nobles are;
How can I therefore think that she will deign
To look on me? I fear I love in vain.

Unto the beauty which I do so desire
   I will make haste, to see how fair she is;
And though I find my betters wooers by her,
   I will be bold, and all my thoughts express;
Which when I have done, will she therefore deign
To pity me?   I fear I love in vain.

I 'll tell her that her hairs are golden twines
   Able to enamour all the deities;
And that her eyes are two celestial signs,
   More glorious than the twelve within the skies.
When I have told her this, will she then deign
To love me too?   I fear I love in vain.

If (when that I have said what I can say,
   And made what protestations I can make)
She will be proud, and coy, and say me nay,
   Though ne'er so fair, my heart from her I 'll take.
I will not subject be to her disdain:
The world shall never say I love in vain.   *Cokayne.*

A Chain of Golden Poems, 1658.*

SONG

Trust the form of airy things,
Or a siren when she sings:
Trust the sly hyena's voice,
Or of all distrust make choice:
And believe these sooner then
Truth in women, faith in men.   *Harington.*

H. Lawes' *Airs and Dialogues, III.*, 1658.*

then] than.

CHLORIS A CONSTANT COMFORT

Stay, stay, ye greedy merchants, stay,
Send not your ships so fast away
To trade for gems or precious ore,
For now they 'll be esteemed no more:
Sail to the Indies of my Chloris' eyes,
Cheeks, hair, and lips, there perfect treasure lies.

Come here, love's heretics that can
Believe there 's no true joy for man,
See what refinëd pleasure flies
From every motion of her eyes;
Gaze on my Chloris freely, then go tell
To all the world where true content doth dwell.

Forgive me, heavens, if I adore
Your sun, or moon, or stars no more;
Those often are eclipsed, and can
As soon destroy as cherish man:
But Chloris like a constant comfort shines,
Not only to our bodies but our minds.   *Hughes.*

H. Lawes' *Airs and Dialogues, III.,* 1658.*

SONNET

Methought I saw my late espousëd saint
Brought to me like Alcestis from the grave,
Whom Jove's great son to her glad husband gave,
Rescued from death by force though pale and faint.
Mine, as whom washed from spot of child-bed taint
Purification in the old law did save,
And such, as yet once more I trust to have

Full sight of her in heaven without restraint,
Came vested all in white, pure as her mind:
Her face was veiled, yet to my fancied sight,
Love, sweetness, goodness, in her person shined
So clear, as in no face with more delight.
But oh, as to embrace me she inclined,
I waked, she fled, and day brought back my night.

Milton.

Poems, &c., upon Several Occasions, 1673. (Poem written 1658.)

THE RESOLUTE COURTIER

Prithee, say aye or no;
If thou 'lt not have me, tell me so;
I cannot stay,
Nor will I wait upon
A smile or frown.
If thou wilt have me, say;
Then I am thine, or else I am mine own.

Be white or black; I hate
Dependence on a checkered fate;
Let go, or hold;
Come, either kiss or not:
Now to be hot,
And then again as cold,
Is a fantastic fever you have got.

A tedious woo is base,
And worse by far than a long grace:
For whilst we stay,
Our lingering spoils the roast,

thou 'lt] thou 't, 1658.

Or stomach 's lost;
Nor can, nor will I stay;
For if I sup not quickly, I will fast.

Whilst we are fresh and stout
And vigorous, let us to 't:
Alas, what good
From wrinkled man appears,
Gelded with years,
When his thin wheyish blood
Is far less comfortable than his tears?   *Shipman.*

Carolina: or, Loyal Poems, 1683. (Poem dated 1658.)

AN EPITAPH ON HIS GRANDFATHER

Here lies an aged corpse, which late
Incaged a soul, whom neither fate
Nor times could change from its first state.

Oppressëd more with age than cares;
Respected more for silver hairs
Than gold; for wisdom more than years.

Happy in every child he had;
Happy in self; and only sad
Being born in good days, but deceased in bad.

Ibid.   *Shipman.*

TO SORROW

Sorrow, in vain why dost thou seek to tempt
My quiet soul to misery and woe?

My constant mind from thine assault 's exempt,
    Innured to fortune's crosses long ago;
Go, seek out some who may affect thy pain;
If none thou find, return to me again.

When elder years witness my race is run,
    And hoary locks my hollow temples fill,
When I shall sit and say the world is done,
    Sorrow, return, and satisfy thy will:
Till then seek some who may affect thy pain;
If none thou find, return to me again.   *Anon.*

E. P.'s *The Mysteries of Love and Eloquence*, 1658. (Text from MS.)*

OF DEATH

The glories of our blood and state
    Are shadows, not substantial things;
There is no armour against fate;
    Death lays his icy hand on kings:
            Sceptre and crown
            Must tumble down,
And in the dust be equal made
With the poor crooked scythe and spade.

Some men with swords may reap the field,
    And plant fresh laurels where they kill;
But their strong nerves at last must yield;
    They tame but one another still:
            Early or late,
            They stoop to fate,
And must give up their murmuring breath,
When they, pale captives, creep to death.

The garlands wither on your brow,
   Then boast no more your mighty deeds;
Upon Death's purple altar now,
   See where the victor-victim bleeds:
         Your heads must come
         To the cold tomb;
Only the actions of the just
Smell sweet and blossom in their dust.   *Shirley.*

The Contention of Ajax and Ulysses, 1659. (Poem written before 1659?)*

WHEN, DEAREST, I BUT THINK ON THEE

When, dearest, I but think on thee,
Methinks all things that lovely be
Are present, and my soul delighted:
   For beauties that from worth arise
   Are, like the grace of deities,
Still present with us, though unsighted.

Thus while I sit and sigh the day
With all his spreading lights away,
Till night's black wings do overtake me:
   Thinking on thee, thy beauties then,
   As sudden lights do sleeping men,
So they by their bright rays awake me.

Thus absence dies, and dying proves
No absence can consist with loves
That do partake of fair perfection:
   Since in the darkest night they may
   By their quick motion find a way
To see each other by reflection.

The waving sea can with such flood
Bathe some high palace that hath stood
Far from the main up in the river:
    Oh, think not then but love can do
    As much, for that 's an ocean too,
That flows not every day, but ever.   *Felltham.*

Lusoria, 1661. (And Suckling's *Last Remains*, 1659.)*

THE WISH

Not to the hills where cedars move
Their cloudy head, not to the grove
Of myrtles in the Elysian shade,
Nor Tempe which the poets made;
Not on the spicy mountains play,
Or travel to Arabia:
I aim not at the careful throne
Which Fortune's darlings sit upon;
No, no, the best this fickle world can give
Has but a little, little time to live.

But let me soar, O let me fly
Beyond poor earth's benighted eye,
Beyond the pitch swift eagles tower,
Above the reach of human power;
Above the stars, above the way
Whence Phoebus darts his piercing ray:
O let me tread those courts that are
So bright, so pure, so blest, so fair,
As neither thou nor I must ever know
On earth: 'tis thither, thither would I go.   *Flatman.*

Poems and Songs, 1674. (Text 1686. Poem written 1659.)*

A LOVER'S LEGACY

Fain would I, Chloris, ere I die,
Bequeath you such a legacy
As you might say when I am gone,
'None has the like!' My heart alone
Were the best gift I could bestow,
But that's already yours, you know.
So that till you my heart resign,
Or fill with yours the place of mine
And by that grace my store renew,
I shall have nought worth giving you,
Whose breast has all the wealth I have,
Save a faint carcase, and a grave.
But had I as many hearts as hairs,
As many loves as love has fears,
As many lives as years have hours:
They should be all and only yours.   *Anon.*

J. Playford's *Select Airs and Dialogues*, 1659.*

A CATCH

Ne'er trouble thyself at the times or their turnings,
Afflictions run circular and wheel about;
Away with thy murmurings and thy heart-burnings,
With the juice of the grape we'll quench the fire out.
  Ne'er chain nor imprison thy soul up in sorrow,
  What fails us to-day may befriend us to-morrow,
  Let us scorn our content from others to borrow.

                                                       Anon.

J. Gamble's *Airs and Dialogues, II.*, 1659. (Text 1670.)*

LAURA SLEEPING

Winds, whisper gently whilst she sleeps,
    And fan her with your cooling wings;

Whilst she her drops of beauty weeps
   From pure and yet-unrivalled springs.

Glide over beauty's field, her face,
   To kiss her lip and cheek be bold,
But with a calm and stealing pace,
   Neither too rude, nor yet too cold.

Play in her beams, and crisp her hair,
   With such a gale as wings soft love,
And with so sweet, so rich an air,
   As breathes from the Arabian grove.

A breath as hushed as lover's sigh,
   Or that unfolds the morning door;
Sweet as the winds that gently fly
   To sweep the spring's enamelled floor.

Murmur soft music to her dreams,
   That pure and unpolluted run
Like to the new-born crystal streams
   Under the bright enamoured sun.

But when she waking shall display
   Her light, retire within your bar:
Her breath is life, her eyes are day,
   And all mankind her creatures are.   *Cotton.*

Poems, 1689. (Poem written before 1660 ?)*

RONDEAU

Thou fool! if madness be so rife
That, spite of wit, thou 'lt have a wife,
I 'll tell thee what thou must expect:

After the honey-moon neglect
All the sad days of thy whole life:

To that a world of woe and strife,
Which is of marriage the effect;
And thou thy woe's own architect,
                Thou fool!

Thou 'lt nothing find but disrespect,
Ill words i' the scolding dialect,
For she 'll all tabor be, or fife.
Then prithee go and whet thy knife,
And from this fate thyself protect,
                Thou fool!

Cotton.

Poems, 1689. (Poem written before 1660 ?)

THE RETREAT

I am returned, my fair, but see
Perfectïon in none but thee:
    Yet many beauties have I seen,
    And in that search a truant been,
Through fruitless curiosity.

I 've been to see each blear-eyed star,
Fond men durst with thy light compare;
    And, to my admiration, find
    That all, but I, in love are blind,
And none but thee divinely fair.

Here then I fix, and now grown wise,
All objects, but thy face, despise;

Taught by my folly, now I swear,
If you forgive me, ne'er to err,
Nor seek impossibilities.

Cotton.

Ibid.

VIRELAY

Thou cruel fair, I go
To seek out any fate but thee,
Since there is none can wound me so,
Nor that has half thy cruelty;
Thou cruel fair, I go.

For ever, then, farewell,
'Tis a long leave I take, but oh!
To tarry with thee here is hell,
And twenty thousand hells to go;
For ever, though, farewell.

Cotton.

Ibid.

SONG

See how like twilight slumber falls
To obscure the glory of those balls,
And, as she sleeps,
See how light creeps
Thorough the chinks, and beautifies
The rayey fringe of her fair eyes.

Observe love's feuds, how fast they fly
To every heart from her closed eye;
What then will she,
When waking, be?

A glowing light for all to admire,
Such as would set the world on fire.

Then seal her eyelids, gentle sleep,
Whiles cares of her mine open keep;
    Lock up, I say,
    Those doors of day,
Which with the morn for lustre strive,
That I may look on her, and live.   *Cotton.*

Poems, 1689. (Poem written before 1660?)

UPON A PATCH FACE

No beauty spots should ladies wear,
They but the spots of beauty are:
Who knows not this (save foolish sots)
That beauty ought to have no spots.
Some note a spot that Venus had:
Admit it were in one so bad,
Yet should not she have spots upon her
That would be held a maid of honour.   *Fairfax.*

Bodley MS. Fairfax 40. (Poem written before 1660.)*

UPON THE NEW-BUILT HOUSE AT APPLETON

Think not, O man that dwells herein,
This house 's a stay, but as an inn
Which for convenience fitly stands
In way to one not made with hands;
But if a time here thou take rest
Yet think eternity 's the best.   *Fairfax.*

Ibid.

THE LARK

Swift through the yielding air I glide
While night's sable shades abide,
Yet in my flight, though ne'er so fast,
I tune and time the wild wind's blast:

And e'er the sun be come about,
Teach the young lark his lesson out;
Who, early as the day is born,
Sings his shrill *Ave* to the rising morn.

Let never mortal lose the pain
To imitate my airy strain,
Whose pitch, too high for human ears,
Was set me by the tuneful spheres.

I carol to the fairy king,
Wake him a-mornings when I sing,
And when the sun stoops to the deep,
Rock him again and his fair queen asleep.   *Anon.*

B.M. Add. MS. 11608, [Before 1660]. (Poem printed 1669.)*

THE WISH

No! my desires are limited; nor expand
      They half so far: I do not crave
To have dominion o'er a mighty land,
      Nor Crassus' riches would I have;
The Grecian empire would not be
Of any comfort or content to me.

---

his lesson] 1669;   her lesson, MS.

While she, dear she, deigns not to cast an eye
    Of pity, or regard my grief,
Rather insults upon my misery;
    So far, so far she 's from relief.
Ah, fairest nymph! all that I crave
Is that one look of pity I might have.

Wouldst thou be pleased but once to smile on me,
    For that smile I 'd the Indies slight;
In them there could not half that comfort be,
    Not half that pleasure or delight:
No, the whole world to me would seem,
For such a favour, of too small esteem.

One smile I wish, nor would I have thee be
    Too lavish of such boons as those.
Ah! how much would poor one recomfort me!
    One smile enough thy pity shows:
And shouldst thou not it then withhold
With joy I die, or else grow overbold.   *Dancer.*

Aminta . . . Together with divers ingenious poems, 1660.

ON MARY, DUCHESS OF RICHMOND

Whether a cheerful air does rise
And elevate her fairer eyes,
Or a pensive heaviness
Her lovely eyelids does depress,
Still the same becoming grace
Accompanies her eyes and face,
Still you 'd think that habit best

elevate] 1673;   elevates, 1660.

In which her countenance last was dressed.
Poor beauties! whom a blush or glance
Can sometimes make look fair by chance,
Or curious dress or artful care
Can make seem fairer than they are.
Give me the eyes, give me the face
To which no art can add a grace;
Give me the looks, no garb nor dress
Can ever make more fair, or less.   *Flecknoe.*

Heroic Portraits, 1660.*

FOND LOVE, NO MORE

Fond love, no more
Will I adore
   Thy feignèd deity;
Go throw thy darts
At simple hearts,
   And prove thy victory.

Whilst I do keep
My harmless sheep
   Love hath no power on me:
'Tis idle souls
Which he controls;
   The busy man is free.   *T. Forde.*

Love's Labyrinth, 1660.

TO THE UNCONSTANT CYNTHIA

You are not, Cynthia, better pleased than I,
   That you first led the way

Through this dark night of blind inconstancy
    And first found break of day:
To freedom now we 'll sacrifice dreams past,
'Twas my good fate to cry Good-morrow last

Perhaps so soon I could not disengage,
    Having a greater score:
Some birds will longer hover round the cage
    Though 'twas their jail before:
Yet sure I meant not long to sit about
The ashes, when the fire was quite burnt out.

Since now my jailor has my chains untied,
    I 'll hold my hands no more
Up at Love's bar; he is condemned untried
    That has been burnt before:
Now that heart-sickness, which she gave, protects;
'Tis seldom that the same plague twice infects.

Breasts that have known Love's cruel slavery
    Are better fortified
By that experience, than they e'er can be
    By reason or by pride:
Then blush not that you quenched this amorous flame,
But blush with me if we two love again.

Sir Robert Howard.

Poems, 1660.*

ON CHRISTMAS DAY

To my heart

To-day,
Hark! Heaven sings;
Stretch, tune, my heart!

(For hearts have strings
May bear their part)
And though thy lute were bruised i' the fall,
Bruised hearts may reach an humble pastoral.

To-day,
Shepherds rejoice,
And angels do
No more: thy voice
Can reach that too:
Bring then at least thy pipe along,
And mingle consort with the angels' song.

To-day,
A shed that 's thatched
(Yet straws can sing)
Holds God; God matched
With beasts; beasts bring
Their song their way: for shame then raise
Thy notes! lambs bleat, and oxen bellow praise.

To-day,
God honoured man
Not angels: yet
They sing; and can
Raised man forget?
Praise is our debt to-day, now shall
Angels (man 's not so poor) discharge it all?

To-day,
Then, screw thee high,
My heart, up to
The angels' cry;
Sing 'Glory,' do:

> What if thy strings all crack and fly?
> On such a ground, music 'twill be to die.   *Paman.*

B.M. Add. MS. 18220. (Poem written 1660.)*

TO LUCIA PLAYING ON HER LUTE

When last I heard your nimble fingers play
Upon your lute, nothing so sweet as they
Seemed: all my soul fled ravished to my ear
That sweetly animating sound to hear.
My ravished heart with play kept equal time,
Fell down with you, with you did Ela climb,
Grew sad or lighter, as the tunes you played,
And with your lute a perfect measure made:
If all, so much as I, your music love,
The whole world would at your devotion move;
And at your speaking lute's surpassing charms
Embrace a lasting peace, and fling by arms.   *Pordage.*

Poems upon Several Occasions, 1660.

A MOCK SONG

'Tis true, I never was in love,
But now I mean to be;
For there 's no art
Can shield a heart
From love's supremacy.

Though in my nonage I have seen
A world of taking faces,
I had not age nor wit to ken
Their several hidden graces.

Their] 1664 and 1668;   There, 1661.

Those virtues which, though thinly set,
 In others are admirëd,
In thee are all together met,
 Which make thee so desirëd,

That though I never was in love,
 Nor never meant to be,
  Thy self and parts
  Above my arts
Have drawn my heart to thee. *A. Brome.*

Songs and other Poems, 1661.

THE RESOLVE

Tell me not of a face that 's fair,
 Nor lip and cheek that 's red,
Nor of the tresses of her hair,
 Nor curls in order laid,
Nor of a rare seraphic voice
 That like an angel sings;
Though, if I were to take my choice,
 I would have all these things.
But if that thou wilt have me love,
 And it must be a she,
The only argument can move
 Is that she will love me.

The glories of your ladies be
 But metaphors of things,
And but resemble what we see
 Each common object brings.

all together] altogether, all Eds.   if that thou] 1661 and 1668;   if thou, 1664.

Roses out-red their lips and cheeks,
    Lilies their whiteness stain:
What fool is he that shadows seeks
    And may the substance gain!
Then if thou 'lt have me love a lass,
    Let it be one that 's kind,
Else I 'm a servant to the glass
    That 's with Canary lined.   *A. Brome.*

Songs and other Poems, 1661.

THE SYMPATHY

Soul of my soul! it cannot be
That you should weep, and I from tears be free.
    All the vast room between both poles
    Can never dull the sense of souls
        Knit in so fast a knot.
    Oh! can you grieve, and think that I
    Can feel no smart because not nigh,
        Or that I know it not?

They 're heretic thoughts.   Two lutes are strung
And on a table tuned alike for song;
    Strike one, and that which none did touch
    Shall sympathising sound as much
        As that which touched you see.
    Think then this world, which heaven inrolls,
    Is but a table round, and souls
        More apprehensive be.

Know they, that in their grossest parts
Mix by their hallowed loves entwinèd hearts,

They 're] Th' are, 1661.

This privilege boast, that no remove
Can e'er infringe their sense of love.
            Judge hence then our estate,
Since when we loved there was not put
Two earthen hearts in one breast, but
            Two souls co-animate.   *Felltham.*

Lusoria, 1661.

UPON A RARE VOICE

When I but hear her sing, I fare
Like one that, raisëd, holds his ear
To some bright star in the supremest round;
    Through which, besides the light that 's seen,
    There may be heard, from heaven within,
The rests of anthems that the angels sound.   *Felltham.*

Ibid.

TO THE SUN

Go, glorious sun,
    Set in perpetual night;
    I shun thy light:
Now she is gone
    In whom all joys did shine,
My darkened sight
    Can see no thing that is divine.

Go, glorious sun,
    And tell her brighter ray
    I come away;
Tell her I run,
    My coming is not far:

The message can be done
By none but thee unto a star.   *Jenkyn.*

Amorea, the Lost Lover . . . being Poems, Sonnets, Songs, etc., 1661.

THE ANGLER'S WISH

I in these flowery meads would be;
These crystal streams should solace me;
To whose harmonious bubbling noise,
I with my angle would rejoice:
Sit here, and see the turtle-dove
Court his chaste mate to acts of love;
Or, on that bank, feel the west wind
Breathe health and plenty; please my mind
To see sweet dew-drops kiss these flowers,
And then washed off by April showers:
Here, hear my Kenna sing a song;
There, see a blackbird feed her young,
Or a laverock build her nest:
Here give my weary spirits rest,
And raise my low-pitched thoughts above
Earth, or what poor mortals love:
        Thus, free from lawsuits and the noise
        Of princes' courts, I would rejoice.

Or, with my Bryan and a book,
Loiter long days near Shawford brook;
There sit by him, and eat my meat,
There see the sun both rise and set;
There bid good morning to next day,
There meditate my time away:

Kenna] 1676;   Clora, 1661 and 1668.

And angle on; and beg to have
A quiet passage to a welcome grave.   *Walton.*

The Complete Angler, 1661. (Text 1676.)

A RHAPSODY

Now, I confess, I am in love,
Although I thought I never should;
But 'tis with one dropped from above,
Whom Nature framed of better mould:
    So fair, so sweet, so all divine,
    I 'd quit the world to make her mine.

Have you not seen the stars retreat
When Sol salutes our hemisphere?
So shrink the beauties, callèd great,
When fair Rosella doth appear;
    Were she as other women are,
    I should not love, or not despair.

Yet I could never bear a mind
Willing to stoop to common faces,
Nor confidence enough could find
To aim at one so full of graces:
    Fortune and Nature did decree
    No woman should be fit for me.   *Anon.*

B.M. Harl. MS. 3991. (Variant in *Merry Drollery,* 1661.)*

CAROL
FOR CANDLEMAS DAY

Christmas hath made an end,
Welladay, welladay;

Which was my dearest friend,
　　More is the pity:
For with an heavy heart
Must I from thee depart
To follow plough and cart
　　All the year after.

Lent is fast coming on,
　　Welladay, welladay;
That loves not any one,
　　More is the pity;
For I doubt both my cheeks
Will look thin eating leeks,
Wise is he then that seeks
　　For a friend in a corner.

All our good cheer is gone,
　　Welladay, welladay;
And turnëd to a bone,
　　More is the pity:
In my good master's house
I shall eat no more souse,
Then give me one carouse,
　　Gentle kind butler.

It grieves me to the heart,
　　Welladay, welladay;
From my friend to depart,
　　More is the pity:
Christmas, I mean 'tis thee
That thus forsaketh me,
Yet till one hour I see,
　　Will I be merry.

Anon.

New Carols, 1661.

WAKE ALL THE DEAD! WHAT HO! WHAT HO!

Wake all the dead! what ho! what ho!
How soundly they sleep whose pillows lie low!
They mind not poor lovers who walk above
On the decks of the world in storms of love.
  No whisper now nor glance can pass
  Through wickets or through panes of glass;
For our windows and doors are shut and barred.
Lie close in the church, and in the churchyard.
  In every grave make room, make room!
  The world 's at an end, and we come, we come.

The state is now Love's foe, Love's foe;
Has seized on his arms, his quiver and bow;
Has pinioned his wings, and fettered his feet,
Because he made way for lovers to meet.
  But, O sad chance, his judge was old;
  Hearts cruel grow when blood grows cold.
No man being young his process would draw.
O heavens, that love should be subject to law!
  Lovers go woo the dead, the dead!
  Lie two in a grave, and to bed, to bed!

Davenant.

The Law against Lovers, in *The Works,* 1673. (Acted 1662.)*

SERENADE,

TO TWO LADIES

See where Calisto wheels about
    The northern axle-tree of heaven,
And swift Boötes still does rout
    Before his lash the glittering seven:

View then those eyes that are more fair
Than any star that glitters there.

Fair Cassiopeia, wouldst thou gain
    The prize of glory in thy sphere?
Try then to borrow of these twain
    Two pair of eyes that shine more clear:
        For whilst they sparkle here below,
        Obscurer lights we cannot know.

In nights they far out-shine the moon
    And render them like glorious days,
They may contend at height of noon
    To equalise the sun's bright rays:
        Their coronet of hair, though brown,
        Does far out-shine Ariadne's crown.

Then gently dart those beams; for know
    How quick and fiercely they surprise
The sentinels that expect below
    The dawning of your beauteous eyes.
        We are your plants, and if we thrive
        'Tis by your influence that we live.   *Porter.*

The Villain, 1663. (Acted 1662.) *

THE LEATHER BOTTEL

Now God alone that made all things,
Heaven and earth and all that 's in,
The ships that in the seas do swim
To keep out foes from coming in,

to borrow] 1670; to morrow, 1663.

Then every one does what he can,
All for the good and use of man:
    And I wish in Heaven his soul may dwell
    That first devised the Leather Bottel.

Now what d' ye say to cans of wood?
Faith, they 're naught, they cannot be good;
For when a man for beer doth send,
To have them filled he doth intend;
The bearer stumbles by the way
And on the ground the beer doth lay;
Then doth the man begin to ban,
And swears 'twas long o' the wooden can;
But had it been in a Leather Bottel
It had not been so, for all had been well,
And safe therein it would remain
Until the man got up again:
    And I wish in Heaven his soul may dwell, &c.

What do you say to glasses fine?
Faith, they shall have no praise of mine;
For when a man 's at table set
And by him several sorts of meat,
The one loves flesh, the other fish,
Then with your hand remove a dish,
Touch but the glass upon the brim,
The glass is broke, and naught left in;
The table-cloth though ne'er so fine
Is soiled with beer, or ale, or wine,
And doubtless for so small abuse
A servant may his service lose:
    But I wish in Heaven his soul may dwell, &c.

What say you to the handled pot?
No praise of mine shall be its lot;
For when a man and wife 's at strife,
As many have been in their life,
They lay their hands upon it both
And break the same although they 're loth;
But woe to them shall bear the guilt,
Between them both the liquor 's spilt,
For which they shall answer another day,
Casting so vainly their liquor away;
But if it had been Leather-bottel'd,
One might have tugged, the other have held,
Both might have tugged till their hearts should break,
No harm the Leather Bottel could take:
  Then I wish in Heaven his soul may dwell, &c.

What say you to flagons of silver fine?
Why, faith, they shall have no praise of mine;
For when a lord for sack doth send,
To have them filled he doth intend,
The man with the flagon runs away
And never is seen after that day;
The lord then begins to swear and ban
For having lost both flagon and man;
But had it been either by page or groom
With a Leather Bottel it had come home:
  And I wish in Heaven his soul may dwell, &c.

And when this Bottel is grown old
And that it will no longer hold,
Out o' the side you may cut a clout
To mend your shoes when they 're worn out;
Then hang the rest up on a pin,
'Twill serve to put odd trifles in,

As rings, and awls, and candles' ends,
For young beginners have such things:
And I wish in Heaven his soul may dwell
That first devised the Leather Bottel.   *Wade.*

The New Academy of Compliments, 1671. (Poem written c. 1662.) *

SONG

So, so,
Lo, lilies fade, before the roses show
Themselves in Bow-dye, summer's livery,
Feasting the curious eye
With choice variety;
While as before
We did adore
Narcissus in his prime,
Now roses do delight
The nicer appetite:
Such is the vast disparity of time.

So, so,
One woman fades, before another know
What 'tis to be in love; but in a trice
All men do sacrifice
To the latter, and despise
Her whom before
They did adore
Like lilies in their prime;
Since now her sparkling eyes
Are darkened in disguise:
Such is the sad disparity of time.   *Clerke.*

Marciano, 1663.

Bow-dye] scarlet dye made at Bow, near Stratford, Essex.

SONG

See, O see!
How every tree,
Every bower,
Every flower,
A new life gives to others' joys,
Whilst that I
Grief-stricken lie,
Nor can meet
With any sweet
But what faster mine destroys.
What are all the senses' pleasures
When the mind has lost all measures?

Hear, O hear!
How sweet and clear
The nightingal
And waters' fall
In consort join for others' ears,
Whilst to me,
For harmony,
Every air
Echoes despair,
And every drop provokes a tear.
What are all the senses' pleasures
When the mind has lost all measures?

G. Digby, Earl of Bristol.

Elvira, 1667. (Acted c. 1663.)*

ORINDA TO LUCASIA

Observe the weary birds ere night be done,
How they would fain call up the tardy sun:

With feathers hung with dew,
And trembling voices too,
They court their glorious planet to appear,
That they may find recruits of spirits there.
The drooping flowers hang their heads,
And languish down into their beds;
While brooks more bold and fierce than they,
Wanting those beams from whence
All things drink influence,
Openly murmur and demand the day.

Thou, my Lucasia, art far more to me,
Than he to all the under-world can be;
From thee I 've heat and light,
Thy absence makes my night.
But ah! my friend, it now grows very long,
The sadness weighty, and the darkness strong:
My tears (its dew) dwell on my cheeks,
And still my heart thy dawning seeks,
And to thee mournfully it cries,
That if too long I wait,
Ev'n thou may'st come too late,
And not restore my life, but close my eyes.   *K. Philips.*

Poems, 1667. (Written before 1664.)

TO MY EXCELLENT LUCASIA, ON OUR FRIENDSHIP

I did not live until this time
Crowned my felicity,
When I could say without a crime,
I am not thine, but thee.

---

its dew] 1667 and 1669;   its due, 1678.

This carcase breathed, and walked, and slept,
    So that the world believed
There was a soul the motions kept;
    But they were all deceived.

For as a watch by art is wound
    To motion, such was mine:
But never had Orinda found
    A soul till she found thine;

Which now inspires, cures and supplies,
    And guides my darkened breast:
For thou art all that I can prize,
    My joy, my life, my rest.

No bridegroom's nor crown-conqueror's mirth
    To mine compared can be:
They have but pieces of this earth,
    I 've all the world in thee.

Then let our flames still light and shine,
    And no false fear control,
As innocent as our design,
    Immortal as our soul.   *K. Philips.*

Poems, 1667. (Written before 1664.)

THE MAD LOVER

I have been in love, and in debt, and in drink,
    This many and many a year;
And those three are plagues enough, one would think,
    For one poor mortal to bear.
'Twas drink made me fall into love,

And love made me run into debt,
And though I have struggled and struggled and strove,
    I cannot get out of them yet.

There 's nothing but money can cure me,
    And rid me of all my pain;
        'Twill pay all my debts,
        And remove all my lets,
And my mistress, that cannot endure me,
    Will love me, and love me again:
Then I 'll fall to loving and drinking amain.   *A. Brome.*

Songs and other Poems, 1664.*

SONG

My lodging it is on the cold ground,
    And very hard is my fare,
But that which troubles me most is
    The unkindness of my dear.
Yet still I cry, 'O turn, Love,
    And I prithee, Love, turn to me;
For thou art the man that I long for,
    And, alack! what remedy?

'I 'll crown thee with a garland of straw then;
    And I 'll marry thee with a rush ring;
My frozen hopes shall thaw then,
    And merrily we will sing.
O turn to me, my dear Love,
    And prithee, Love, turn to me;
For thou art the man that alone canst
    Procure my liberty.

'But if thou wilt harden thy heart still,
　　And be deaf to my pitiful moan,
Then I must endure the smart still
　　And tumble in straw alone.
Yet still I cry, O turn, Love,
　　And I prithee, Love, turn to me;
For thou art the man that alone art
　　The cause of my misery.'　　　　*Davenant.*

The Rivals, 1668. (Acted 1664.)*

WRITTEN AT SEA,
IN THE FIRST DUTCH WAR

To all you ladies now at land,
　　We men at sea do write;
But first I hope you 'll understand
　　How hard 'tis to indite:
The Muses now, and Neptune too,
We must implore, to write to you.

For though the Muses should be kind,
　　And fill our empty brain;
Yet when rough Neptune calls the wind
　　To rouse the azure main,
Our paper, ink, and pen, and we
Roll up and down our ship at sea.

Then, if we write not by each post,
　　Think not we are unkind;
Nor yet conclude that we are lost
　　By Dutch or else by wind;
Our tears we 'll send a speedier way:
The tide shall bring them twice a day.

With wonder and amaze the king
    Will vow his seas grow bold;
Because the tides more water bring
    Than they were wont of old:
But you must tell him that our cares
Send floods of grief to Whitehall Stairs.

To pass the tedious hours away,
    We throw the merry main;
Or else at serious ombre play:
    But why should we in vain
Each other's ruin thus pursue?
We were undone when we left you.

If foggy Opdam did but know
    Our sad and dismal story,
The Dutch would scorn so weak a foe,
    And leave the port of Goree;
For what resistance can they find
From men that left their hearts behind?

Let wind and weather do their worst,
    Be you to us but kind;
Let Frenchmen vapour, Dutchmen curse,
    No sorrow shall we find:
'Tis then no matter how things go,
Nor who 's our friend, nor who 's our foe.

In justice, you cannot refuse
    To think of our distress,
Since we in hope of honour lose
    Our certain happiness;
All our designs are but to prove
Ourselves more worthy of your love.

Alas! our tears tempestuous grow
   And cast our hopes away;
While you, unmindful of our woe,
   Sit careless at a play:
And now permit some happier man
To kiss your busk, and wag your fan.

When any mournful tune you hear,
   That dies in every note
As if it sighed for each man's care
   For being so remote,
Think then how oft our love we made
To you, while all those tunes were played.

And now we have told all our love,
   And also all our tears,
We hope our declarations move
   Some pity for our cares;
Let 's hear of no unconstancy,
We have too much of that at sea.   *Dorset.*

B.M. Harl. MS. 3991, [temp. Chas. II.] (Ballad registered Dec. 30, 1664.)*

IF SHE BE NOT AS KIND AS FAIR

If she be not as kind as fair,
   But peevish and unhandy,
Leave her, she 's only worth the care
   Of some spruce Jack-a-dandy.

I would not have thee such an ass,
   Hadst thou ne'er so much leisure,
To sigh and whine for such a lass
   Whose pride 's above her pleasure.   *Etherege.*

The Comical Revenge, 1664.*

TO HIS MISTRESS

Phyllis, though your all powerful charms
Have forced me from my Celia's arms,
That sure defence against all powers
But those resistless eyes of yours,
Think not your conquest to maintain
By rigour or unjust disdain;
In vain, fair nymph, in vain you strive,
Since love does seldom hope survive:
Or if I languish for a time,
While all your glories in their prime
May justify such cruelty
By the same force that conquered me;
When age shall come, at whose command
Those troops of beauties must disband,
A tyrant's strength once took away,
What slave so dull as to obey?
These threatening dangers then remove:
Make me at least believe you love;
Dissemble, and by that sly art
Preserve and govern well my heart;
Or, if you 'll learn a nobler way
To keep your empire from decay,
And here for ever fix your throne,
Be kind, but kind to me alone.

G. Villiers, Duke of Buckingham(?)

B.M. Harl. MS. 3991. (And Bodley MS. Ashm. 36–7. Poem written 1665,
printed 1671.)*

THE SLIGHT

I did but crave that I might kiss,
    If not her lip, at least her hand,

The coolest lover's frequent bliss;
      And rude is she that will withstand
      That inoffensive liberty:
She (would you think it?) in a fume
Turned her about and left the room;
      Not she, she vowed, not she.

Well, Chariessa, then said I,
      If it must thus for ever be,
I can renounce my slavery
      And, since you will not, can be free.
      Many a time she made me die,
Yet (would you think 't?) I loved the more;
But I 'll not take 't as heretofore,
      Not I, I 'll vow, not I.   *Flatman.*

Poems and Songs, 1674. (Text 1686. Poem written 1666.)*

LADIES, FAREWELL!

Ladies, farewell! I must retire,
Though I your faces all admire,
And think you heavens in your kinds,
Some for beauties, some for minds:
If I stay and fall in love,
One of these heavens, hell would prove.

Could I know one, and she not know it,
Perhaps I then might undergo it;
But if the least she guess my mind,
Straight in a circle I 'm confined;
By this I see, who once doth dote,
Must wear a woman's livery coat.

Therefore, this danger to prevent,
And still to keep my heart's content,
Into the country I 'll with speed,
With hounds and hawks my fancy feed:
Both safer pleasures to pursue,
Than staying to converse with you.

                                                    Hon. James Howard.

The English Monsieur, 1674. (Acted 1666.) *

OF SOLITUDE

Hail, old patrician trees, so great and good!
    Hail, ye plebeian underwood!
    Where the poetic birds rejoice,
And for their quiet nests and plenteous food,
    Pay with their grateful voice.

Hail, the poor Muse's richest manor seat!
    Ye country houses and retreat
    Which all the happy gods so love,
That for you oft they quit their bright and great
    Metropolis above.

Here Nature does a house for me erect,
    Nature the wisest architect,
    Who those fond artists does despise
That can the fair and living trees neglect,
    Yet the dead timber prize.

Here let me, careless and unthoughtful lying,
    Hear the soft winds above me flying
    With all their wanton boughs dispute,
And the more tuneful birds to both replying,
    Nor be myself too mute.

A silver stream shall roll his waters near,
    Gilt with the sunbeams here and there,
    On whose enamelled bank I 'll walk,
And see how prettily they smile, and hear
    How prettily they talk.

Ah wretched, and too solitary he
    Who loves not his own company!
    He 'll feel the weight of 't many a day
Unless he call in sin or vanity
    To help to bear 't away.

O Solitude, first state of human-kind!
    Which blest remained till man did find
    Even his own helpers company.
As soon as two (alas!) together joined,
    The serpent made up three.

Though God himself, through countless ages thee
    His sole companion chose to be,
    Thee, sacred Solitude alone,
Before the branchy head of number's tree
    Sprang from the trunk of one.

Thou (though men think thine an unactive part)
    Dost break and tame th' unruly heart,
    Which else would know no settled pace,
Making it move well managed by thy art,
    With swiftness and with grace.

Thou the faint beams of reason's scattered light,
    Dost like a burning-glass unite,
    Dost multiply the feeble heat,

And fortify the strength, till thou dost bright
        And noble fires beget.

Whilst this hard truth I teach, methinks I see
        The monster London laugh at me:
        I should at thee too, foolish city,
If it were fit to laugh at misery,
        But thy estate I pity.

Let but thy wicked men from out thee go,
        And all the fools that crowd thee so,
        Even thou who dost thy millions boast,
A village less than Islington wilt grow,
        A solitude almost.   *Cowley.*

Several Discourses by way of Essays, in *The Works,* 1668. (Written before 1667.)

I FEED A FLAME WITHIN

I feed a flame within, which so torments me
That it both pains my heart and yet contents me:
'Tis such a pleasing smart, and I so love it,
That I had rather die than once remove it.

Yet he for whom I grieve shall never know it,
My tongue does not betray, nor my eyes show it:
Not a sigh, nor a tear, my pain discloses,
But they fall silently like dew on roses.

Thus, to prevent my love from being cruel,
My heart 's the sacrifice, as 'tis the fuel:
And while I suffer this to give him quiet,
My faith rewards my love, though he deny it.

On his eyes will I gaze and there delight me;
While I conceal my love no frown can fright me:
To be more happy I dare not aspire;
Nor can I fall more low, mounting no higher.   *Dryden.*

Secret Love: or, The Maiden Queen, 1668. (Acted 1667.)*

TO A LADY, ASKING HIM HOW LONG HE WOULD LOVE HER

It is not, Celia, in our power
    To say how long our love will last;
It may be we within this hour
    May lose those joys we now do taste:
The blessèd, that immortal be,
From change in love are only free.

Then, since we mortal lovers are,
    Ask not how long our love will last;
But, while it does, let us take care
    Each minute be with pleasure passed.
Were it not madness to deny
To live, because we 're sure to die?   *Etherege.*

J. Playford's *Catch that Catch can,* 1667. (Text 1672.)*

THE CASKET

What spendthrifts are we of the day,
    Wasting it vainly while
We deck a cottage made of clay
    Or somewhat yet more vile!

we 're] w' are, 1672.

We prize and hug this idle breath,
        As if more than a span;
And pamper up these slaves of death—
        Carcasses of the man.

We think all little to entrust
        With bodies which yet shall
Shrink to a scuttle-full of dust
        And worthless ashes fall.

But the imprisoned soul distressed
        Languishes quite forgot:
Thus are the caskets gilt and dressed,
        When jewels rust and rot.   *Wanley.*

Scintillulae Sacrae, B.M. Add. MS. 22472. (MS. dated 1667.)*

HUMAN CARES

These pretty little birds, see how
    They skip from bough to bough,
Tuning their sweet melodious notes
    Through warbling slender throats;
Not caring where they next shall feed
Upon what little worm or seed.

The glittering sparkles of the night
    How free they spend their light!
As nimble fairies on the ground
    They smile and dance the round;
Careless where 'tis they shall repair
That oil that makes them shine so fair.

The purling waters glide away
    And o'er blue pebbles stray;

They leave their fountains far behind,
    And thousand circles wind
About the flowery meadows' side,
Not doubting but to be supplied.

The trees do bud and bloom and grow
    And boast their plenty so,
As if they feared no pilfering hand,
    Or blustering wind's command,
Or nipping frosts should then undress.
And make their leavy glories less.

But man alone, poor foolish man!
    Who scarce lives out a span,
Is stocked with cares and idle fears
    For full one hundred years,
And, as if wanting grief, he must
Go take up sorrow upon trust.   *Wanley.*

Scintillulae Sacrae, B.M. Add. MS. 22472. (MS. dated 1667.)

ONE AND HIS MISTRESS A-DYING

Shall we die, both thou and I,
    And leave the world behind us?
Come, I say, and let 's away,
    For nobody here doth mind us.

Why do we gape? we cannot 'scape
    The doom that is assigned us;
When we are in grave, although we rave,
    There nobody needs to bind us.

The clerk shall sing, the sexton ring,
    And old wives they shall wind us;
The priest shall lay our bones in clay,
    And nobody there shall find us.

Farewell wits, and folly's fits,
    And griefs that often pined us!
When we are dead we 'll take no heed
    What nobody says behind us.

Merry nights and false delights
    Adieu, ye did but blind us;
We must to mould, both young and old,
    Till nobody 's left behind us.   *Anon.*

Westminster Drollery, II., 1672. (Short variant printed 1667.)*

HIS MAJESTY'S HEALTH

Here 's a health unto his Majesty!
    With a fa, la, la, &c.
Conversion to his enemies!
    With a fa, la, la, &c.
And he that will not pledge this health,
I wish him neither wit, nor wealth;
Nor yet a rope to hang himself!
    With a fa, la, la, &c.   *Anon.*

J. Playford's *Catch that Catch can*, 1667.*

LOVE

'Tis, in good truth, a most wonderful thing
    (I am e'en ashamed to relate it)
That love so many vexations should bring,
    And yet few have the wit to hate it.

Love's weather in maids should seldom hold fair:
  Like April's mine shall quickly alter.
I 'll give him to-night a lock of my hair,
  To whom next day I 'll send a halter.

I cannot abide these malapert males,
  Pirates of love, who know no duty;
Yet love with a storm can take down their sails,
  And they must strike to Admiral Beauty.

Farewell to that maid who will be undone,
  Who in markets of men (where plenty
Is cried up and down) will die even for one,—
  I will live to make fools of twenty.   *Davenant.*

The Unfortunate Lovers, as revised in *The Works,* 1673. (Written before 1668.) *

BONNY BLACK BESS

Methinks the poor town has been troubled too long
With Phyllis and Chloris in every song,
By fools who at once can both love and despair,
And will never leave calling them cruel and fair;
Which justly provokes me in rhyme to express
The truth that I know of bonny Black Bess.

This Bess of my heart, this Bess of my soul,
Has a skin white as milk and hair black as coal;
She 's plump, yet with ease you may span round her waist,
But her round swelling thighs can scarce be embraced:
Her belly is soft, not a word of the rest,
But I know what I think when I drink to the best.

The ploughman and squire, the arranter clown,
At home she subdued in her paragon gown;

But now she adorns the boxes and pit,
And the proudest town-gallants are forced to submit;
· All hearts fall a-leaping wherever she comes,
And beat day and night, like my Lord Craven's drums.

I dare not permit her to come to Whitehall,
For she 'd outshine the ladies, paint, jewels, and all;
If a lord should but whisper his love in the crowd,
She 'd sell him a bargain, and laugh out aloud;
Then the Queen, overhearing what Betty did say,
Would send Mr. Roper to take her away.

But to these that have had my dear Bess in their arms,
She 's gentle, and knows how to soften her charms;
And to every beauty can add a new grace,
Having learned how to lisp and to trip in her pace,
And, with head on one side and a languishing eye,
To kill *us* by looking as if *she* would die.   *Dorset.*

Methinks the Poor Town, 1673. (And *Miscellany Poems, V.*, 1704. Poem
written 1668.)*

DAMON AND CELIMENA

Damon.   Celimena, of my heart
             None shall e'er bereave you,
             If with your good leave I may
             Quarrel with you once a day,
             I will never leave you.

Celimena. Passion 's but an empty name
             Where respect is wanting:
             Damon, you mistake your aim;

---

dear Bess] 1704;   dear dear Bess, 1673.

Hang your heart, and burn your flame,
If you must be ranting.

Damon.   Love as dull and muddy is
As decaying liquor:
Anger sets it on the lees,
And refines it by degrees,
Till it works it quicker.

Celimena. Love by quarrels to beget
Wisely you endeavour,
With a grave physician's wit,
Who to cure an ague-fit
Put me in a fever.

Damon.   Anger rouses Love to fight,
And his only bait is;
'Tis the spur to dull delight,
And is but an eager bite
When desire at height is.

Celimena. If such drops of heat can fall
In our wooing weather,
If such drops of heat can fall
We shall have the Devil and all
When we come together.   Dryden.

An Evening's Love, 1671. (Acted 1668.)*

TO LITTLE OR NO PURPOSE I SPENT MANY DAYS

To little or no purpose I spent many days
In ranging the Park, the Exchange, and the Plays;
For ne'er in my rambles, till now, did I prove

So lucky to meet with the man I could love.
   Oh! how I am pleased when I think on this man,
   That I find I must love, let me do what I can!

How long I shall love him, I can no more tell,
Than, had I a fever, when I should be well.
My passion shall kill me before I will show it,
And yet I would give all the world he did know it:
   But oh, how I sigh when I think, should he woo me,
   I cannot deny what I know would undo me!

Etherege.

She would if she could, 1668.*

THE SEA-GODDESS

My cabinets are oyster-shells,
In which I keep my orient pearls;
To open them I use the tide,
As keys to locks, which opens wide
The oyster shells, then out I take
Those orient pearls and crowns do make;
And modest coral I do wear,
Which blushes when it touches air.
On silver waves I sit and sing,
And then the fish lie listening:
Then sitting on a rocky stone
I comb my hair with fishes' bone;
The whilst Apollo with his beams
Doth dry my hair from watery streams.
His light doth glaze the water's face,
Make the large sea my looking-glass:
So when I swim on waters high,
I see myself as I glide by:
But when the sun begins to burn,

I back into my waters turn,
And dive unto the bottom low:
Then on my head the waters flow
In curlëd waves and circles round,
And thus with waters am I crowned.

Duchess of Newcastle.

The Convent of Pleasure, in *Plays never before printed*, 1668.

TO CHLORIS

Ah, Chloris! that I now could sit
    As unconcerned as when
Your infant beauty could beget
    No pleasure, nor no pain.

When I the dawn used to admire,
    And praised the coming day,
I little thought the growing fire
    Must take my rest away.

Your charms in harmless childhood lay
    Like metals in the mine:
Age from no face took more away
    Than youth concealed in thine.

But as your charms insensibly
    To their perfection pressed,
Fond Love, as unperceived, did fly
    And in my bosom rest.

My passion with your beauty grew,
    And Cupid at my heart,
Still as his mother favoured you,
    Threw a new flaming dart.

Each gloried in their wanton part:
  To make a lover, he
Employed the utmost of his art;
  To make a beauty, she.

Though now I slowly bend to love,
  Uncertain of my fate,
If your fair self my chains approve,
  I shall my freedom hate.

Lovers, like dying men, may well
  At first disordered be,
Since none alive can truly tell
  What fortune they must see.   *Sedley.*

Mulberry Garden, 1668.*

AN EPITAPH

FOR A GODLY MAN'S TOMB

Here lies a piece of Christ; a star in dust;
A vein of gold; a china dish that must
Be used in heaven, when God shall feast the just.

Iter Boreale, 1668.   *Wild.*

SONG

I pass all my hours in a shady old grove,
And I live not the day that I see not my Love.
I survey every walk now my Phyllis is gone,
And sigh when I think we were there all alone.
  Oh, then 'tis! oh, then I think there's no such hell
  Like loving, like loving too well!

But each shade and each conscious bower when I find,
Where I once have been happy and she has been kind,
And I see the print left of her shape in the green,
And imagine the pleasure may yet come again;
    Oh, then 'tis! oh, then I think no joy 's above
    The pleasures, the pleasures of love!

While alone to myself I repeat all her charms,
She I love may be locked in another man's arms:
She may laugh at my cares, and so false she may be
To say all the kind things she before said to me.
    Oh, then 'tis! oh, then I think there 's no such hell
    Like loving, like loving too well!

But when I consider the truth of her heart,
Such an innocent passion, so kind, without art,
I fear I have wronged her, and hope she may be
So full of true love to be jealous of me.
    Oh, then 'tis! oh, then I think no joy 's above
    The pleasures, the pleasures of love!   *King Charles II(?)*

Westminster Drollery, I., 1671. (And in *Windsor Drollery,* 1671. Poem dated
1670 in B.M. Harl. MS. 3991.)*

PHYLLIS

Wherever I am, and whatever I do,
    My Phyllis is still in my mind:
When angry I mean not to Phyllis to go,
    My feet of themselves the way find:
Unknown to myself I am just at her door,
And when I would rail I can bring out no more
    Than, 'Phyllis, too fair and unkind!'

when I find,] *Windsor D.*;   that I find, *Westminster D.*

When Phyllis I see, my heart bounds in my breast,
  And the love I would stifle is shown:
But, asleep or awake, I am never at rest
  When from my eyes Phyllis is gone!
Sometimes a sad dream does delude my sad mind:
But, alas, when I wake and no Phyllis I find,
  How I sigh to myself all alone!

Should a king be my rival in her I adore,
  He should offer his treasure in vain:
O let me alone to be happy and poor,
  And give me my Phyllis again:
Let Phyllis be mine, and but ever be kind,
I could to a desert with her be confined,
  And envy no monarch his reign.

Alas, I discover too much of my love,
  And she too well knows her own power!
She makes me each day a new martyrdom prove,
  And makes me grow jealous each hour.
But let her each minute torment my poor mind,
I had rather love Phyllis both false and unkind,
  Than ever be freed from her power.   *Dryden.*

The Conquest of Granada, I., 1672. (Acted 1670. Song printed 1671.)*

TO HIS MISTRESS,
WHO SAID SHE HATED HIM FOR HIS GREY HAIRS

  Oh, hate me not for my grey hair
    Since you love still variety,
  The black, the red, the brown, the fair,
    All in their turns delight your eye.

Knots of two colours, nay of three.
    Can please you better than of one;
My parti-colours then should be
    Better than all white, or all brown.

You, when a garland you would make,
    Not flowers of the same colour choose,
But various-coloured ones would take:
    Change but in me you would refuse.

Would you a bracelet weave, or brede,
    You 'd different coloured ribbons take;
To set off your hair of your head,
    With powder, grey you make of black.

You the grey morning used to love,
    Which promised you good days and bright;
Why then a grey head disapprove,
    Promising you a pleasant night?

Then hate me not for my grey hairs,
    Which are not so much mine as thine,
Since caused but by the grief and cares
    Thy love gave me, so thine, not mine.

Wycherley.

Miscellany Poems, 1704. (Poem written c. 1670?)*

THE ADVICE

Phyllis, for shame, let us improve
    A thousand several ways
These few short minutes stol'n by love
    From many tedious days. ·

Change but in me] *i.e.* Change only in me.   brede] braid.

Whilst you want courage to despise
    The censure of the grave,
For all the tyrants in your eyes,
    Your heart is but a slave.

My love is full of noble pride,
    And never will submit
To let that fop, discretion, ride
    In triumph over wit.

False friends I have, as well as you,
    That daily counsel me
Vain frivolous trifles to pursue,
    And leave off loving thee.

When I the least belief bestow
    On what such fools advise,
May I be dull enough to grow
    Most miserably wise.   *Dorset.*

Westminster Drollery, I., 1671. (And in *Windsor Drollery*, 1671.)*

HOW UNHAPPY A LOVER AM I
(*Song, in Two Parts*)

He. How unhappy a lover am I
        While I sigh for my Phyllis in vain!
    All my hopes of delight
    Are another man's right
        Who is happy while I am in pain

She. Since her honour allows no relief,
        But to pity the pains which you bear,

'Tis the best of your fate,
In a hopeless estate,
　　To give o'er, and betimes to despair.

He. I have tried the false medicine in vain;
　　For I wish what I hope not to win:
From without, my desire
Has no food to its fire;
　　But it burns and consumes me within.

She. Yet at least 'tis a pleasure to know
　　That you are not unhappy alone:
For the nymph you adore
Is as wretched, and more,
　　And accounts all your sufferings her own.

He. O ye gods, let me suffer for both!
　　At the feet of my Phyllis I 'll lie:
I 'll resign up my breath,
And take pleasure in death,
　　To be pitied by her when I die.

She. What her honour denied you in life,
　　In her death she will give to your love.
Such a flame as is true
After fate will renew
　　For the souls to meet closer above.　　　　*Dryden.*

The Conquest of Granada, II., 1672. (Song printed 1671.)*

TO A VERY YOUNG LADY

Sweetest bud of beauty, may
No untimely frost decay

The early glories, which we trace
Blooming in thy matchless face;
But kindly opening, like the rose,
Fresh beauties every day disclose,
Such as by Nature are not shown
In all the blossoms she has blown:
And then, what conquest shall you make,
Who hearts already daily take!
Scorched in the morning with thy beams,
How shall we bear those sad extremes
Which must attend thy threatening eyes
When thou shalt to thy noon arise?   *Etherege.*

A Collection of Poems, 1672. (Poem printed 1671.)*

OF HIS MISTRESS GROWN OLD

When I wooed Carinda first
    She had wit and beauty store,
But Time hath now done all his worst,
    He never can assault her more:
She was handsome then, benighted now,
She was gamesome then, but slighted now;
There 's none can be delighted now
                With her as heretofore.

Her eyes, that had inflaming power,
    Now are eclipsed and shine no more;
Her cheeks like roses when in flower,
    Now are cerusëd o'er and o'er:
She was pretty then, she 's painted now,

cerusëd] ceruss'd, 1671.

She was witty then, she 's tainted now,
And I 'll no more be acquainted now
        With her as heretofore.

Her airy fancy 's only left her
    Which can help beget a flame,
Of all the rest Time hath bereft her
    Which did still support the same.
'Tis pity then she 's grown so old,
She 'd fit ye when her tale she told,
She has nought but wealth now can uphold
        Her glory and her fame.   *Hicks.*

Oxford Drollery, 1671.

SHE THAT WITH LOVE IS NOT POSSESSED

She that with love is not possessed,
    Has not for that the harder heart:
I think the softer and more tender breast
Would dull, would dull, would dull and damp the dart.

Away with melancholy fits,
    Whose strange effect our eyes disarms,
Deposes beauty, and distracts our wits,
Whilst we grow pale, grow pale, and lose our charms.

Love does against itself conspire:
    Such languishing, desires imparts,
That quench the fuel yet preserve the fire,
Clouding those eyes, those eyes, whence love takes darts.
                                Settle.

Cambyses, 1671.*

A WIFE I DO HATE

A wife I do hate,
For either she 's false or she 's jealous;
   But give me a mate
That nothing will ask or tell us:
   She stands on no terms,
Nor chaffers by way of indenture;
   Her love 's for your farms,
But takes the kind man at a venture.

   If all prove not right,
Without act, process, or warning,
   From a wife for a night
You may be divorced in the morning.
   Where parents are slaves
Their brats cannot be any other:
   Great wits and great braves
Have always a punk to their mother.   *Wycherley.*

Westminster Drollery, I., 1671. (And *Love in a Wood,* 1672.)*

A LOVER I AM

A lover I am, and a lover I 'll be,
And hope from my love I shall never be free:
Let wisdom be blamed in the grave woman-hater,
Yet never to love is a sin of ill nature:
But he who loves well, and whose passion is strong,
Shall never be wretched, but ever be young.

With hopes and with fears, like a ship in the ocean,
Our hearts are kept dancing and ever in motion;
When our passion is pallid, and our fancy would fail,

A little kind quarrel supplies a fresh gale:
But when the doubt 's cleared, and the jealousy 's gone,
How we kiss and embrace, and can never have done!

Anon.

Westminster Drollery, I., 1671.*

ON A GENTLEMAN IN A LATE ENGAGEMENT AGAINST THE TURKS, WAS SLAIN AND THROWN OVERBOARD, AND SHE SINCE MAD

I 'll go to my Love where he lies in the deep,
And in my embraces my dearest shall sleep:
When we wake, the kind dolphins about us shall throng,
And in chariots of shell shall draw us along.
The orient pearl that the ocean bestows,
We 'll mix with the coral, our crowns to compose.
Then the sea-nymphs shall grieve and envy our bliss,
We 'll teach them to love, and the cockles to kiss.

For my Love sleeps now in his watery grave,
Has nothing to show for his tomb but a wave;
I 'll kiss his dear lips, than the coral more red
That grows where he lies in his watery bed:
     Ah! ah! ah! my Love is dead.
There was not a bell, but a tortoise-shell
To ring, to ring, to ring my Love's knell.
Ah, my Love 's dead! There was not a bell,
But a tortoise-shell to ring my Love's knell.   *Anon.*

Windsor Drollery, 1671.*

HAPPY, HAPPY COUNTRY SWAINS

Happy, happy country swains,
  If they knew their happiness;

Sport is sweetened by their pains,
    Sure hope their labour relishes:
        The plough their living, when they eat
        Labour finds appetite and meat.

When the seas and tempests roar,
    Work at night brings quiet sleep;
Dancing along the golden shore,
    This course night and day they keep:
        In merriment, a pipe, musician;
        Labour their physic, no physician.

Thus they quiet fearless reign,
    Rich in that they are content;
Their children are a moving train,
    Their life in innocence is spent;
        Under whose low roofs peace doth hide,
        And shut out Fortune's wants and pride.   *Anon.*

Poor Robin, An Almanac, 1671.

TO PHYLLIS

Phyllis, I pray,
Why did you say
    That I did not adore you?
I durst not sue
As others do,
    Nor talk of love before you.

Should I make known
My flame, you 'd frown,
    No tears could e'er appease you;
'Tis better I
Should silent die,
    Than, talking, to displease you.   *Anon.*

The New Academy of Compliments, 1671.*

LONG BETWIXT LOVE AND FEAR

Long betwixt love and fear, Phyllis, tormented,
Shunned her own wish, yet at last she consented:
But loth that day should her blushes discover,
     'Come, gentle Night,' she said,
     'Come quickly to my aid,
     And a poor shame-faced maid
        Hide from her lover.

'Now cold as ice I am, now hot as fire,
I dare not tell myself my own desire;
But let day fly away, and let night haste her:
     Grant, ye kind Powers above,
     Slow hours to parting love;
     But when to bliss we move,
        Bid 'em fly faster.

'How sweet it is to love when I discover
That fire which burns my heart, warming my lover;
'Tis pity love so true should be mistaken:
     But if this night he be
     False or unkind to me,
     Let me die ere I see
        That I 'm forsaken.'   *Dryden.*

The Assignation, 1673. (Acted 1672.)*

FAREWELL, FAIR ARMIDA

Farewell, fair Armida, my joy and my grief,
In vain I have loved you, and find no relief;
Undone by your virtue too strict and severe,
Your eyes gave me love, and you gave me despair;
Now called by my honour, I seek with content

A fate which in pity you would not prevent:
To languish in love were to find by delay
A death that 's more welcome the speediest way.

On seas and in battles, in bullets and fire,
The danger is less than in hopeless desire;
My death's wound you gave me, though far off I bear
My fall from your sight, not to cost you a tear:
But if the kind flood on a wave should convey
And under your window my body should lay,
The wound on my breast when you happen to see,
You 'll say with a sigh, 'It was given by me.'   *Dryden(?)*

R. V.'s *New Court Songs and Poems*, 1672. (And *Covent Garden Drollery*, 1672.)*

SILVIA

The nymph that undoes me is fair and unkind,
No less than a wonder by Nature designed;
She 's the grief of my heart, the joy of my eye,
And the cause of a flame that never can die.

Her mouth, from whence wit still obligingly flows,
Has the beautiful blush and the smell of the rose;
Love and destiny both attend on her will,
She wounds with a look, with a frown she can kill.

The desperate lover can hope no redress,
Where beauty and rigour are both in excess;
In Silvia they meet, so unhappy am I,
Who sees her must love, and who loves her must die.

                                        Etherege.

A Collection of Poems, 1672.*

My fall] *Cov. Gar.*, and 1673;   My fate, *Court Songs*.

DEATH

Oh, the sad day!
When friends shall shake their heads, and say
Of miserable me—
'Hark, how he groans, look how he pants for breath,
See how he struggles with the pangs of death!'
When they shall say of these poor eyes—
'How hollow and how dim they be!
Mark how his breast does swell and rise
Against his potent enemy!'
When some old friend shall step to my bedside,
Touch my chill face, and then shall gently slide,
And—when his next companions say
'How does he do?   What hopes?'—shall turn away,
Answering only, with a lift-up hand—
'Who can his fate withstand?'
Then shall a gasp or two do more
Than e'er my rhetoric could before:
Persuade the peevish world to trouble me no more!

Flatman.

Poems and Songs, 1674. (Text 1686. Poem printed 1672.)*

I SIGH ALL THE NIGHT

I sigh all the night and I languish all day,
And much to be pitied I am:
Ever since your bright eyes my heart did surprise
I could not extinguish the flame:
But you, since you 've known my heart was your own,
Though before you was kind, now scornful are grown:
If so cruel you prove

you 've] y 'ave;   in both texts.

To the man that you love,
Ah, Phyllis! Ah, Phyllis! what fate
Have you in reserve for the wretch that you hate?

Ravenscroft.

The Citizen turned Gentleman, 1672. (Text from *Mamamouchi,* 1675.)*

LOVE STILL HAS SOMETHING OF THE SEA

Love still has something of the sea
From whence his mother rose;
No time his slaves from doubt can free,
Nor give their thoughts repose:

They are becalmed in clearest days,
And in rough weather tossed;
They wither under cold delays,
Or are in tempests lost.

One while they seem to touch the port,
Then straight into the main
Some angry wind in cruel sport
The vessel drives again.

At first disdain and pride they fear,
Which if they chance to 'scape,
Rivals and falsehood soon appear
In a more dreadful shape.

By such degrees to joy they come,
And are so long withstood,
So slowly they receive the sum,
It hardly does them good.

'Tis cruel to prolong a pain;
    And, to defer a joy,
Believe me, gentle Celemene,
    Offends the wingèd boy.

An hundred thousand oaths your fears
    Perhaps would not remove;
And if I gazed a thousand years
    I could no deeper love.   *Sedley.*

The Miscellaneous Works, 1702. (Poem printed 1672.)*

TO CELIA

Not, Celia, that I juster am
    Or better than the rest;
For I would change each hour, like them,
    Were not my heart at rest.

But I am tied to very thee
    By every thought I have;
Thy face I only care to see,
    Thy heart I only crave.

All that is woman is adored
    In thy dear self I find:
For the whole sex can but afford
    The handsome and the kind.

Why then should I seek farther store,
    And still make love anew?

Stz. 6, in 1672, ran—   'Tis cruel to prolong a pain;
                                And to defer a bliss,
                             Believe me, gentle Hermione,
                                No less inhuman is.

When change itself can give no more,
    'Tis easy to be true.   *Sedley.*

*Ibid.**

THE RURAL DANCE ABOUT THE MAYPOLE

Come, lasses and lads,
Take leave of your dads,
And away to the maypole hie!
For every he
Has got him a she,
With a minstrel standing by:
For Willy has gotten his Jill, and Johnny has got his Joan,
To jig it, jig it, jig it, jig it, jig it up and down!

'Strike up!' says Wat,
'Agreed!' says Kate,
'And I prithee, fiddler, play!'
'Content!' says Hodge,
And so says Madge,
'For this is a holiday.'
Then every man did put his hat off to his lass,
And every girl did curchy, curchy, curchy on the grass.

'Begin!' says Hal,
'Ay, ay!' says Mall,
'We 'll lead up *Packington's Pound*';
'No, no!' says Noll,
And so says Doll,
'We 'll first have *Sellenger's Round*.'
Then every man began to foot it round about,
And every girl did jet it, jet it, jet it in and out.

hie] hey, 1672.   Ay, ay!] I, I, 1672.

'You 're out!' says Dick,
''Tis a lie!' says Nick,
'The fiddler played it false';
''Tis true!' says Hugh,
And so says Sue,
And so says nimble Alice.
The fiddler then began to play the tune again,
And every girl did trip it, trip it, trip it to the men.

'Let 's kiss!' says Jane,
'Content!' says Nan,
And so says every she;
'How many?' says Batt,
'Why, three,' says Matt,
'For that 's a maiden's fee;'
But they, instead of three, did give 'em half a score;
And they in kindness gave 'em, gave 'em, gave 'em as many
more.

Then, after an hour,
They went to a bower,
And played for ale and cakes,
And kisses too
Until they were due,
The lasses kept the stakes:
The girls did then begin to quarrel with the men,
And bid 'em take their kisses back, and give 'em their own
again.

Yet there they sate
Until it was late,

You 're] Y' are, 1672.

And tired the fiddler quite,
　　With singing and playing,
　　Without any paying,
　From morning until night.
They told the fiddler then, they 'd pay him for his play;
And each a two-pence, two-pence, two-pence gave him, and
　went away.   *Anon.*

*Westminster Drollery, II., 1672.**

THE MOON'S LOVE

The Moon, in her pride, once glancëd aside
　　Her eyes and espied the Day,
As unto his bed, in waistcoat of red,
　　Fair Phoebus him led the way;
Such changes of thought in her chastity wrought,
　　That thus she besought the boy:
　　　'O tarry and marry the starry Diana
　　　That will be thy gem and joy!

'I will be as bright at noon as at night,
　　If that may delight the Day;
Come hither and join thy glories with mine,
　　Together we 'll shine for aye:
The night shall be noon, and every moon
　　As pleasant as June or May;
　　　O tarry and marry the starry Diana
　　　That will be thy gem and joy!

'Enamoured of none, I live chaste and alone,
　　Though courted of one, some say;
And true if it were, so frivolous fear

    Let never my dear dismay;
I 'll change my opinion, and turn my old minion,
    The sleepy Endymion, away;
        O tarry and marry the starry Diana
        That will be thy gem and joy!'

And but that the night should have wanted her light,
    Or lovers in sight should play,
Or Phoebus should shame to bestow such a dame
    (With a dower of his flame) on a boy,
Or day should appear eternally here,
    And night otherwhere, the Day
        Had tarried and married the starry'd Diana,
        And she been his gem and joy.   *Anon.*

Westminster Drollery, II., 1672.

ON HIS MISTRESS' GARDEN OF HERBS

Heart's-ease, an herb that sometimes hath been seen
In my love's garden plot to flourish green,
Is dead and withered with a wind of woe;
And bitter rue in place thereof doth grow.
The cause I find to be, because I did
Neglect the herb called time, which now doth bid
Me never hope, nor look once more again
To gain heart's-ease, to ease my heart of pain.
One hope is this, in this my woeful case,
My rue, though bitter, may prove herb of grace.   *Anon.*

Ibid.

FAIRER THAN FAIREST

    Fairer than fairest, if your eyes,
    Clearer than the clearest skies,

Deign to look upon a lover
Who this bold truth dares discover,
That he loves, and loves most true,
And ne'er loved but only you:
Behold, of all your sex the fairest,
Dearest, sweetest, and the rarest,
The humblest of your servants here,
Suspended betwixt hope and fear,
Awaits from you his destiny,
Whether he should live or die.   *Anon.*

Emilia, 1672.

CHRIST CHURCH BELLS

O the bonny Christ Church bells!
   One, two, three, four, five, six;
They sound so wondrous great,
   So woundy sweet,
And they troll so merrily, merrily.
O the first and second bell!
That every day at four and ten
Cry, Come, come, come, come, come to prayers;
And the verger troops before the dean:
Tinkle, tinkle, ting, goes the small bell at nine
   To call the beerers home,
     But the devil a man
     Will leave his can
Till he hears the mighty *Tom.*   *Aldrich* (?)

J. Playford's *The Musical Companion,* 1673.*

TO CHLORIS

Fie, Chloris! 'Tis silly to sigh thus in vain,
'Tis silly to pity the lovers you 've slain;

If still you continue your slaves to deride,
The compassion you feign will be taken for pride:
And sorrow for sin can never be true
In one that does daily commit it anew.

If, while you are fair, you resolve to be coy,
You may hourly repent, as you hourly destroy;
Yet none will believe you, protest what you will,
That you grieve for the dead, if you daily do kill:
And where are our hopes when we zealously woo,
If you vow to abhor what you constantly do?

Then, Chloris, be kinder, and tell me my fate,
For the worst I can suffer 's to die by your hate:
If thus you design, never fancy in vain
By your sighs and your tears to recall me again;
Nor weep at my grave, for (I swear) if you do,
As you now laugh at me, I will then laugh at you.

Waldren(?)

Methinks the Poor Town, 1673.*

MY YOUTH IT WAS FREE

My youth it was free
From horror and terror;
I ne'er did agree
    With the black nor the fair:
So stubborn I grew,
I laughed at, and scoffed at
Those men that I knew
    Were brought in Love's snare.
Nay, more than this, I laughed at the pains
Men took to be wretched, and loaded with chains.

But when I the charms of my Phyllis did see,
I resigned up my heart and refused to be free.

    My heart then began
    To be firëd and mirëd
    With love: never man
      Was in fetters so fast;
    Yet forgot that she was
    A woman, for no man
    Could yet know the cause
      Why their love does not last.
I never considered the tricks nor the art
She used to entangle and captive each heart.
At length I discovered and presently knew
That my Phyllis was fickle, and could not be true.

    I cursed my hard fate
    That taught me and brought me
    Into this sad state,
      Thus to kindle my flame:
    When I did begin
    To pause on 't, the cause on 't
    I knew it was mine,
      Not my Phyllis to blame.
I bore such respect to her, that I thought
Whatever she did, 'twas I was in fault.
At length I resolved that I never would be
So mad as to love, but would ever be free.   *Anon.*

W. Hick's *London Drollery*, 1673.

THE SALUTATION

    These little limbs,
These eyes and hands which here I find,

This panting heart wherewith my life begins,
    Where have ye been?   Behind
What curtain were ye from me hid so long?
Where was, in what abyss, my new-made tongue?

    When silent I
So many thousand thousand years
Beneath the dust did in a chaos lie,
    How could I, smiles or tears,
Or lips or hands or eyes or ears, perceive?
Welcome ye treasures which I now receive.

    I that so long
Was nothing from eternity,
Did little think such joys as ear or tongue
    To celebrate or see:
Such sounds to hear, such hands to feel, such feet,
Such eyes and objects, on the ground to meet.

    New burnished joys
Which finest gold and pearl excel!
Such sacred treasures are the limbs of boys,
    In which a soul doth dwell;
Their organizëd joints and azure veins
More wealth include than the dead world contains.

    From dust I rise,
And out of nothing now awake;
These brighter regions which salute mine eyes,
    A gift from God I take.
The earth, the seas, the light, the lofty skies,
The sun and stars are mine; if these I prize.

                   A stranger here
              Strange things doth meet, strange glory see;
              Strange treasures lodged in this fair world appear,
                   Strange all and new to me:
              But that they mine should be, who nothing was,
              That strangest is of all, yet brought to pass.   *Traherne.*

Poems of Felicity. B.M. Burney MS. 392. (Written before 1674.)*

                        WONDER

                   How like an angel came I down!
                        How bright are all things here!
              When first among his works I did appear
                   Oh, how their glory did me crown!
              The world resembled his eternity,
                        In which my soul did walk;
                   And every thing that I did see
                        Did with me talk.

                   The skies in their magnificence,
                        The lovely, lively air,
              Oh, how divine, how soft, how sweet, how fair!
                   The stars did entertain my sense,
              And all the works of God so bright and pure,
                        So rich and great, did seem
                   As if they ever must endure
                        In my esteem.

                   A native health and innocence
                        Within my bones did grow,
              And while my God did all his glories show,
                   I felt a vigour in my sense
              That was all spirit: I within did flow

With seas of life like wine;
I nothing in the world did know
        But 'twas divine.

Harsh rugged objects were concealed,
        Oppressions, tears and cries,
Sins, griefs, complaints, dissensions, weeping eyes
        Were hid, and only things revealed
Which heavenly spirits and the angels prize.
        The state of innocence
        And bliss, not trades and poverties,
                Did fill my sense.

The streets seemed paved with golden stones,
        The boys and girls all mine;
To me how did their lovely faces shine!
        The sons of men all holy ones,
In joy and beauty, then appeared to me;
        And every thing I found
        (While like an angel I did see)
                Adorned the ground.

Rich diamonds, and pearl, and gold
        Might every where be seen;
Rare colours, yellow, blue, red, white and green,
        Mine eyes on every side behold:
All that I saw, a wonder did appear,
        Amazement was my bliss:
        That and my wealth met every where:
                No joy to this!

Cursed, ill-devised proprieties,
        With envy, avarice

And fraud (those fiends that spoil ev'n Paradise),
   Were not the object of mine eyes,
Nor hedges, ditches, limits, narrow bounds:
     I dreamt not aught of those,
    But in surveying all men's grounds
      I found repose.

    For property its self was mine,
     And hedges, ornaments;
Walls, houses, coffers, and their rich contents,
   To make me rich combine.
Clothes, costly jewels, laces, I esteemed
    My wealth by others worn;
   For me they all to wear them seemed
     When I was born.   *Traherne.*

Poems of Felicity. B.M. Burney MS. 392. (Written before 1674.)

SHADOWS IN THE WATER

In unexperienced infancy
Many a sweet mistake doth lie:
Mistake though false, intending true;
A seeming somewhat more than view;
   That doth instruct the mind
   In things that lie behind,
And many secrets to us show
Which afterwards we come to know.

Thus did I by the water's brink
Another world beneath me think;
And, while the lofty spacious skies
Reversèd there abused mine eyes,

I fancied other feet
Came mine to touch or meet;
As by some puddle I did play
Another world within it lay.

Beneath the water, people, drowned
Yet with another heaven crowned,
In spacious regions seemed to go
As freely moving to and fro:
In bright and open space
I saw their very face;
Eyes, hands, and feet they had like mine;
Another sun did with them shine.

'Twas strange that people there should walk
And yet I could not hear them talk:
That through a little watery chink,
Which one dry ox or horse might drink,
We other worlds should see,
Yet not admitted be;
And other confines there behold
Of light and darkness, heat and cold.

I called them oft, but called in vain;
No speeches we could entertain:
Yet did I there expect to find
Some other world, to please my mind.
I plainly saw by these
A new Antipodes,
Whom, though they were so plainly seen,
A film kept off that stood between.

By walking men's reversèd feet
I chanced another world to meet;

Though it did not to view exceed
A phantasm, 'tis a world indeed,
    Where skies beneath us shine,
    And earth by art divine
Another face presents below,
Where people's feet against ours go.

Within the regions of the air,
Compassed about with heavens fair,
Great tracts of land there may be found
Enriched with fields and fertile ground;
    Where many numerous hosts
    In those far distant coasts,
For other great and glorious ends,
Inhabit, my yet unknown friends.

O ye that stand upon the brink,
Whom I so near me, through the chink,
With wonder see, what faces there,
Whose feet, whose bodies, do ye wear?
    I my companions see
    In you, another me.
They seemèd others, but are we;
Our second selves those shadows be.

Look how far off those lower skies
Extend themselves! scarce with mine eyes
I can them reach.   O ye my friends!
What secret borders on those ends?
    Are lofty heavens hurled
    'Bout your inferior world?
Are ye the representatives
Of other people's distant lives?

Of all the playmates which I knew
That here I do the image view
In other selves, what can it mean
But that below the purling stream
  Some unknown joys there be
  Laid up in store for me,
To which I shall, when that thin skin
Is broken, be admitted in?   *Traherne.*

Poems of Felicity. B.M. Burney MS. 392. (Written before 1674.)

WALKING

To *walk* abroad is, not with eyes,
But thoughts, the fields to see and prize;
  Else may the silent feet,
    Like logs of wood,
Move up and down, and see no good,
    Nor joy nor glory meet.

Ev'n carts and wheels their place do change,
But cannot see, though very strange
  The glory that is by:
    Dead puppets may
Move in the bright and glorious day,
    Yet not behold the sky.

And are not men than they more blind,
Who having eyes yet never find
  The bliss in which they move?
    Like statues dead
They up and down are carrïed,
    Yet neither see nor love.

To *walk* is by a thought to go,
To move in spirit to and fro,
   To mind the good we see,
      To taste the sweet,
Observing all the things we meet
      How choice and rich they be:

To note the beauty of the day,
And golden fields of corn survey,
   Admire each pretty flower
      With its sweet smell
To praise their Maker, and to tell
      The marks of his great power:

To fly abroad, like active bees,
Among the hedges and the trees,
   To cull the dew that lies
      On every blade,
From every blossom, till we lade
      Our minds, as they their thighs:

Observe those rich and glorious things,
The rivers, meadows, woods, and springs,
   The fructifying sun,
      To note from far
The rising of each twinkling star
      For us his race to run.

A little child these well perceives,
Who, tumbling in green grass and leaves,
   May rich as kings be thought:
      But there 's a sight
Which perfect manhood may delight,
      To which we shall be brought:

While in those pleasant paths we talk
'Tis *that* towards which at last we walk;
 For we may by degrees
  Wisely proceed
Pleasures of love and praise to heed,
 From viewing herbs and trees.   *Traherne.*

Poems of Felicity. B.M. Burney MS. 392. (Written before 1674.)

I GRANT YOUR EYES ARE MUCH MORE BRIGHT

I grant your eyes are much more bright
Than ever was unclouded light;
And that love in your charming voice
As much of reason finds for choice:
Yet if you hate when I adore,
To do the like I find much more.

A voice would move all but a stone
Without kind love shall find me one;
And eyes the brightest ever shined
On me have power but as they 're kind:
You must, to throw down all defence,
As much my reason please as sense.

I clearly know, say what you will,
To read my heart you want the skill;
And of this 'tis a pregnant sign,
Since you see not these truths of mine:
Which if you did, you would despair,
Without your love, to form one there. *Bulteel (?)*

A New Collection of Poems and Songs, 1674.*

they 're] W. J. Linton, 1883; their, 1674.

SONG

Kind lovers, love on,
Lest the world be undone,
And mankind be lost by degrees:
For if all from their loves
Should go wander in groves,
There soon would be nothing but trees.   *Crowne.*

Calisto, 1675. (Written 1674.)*

NOW HAVING PROVED THY FOND DELAYS

Now having proved thy fond delays
With all thy pride and scorn,
No more my love shall make essays,
Since, to be still forlorn,
What soldier, that would honour win,
Will teach his prowess such a sin?

I 'll find some easy thing to love,
Unpractised in disdain;
Or else thy sex throughout I 'll prove,
And hundreds for thee gain.
He limits too much Nature's power
That courts the spring but in one flower.

But if I thus thy charms can slight,
Well may some other too:
And then perhaps thou 'lt quit thy height
As froward haggards do,
That fly the watchful falconer's call
Till their own pride compels their fall.
                                   Hon. Edward Howard.

Poems and Essays, 1674. (Published anonymously.)*

LIFE

We are born, then cry
We know not for why;
And all our lives long
Still but the same song.
Our lives are but short,
We 're made Fortune's sport,
We spend them in care,
In hunting the hare,
In tossing the pot,
In venturing our lot
At dice, when we play
To pass time away.
We dress ourselves fine,
At noon we do dine,
We walk then abroad,
Or ride on the road;
With women we dally,
Retreat and rally,
And then in the bed
We lay down our head.
And all this and more
We do o'er and o'er,
Till at last we all die,
And in the cold grave lie.

Then let us be merry,
Send down to the ferry
A bottle for him—
Old Charon the grim—
A bribe for our stay,
Till we must away.   *N. C.*

N. C.'s *Bristol Drollery*, 1674.

THE PASSING-BELL

Come, honest Sexton, take thy spade,
And let my grave be quickly made:
Thou still art ready for the dead,
Like a kind host to make a bed.
I now am come to be thy guest,
Let me in some dark lodging rest,
For I am weary, full of pain,
And of my pilgrimage complain.
On Heaven's decree I waiting lie,
And all my wishes are to die.
    Hark! hark! I hear my passing-bell,
    Farewell, my loving friends, farewell!

Make my cold bed, good Sexton, deep,
That my poor bones may safely sleep;
Until that sad and joyful day
When from above a voice shall say,
'Wake, all ye Dead, lift up your eyes,
The great Creator bids you rise.'
Then do I hope, among the just,
To shake off this polluted dust;
And with new robes of glory dressed
To have access among the Blest.
    Hark! hark! I hear my passing-bell,
    Farewell, my loving friends, farewell!   *Anon.*

H. Playford's *Harmonia Sacra*, 1688. (Variant printed 1674.)*

FADING BEAUTY

Take Time, my dear, ere Time takes wing:
Beauty knows no second spring.

Marble pillars, tombs of brass,
Time breaks down, much more this glass;
Then ere that tyrant Time bespeak it,
Let 's drink healths in 't first, then break it.
At twenty-five in women's eyes
Beauty does fade, at thirty dies.   *Anon.*

*A New Collection of Poems and Songs, 1674.**

ENGLAND

Oh, England!
  Sick in head and sick in heart,
  Sick in whole and every part:
  And yet sicker thou art still
  For thinking that thou art not ill.   *Anon.*

Bodley MS. Rawl. Poet. 66. (Written before 1675.)*

CUPID, I SCORN TO BEG THE ART

Cupid, I scorn to beg the art
  From thy imaginary throne,
To learn to wound another's heart,
  Or how to heal my own.
If she be coy, my airy mind
Brooks not a siege: if she be kind,
She proves my scorn, that was my wonder;
For towns that yield I hate to plunder.

Love is a game, hearts are the prize,
Pride keeps the stakes, art throws the dice:
  When either 's won,
  The game is done.

> Love is a coward, hunts the flying prey;
> But when it once stands still, Love runs away.   *Fane.*

Love in the Dark, 1675.

THE CARELESS GALLANT

Let us drink and be merry, dance, joke and rejoice,
With claret and sherry, theorbo and voice;
The changeable world to our joy is unjust,
All treasure 's uncertain, then down with your dust;
In frolics dispose your pounds, shillings, and pence,
For we shall be nothing a hundred years hence.

We 'll sport and be free with Frank, Betty, and Dolly,
Have lobsters and oysters to cure melancholy;
Fish dinners will make a man spring like a flea,
Dame Venus, love's lady, was born of the sea,
With her and with Bacchus we 'll tickle the sense,
For we shall be past it a hundred years hence.

Your beautiful bit who hath all eyes upon her,
That her honesty sells for a hogo of honour,
Whose lightness and brightness doth cast such a splendour,
That none are thought fit but the stars to attend her,
Though now she seems pleasant and sweet to the sense,
Will be damnable mouldy a hundred years hence.

Your usurer that in the hundred takes twenty,
Who wants in his wealth and pines in his plenty,
Lays up for a season which he shall ne'er see,
The year of one thousand eight hundred and three,

---

hogo] a flavour, (*haut goût*).

Shall have changed all his bags, his houses and rents
For a worm-eaten coffin a hundred years hence.

Your Chancery lawyer, who by conscience thrives
In spinning a suit to the length of three lives,
A suit which the client doth wear out in slavery,
Whilst pleader makes conscience a cloak for his knavery,
Can boast of his cunning i' the present tense,
For *non est inventus* a hundred years hence.

Then why should we turmoil in cares and fears,
And turn our tranquillity to sighs and tears?
Let 's eat, drink and play ere the worms do corrupt us,
For I say that *Post mortem nulla voluptas*;
Let 's deal with our damsels that we may from thence
Have broods to succeed us a hundred years hence.   *Jordan.*

The Triumphs of London, 1675. (Text from Bodley, 4to. Rawl. 566.)*

HER WINDOW

Here first the day does break,
And for access does seek,
Repairing for supplies
To her new-opened eyes;
Then, with a gentle light
Gilding the shades of night,
Their curtains drawn, does come
To draw those of her room;
Both open, a small ray
Does spread abroad the day,

non est inventus] equivalent to 'Not to be found.'   *Post . . . voluptas*]
There is no pleasure after death.

Which peeps into each nest
Where neighbouring birds do rest;
Who, spread upon their young,
Begin their morning song,
And from their little home
Nearer her window come,
While from low boughs they hop
And perch upon the top;
And so from bough to bough
Still singing, as they go,
In praise of light and her
Whom they to light prefer;
By whose protection blessed,
So quietly they nest,
Secure as in the wood
In such a neighbourhood:
While undisturbed they sit
Fearing no hawk nor net,
And here the first news sing
Of the approaching spring:
The spring which ever here
Does first of all appear;
Its fair course still begun
By her and by the sun.   *Leigh.*

Poems upon Several Occasions, 1675.

LOVE ARMED

Love in fantastic triumph sat,
    Whilst bleeding hearts around him flowed,
For whom fresh pains he did create,
    And strange tyrannic power he showed.
From thy bright eyes he took his fire,

Which round about in sport he hurled;
But 'twas from mine he took desire
Enough to undo the amorous world.

From me he took his sighs and tears,
From thee his pride and cruelty;
From me his languishments and fears,
And every killing dart from thee:
Thus thou and I the god have armed,
And set him up a deity;
But my poor heart alone is harmed,
Whilst thine the victor is, and free.   *Behn.*

Abdelazer, 1677. (Acted 1676. Text from *Poems*, 1684.)*

CELIA

Since Celia 's my foe,
To a desert I 'll go,
  Where some river
    For ever
Shall echo my woe.

The trees shall appear
More relenting than her;
  In the morning
    Adorning
Each leaf with a tear.

When I make my sad moan
To the rocks all alone,
  From each hollow
    Will follow
Some pitiful groan.

> But with silent disdain
> She requites all my pain,
> To my mourning
> Returning
> No answer again.   *Duffett.*

*New Poems, 1676.**

WHILE ON THOSE LOVELY LOOKS I GAZE

> While on those lovely looks I gaze,
> To see a wretch pursuing,
> In raptures of a blest amaze,
> His pleasing, happy ruin;
> 'Tis not for pity that I move:
> His fate is too aspiring,
> Whose heart, broke with a load of love,
> Dies wishing and admiring.
>
> But if this murder you 'd forgo,
> Your slave from death removing,
> Let me your art of charming know,
> Or learn you mine of loving.
> But, whether life or death betide,
> In love 'tis equal measure;
> The victor lives with empty pride,
> The vanquished die with pleasure.   *Rochester.*

Poems on Several Occasions, [1680]. (Variant printed 1676.)*

AS AMORET WITH PHYLLIS SAT

> As Amoret with Phyllis sat
> One evening on the plain,

His pleasing] 1676 and 1696;   This pleasing, [1680] and 1685.

And saw the charming Strephon wait
   To tell the nymph his pain;
The threatening danger to remove
   She whispered in her ear,
'Ah! Phyllis, if you would not love,
   This shepherd do not hear.
None ever had so strange an art
   His passion to convey
Into a listening virgin's heart,
   And steal her soul away.
Fly! fly betimes! for fear you give
   Occasion for your fate.'
'In vain,' said she, 'in vain I strive,
   Alas! 'tis now too late.'   *Scrope.**

G. Etherege's *The Man of Mode*, 1676.

I LIKED BUT NEVER LOVED BEFORE

I liked but never loved before
   I saw that charming face,
Now every feature I adore,
   And dote on every grace.
She ne'er shall know that kind desire
   Which her cold look denies,
Unless my heart, that 's all on fire,
   Should sparkle through my eyes.
Then if no gentle glance return
   A silent leave to speak,
My heart, which would for ever burn,
   Alas! must sigh and break.   *Anon.*

A New Collection of the Choicest Songs, 1676. (Text 1678.)*

DORINDA

Dorinda's sparkling wit, and eyes,
    Uniting cast too fierce a light,
Which blazes high, but quickly dies,
    Pains not the heart, but hurts the sight.

Love is a calmer, gentler joy,
    Smooth are his looks and soft his pace,
Her Cupid is a black-guard boy
    That runs his link full in your face.   *Dorset.*

C. Gildon's *A New Miscellany*, 1701. (Poem written c. 1677 ?)*

LOVE AND LIFE

All my past life is mine no more,
    The flying hours are gone,
Like transitory dreams given o'er,
Whose images are kept in store
    By memory alone.

Whatever is to come, is not;
    How can it then be mine?
The present moment 's all my lot,
And that, as fast as it is got,
    Phyllis, is wholly thine.

Then talk not of inconstancy,
    False hearts, and broken vows;
If I, by miracle, can be

---

sight] MS. and 1779; eyes, 1701.   gentler] 1779; gentle, 1701.

This live-long minute true to thee,
   'Tis all that heaven allows.   *Rochester.*

Poems on Several Occasions, [1680]. (Poem printed 1677.)*

THE BULLY

Room, room for a Blade of the Town
   That takes delight in roaring,
And daily rambles up and down,
   And at night in the street lies snoring:
That for the noble name of Spark
   Dares his companions rally;
Commits an outrage in the dark,
   Then slinks into an alley.

To every female that he meets
   He swears he bears affection,
Defies all laws, arrests, and 'cheats,
   By the help of a kind protection.
Then he, intending further wrongs,
   By some resenting cully
Is decently run through the lungs,
   And there 's an end of bully.

*Ibid.**   *Rochester* or *D'Urfey.*

PEACE

I sought for Peace, but could not find;
   I sought it in the city,
But they were of another mind,
   The more 's the pity!

'cheats] 1709 and 1721; fears, [1680].

I sought for Peace of country swain,
       But yet I could not find;
So I, returning home again,
       Left Peace behind.

Sweet Peace, where dost thou dwell? said I.
       Methought a voice was given;
Peace dwelt not here, long since did fly
       To God in Heaven.

Thought I, this echo is but vain,
       To folly 'tis of kin;
Anon I heard it tell me plain,
       'Twas killed by sin.

Then I believed the former voice,
       And rested well content,
Laid down and slept, rose, did rejoice,
       And then to heaven went.
There I enquired for Peace, and found it true,
An heavenly plant it was, and sweetly grew.

                                           Speed (?)

S. Speed's *Prison Piety*, 1677.

THE FLOWER

Oh, that I were a lovely flower
       In Christ his bower;
Or that I were a weed, to fade
       Under his shade.
But how can I a weed become
If I am shadowed with the Son?   *Speed* (?)

Ibid.

THE AMORIST

See where enamoured Thyrsis lies,
And cannot cease to gaze
On his Larissa's sparkling eyes,
But takes delight to see those comets blaze,
Whose lustre still is fatal to the swain,
O'er whom they reign;
For by their influence the poor shepherd dies,
Or (more to be lamented) lives in pain.   *Tate.*

Poems, 1677.

SONG

How blest he appears
That revels and loves out his happy years,
That fiercely spurs on till he finish his race,
And knowing life 's short, chooses living apace!
To cares we were born, 'twere a folly to doubt it,
Then love and rejoice, there 's no living without it.

Each day we grow older;
But as fate approaches, the brave still are bolder.
The joys of love with our youth slide away,
But yet there are pleasures that never decay:
When beauty grows dull, and our passions grow cold,
Wine still keeps its charms, and we drink when we 're old.

Friendship in Fashion, 1678.   *Otway.*

WIT PREDOMINANT

Ah! lay by your lute;
Ah! Lucasia, forbear.

Whilst your tongue I may hear,
Other music is mute.
Ah! lay by your lute,
For the heavens have decreed that my heart should submit
To none but the charms of your wit.

The conflict was hot
When I first met your eyes;
Yet my heart would still rise
Though through and through shot.
The conflict was hot;
But your wit's great artillery when drawn to the field,
Oh, then 'twas my glory to yield!

To satisfy all,
When an empire is due
To each beauty in you,
The world is too small,
To satisfy all.
With the rest you in triumph shall sit and survey;
But give wit all the spoils of the day.   *Rymer.*

Edgar, 1678.*

A GOOD-MORROW

The fringëd vallance of your eyes advance,
Shake off your canopied and downy trance;
Phoebus already quaffs the morning dew,
Each does his daily lease of life renew.
He darts his beams on the lark's mossy house,
And from his quiet tenement does rouse
The little, charming, and harmonious fowl,
Which sings its lump of body to a soul:
Swiftly it clambers up in the steep air
With warbling throat, and makes each note a stair.

This the solicitous lover straight alarms,
Who too long slumbered in his Celia's arms:
And now the swelling spunges of the night
With aching heads stagger from their delight:
Slovenly tailors to their needles haste:
Already now the moving shops are placed
By those who crop the treasures of the fields
And all those gems the ripening summer yields.

Shadwell.

Timon of Athens, 1678.

THE REVIVAL

Unfold, unfold; now take in his light,
Who makes thy cares more short than night.
The joys which with his day-star rise
He deals to all but drowsy eyes;
And, what the men of this world miss,
Some drops and dews of future bliss.

Hark how his winds have changed their note,
And with warm whispers call thee out!
The frosts are past, the storms are gone,
And backward life at last comes on.
    The lofty groves in express joys
    Reply unto the turtle's voice;
    And here in dust and dirt, oh, here
    The lilies of his love appear!   *Vaughan.*

Thalia Rediviva, 1678.

MORE LOVE OR MORE DISDAIN

More love or more disdain I crave;
    Sweet, be not still indifferent:

Oh! send me quickly to my grave,
   Or else afford me more content.
Or love or hate me more or less,
For love abhors all lukewarmness.

Give me a tempest if 'twill drive
   Me to the place where I would be;
Or if you 'll have me still alive,
   Confess you will be kind to me.
Give hopes of bliss or dig my grave:
More love or more disdain I crave.   *Webbe.*

Banister and Low's *New Airs and Dialogues*, 1678.*

SWEET, BE NO LONGER SAD

Sweet, be no longer sad,
   Prithee be wise!
Recall that quickness once you had
   In those fair eyes:
Methinks they 're heavy grown
As they were not your own,
And had forgot hearts to surprise.

Tell me, oh, tell me now,
   Where have you sent
The roses, in your cheeks did grow?
   Where 's the content
You once enjoyed?   Say where
Those pleasing charms now are
Which daily do my heart torment?   *Webbe.*

Ibid.

WHEN I A LOVER PALE DO SEE

When I a lover pale do see
Ready to faint and sickish be,
With hollow eyes, and cheeks so thin
As all his face is nose and chin;
When such a ghost I see in pain
Because he is not loved again,
And pule and faint and sigh and cry,—
Oh, there 's your loving fool! say I.

'Tis love with love should be repaid
And equally on both sides laid;
Love is a load a horse would kill
If it do hang on one side still;
But if he needs will be so fond
As rules of reason go beyond,
And love where he 's not loved again,
Faith, let him take it for his pain.   *Anon.*

Banister and Low's *New Airs and Dialogues.* 1678.*

CAN LIFE BE A BLESSING

Can life be a blessing,
Or worth the possessing,
Can life be a blessing if love were away?
Ah, no! though our love all night keep us waking,
And though he torment us with cares all the day,
Yet he sweetens, he sweetens our pains in the taking;
There 's an hour at the last, there 's an hour to repay.

hollow] hallow, 1678;   (old spelling, *O.E.D.*)   repay] 1679;   repray, 1695.

In every possessing,
The ravishing blessing,
In every possessing the fruit of our pain,
Poor lovers forget long ages of anguish,
Whate'er they have suffered and done to obtain;
'Tis a pleasure, a pleasure to sigh and to languish,
When we hope, when we hope to be happy again.

Dryden.

Troilus and Cressida, 1679. (Text from *The Works*, 1695.)*

BLUSH NOT REDDER THAN THE MORNING

Blush not redder than the morning,
Though the virgins gave you warning;
Sigh not at the chance befell ye,
Though they smile and dare not tell ye.

Maids, like turtles, love the cooing,
Bill and murmur in their wooing.
Thus like you, they start and tremble
And their troubled joys dissemble.

Grasp the pleasure while 'tis coming;
Though your beauties now are blooming,
Time at last your joys will sever,
And they 'll part, they 'll part for ever.

Lee.

Caesar Borgia, 1680. (Acted 1679.)*

CONSTANCY

I cannot change, as others do,
Though you unjustly scorn;
Since that poor swain that sighs for you,

For you alone was born.
No, Phyllis, no! your heart to move,
A surer way I 'll try,
And to revenge my slighted love,
Will still love on, will still love on and die!

When, killed with grief, Amyntas lies,
And you to mind shall call
The sighs that now unpitied rise,
The tears that vainly fall:
That welcome hour that ends this smart,
Will then begin your pain,
For such a faithful, tender heart
Can never break, can never break in vain.

Rochester.

Poems on Several Occasions [1680]. (Poem printed 1679.)*

PHYLLIS

Smiling Phyllis has an air
So engaging all men love her,
But her hidden beauties are
Wonders I dare not discover,
So bewitching, that in vain
I endeavour to forget her;
Still she brings me back again,
And I daily love her better.

Kindness springs within her eyes,
And from thence is always flowing;
Every minute does surprise
With fresh beauties still a-blowing;
Were she but as true as fair,

Never man had such a treasure;
But I die with jealous care
In the midst of all my pleasure.

Free and easy without pride
    Is her language and her fashion,
Setting gentle love aside
    She 's unmoved with any passion;
When she says I have her heart,
    Though I ought not to believe her,
She so kindly plays her part
    I could be deceived for ever.   *Anon.*

J. Playford's *Choice Airs and Songs, II.*, 1679.*

TO HIS MISTRESS

Do not unjustly blame
    My guiltless breast,
For venturing to disclose a flame
    It had so long suppressed.

In its own ashes it designed
    For ever to have lain,
But that my sighs, like blasts of wind,
    Made it break out again.   *Butler.*

The Genuine Remains, 1759. (Written before 1680.)

LOVE

All love at first, like generous wine,
Ferments and frets, until 'tis fine;
But when 'tis settled on the lee,

And from the impurer matter free,
Becomes the richer still, the older,
And proves the pleasanter, the colder.   *Butler.*

The Genuine Remains, 1759. (Written before 1680.)

ABSENT FROM THEE

Absent from thee I languish still,
    Then ask me not, when I return?
The straying fool 'twill plainly kill
    To wish all day, all night to mourn.

Dear, from thine arms then let me fly,
    That my fantastic mind may prove
The torments it deserves to try,
    That tears my fixed heart from my Love.

When wearied with a world of woe,
    To thy safe bosom I retire,
Where love, and peace, and truth does flow,
    May I contented there expire:

Lest once more wandering from that heaven
    I fall on some base heart unblessed,
Faithless to thee, false, unforgiven,
    And lose my everlasting rest.   *Rochester.*

Poems, &c., 1696. (Written before 1680; Poem not in earlier Eds.)

MY DEAR MISTRESS

My dear mistress has a heart
    Soft as those kind looks she gave me,

When, with love's resistless art
    And her eyes, she did enslave me;
But her constancy 's so weak,
    She 's so wild and apt to wander,
That my jealous heart would break
    Should we live one day asunder.

Melting joys about her move,
    Killing pleasures, wounding blisses;
She can dress her eyes in love,
    And her lips can arm with kisses;
Angels listen when she speaks,
    She 's my delight, all mankind's wonder:
But my jealous heart would break
    Should we live one day asunder.   *Rochester.*

Ibid. (Poem not in earlier Eds; written before 1680.)*

MAY THE AMBITIOUS EVER FIND

May the ambitious ever find
    Reward in crowds and noise,
Whilst gentle love does fill my mind
    With silent real joys.

May fools and knaves grow rich and great,
    And the world think 'em wise,
Whilst I lie dying at her feet,
    And all that world despise.

Let conquering kings new trophies raise,
    And melt in court delights:
Her eyes shall give me brighter days,
    Her arms much softer nights.   *Rochester* or *Dorset.*

B.M. Add. MS. 19759, [c. 1681]. (Poem printed 1684; written before 1680?)*

TO MISTRESS SARAH HICKFORD

Though when I cry
You not resent it,
But seem to joy and glory in my pain;
Yet when I die
You will repent it,
And wish, too late, I were alive again.

Then will you mourn
With eyes o'erflowing
The early fall of him whose love you blame;
And on my urn
Your tears bestowing
Pity my ashes, thought you scorn my flame.

'Tis vain relief
Then to deplore me
And wish, too late, that I might breathe this air:
Not all your grief
Can then restore me,
For Fate and you alike are deaf to prayer.   *Chambers.*

Bodley MS. Eng. Poet. e. 4, [c. 1680].*

FAREWELL, UNGRATEFUL TRAITOR!

Farewell, ungrateful traitor!
    Farewell, my perjured swain!
Let never injured creature
    Believe a man again.
The pleasure of possessing
Surpasses all expressing,

But 'tis too short a blessing,
     And love too long a pain.

'Tis easy to deceive us
     In pity of your pain,
But when we love, you leave us
     To rail at you in vain.
Before we have descried it,
There is no bliss beside it,
But she, that once has tried it,
     Will never love again.

The passion you pretended,
     Was only to obtain;
But when the charm is ended,
     The charmer you disdain.
Your love by ours we measure
Till we have lost our treasure,
But dying is a pleasure
     When living is a pain.   *Dryden.*

The Spanish Friar, 1681. (Acted 1680. Text from *The Works*. 1695.)*

LOVE'S DELIGHTS

Love's delights were past expressing
     Could our happy visions last;
     Pity 'tis they fly so fast!
Pity 'tis so short a blessing!
Love's delights were past expressing
     Could our happy visions last;
Tides of pleasure in possessing
     Sweetly flow, but soon are past.

Calms in love are fleeting treasure,
   Only visit and away;
   Hasty blessing we enjoy,
Tedious hours of grief we measure:
Calms in love are fleeting treasure,
   Only visit and away;
Sighs and tears fore-run the pleasure,
   Jealous rage succeeds the joy.   *Tate.*

The History of King Richard II., 1681. (Acted 1680. Also in *The Sicilian Usurper*, 1691.) *

WOULD YOU BE A MAN OF FASHION?

Would you be a man of fashion?
   Would you lead a life divine?
Take a little dram of passion
   In a lusty dose of wine.
If the nymph has no compassion,
   Vain it is to sigh and groan.
Love was but put in for fashion,
   Wine will do the work alone.   *Anon.*

J. Playford's *Choice Airs and Songs, V.*, 1684. (Poem written before 1681 ?) *

WHAT ART THOU, LOVE?

What art thou, Love? whence are those charms?
   That thus thou bear'st an universal rule:
For thee the soldier quits his arms,
   The king turns slave, the wise man fool.

In vain we chase thee from the field,
   And with cool thoughts resist thy yoke:

Next tide of blood, alas! we yield,
    And all those high resolves are broke.

Can we e'er hope thou shouldst be true,
    Whom we have found so often base?
Cozened and cheated, still we view
    And fawn upon the treacherous face.

In vain our nature we accuse;
    And dote, because she says we must:
This for a brute were an excuse,
    Whose very soul and life is lust.

To get our likeness! what is that?
    Our likeness is but misery;
Why should I toil to propagate
    Another thing as vile as I?

From hands divine our spirits came,
    And gods, that made us, did inspire
Something more noble in our frame,
    Above the dregs of earthly fire.   *Allestry.*

B.M. Add. MS. 33234, [c. 1680–2]. (And *Miscellany Poems, III.*, 1693.)*

TO CLELIA

Coy Clelia, veil those charming eyes,
    From whose surprise there 's none can part;
For he that gazes, surely dies,
    Or leaves behind a conquered heart.

what is that?] 1693;   what 's that? MS.

I durst not once presume to look,
   Or cast my wary eyes aside:
But as a boy that cons his book,
   Close sitting by his master's side,

Dares not presume to look awry
   On toys that catch the wandering sense;
So if I gaze I surely die:
   Against those charms there 's no defence.

Thus heathens, at the sun's up-rise,
   Unto the ground did bow their head,
Not able with their feeble eyes
   To view their god they worshippëd.

                                              Coppinger.

Poems, Songs and Love-Verses, 1682.

THE GODDESSES' GLORY

When the soft winds did blow
   In the fair flourishing spring,
Where silver streams did flow,
   And the sweet small birds did sing:
      The hills enamelled were
      With fragrant flowers fair
         Pleasant and gay;
      Through shades and groves I went
      Then with a full intent
         To gather may.

A pleasant flowery plain
   At length I there did espy,
Where a young female train

Made a most sweet harmony;
   On lutes they played and sung,
   Which were most sweetly strung,
      All the long day;
   The which did charm me so
   That I forgot to go
      To gather may.

Clorona she was there,
   Whom the young swains do adore,
And Floramella fair
   With many youthful nymphs more:
      The one for beauty bright
      Cast such a splendid light,
        Out-shined the day;
      I asked who she might be,
      Straight it was told to me
        The Queen of May.

There was none could compare
   With her among all the rest:
The tresses of her hair
   Shaded her white snowy breast:
      Long did I stand and gaze,
      Words cannot speak her praise,
        Being so gay;
      Then I thought in my mind
      That I should never find
        More sweeter may.

The harmony they made
   My yielding fancy did move,

So that I was betrayed
  In the sweet raptures of love:
    Their voices soft and sweet
    Did with their music meet
      As they did play;
    Thought I, I 'd rather be
    In their sweet company
      Than gather may.

No man felt greater smart
  Than I in all the whole earth,
Being denied a part
  In their sweet innocent mirth:
    The nymph that wounded me
    Would not to that agree,
      But said me nay;
    Fair Flora was her name;
    I wished I ne'er had came
      To gather may.

They were arrayed in white
  With their fine kerchers of lawn;
But e'er the gloomy night
  Her sable curtains had drawn,
    Homeward they did repair,
    And left me wounded there
      Where I did stay,
    Being perplexed in mind,
    Knowing not where to find
      The Queen of May.

Anon.

Bodley, Wood 417, [c. 1682 ?]*

KINGSTON CHURCH

Sweet, use your time, abuse your time
   No longer, but be wise;
Young lovers now discover you
   Have beauty to be prized;
But if you 're coy you 'll lose the joy,
   So curst will be your fate,
The flower will fade, you 'll die a maid,
   And mourn your chance too late.

At thirteen years and fourteen years
   The virgin's heart may range;
'Twixt fifteen years and fifty years
   You 'll find a wondrous change:
Then whilst in tune, in May and June,
   Let love and youth agree,
For if you stay till Christmas day
   The devil shall woo for me.

D'Urfey.

A New Collection of Songs and Poems, 1683.*

TO CELIA

I spend my sad life in sighs and in cries,
And in silent dark shades mourn the frowns of your eyes;
Lewd satyrs and fauns soft pity do show,
And wolves howl in consort to the noise of my woe:
Even mountains and groves are kinder than she;

---

change] 1703; chance, 1683.

Groans rebound from each rock, tears drop from each tree,
And all things, but Celia, show pity, show pity on me.

Come Celia, come learn of these shades to be kind,
Learn to yield when I sigh, trees bend with the wind;
When drops often fall, rocks, stones, will relent,
Ah! learn, cruel maid! when I weep, to repent.
Kind ivies do ne'er from embraces remove,
Rivers mix, and that mixture a marriage may prove;
Learn of trees to embrace; of rivers, cold rivers, to love.

Kenrick.

Miscellany Poems, II., 4th Ed., 1716. (And also J. Playford's *Choice Airs and Songs, IV.,* 1683.)*

ON HER ABSENCE

Boast not your fresh unmingled sweets,
Boast not your noiseless sleepy nights
And such your country dear delights,
Since ye no longer feel the ray,
When all was dull, that made you gay,
And turned your darkness into day.

No doubt the town is nobly great,
No doubt the country purely sweet,
When that we there Clorinda meet;
But all is desert, all despair:
For heaven itself I should not care
Unless I saw Clorinda there.

Rymer.

Curious Amusements, 1714. (Poem written 1683 ?)*

Kind ivies] 1716;   Kind joys, 1683 (an obvious misprint).

TO SILVIA

You I love, by all that 's true,
More than all things here below,
With a passion far more great
Than e'er creature lovëd yet;
And yet still you cry, 'Forbear,
Love no more, or love not here.'

Bid the miser leave his ore,
Bid the wretched sigh no more,
Bid the old be young again,
Bid the nun not think of man:
Silvia, this when you can do,
Bid me then not think of you.

Love 's not a thing of choice, but fate;
That makes me love, that makes you hate:
Silvia then do what you will,
Ease or cure, torment or kill;
Be kind or cruel, false or true,
Love I must, and none but you.   *Anon.*

J. Playford's *Choice Airs and Songs, IV.,* 1683.*

SONG

Oh, why did e'er my thoughts aspire
    To wish for that no crown can buy?
'Tis sacrilege but to desire
    What she in honour will deny.
As Indians do the Eastern skies,
    I at a distance must adore
The brighter glories of her eyes,
    And never dare pretend to more.   *Sackville.*

T. Southerne's *The Disappointment,* 1684.*

A FAREWELL TO WIVES

Once in our lives, ,
Let us drink to our wives,
Though the number of them is but small.
God take the best,
And the devil take the rest,
And so we shall be rid of them all.   *Anon.*

H. Playford's *Wit and Mirth*, 1684.*

THE ENCHANTMENT

I did but look and love awhile,
  'Twas but for one half-hour;
Then to resist I had no will,
  And now I have no power.

To sigh and wish, is all my ease:
  Sighs which do heat impart
Enough to melt the coldest ice,
  Yet cannot warm your heart.

Oh! would your pity give my heart
  One corner of your breast,
'Twould learn of yours the winning art,
  And quickly steal the rest.   *Otway.*

The Works of . . . Rochester and Roscommon, 1709. (Poem written before 1685.)

THE WISH

If I live to be old, for I find I go down,
Let this be my fate: In a country town

May I have a warm house, with a stone at the gate,
And a cleanly young girl to rub my bald pate.
   May I govern my passion with an absolute sway,
   And grow wiser and better as my strength wears away,
   Without gout or stone, by a gentle decay.

Near a shady grove, and a murmuring brook,
With the ocean at distance, whereupon I may look,
With a spacious plain without hedge or stile,
And an easy pad-nag to ride out a mile.
   May I govern, &c.

With *Horace* and *Petrarch*, and two or three more
Of the best wits that reigned in the ages before,
With roast mutton, rather than ven'son or veal,
And clean though coarse linen at every meal.
   May I govern, &c.

With a pudding on Sundays, with stout humming liquor,
And remnants of Latin to welcome the vicar,
With Monte-Fiascone or Burgundy wine,
To drink the King's health as oft as I dine.
   May I govern, &c.

With a courage undaunted may I face my last day,
And when I am dead may the better sort say,
In the morning when sober, in the evening when mellow,
He 's gone, and left not behind him his fellow.
   May I govern my passion with an absolute sway,
   And grow wiser and better as my strength wears away,
   Without gout or stone, by a gentle decay.

                   W. Pope.

Two New Songs, 1685. (Text from *The Wish*, 1697.)*

COME, SWEET LASS

Come, sweet lass!
This bonny weather
   Let 's together;
   Come, sweet lass,
Let 's trip it on the grass:
   Every where
Poor Jockey seeks his dear,
And unless you appear
He sees no beauty there.

   On our green
The loons are sporting,
Piping, courting;
   On our green
The blithest lads are seen:
   There all day
Our lasses dance and play,
And every one is gay,
But I, when you 're away.   *Anon.*

H. Playford's *Wit and Mirth*, 1699. (Poem printed 1685.) *

LUCINDA

When Lucinda's blooming beauty
   Did the wondering town surprise,
With the first I paid my duty,
   Fixing there my wandering eyes.

Her kind spring each hour discloses
   Charms we nowhere else can trace;
Gayer than the blush on roses
   Are the glories on her face.

She alone the life of pleasure
   Makes the Park, and makes the Play,
Scattering her amazing treasure,
   Gives her slaves a golden day.

You whose thoughts are too aspiring
   Hope not she will ease your care;
I have learnt to live admiring,
   Love is vanquished by despair.   *Anon.*

H. Playford's *The Theatre of Music, I.,* 1685.*

OF THE CHILD WITH THE BIRD AT THE BUSH

My little bird, how canst thou sit
   And sing amidst so many thorns?
Let me but hold upon thee get,
   My love with honour thee adorns.

Thou art at present little worth,
   Five farthings none will give for thee;
But prithee, little bird, come forth,
   Thou of more value art to me.

'Tis true it is sun-shine to-day,
   To-morrow birds will have a storm;
My pretty one, come thou away,
   My bosom then shall keep thee warm.

Thou subject art to cold o' nights,
   When darkness is thy covering;
At days thy danger 's great by kites,
   How canst thou then sit there and sing?

Thy food is scarce and scanty too,
   'Tis worms and trash which thou dost eat;
Thy present state I pity do,
   Come, I 'll provide thee better meat.

I 'll feed thee with white bread and milk,
   And sugar-plums, if them thou crave;
I 'll cover thee with finest silk,
   That from the cold I may thee save.

My father's palace shall be thine,
   Yea, in it thou shalt sit and sing;
My little bird, if thou 'lt be mine,
   The whole year round shall be thy spring.

I 'll teach thee all the notes at court;
   Unthought-of music thou shalt play;
And all that thither do resort
   Shall praise thee for it every day.

I 'll keep thee safe from cat and cur,
   No manner o' harm shall come to thee:
Yea, I will be thy succourer,
   My bosom shall thy cabin be.

But lo! behold, the bird is gone;
   These charmings would not make her yield:
The child 's left at the bush alone,
   The bird flies yonder o'er the field.

Bunyan.

A Book for Boys and Girls, 1686.

Dryden's Ode, *To the Pious Memory of . . . Mrs. Anne Killigrew,* was
written and prefixed to her *Poems,* 1686.

OF LOVE

O Love! that stronger art than wine,
Pleasing delusion, witchery divine;
Want, to be prized above all wealth;
Disease, that has more joys than health:
Though we blaspheme thee in our pain
And of thy tyranny complain,
We all are bettered by thy reign.

What reason never can bestow
We to this useful passion owe:
Love wakes the dull from sluggish ease,
And learns a clown the art to please;
Humbles the vain, kindles the cold,
Makes misers free, and cowards bold:
'Tis he reforms the sot from drink,
And teaches airy fops to think.

When full brute appetite is fed,
And choked the glutton lies and dead,
Thou new spirits dost dispense,
And fine the gross delights of sense;
Virtue's unconquerable aid,
That against Nature can persuade;
And makes a roving mind retire
Within the bounds of just desire;
Cheerer of age, youth's kind unrest,
And half the heaven of the blest.

Behn or *Ousley.**

A. Behn's *The Lucky Chance*, 1687. (Acted 1686. Also in H. Playford's *The Theatre of Music, IV.*, 1687.)

dost dispense, And fine] Playford, 1687; does dispense, And fines, Behn, 1687.

OF THE LAST VERSES IN THE BOOK

When we for age could neither read nor write,
The subject made us able to indite.
The soul with nobler resolutions decked,
The body stooping, does herself erect:
No mortal parts are requisite to raise
Her that unbodied can her Maker praise.

The seas are quiet, when the winds give o'er;
So calm are we, when passions are no more:
For then we know how vain it was to boast
Of fleeting things, so certain to be lost.
Clouds of affection from our younger eyes
Conceal that emptiness, which age descries.

The soul's dark cottage, battered and decayed,
Lets in new light through chinks that time has made.
Stronger by weakness, wiser, men become
As they draw near to their eternal home:
Leaving the old, both worlds at once they view
That stand upon the threshold of the new.   *Waller.*

Poems, &c., 1686.

SONG

Pride and ambition, and peevishness too,
    Nay, all the whole sex's legion of ills
I 'd meet in a woman I 'm doomed to woo,
    So wit, damned wit, not the catalogue fills:
To themselves 'tis a plague, to us it is worse,
But poisoned with learning is curse upon curse.   *Anon.*

H. Playford's *The Theatre of Music, III.,* 1686.

'TIS TOO LATE FOR A COACH

'Tis too late for a coach, and too soon to reel home,
We have freedom to stagger when the town is our own.
Let 's while it away and whip sixpences round
Till the drawers are foundered and the hogshead does sound.
The glass stays with you, Tom, save your tide, pull away,
One minute of midnight is worth a whole day.   *Anon.*

J. Playford's *The Pleasant Musical Companion, II.*, 1686.* (Text 1687.)

OF MIDDLE LIFE

My happier state
And blessèd fate
My clearer judgement now doth note:
Am put away
From love to stay,
Too old to love, too young to dote.

So clear my sight
Knows what 's delight,
For this doth keep us both still friends,
And is so kind
Not being blind
As th' other is at both love's ends.   *Anon.*

B.M. Add. MS. 32339. (Poem written before 1687.)*

WHEN THOU DOST DANCE

When thou dost dance the spheres do play,
By night stars' torches, sun by day;
Each step so loth to wrong thy birth,

    Afraid to hurt thy mother earth;
      The tender blades of grass when thou
      Dost dance upon them do not bow.

    The falling dew too doth thee woo,
    When tripp'st on it scarce wets thy shoe:
    Then, lady like, doth change thy mind
    And dances on the wavering wind:
      The thinner air strives thine to meet
      To tread it with thy gentle feet.   *Anon.*

B.M. Add. MS. 32339. (Poem written before 1687.)*

COMPLAINS, BEING HINDERED THE SIGHT
OF HIS NYMPH

To view these walls each night I come alone,
And pay my adoration to the stone,
Whence joy and peace are influenced on me,
For 'tis the temple of my deity.

As nights and days an anxious wretch by stealth
Creeps out to view the place which hoards his wealth,
So to this house that keeps from me my heart,
I come, look, traverse, weep, and then depart.

She 's fenced so strongly in on every side,
Thought enters, but my footsteps are denied.
Then sighs in vain I breathe, and tears let fall:
Kiss a cold stone sometimes, or hug the wall.

For like a merchant that rough seas has crossed,
Near home is shipwrecked, and his treasure lost,

So, tossed in storms of sorrow, on firm ground,
I in a sea of mine own tears am drowned.   *Ayres.*

Lyric Poems, Made in Imitation of the Italians, 1687.

ON A FAIR BEGGAR

Barefoot and ragged, with neglected hair,
She whom the Heavens at once made poor and fair,
    With humble voice and moving words did stay,
    To beg an alms of all who passed that way.

But thousands viewing her became her prize,
Willingly yielding to her conquering eyes,
    And caught by her bright hairs, whilst careless she
    Makes them pay homage to her poverty.

So mean a boon, said I, what can extort
From that fair mouth, where wantom Love to sport
    Amidst the pearls and rubies we behold?
Nature on thee has all her treasures spread,
Do but incline thy rich and precious head,
    And those fair locks shall pour down showers of gold.

Ibid.   *Ayres.*

SERENADE

When maidens are young, and in their spring,
Of pleasure, of pleasure, let 'em take their full swing,
    Full swing, full swing,
And love, and dance, and play, and sing.
For Silvia, believe it, when youth is done,
There 's nought but hum-drum, hum-drum, hum-drum,
There 's nought but hum-drum, hum-drum, hum-drum.

Then Silvia be wise, be wise, be wise,
The painting and dressing for a while are supplies,
    And may surprise—
But when the fire 's going out in your eyes,
It twinkles, it twinkles, it twinkles, and dies,
And then to hear love, to hear love from you,
I 'd as live hear an owl cry, *Wit to woo! Wit to woo!*
    Wit to woo!

                                    Behn.

The Emperor of the Moon, 1687. (And in *The History of Adolphus, Prince of Russia*, 1691.)*

ONLY TELL HER THAT I LOVE

Only tell her that I love,
    Leave the rest to her and fate;
Some kind planet from above
May, perhaps, her pity move:
    Lovers on their stars must wait,
Only tell her that I love.

Why, oh, why should I despair?
    Mercy 's pictured in her eye;
If she once vouchsafe to hear,
Welcome, hope! and farewell, fear!
    She 's too good to let me die,
Why, oh, why should I despair?   *Cutts.*

Poetical Exercises, 1687.

Dryden's *A Song for St. Cecilia's Day* was written, and printed as a broadside, 1687.

The painting] 1691;   Though painting, 1687.   live] lief.

CANTICLE

'Twas my Beloved spake,
I know his charming voice, I heard him say,
Rise up my Love, my fairest one awake,
    Awake and come away.

    The winter all is past
And stormy winds that with such rudeness blew;
The heavens are no longer overcast,
    But try to look like you.

    The flowers their sweets display,
The birds in short preludiums tune their throat,
The turtle in low murmurs does essay
    Her melancholy note.

    The fruitful vineyards make
An odorous smell, the fig looks fresh and gay,—
Arise my Love, my fairest one awake,
    Awake and come away.   *Norris.*

A Collection of Miscellanies, 1687.

THE VICTORY IN HUNGARY

Hark how the Duke of Lorraine comes,
    The brave victorious soul of war,
With trumpets and with kettle-drums,
    Like thunder rolling from afar.

On the left wing, the conquering horse
    The brave Bavarian Duke does lead;

These heroes with united force,
   Fill all the Turkish host with dread.

Their bright caparisons behold!
   Rich habits, streamers, shining arms,
The glittering steel and burnished gold,
   The pomp of war with all its charms.

With solemn march, and fatal pace,
   They bravely on the foe press on;
The cannons roar, the shot takes place,
   Whilst smoke and dust obscure the sun.

The horses neigh, the soldiers shout,
   And now the furious bodies join;
The slaughter rages all about,
   And men in groans their blood resign.

The weapons' clash, the roaring drum
   With clangour of the trumpets' sound,
The howls and yells of men o'ercome
   And from the neighbouring hills rebound.

Now, now the infidels give place;
   Then, all in routs, they headlong fly;
Heroes, in dust, pursue the chase,
   While deafening clamours rend the sky.

Shadwell.

The Squire of Alsatia, 1688.*

YE GODS, YOU GAVE TO ME A WIFE

Ye Gods, you gave to me a wife,
   Out of your wonted favour,

To be the comfort of my life,
And I was glad to have her:

But if your Providence divine
For something else design her,
To obey your will at any time
I 'm ready to resign her.   *Anon.*

H. Playford's *The Banquet of Music, I.,* 1688.

IF ALL BE TRUE THAT I DO THINK

If all be true that I do think,
There are five reasons we should drink:
Good wine; a friend; or being dry;
Or lest we should be by and by;
Or any other reason why.   *Aldrich.**

H. Playford's *The Banquet of Music, III.,* 1689.

HOW HAPPY 'S THAT LOVER

How happy 's that lover, who, after long years
Of wishing and doubting, despairing and sorrow,
Shall hear his kind mistress say, 'Shake off thy tears,
And prepare to be happy to-morrow.'

Jove of Io possessed, or on Dana's breast,
Was ne'er half so happy, or really blessed,
As Sylvio would be, might he laugh, love, and say,
'Let the sun rise in state, for to-morrow 's the day.'

                                                   Anon.

Comes Amoris . . . The Third Book, 1689. (Text 1690.)*

Dana's] *i.e.* Danae's.   Sylvio] Sylvia, 1690, corrected in MS.

THE HAPPIEST MORTALS ONCE WERE WE

The happiest mortals once were we,
I loved Myra, Myra me;
Each desirous of the blessing,
Nothing wanting but possessing;
I loved Myra, Myra me:
The happiest mortals once were we.

But since cruel fates dissever,
Torn from love, and torn for ever,
Tortures end me,
Death befriend me!
Of all pains, the greatest pain
Is to love, and love in vain.   *Lansdowne.*

The Genuine Works, 1732. (Poem written before 1690.)

JEALOUSY

Vain Love, why dost thou boast of wings
That cannot help thee to retire
When such quick flames suspicion brings
As do the heart about thee fire?
Still swift to come, but when to go
Thou shouldst be more—alas, how slow!

Lord of the world must surely be
But thy bare title at the most;
Since Jealousy is lord of thee
And makes such havoc on thy coast
As does thy pleasant land deface,
Yet binds thee faster to the place.   *Winchilsea.*

Miscellany Poems, 1713. (Written before 1690.) *

WHAT SHALL I DO?

What shall I do to show how much I love her?
　　How many millions of sighs can suffice?
That which wins other hearts, never can move her,
　　Those common methods of love she 'll despise.

I will love more than man e'er loved before me,
　　Gaze on her all the day, melt all the night,
Till for her own sake at last she 'll implore me
　　To love her less, to preserve our delight.

Since gods themselves could not ever be loving,
　　Men must have breathing recruits for new joys;
I wish my love could be always improving,
　　Though eager love, more than sorrow, destroys.

In fair Aurelia's arms leave me expiring
　　To be embalmed by the sweets of her breath,
To the last moment I 'll still be desiring:
　　Never had hero so glorious a death.

　　　　　　　　　　　　　　Dryden(?) or *Betterton(?)*

The Prophetess: or, The History of Dioclesian, 1690.*

THE FIRE OF LOVE

The fire of love in youthful blood,
Like what is kindled in brushwood,
　　But for a moment burns;
Yet in that moment makes a mighty noise,
It crackles, and to vapour turns,
　　And soon itself destroys.

But when crept into aged veins
It slowly burns, and long remains;
   And with a sullen heat,
Like fire in logs, it glows, and warms 'em long,
And though the flame be not so great,
   Yet is the heat as strong.   *Shadwell* or *Dorset.*

The Amorous Bigot, 1690.*

SONG

Pursuing beauty, men descry
   The distant shore and long to prove
(Still richer in variety)
   The treasures of the land of love.

We women, like weak Indians, stand
   Inviting from our golden coast
The wandering rovers to our land:
   But she who trades with 'em is lost.

With humble vows they first begin,
   Stealing unseen into the heart;
But, by possession settled in,
   They quickly act another part.

For beads and baubles we resign
   In ignorance our shining store;
Discover nature's richest mine,
   And yet the tyrants will have more.

Be wise, be wise, and do not try
   How he can court, or you be won:
For love is but discovery,
   When that is made, the pleasure 's done.

Sir Antony Love, 1691. (Acted 1690.)   *Southerne.**

WERE I TO TAKE WIFE

Were I to take wife,
As 'tis for my life,
She should be brisk, pleasant, and merry;
A lovely fine brown,
A face all her own,
With a lip red and round as a cherry.

Not much of the wise,
Less of the precise,
Nor over-reserved, nor yet flying;
Hard breasts, a straight back,
An eye full and black,
But languishing as she were dying.

And then for her dress,
Be 't more or be 't less,
Not tawdry set out, nor yet meanly;
And, one thing beside,
Just, just so much pride
As may serve to keep honest and cleanly.   *Wilson.*

Belphegor: or, The Marriage of the Devil, 1691. (Licensed, 1690.)

SONG
TO A MINUET

How happy the lover,
How easy his chain,
How pleasing his pain!
How sweet to discover
He sighs not in vain!
For love, every creature
Is formed by his nature;

No joys are above
The pleasures of love.

In vain are our graces,
    In vain are your eyes,
    If love you despise;
When age furrows faces,
    'Tis time to be wise.
Then use the short blessing
That flies in possessing:
    No joys are above
    The pleasures of love.   *Dryden.*

King Arthur, 1691. (Text from *The Works*, 1695.)*

I'LL TELL HER

I 'll tell her the next time, said I—
In vain, in vain, for when I try
Upon my timorous tongue the trembling accents die.

Alas! A thousand thousand fears
Still over-awe when she appears,
My breath is spent in sighs, my eyes are drowned in tears.
                                            Lansdowne.

The History of Adolphus, Prince of Russia, 1691.

STREPHON

Strephon the brisk and gay,
    Young Strephon 's Nature's wonder,
Whose eyes let forth bright flames of day,
Whose every look does souls betray,
    Or splits an heart asunder.

Strephon has every grace
   And wears 'em still about him;
The nymph whose greedy eye does trace
The swarming beauties of his face
   Yields heaven 's no heaven without him.

Who views his mien or air
   The lovely youth confounds her;
He is so charming and so fair,
The heedless virgin, unaware,
   Plays with the dart that wounds her.   *Smith.*

Win her and take her, 1691.

SONG

Lost is my quiet for ever,
   Lost is life's happiest part;
Lost all my tender endeavour
   To touch an insensible heart.

But though my despair is past curing,
   And much undeserved is my fate,
I 'll show, by a patient enduring,
   My love is unmoved as her hate.   *Anon.*

H. Playford's *The Banquet of Music, V.,* 1691.*

WRITTEN ON THE LEAVES OF A WHITE FAN

Flavia the least and slightest toy
Can with resistless art employ:
This fan, in meaner hands, would prove

---

endeavour] misprinted, endeavours, 1691 and 1698.

An engine of small force in love;
Yet she with graceful air and mien
(Not to be told, or safely seen!)
Directs its wanton motions so
That it wounds more than Cupid's bow:
Gives coolness to the matchless dame,
To every other breast a flame.   *Atterbury.*

The Gentleman's Journal, 1692.*

NO, NO! I NE'ER SHALL LOVE THEE LESS

No, no! I ne'er shall love thee less
    For all thy fierce disdain;
So fast thy blooming charms increase,
Thy sparkling eyes my heart oppress,
    Each glance renews my pain.

Yet must I, (Fate!) like busy flies,
    Still to thy brightness turn;
Pursue thee with my restless eyes,
Till, as each flaming blush does rise,
    Insensibly I burn.   *Cromwell.*

C. Gildon's *Miscellany Poems*, 1692.*

TO MANY DEATHS DECREED

Ah me! to many deaths decreed,
    My Love to war goes every day.
In every wound of his I bleed,
    I die the hour he goes away,
    Yet I would hate him should he stay.

Ah me! to many deaths decreed,
By love or war I hourly die;
If I see not my Love I bleed,
Yet when I have him in my eye
He kills me with excess of joy.   *Crowne.*

Regulus, 1694. (Poem printed 1692.)*

HUNTING SONG

Tantivy! tivy! tivy! tivy! high and low;
Hark! hark! how the merry merry horn does blow
As through the lanes and the meadows we go,
    As Puss has run over the down;
When Ringwood, and Rockwood, and Jowler, and Spring,
And Thunder, and Wonder, made all the woods ring,
And horsemen and footmen, hey ding a ding, ding!
Who envies the splendour and state of a crown?

Then follow, follow, follow, follow, jolly boys,
Keep in with the beagles now whilst the scent lies;
The fiery-faced god is just ready to rise,
    Whose beams all our pleasure control;
Whilst over the mountains and valleys we roll,
And Wat's fatal knell in each hollow we toll,
And, in the next cottage, top off a brown bowl:
What pleasure like hunting can cherish the soul?   *D'Urfey.*

The Marriage-hater matched, 1692.*

Puss] the hare.   control] misprinted, controls, 1692 and 1693.   Wat] the
hare.

UPON A FAVOUR OFFERED

Celia, too late you would repent:
　　The offering all your store
Is now but like a pardon sent
　　To one that 's dead before.

While at the first you cruel proved,
　　And grant the bliss too late;
You hindered me of one I loved,
　　To give me one I hate.

I thought you innocent as fair
　　When first my court I made;
But when your falsehoods plain appear,
　　My love no longer stayed.

Your bounty of those favours shown,
　　Whose worth you first deface,
Is melting valued medals down
　　And giving us the brass.

Oh, since the thing we beg 's a toy
　　That 's prized by love alone,
Why cannot women grant the joy
　　Before our love is gone?　　　　　*Walsh.*

Letters and Poems, Amorous and Gallant, 1692.

DEATH

A SONNET

What has this bugbear Death that 's worth our care?
After a life in pain and sorrow passed,

After deluding hope and dire despair,
   Death only gives us quiet at the last.
How strangely are our love and hate misplaced!
   Freedom we seek, and yet from freedom flee;
Courting those tyrant-sins that chain us fast,
   And shunning Death, that only sets us free.

'Tis not a foolish fear of future pains,
(Why should they fear who keep their souls from stains?)
   That makes me dread thy terrors, Death, to see:
'Tis not the loss of riches, or of fame,
Or the vain toys the vulgar pleasures name;
   'Tis nothing, Celia, but the losing thee.   *Walsh.*

Ibid.

YOU UNDERSTAND

You understand no tender vows
   Of fervent and eternal love;
That lover will his labour lose,
Who does with sighs and tears propose
   Your heart to move.
But if he talk of settling land,
A house in town, and coach maintained,
   You understand.

You understand no charms in wit,
   In shape, in breeding, or in air;
To any fops you will submit,
The nauseous clown, or fulsome cit,
   If rich they are.

if he] 1699; if ye, 1692.

Who guineas can, may you, command;
Put gold, and then put in your hand,
    You understand.   *Anon.*

*The Gentleman's Journal, 1692.**

CORINNA IS DIVINELY FAIR

Corinna is divinely fair,
Easy her shape and soft her air;
Of hearts she had the absolute sway
Before she threw her own away:
The power now languishes by which she charmed;
Her beauty sullied, and her eyes disarmed.

Like Nature, she is apt to waste
Her treasure where 'tis valued least:
So peasants surfeit—where it grows—
On fruit the eastern sun bestows;
But all the delicacy fades before
It can, through oceans, reach our distant shore.   *Anon.*

*Ibid.**

FLY SOFT, YE GENTLE HOURS

Fly soft, ye gentle hours, post not so fast,
    Whilst I Belinda's charming face admire:
For she hath vowed this visit is the last,
    And then, like Time, once gone, she comes no more.
Let the sun slack his pace, be his steeds unregarded;
Whilst he looks on her face, his stay 's well rewarded.

Ah, 'tis in vain!   She fled with eager haste;
    Yet, kindly, to assuage my deadly smart,

Whilst with her lightning eyes she pierced my breast,
 She left her darling image in my heart:
And to show to the last her art of beguiling,
Though my hopes are all past, her picture 's still smiling.
            Anon.

H. Playford's *The Banquet of Music, VI.,* 1692.

FROM ALL UNEASY PASSIONS FREE

From all uneasy passions free,
Revenge, ambition, jealousy,
Contented, I had been too blessed
If love and you had let me rest.
Yet that dull life I now despise;
   Safe from your eyes
I feared no griefs, but then I found no joys.

Amidst a thousand kind desires
Which beauty moves and love inspires,
Such pangs I feel of tender fear,
No heart so soft as mine can bear.
Yet I 'll defy the worst of harms;
   Such are your charms,
'Tis worth a life to die within your arms.
      J. Sheffield, Duke of Buckingham.

A Collection of Poems, 1693. (Text from *The Works,* 1723.) *

ANCIENT PHYLLIS

Ancient Phyllis has young graces,
 'Tis a strange thing but a true one;
  Shall I tell you how?
She herself makes her own faces,

And each morning wears a new one.
    Where 's the wonder now?   *Congreve.*

The Double-Dealer, 1694. (Acted 1693.)*

TO A FAIR YOUNG LADY,
GOING OUT OF THE TOWN IN THE SPRING

Ask not the cause why sullen spring
    So long delays her flowers to bear;
Why warbling birds forget to sing,
    And winter storms invert the year:
Chloris is gone; and fate provides
To make it spring, where she resides.

Chloris is gone, the cruel fair;
    She cast not back a pitying eye,
But left her lover in despair,
    To sigh, to languish, and to die:
Ah! how can those fair eyes endure
To give the wounds they will not cure?

Great god of love, why hast thou made
    A face that can all hearts command,
That all religions can invade,
    And change the laws of every land?
Where thou hadst placed such power before,
Thou shouldst have made her mercy more.

When Chloris to the temple comes,
    Adoring crowds before her fall;
She can restore the dead from tombs,
    And every life but mine recall.

I only am by Love designed
To be the victim for mankind.   *Dryden.*

Miscellany Poems, III., 1693.*

RONDELAY

Chloe found Amyntas lying
　All in tears, upon the plain,
Sighing to himself, and crying,
　'Wretched I, to love in vain!
Kiss me, dear, before my dying,
　Kiss me once, and ease my pain!'

Sighing to himself, and crying,
　'Wretched I, to love in vain!
Ever scorning and denying
　To reward your faithful swain:
Kiss me, dear, before my dying;
　Kiss me once, and ease my pain!'

'Ever scorning and denying
　To reward your faithful swain!'
Chloe, laughing at his crying,
　Told him that he loved in vain.
'Kiss me, dear, before my dying;
　Kiss me once, and ease my pain!'

Chloe, laughing at his crying,
　Told him that he loved in vain;
But repenting, and complying,
　When he kissed, she kissed again:
Kissed him up, before his dying;
　Kissed him up, and eased his pain.   *Dryden.*

Ibid.

SONG

No, no, no, no, resistance is but vain,
And only adds new weight to Cupid's chain:
A thousand ways, a thousand arts
The tyrant knows to captivate our hearts:
Sometimes he sighs employs, and sometimes tries
The universal language of the eyes:
The fierce with fierceness he destroys,
The weak with tenderness decoys:
He kills the strong with joy, the weak with pain:
No, no, no, no, resistance is but vain.   *Henly.*

The Maid's Last Prayer, 1693.*

YOU SAY YOU LOVE

You say you love!   Repeat again,
    Repeat the amazing sound;
Repeat the ease of all my pain,
    The cure of every wound.

What you to thousands have denied,
    To me you freely give:
Whilst I in humble silence died,
    Your mercy bids me live.

So upon Latmos' top each night
    Endymion sighing lay,
Gazed on the moon's transcendent light,
    Despaired, and durst not pray.

But divine Cynthia saw his grief,
    The effect of conquering charms;

So upon Latmos'] 1704;   So on cold Latmos', 1693.

Unasked, the goddess brings relief,
　　And falls into his arms.　　　　　　　. W. King.

Miscellany Poems, III., 1693. (Text from Miscellanies in Prose and Verse,
[1709 ?].) *

THOUGH YOU MAKE NO RETURN

Though you make no return to my passion,
　　Still, still I presume to adore;
'Tis in love but an odd reputation,
　　When faintly repulsed, to give o'er.
　　　　When you talk of your duty
　　　　I gaze on your beauty,
Nor mind the dull maxim at all:
　　　　Let it reign in Cheapside
　　　　With a citizen's bride,
It will ne'er be received at Whitehall.

What apocryphal tales are you told
　　By one who would make you believe
That, because of 'to have and to hold,'
　　You still must be pinned to his sleeve!
　　　　'Twere apparent high treason
　　　　'Gainst love and good reason,
Should one such a treasure engross:
　　　　He who knows not the joys
　　　　That attend such a choice,
Should resign to another who does.　　　Southerne.

The Gentleman's Journal, 1693. (Slight variant in The Maid's Last Prayer,
1693.) *

ON HIS MISTRESS DROWNED

Sweet stream, that dost with equal pace
Both thyself fly and thyself chase,

Forbear a while to flow,
And listen to my woe.

Then go, and tell the sea that all its brine
Is fresh, compared to mine;
Inform it that the gentler dame,
Who was the life of all my flame,
In the glory of her bud
Has passed the fatal flood:
Death, by this only stroke, triumphs above
The greatest power of Love.

Alas, alas!   I must give o'er,
My sighs will let me add no more.
Go on, sweet stream, and henceforth rest
No more than does my troubled breast;
And if my sad complaints have made thee stay,
These tears, these tears shall mend thy way.

Sprat.

Miscellany Poems, III., 1693.

ON LOVE

Love, thou art best of human joys,
Our chiefest happiness below:
All other pleasures are but toys,
Music without thee is but noise,
And beauty but an empty show.

Heaven, who knew best what man would move
And raise his thoughts above the brute,
Said, Let him be, and let him love!

---

what man would move] *i.e.* what would move man.

That must alone his soul improve,
    Howe'er philosophers dispute.   *Winchilsea.*

Miscellany Poems, 1713. (Poem printed 1693.)*

YOUNG SILVIA

All own the young Silvia is fatally fair,
    All own the young Silvia is pretty;
Confess her good nature, and easy soft air,
    Nay more, that she 's wanton and witty:
Yet all these keen arrows at Damon still cast
    Could never his quiet destroy,
Till the cunning coquette shot me flying at last,
    By a *Je ne say, Je ne say quoy.*

So though the young Silvia were not very fair,
    Though she were but indiff'rently pretty;
Much wanting Aurelia's, or Celia's, soft air,
    But not the dull sense of the city:
Yet still the dear creature would please without doubt,
    And give one abundance of joy,
Since all that is missing is mainly made out
    By a *Je ne say, Je ne say quoy.*   *De la Sale.*

The Gentleman's Journal, 1694.

IMPATIENT WITH DESIRE

Impatient with desire, at last
    I ventured to lay forms aside;
'Twas I was modest, not she chaste,
    The nymph as soon as asked complied.

Chaste] chast, 1694.

With amorous awe, a silent fool,
    I gazed upon her eyes with fear:
Speak, Love, how came your slave so dull
    To read no better there?

Thus, to ourselves the greatest foes,
    Although the fair be well inclined,
For want of courage to propose,
    By our own folly, she 's unkind.   *Lansdowne.*

*Miscellany Poems, IV., 1694.**

TO A LADY: SHE REFUSING TO CONTINUE
A DISPUTE WITH ME, AND LEAVING
ME IN THE ARGUMENT

Spare, generous Victor, spare the slave
    Who did unequal war pursue,
That more than triumph he might have
    In being overcome by you.

In the dispute whate'er I said,
    My heart was by my tongue belied;
And in my looks you might have read
    How much I argued on your side.

You, far from danger as from fear,
    Might have sustained an open fight;
For seldom your opinions err,
  · Your eyes are always in the right.

Why, fair one, would you not rely
    On reason's force with beauty's joined?

Could I their prevalence deny,
  I must at once be deaf and blind.

Alas! not hoping to subdue,
  I only to the fight aspired:
To keep the beauteous foe in view
  Was all the glory I desired.

But she, howe'er of victory sure,
  Contemns the wreath too long delayed;
And, armed with more immediate power,
  Calls cruel silence to her aid.

Deeper to wound, she shuns the fight:
  She drops her arms, to gain the field:
Secures her conquest by her flight,
  And triumphs when she seems to yield.

So when the Parthian turned his steed,
  And from the hostile camp withdrew,
With cruel skill the backward reed
  He sent; and as he fled, he slew.   *Prior.*

Poems on Several Occasions, 1721. (Poem written c. 1694?) *

THE KNOTTING SONG

Hears not my Phyllis how the birds
  Their feathered mates salute?
They tell their passion in their words;
  Must I alone be mute?
      Phyllis, without frown or smile,
      Sat and knotted all the while.

The god of love, in thy bright eyes,
   Does like a tyrant reign;
But in thy heart a child he lies,
   Without his dart or flame.
     Phyllis, without frown or smile,
     Sat and knotted all the while.

So many months, in silence past
   And yet in raging love,
Might well deserve one word at last
   My passion should approve.
     Phyllis, without frown or smile,
     Sat and knotted all the while.

Must then your faithful swain expire,
   And not one look obtain,
Which he, to soothe his fond desire,
   Might pleasingly explain?
     Phyllis, without frown or smile,
     Sat and knotted all the while.   *Sedley.*

The Miscellaneous Works, 1702. (Poem printed 1694.)*

A SHORT VISIT

So the long absent winter sun,
   When of the cold we most complain,
Comes slow, but swift away does run;
   Just shows the day, and sets again.

So the prime beauty of the spring,
   The virgin lily, works our eyes;
No sooner blown, but the gay thing
   Steals from the admirer's sight, and dies.

The gaudy sweets o' the infant year,
   That ravish both the smell and view,
Do thus deceitfully appear,
   And fade as soon as smelt unto.

Aminta, though she be more fair
   Than untouched lilies, chaste as those,
Welcome as suns in winter are,
   And sweeter than the blowing rose:

Yet, when she brought, as late she did,
   All that a dying heart could ease,
And by her swift return forbid
   The joys to last, she 's too like these.

Ah, tryrant beauty! do you thus
   Increase our joy to make it less?
And do you only show to us
   A heaven, without design to bless?

This was unmercifully kind,
   And all our bliss too dear has cost:
For is it not a hell to find
   We had a paradise that 's lost?   *Anon.*

Miscellany Poems, IV., 1694.

WHAT CAN WE POOR FEMALES DO

   What can we poor females do,
   When pressing teasing lovers sue?
   Fate affords no other way
      But denying, or complying;

And resenting, or consenting,
            Does alike our hopes betray.   *Anon.*

H. Purcell's *Orpheus Britannicus, II.,* 1702. (Earlier in *Comes Amoris . . .
The Fifth Book,* 1694.)

A NYMPH AND A SWAIN

A nymph and a swain to Apollo once prayed,
The swain had been jilted, the nymph been betrayed:
Their intent was to try if his oracle knew
E'er a nymph that was chaste, or a swain that was true.

Apollo was mute, and had like t' have been posed,
But sagely at length he this secret disclosed:
'He alone won't betray in whom none will confide;
And the nymph may be chaste that has never been tried.'

Love for Love, 1695.*   *Congreve.*

SONG

Fair, and soft, and gay, and young,
All charm! she played, she danced, she sung!
There was no way to 'scape the dart,
No care could guard the lover's heart.
'Ah! why,' cried I, and dropped a tear
(Adoring, yet despairing e'er
To have her to myself alone),
'Was so much sweetness made for one?'

But growing bolder, in her ear
I in soft numbers told my care:
She heard, and raised me from her feet,
And seemed to glow with equal heat.

Like heaven's, too mighty to express,
My joys could but be known by guess.
'Ah, fool!' said I, 'what have I done,
To wish her made for more than one?'

But long she had not been in view,
Before her eyes their beams withdrew:
Ere I had reckoned half her charms,
She sank into another's arms.
But she, that once could faithless be,
Will favour him no more than me:
He, too, will find he is undone,
And that she was not made for one.   *Gould.*

The Rival Sisters, 1696. (Acted 1695.)*

AN ODE

The merchant, to secure his treasure,
    Conveys it in a borrowed name:
Euphelia serves to grace my measure,
    But Chloe is my real flame.

My softest verse, my darling lyre,
    Upon Euphelia's toilet lay;
When Chloe noted her desire
    That I should sing, that I should play.

My lyre I tune, my voice I raise;
    But with my numbers mix my sighs:
And whilst I sing Euphelia's praise,
    I fix my soul on Chloe's eyes.

Fair Chloe blushed, Euphelia frowned;
   I sung and gazed, I played and trembled;
And Venus to the Loves around
   Remarked, how ill we all dissembled.   *Prior.*

Poems on Several Occasions, 1721. (Poem written c. 1695 ?)*

PASTORELLA

A lass there lives upon the green,
   Could I her picture draw;
A brighter nymph was never seen;
That looks and reigns a little queen
   And keeps the swains in awe.

Her eyes are Cupid's darts and wings,
   Her eyebrows are his bow;
Her silken hair the silver strings
Which sure and swift destruction brings
   To all the vale below.

If Pastorella's dawning light
   Can warm and wound us so,
Her noon will shine so piercing bright
Each glancing beam will kill outright
   And every swain subdue.   *Sheers(?)*

Oroonoko, 1696. (Acted 1695.)

CELIA AND BELINDA

'Tell me, Belinda, prithee do,'
   The wanton Celia said,
'Since you 'll allow no lover true,
   Inform a tender maid,

Are not we women fools then to be so?'
Belinda, smiling, thus her sex betrayed:
  'Men have their arts, and we have eyes,
  We both believe and both tell lies;
  Though they a thousand hearts pursue,
  We love to wound as many too;
Yet still with virtue! virtue! keep a pother:
      We look, we love,
      We like, we leave,
      We both deceive,
And thus are fools to one another.'   *Cibber.*

Woman's Wit, 1697. (Acted 1696.)*

LONDON

Slaves to London, I 'll deceive you;
For the country now I leave you.
Who can bear, and not be mad,
Wine so dear and yet so bad?
Such a noise, an air so smoky,
That to stun ye, this to choke ye?
Men so selfish, false and rude,
Nymphs so young and yet so lewd?

If we play, we 're sure of losing;
If we love, our doom we 're choosing.
At the playhouse tedious sport,
Cant in city, cringe at court,
Dirt in streets, and dirty bullies,
Jolting coaches, whores and cullies,
Knaves and coxcombs everywhere:
Who that 's wise would tarry here?

Quiet harmless country pleasure
Shall at home engross my leisure.
Farewell, London! I 'll repair
To my native country air:
I leave all thy plagues behind me—
But at home my wife will find me?
O ye gods! 'Tis ten times worse!
London is a milder curse.   *Motteux.*

Love's a Jest, 1696.*

PRITHEE, CHLOE, NOT SO FAST

Prithee, Chloe, not so fast,
Let 's not run and wed in haste;
We 've a thousand things to do:
You must fly, and I pursue;
You must frown, and I must sigh;
I intreat, and you deny.
Stay!—If I am never crossed,
Half the pleasure will be lost:
Be, or seem to be, severe,
Give me reason to despair;
Fondness will my wishes cloy,
Make me careless of the joy.
Lovers may of course complain
Of their trouble and their pain;
But if pain and trouble cease,
Love, without it, will not please.   *Oldmixon.*

Poems on Several Occasions, 1696.

TO CORINNA

Those arts which common beauties move,
Corinna, you despise;

haste] hast, 1696.

You think there 's nothing wise in love,
    Or eloquent in sighs:
You laugh at ogle, cant, and song,
    And promises abuse;
But say—for I have courted long—
    What methods shall I use?

We must not praise your charms and wit,
    Nor talk of dart and flame;
But sometimes you can think it fit
    To smile at what you blame.
Your sex's forms, which you disown,
    Alas! you can't forbear,
But, in a minute, smile and frown,
    Are tender and severe.

Corinna, let us now be free,
    No more your arts pursue,
Unless you suffer me to be
    As whimsical as you.
At last the vain dispute desist,
    To love resign the field;
'Twas custom forced you to resist,
    And custom bids you yield.   *Oldmixon.*

Ibid.

TO A VERY YOUNG GENTLEMAN AT A DANCING-SCHOOL

So when the Queen of Love rose from the seas
Divinely fair, in such a blest amaze
The enamoured watery deities did gaze:

As we when charming Flammin did surprise,
More heavenly bright, our whole seraglio's eyes;
And not a nymph her wonder could disguise:

Whilst with a graceful pride the lovely boy
Passed all the ladies (like a sultan) by,
Only he looked more absolute and coy.

When with an haughty air he did advance
To lead out some transported she to dance,
He gave his hand as carelessly as chance:

Attended with a universal sigh,
On her each beauty cast a jealous eye,
And quite fell out with guiltless destiny.

                                                          E. Rowe.

Poems on Several Occasions, 1696.

Dryden's *Alexander's Feast: or, The Power of Music; An Ode in Honour of
St. Cecilia's Day*, was written and printed 1697.

TO CHLOE

When, Chloe, I your charms survey,
My wandering senses run away,
My trembling heart goes pit-a-pat:
Can you not guess what I 'd be at?
Sometimes in gentle sighs I move
The air with softest breeze of love:
Sometimes like gun of largest bore
I vent my sighs with dismal roar:
Disordered, know not what I do,
And all, my dear, for love of you.

                                                          *Cheek.**

A Plot and no Plot, [1697].

fell] misprinted, fall, 1696.

IN DERISION OF A COUNTRY LIFE

Fond nymphs, from us true pleasure learn:
There is no music in a churn,
The milkmaids sing beneath the cow,
The sheep do bleat, the oxen low:
    If these are comforts for a wife,
    Defend, defend me from a country life.

The team comes home, the ploughman whistles,
The great dog barks, the turkey-cock bristles,
The jackdaws caw, the magpies chatter,
Quack, quack, cry the ducks that swim in the water:
    If these are comforts for a wife,
    Defend, defend me from a country life.

Then melancholy crows the cock,
And dull is the sound of the village clock;
The leaden hours pass slow away;
Thus yawning mortals spend the day:
    If these are comforts for a wife,
    Defend, defend me from a country life.

Ravenscroft.

The Italian Husband, 1698. (Acted 1697.)*

PHILIRA

Fly, fly, you happy shepherds, fly!
    Avoid Philira's charms;
The rigour of her heart denies
    The heaven that 's in her arms.
Ne'er hope to gaze and then retire,
    Nor, yielding, to be blessed:

Nature, who formed her eyes of fire,
  Of ice composed her breast.

Yet, lovely maid, this once believe
  A slave whose zeal you move;
The gods, alas! your youth deceive,
  Their heaven consists in love.
In spite of all the thanks you owe,
  You may reproach 'em this,
That where they did their form bestow
  They have denied their bliss.

                                    Vanbrugh.

The Provoked Wife, 1697. (Text 1698.)

THE NIGHTINGALE

Once on a time, a nightingale
  To changes prone,
Unconstant, fickle, whimsical,
  (A female one),
Who sung like others of her kind,
Hearing a well-taught linnet's airs,
Had other matters in her mind,
To imitate him she prepares.
Her fancy straight was on the wing:
    I fly, quoth she,
    As well as he;
    I don't know why
    I should not try,
As well as he, to sing.
From that day forth she changed her note,
She spoiled her voice, she strained her throat:
She did, as learned women do,

Till every thing
That heard her sing
Would run away from her—as I from you.

Vanbrugh.

Aesop, 1697.

DIANA'S HUNTING-SONG

With horns and hounds, I waken the day,
And hie to my woodland-walks away;
I tuck up my robe, and am buskined soon,
And tie to my forehead a wexing moon.
I course the fleet stag, unkennel the fox,
And chase the wild goats o'er summits of rocks;
With shouting and hooting we pierce through the sky
And Echo turns hunter and doubles the cry.
   With shouting and hooting we pierce through the sky
   And Echo turns hunter and doubles the cry.

Dryden.

The Secular Masque, 1700. (Song printed 1699.)*

SONG

How blest are lovers in disguise!
   Like gods they see, as I do thee,
Unseen by human eyes.
   Exposed to view, I 'm hid from you,
I 'm altered, yet the same:
   The dark conceals me, love reveals me—
Love which lights me by its flame.

Were you not false, you me would know;
   For though your eyes could not devise,

---

wexing] waxing.

Your heart had told you so.
　Your heart would bear with eager heat,
And me by sympathy would find:
　True love might see one changed like me,
False love is only blind.   *Farquhar.*

Love and a Bottle, 1699.

SONG

Find me a lonely cave,
　Remote from human-kind,
Dark as the midnight grave,
　And dismal as my mind;
　　There let me sigh my soul away,
　　And mourn at cruel death's delay.   *Anon.*

H. Playford's *Mercurius Musicus*, 1699.

UPON A SICKLY LADY

Corinna with a graceful air
　Her symptoms does reveal:
Such charms adorn the sickly fair
　We scarce can wish her well.

How does the pale complexion please!
　Faint looks and languid eye!
New beauties rise with her disease,
　And when she 's sick we die.   *Burnaby.*

The Reformed Wife, 1700.

LOVE 'S BUT THE FRAILTY OF THE MIND

Love 's but the frailty of the mind,
When 'tis not with ambition joined;

A sickly flame, which if not fed expires,
And feeding, wastes in self-consuming fires.

   'Tis not to wound a wanton boy,
   Or amorous youth, that gives the joy;
But 'tis the glory to have pierced a swain,
For whom inferior beauties sighed in vain.

   Then I alone the conquest prize
   When I insult a rival's eyes:
If there 's delight in love, 'tis when I see
That heart, which others bleed for, bleed for me.

Congreve.

The Way of the World, 1700.

FAIR, SWEET, AND YOUNG

Fair, sweet, and young, receive a prize
Reserved for your victorious eyes.
From crowds, whom at your feet you see,
Oh, pity and distinguish me;
As I from thousand beauties more
Distinguish you, and only you adore!

Your face for conquest was designed;
Your every motion charms my mind.
Angels, when you your silence break,
Forget their hymns to hear you speak;
But when at once they hear and view,
Are loth to mount, and long to stay with you.

No graces can your form improve,
But all are lost unless you love;

> While that sweet passion you disdain,
> Your veil and beauty are in vain.
> In pity then prevent my fate,
> For, after dying, all reprive 's too late.   *Dryden.*

Miscellany Poems, V., 1704. (Poem written not later than 1700.)

ANSWER TO CHLOE JEALOUS

Dear Chloe, how blubbered is that pretty face!
   Thy cheek all on fire, and thy hair all uncurled:
Prithee quit this caprice; and, as old Falstaff says,
   Let us e'en talk a little like folks of this world.

How canst thou presume thou hast leave to destroy
   The beauties which Venus but lent to thy keeping?
Those looks were designed to inspire love and joy:
   More ord'nary eyes may serve people for weeping.

To be vexed at a trifle or two that I writ,
   Your judgement at once, and my passion, you wrong;
You take that for fact, which will scarce be found wit:
   Od's life! must one swear to the truth of a song?

What I speak, my fair Chloe, and what I write, shows
   The difference there is betwixt nature and art:
I court others in verse, but I love thee in prose;
   And they have my whimsies, but thou hast my heart.

The god of us verse-men (you know, child) the Sun,
   How after his journeys he sets up his rest:

---

reprive 's] reprieve 's.

If at morning o'er earth 'tis his fancy to run;
   At night he reclines on his Thetis's breast.

So when I am wearied with wandering all day,
   To thee, my delight, in the evening I come;
No matter what beauties I saw in my way:
   They were but my visits, but thou art my home.

Then finish, dear Chloe, this pastoral war;
   And let us like Horace and Lydia agree;
For thou art a girl as much brighter than her,
   As he was a poet sublimer than me.   *Prior.*

Poems on Several Occasions, 1721. (Poem written not later than 1700 ?)*

A LOVER'S ANGER

As Chloe came into the room t'other day,
I peevish began, 'Where so long could you stay?
In your life-time you never regarded your hour:
You promised at two; and (pray look, child) 'tis four.
A lady's watch needs neither figures nor wheels:
'Tis enough, that 'tis loaded with baubles and seals.
A temper so heedless no mortal can bear——'
Thus far I went on with a resolute air.
'Lord bless me!' said she; 'let a body but speak:
Here 's an ugly hard rose-bud fall'n into my neck;
It has hurt me and vexed me to such a degree—
See here! for you never believe me; pray see,
On the left side my breast what a mark it has made!'
So saying, her bosom she careless displayed.
That seat of delight I with wonder surveyed,
And forgot every word I designed to have said.   *Prior.*

Ibid.

THE GARLAND

The pride of every grove I chose,
  The violet sweet, and lily fair,
The dappled pink, and blushing rose,
  To deck my charming Chloe's hair.

At morn the nymph vouchsafed to place
  Upon her brow the various wreath;
The flowers less blooming than her face,
  The scent less fragrant than her breath.

The flowers she wore along the day;
  And every nymph and shepherd said,
That in her hair they looked more gay,
  Than glowing in their native bed.

Undressed at evening, when she found
  Their odours lost, their colours past;
She changed her look, and on the ground
  Her garland and her eye she cast.

That eye dropped sense distinct and clear
  As any muse's tongue could speak,
When from its lid a pearly tear
  Ran trickling down her beauteous cheek.

Dissembling what I knew too well,
  'My love, my life,' said I, 'explain
This change of humour: prithee tell,
  That falling tear—what does it mean?'

She sighed; she smiled: and to the flowers
  Pointing, the lovely moralist said:

'See! friend, in some few fleeting hours,
    See yonder, what a change is made.

'Ah, me! the blooming pride of May
    And that of beauty are but one;
At morn both flourish bright and gay,
    Both fade at evening, pale, and gone.

'At dawn poor Stella danced and sung;
    The amorous youth around her bowed:
At night her fatal knell was rung;
    I saw, and kissed her in her shroud.

'Such as she is, who died to-day,
    Such I, alas! may be to-morrow:
Go, Damon, bid thy muse display
    The justice of thy Chloe's sorrow.'   *Prior.*

Poems on Several Occasions, 1721. (Poem written not later than 1700 ?)

TO HIS SOUL

Poor little, pretty, fluttering thing,
    Must we no longer live together?
And dost thou prune thy trembling wing,
    To take thy flight thou know'st not whither?

Thy humorous vein, thy pleasing folly,
    Lies all neglected, all forgot:
And pensive, wavering, melancholy,
    Thou dread'st and hop'st thou know'st not what.
                                                              Prior.
*Ibid.**

PHYLLIS

Phyllis is my only joy,
   Faithless as the winds or seas;
Sometimes coming, sometimes coy,
   Yet she never fails to please;
     If with a frown
     I am cast down,
     Phyllis smiling,
     And beguiling,
Makes me happier than before.

Though, alas! too late I find
   Nothing can her fancy fix,
Yet the moment she is kind,
   I forgive her all her tricks;
     Which though I see,
     I can't get free;
     She deceiving,
     I believing;
What need lovers wish for more?   *Sedley.*

The Miscellaneous Works, 1702. (Poem written not later than 1700?)*

AMONG THE VIOLETS, FAIR LILIES AND ROSES

Among the violets, fair lilies and roses,
   There a fair beauty lay all alone,
While to the valley her mind she discloses
   With many a passionate sigh and groan:
Said she, I once my promise plighted
   To one that did the like to me:
There is no torment like true love when slighted,
   I am a-weary of life, said she.

My Love takes pleasure to torture and grieve me,
　　Or else he 'd ne'er let me feel the smart;
For more than cruel he was sure to leave me
　　When he had conquered my yielding heart:
Long did he woo and was refusëd;
　　At length I did to love agree,
But my good nature he now has abusëd,
　　I am a-weary of life, said she.

In sleepy raptures I often am taken,
　　For then my Love he does pleasant seem;
But when from slumbers, at length I awaken
　　And find it is but a golden dream,
Then is my passion soon increasëd
　　To such a vast and high degree,
That by pale death I would fain be releasëd,
　　Being a-weary of life, said she.

Was I to wander from this land and nation,
　　Yet he would always be in my mind;
Love in my heart has made a deep impression;
　　I cannot waver with every wind:
Therefore it is my whole desire
　　This very minute to be free,
Here in this valley alone to expire,
　　Being a-weary of life, said she.

How many sorrowful sighs did he send me
　　Before I ever would grant him love!
And many thousand soft kisses did lend me,
　　Calling to witness the powers above,
That if I would but once believe him,
　　Never was man more true than he;

Thus to my grief I too soon did receive him,
   Now I am weary of life, said she.

When he first saw me, he called it his duty,
   To love and honour me every way,
Then he 'd admire the charms of my beauty,
   And in these words he would often say
That I an angel did resemble,
   Let me not die for love of thee:
Thus you may see how young men can dissemble;
   I am a-weary of life, said she.

While he did flatter I thought he was loyal,
   And loth that he should love's pains endure;
Yet found him false, when once come to the trial,
   Never was man more ungrateful sure:
Here do I languish unregarded
   By him that ought to pity me;
Thus for good will I am evil rewarded,
   Now I am weary of life, said she.

Then a keen blade to her breast she directed,
   Giving a deep and a fatal wound;
Dying, she on her false lover reflected,
   You did my blessings and joys confound.
Then as the blood in streams was flowing,
   In tears she wept most bitterly,
Farewell, false lover, for now I am going
   To the Elysium shades, said she.   *Anon.*

Bodley, Douce Ballads, I. 66. (Poem written not later than 1700.)*

A LOVE SONG

Sabina has a thousand charms
   To captivate my heart;
Her lovely eyes are Cupid's arms,
   And every look a dart:
But when the beauteous idiot speaks,
   She cures me of my pain;
Her tongue the servile fetters breaks
   And frees her slave again.

Had Nature to Sabina lent
   Beauty with reason crowned,
Each single shaft her eyes had sent
   Had given a mortal wound;
Now though each hour she gains a heart,
   And makes mankind her slave,
Yet like the Grecian hero's dart,
   She heals the wounds she gave.   *Anon.*

J. Blow's *Amphion Anglicus*, 1700.*

ODE ON SOLITUDE

Happy the man, whose wish and care
A few paternal acres bound,
Content to breathe his native air
    In his own ground:

Whose herds with milk, whose fields with bread,
Whose flocks supply him with attire;
Whose trees in summer yield him shade,
    In winter, fire:

Blest, who can unconcern'dly find
Hours, days, and years, slide soft away
In health of body, peace of mind,
     Quiet by day,

Sound sleep by night; study and ease
Together mixed; sweet recreation,
And innocence which most does please,
     With meditation.

Thus let me live, unseen, unknown;
Thus unlamented let me die,
Steal from the world, and not a stone
     Tell where I lie.

                                 A. Pope.

The Works, 1735–7. (Poem written 1700.)*

ABBREVIATIONS,
NOTES TEXTUAL
& BIOGRAPHICAL,
& INDEXES

ABBREVIATIONS AND REFERENCES

[n.d.] No date printed on title-page or colophon of book.

[c. 1667] The approximate date of an undated book or MS.

[1667] Date, originally omitted, supplied by extraneous evidence.

(Registered 1667) Year of Entry in Registers of the Stationers' Company.

(?) A Note of Interrogation implies a doubtful ascription of date or author, according to position.

* An Asterisk refers to a note dealing with authorship, date, text, or source, or with the reprinting of the poem in the various poetical collections of the period. To save repetition, however, any question affecting a group of poems (*e.g.* several poems from the same MS.) is discussed in a note to the *first* poem of the particular group; and accordingly an asterisk is affixed to that poem only.

B.M.——British Museum.

Bodley——Bodleian Library.

G. E. Bentley——*The Jacobean and Caroline Stage.*

C.B.E.L.——*Cambridge Bibliography of English Literature.*

Camb.——*Cambridge History of English Literature.*

Ch. Ch.——Christ Church, Oxford.

Coll.——Poetical Collection cited in 'A Short-Title List' on pp. 519 ff.

D.N.B.——*Dictionary of National Biography.*

A. Nicoll.——*A History of Restoration Drama.*

O.E.D.——*Oxford English Dictionary.*

Pepys——Quotation from 'The Diary' Ed. by H. B. Wheatley.

R.E.S.——*Review of English Studies.*

Times Lit. Sup.——*Times Literary Supplement.*

NOTES

(The initial numbers refer to the pages on which an asterisk appears. When a poem is stated to occur in the Collections—e.g. 'in Colls. 27, 36, 104' —the reference is the numbered Short-Title List appended to these Notes; such references including also variants of the poem concerned in the note)

2. The following note (the reader should perhaps be reminded), which details my discoveries about the Countess of Pembroke's epitaph, was written in 1927, when Jonson was, more often that not, still credited with its authorship. These famous lines appeared in print at a much earlier date than had previously been recorded. The text I follow was published in 1623, that is, in the second year after the Countess's death. But, as in all the early printed texts, no author's name is appended to the poem. In addition to this new text, I was able to cite a manuscript attribution of these verses to Browne, likewise earlier than any yet recorded, which, in connection with the known evidence, may, I think, be fairly said to establish his claim to them. These verses, subscribed 'W. Browne,' appear in *Bodley MS. Rawl. Poet. 160*, the actual transcription of which is officially stated to be c. 1640; and I have not found anything in it which would conflict with the assigned date in any way. The earliest known association of the poem with Browne's name has until now been its presence among his miscellaneous verse in the well-known *B.M. Lansdowne MS. 777* (43b), said to be in his autograph; a little later ascription being the copy of the epitaph subscribed 'William Browne' in the Trinity College, Dublin, MS. [date c. 1650], mentioned in *Poems of William Browne*, Ed. by G. Goodwin, [n.d.]. There is also John Aubrey's testimony in his manuscript *Naturall Historie of Wiltshire (Bodley MS. Aubrey 1-2)*, in which he has copied out the first stz. and written beneath it:—'These verses were made by Mr. Browne who wrote the Pastoralls: and they are inserted there'; the latter part of the statement being obviously incorrect. Aubrey's MS. is dated 1685 on the title-page; but there are later additions, almost down to the time of his death in 1697. Lastly, Browne himself is thought by Mr. Goodwin (*op. cit.*) to have referred to this epitaph in the concluding lines of his *Elegy* on the Countess's grandson, Charles, Lord Herbert of Cardiff:

> And since my weak and saddest verse
> Was worthy thought thy grandam's herse,
> Accept of this!

It is possible of course; but it must be admitted that Browne had also written an *Elegy* on the Countess (180 lines), to which the lines in question may equally refer. That the epitaph has often been attributed to Ben Jonson, is due first and last to Whalley, who included a variant of the first stz. in his edition of Jonson's *Works*, 1756, because it was 'universally assigned' to him 'tho' it hath never yet been printed with his works.' The epitaph was also included in the posthumous *Poems* of Pembroke (son of the Countess) and Ruddier (Rudyerd), 1660; but as this volume contains a number of pieces not written by them, Pembroke's claim cannot seriously be upheld in face of the cumulative evidence, above summarized, of Browne's authorship. The poem appears in many MSS., the earliest I have seen being *Bodley MS. Ashm. 781*, in which it was written before 1630; and it is also to be found in Colls. 11, 24, 26.

3. For date, see *The Poems . . . of Edward, Lord Herbert*, Ed. by G. C. M. Smith, 1923.

5. The song is indicated, but not printed, in the 1647 folio. It was ascribed to H. Harrington when first printed in Coll. 37. It is also found in Colls. 47, 74a, 86, 95.

8. Hanney's 'Song' reappears later in Coll. 39a.

10. Wither's poem appears in Colls. 45, 47, 74a, 95.

12. Walton says Donne wrote this 'on his former sick-bed'; this illness is dated 1623 by the *D.N.B.* and by other biographies; (see also note 74). The Hymn appears late in the century in Colls. 171, 248.

14. Line 5, Your beds of wanton down the best, 1647; Your bed of wanton down 's the best, 1679. The apostrophe marking the abbreviated 'is' was often omitted. I have supplied it in 'bed's'; in which connection note also, 'your horse,' l. 16, is in the singular too. Line 9, both editions omit the comma after 'best' which I print to clarify the meaning of 'ring': *cf.* the 1661 text (Coll. 73), 'Call for the best till the house doth ring.' The poem appears in Colls. 48, 73, 90a, 92, 94, 123, 146a, 262.

14. *D.N.B.* cites the 'Office Book' of Sir H. Herbert, Master of the Revels, as the authority for the joint authorship of this play. The song appears in Colls. 90a, 94, 146a.

16. Dated by E. Malone's Note in his copy of the play, in which he quotes Sir H. Herbert (see above).

16. 'These Juvenilia, most of them the issues of your youthful Muse,' is the Publishers' description of the 1657 volume. King was aged 32 in 1624, the probable year of his wife's death; before which date it is generally agreed that his lighter lyrics, this among them, had been written. This song appears in Colls. 109, 162.

18. This song was included after I had made the final examination of the Collections; but I do not remember its occurence in any of them.

19. Variant also in Coll. 39a.

23. It seems to be practically certain that King's wife died in 1624; but actual evidence is, I believe, still lacking.

24. This song has not, I think, been printed before. Stz. 1, also occurs in *Ch. Ch. MS. 87*, which is dated on flyleaf 1624.

26. Except for the extra stz., omitted in 1647, the 1648 text is inferior to the one I print. The poem also occurs in *Bodley MS. Mal. 19*. Date: *temp.* Jas. I, before Charles I 'came in,' (see stz. 4).

27. This play is not included in 1647 folio. The song appears in Colls. 29, 45, 90a.

28. Claimed for Strode by B. Dobell (see *The Poetical Works of William Strode*, 1907), and also by Malone on the evidence of *Bodley MS. Mal. 21*. In this MS. however the poem itself is not signed, but is followed by a reply 'Against Melancholy' subscribed 'Dr. Strode.' *Wit Restored*, 1658, also has both poems; the first is anonymous, as in the MS.; and the second is en-

titled 'The answer, by Dr. Stroad.' The song itself was very popular, and is said to have inspired Milton's *Il Penseroso*. I have found it in many MSS., the earliest I have noted being *Bodley MS. Eng. Poet, e. 14* [c. 1620–30]; and *B.M. Add. MS. 15227* [c. 1630]. It was first printed in Coll. 16; and is found later in Colls. 26a, 29, 45, 47, 61, 74a, 95.

30. In the broadsides, six extra stzs. occur between stzs. 5 and 6. The Forbes' text, 1666, is my authority for their omission; he however makes stz. 2 the penultimate. In the order of stzs. and in text I follow Roxb. For date, see W. Chappell's *Popular Music* [1855–7], and 1893. The poem appears in Colls. 80, 133, 264, 266, 267.

31. I have found three MS. volumes of Austin's poems, all containing this 'Carol,' and all transcribed by R. Crane; the others being *B.M. Add. MS. 34752, and B.M. Harl. MS. 3357.* The text of the carol is identical in all three.

35. Date: MS. written 1615–26; the poem occurs towards the end. It is also in *B.M. Add. MS. 27879,* and, with a different last stz., in a MS. in the possession of Mr. J. W. Brown (see the article by him, *Cornhill Magazine*, Sept. 1921). Expanded as a broadside, it also appears in Colls. 264, 276.

36. Stz. 1, also appears in *B.M. Add. MS. 24665* [1615–26].

37. No completely satisfactory text of this poem has yet come to light, though I have found two not noted in *The Poetical Works of William Basse*, Ed. by R. W. Bond, 1893. There are therefore now four known texts: *Sportive Wit*, 1656; *Wit and Drollery*, 1682; the Pepys ballad [before 1640]; and the MS. version [c. 1648–60]. The new 1656 text being on the whole the best, I reprint that, but include seven slight emendations from the others, as follows. Stz. 1, l. 6, welkin is seen, Pepys and MS.; welkin seen, 1656 and 1682. Stz. 2, l. 2, his foam, Pepys and MS.; his Son, 1656; his foine, 1682. Stz. 2, l. 6, And Black, 1682; And the Black, 1656; Black, Pepys and MS. Stz. 3, l. 5, The[y] spring from, R. W. Bond; The spring from, Pepys; That springs with, 1656; That drop from, 1682; Revived by, MS. Stz. 4, l. 7, His sport, 1682; Sports, 1656, Pepys and MS. Stz. 4, l. 9, Home again to, 1682; Home to, 1656 and Pepys; Unto, MS. Stz. 4, l. 12, carouses to, MS.; carouseth to, Pepys; carouses in, 1656 and 1682. The song is dated by a now vanished MS., known both as *The Gordon Lute Book*, and as the *Straloch MS.* There is however a description of it, with a list of its contents, in the *Gentleman's Magazine*, Feb. 1823. Its title-page ran: 'An Playing Booke for the Lute . . . Notted and collected by Robert Gordon . . . , 1627, In Februarie'; and at the end of the MS. are the words 'Finis huic libro impositus. Anno D. 1629. Ad finem. Decem. 6.' It is possible therefore for the song to be a year or two later than 1627. A transcript of the MS. by Graham is said to be in the Advocates' Library, Edinburgh. Among the tunes it contained appears 'Hunter's carrerre' (*i.e.* career), which was identified by W. Chappell (*op. cit.* note 30) with *Basse's Career*, or *Basse his careere*, the tune of this song, from which it took its name, and to which several ballads were afterwards made. The title of the song in the ballad text is 'Maister Basse his Careere'; and Izaac Walton refers to it in *The Complete Angler*, 1653, as the 'Hunter in his carrere.' 'The Hunter's Song' is the title in Colls. 51, 135.

44. This famous poem is here reprinted from the oldest printed text yet recorded—the 7th Edition of *The Crums of Comfort*, 1628, in the B.M. The book was registered Oct. 7th, 1623, but none of the early editions seems to have survived; a copy of the 10th Edition, 1629, is in Bodley. In both the 7th and 10th Editions the poem has another and very inferior stz. appended, entitled 'Verses of Man's Resurrection,' which I have relegated to this place. It runs as follows:

> Like to the seed put in earth's womb,
> Or like dead Lazarus in his tomb,
> Or like Tabitha being asleep,
> Or Jonas-like within the deep,
> Or like the night, or stars by day
> Which seem to vanish clean away:
> Even so this death man's life bereaves,
> But, being dead, man death deceives.
> The seed it springeth, Lazarus standeth,
> Tabitha wakes, and Jonas landeth,
> The night is past, the stars remain;
> So man that dies shall live again.

This stz. is also to be found, with all the others, in *B.M. Egerton MS. 923*, and, with the first stz. only, in *Ch. Ch. MS. 87*. In part or in whole, or with other stzs. on the same model, the poem has the following claimants. Quarles, in *Argalus and Parthenia . . . Newly perused, perfected and written* [1629]; (Hazlitt cites an earlier edition [London, 1622], which I have failed to trace). Wastell, in *Microbiblion*, 1629, (where the poem is appended to his metrical summary of the Bible, with one of Southwell's poems, both without ascription). Strode, in *Bodley MS. Mal. 16* [c. 1620–30], and in Dobell's MS. Francis Beaumont, in *Poems*, 1640. W. Browne, in *B.M. Lansdowne MS. 777*, 1650. H. King, in *Poems*, etc., 1657. One or more stzs. appear anonymously in numerous MSS., and also, ascribed to Quarles, in Coll. 125.

47. This appears in Colls. 31, 42, 77, 83, 85.

48. The song appears in Coll. 64.

48. Reprinted by Shirley as the second of two stzs. in *Poems*, 1646. It also occurs in Colls. 26a, 29, 90a.

49. There is in *Bodley MS. Rawl. Poet. 147*, a variant of this with four extra stzs. following stz. 4, and another at the end, all rather feeble, and subscribed 'Tho. Bonham.' Bonham died in 1629 (?)—*D.N.B.* This attribution is corroborated by John Aubrey who wrote that 'Tom Bonham . . . haz made many a good Song & Epitaph, when yᵉ shrill Sirocco blows &c.' (*Bodley MS. Wood F 39, fol. 199*). 'Swedish drum' is evidently a topical reference to Gustavus Adolphus's campaigns, probably that against the Poles, 1626–9. Charocco—Scirocco? but that of course is a warm wind in Italy. 'Rumkin' is misprinted 'Kumkin,' in 1650; it is 'Rumkin' or 'Rumken' in the other texts. The song appears also in Colls. 52, 70, 73, 89, 90a, 190, some having variant readings.

51. Most of Browne's love lyrics are supposed to have been written before his second marriage on Dec. 24th, 1628. A H. Bullen thought the Sonnets to Celia especially are assignable to the long period of betrothal, (*op. cit.* note 2). This song, also of Celia, is in much the same key and probably of the same date; and Browne included it, changing the name to 'Marina,' in Book III of *Britannia's Pastorals* (written c. 1635 ?) which he left unpublished. The two poems which follow this, are probably not later in date, and so are grouped with it for convenience.

53. This poem, 'To Chloris,' hitherto unprinted, is taken from a MS., written in the years 1625-8, on the cover of which is inscribed 'Verses by John Cobbes.'

54. Little or nothing is known of Dr. Francis Andrewes, but this MS. contains a number of his poems, two of which are dated 1629. The poem, now printed in its complete form for the first time, has hitherto been wrongly ascribed to Lancelot Andrewes, Bishop of Winchester.

56. Jonson wrote this ode after the failure of the performance of *The New Inn*, 1629. There is printed in *Reliquiae Antiquae*. Vol. I, 1841, a short poem from *B.M. M.S. Bib. Reg. 12. B.I.*, said to be in Ben Jonson's handwriting. I am however informed by the British Museum authorities that it is emphatically not Jonson's autograph. But though there can be no other reason for ascribing it to him, it remains nevertheless interesting on its own account. A slight variant of it appears later in *Merry Drollery*, 1661. In the MS. it runs as follows:

MIRTH

There was a mad lad had an acre of ground,
    And he sold it for five pounds;
He went to the tavern and drank it all out,
    Unless it were one half-crown.
        And as he went thence
        He met with a wench
            And asked her if she were willing
        To go to the tavern
        And spend eighteenpence
            And kiss for the t'other odd shilling.   *Anon.*

57. Massinger's song appears in Colls. 26a, 29, 90a.

57. There is an older and graver note about this, quite unlike Henry King's earlier love lyrics. It is frequently found in the MSS., where it is sometimes subscribed Dr. John King, or J. K., as in *Bodley MSS. Mal. 16* and *21*. It is in two MSS. written c. 1620-30, *viz. Bodley MS. Mal. 16*, and *Bodley MS. Eng. Poet. e. 14;* and it also appears in Colls. 50, 253.

58. This poem, I believe, exists in one MS. only, and there it is subscribed H. King. There is nothing by which to date it; but being in the sombre key of the preceding poem, I have placed them together. The actual MS. was written c. 1650, but it contains at least one poem dated 1630.

58. May's drama mostly dates from about 1620 to 1630, and was very un-

successful. This song however was popular enough to be retained in Colls. 24, 26, 31, 42, 77, 83; and it occurs also in Colls. 26a, 29, 90a, 146a.

59. I have included two emendations from the MS. cited. The 1655 text in l. 2, is a foot short, omitting the 'and white' of the MS.; it also loses the rhyme entirely in l. 15 with the reading: 'Are not men made for maids and maids for men?' whereas the MS. line which I print keeps it. As regards date, the MS. was written c. 1620–30. And an expanded variant of the poem, having 15 six-line stzs., was printed as a broadside (in Coll. 264) 'by the Assigns of Thos. Symcocke,' who ceased to print after their patent was cancelled by the Court of Chancery, June 30th, 1629. In addition to the texts already mentioned, the poem appears, with innumerable variants, in several MSS., and in Colls. 74a, 92, 95, 109, 162, 262.

60. Vincent was born in 1627, but there is some doubt about the date of the poem. *D.N.B.* says it was written 3 years later. The MSS. differ: *B.M. Add. MS. 25707* entitles the poem 'Upon the birth of my son Vincent Corbett'; *Bodley MS. Rawl. Poet. 147* reads 'Dr. Corbett to his son Vincent on his birthday, Novemb. 10. 1630'; other MSS. are non-committal like *Bodley MS. Ashm. 47,* with 'To his son Vincent Corbet on his birthday, R.C.' The poem was omitted in *Poetica Stromata,* 1648; but included in *Poems,* 3rd Ed., 1672.

62. From 'Nymphal III'; where the song is set for two nymphs singing alternate quatrains.

64. Seven parenthetic stzs. of invocation, not descriptive of the Ascension, follow stz. 3 in the original, but are here omitted. A final couplet follows the Song proper:

> From top of Olivet such notes did rise,
> When man's Redeemer did transcend the skies.

65. 'The Passing Bell' is found in Coll. 39a.

66. 'On Shakespeare' was first reprinted in *Poems . . . by Wil. Shakespeare. Gent. 1640.*

66. Date: the 1645 volume seems to be approximately chronological in its arrangement. This 'Sonnet,' and 'At a Solemn Music,' both occur earlier than the 1631 'Sonnet,' on reaching 'my three and twentieth year.'

68. Randolph's second stz. appears in Colls. 81, 94, 110.

68. This and the following piece are from an unprinted MS. recently acquired by the British Museum, and, at the time of writing, not yet described. It is a long allegorical pastoral in rhymed couplets with songs interspersed, divided into five books, each ending with a masque. It was written about 1630, and contains a reference to the birth of Charles II. Here is yet another song from the same source:

SONG

> Draw near, and see,
> Fond man, what joys they be
> That do attend
> To crown the end

Of toil, with soft security.
   Here no sorrows are
      To oppress;
   Nor no pinching care
To clog the soul with heaviness:
But sweet delight shall dandle thee.

   Cease to torment
Thine heart with discontent:
     Thy sweat and pain
     Will be in vain
When greedy worms thy bosom rent.
   See, delightful time
      Posts away,
   And thy beauty's prime
The wrinkled age will soon decay:
What are thou then when youth is spent?

   Stay, stay, and taste
Of joy while day doth last,
     Ere crazy night
     Bury delight:
O stay, thy time is quickly past.
   Taste, and thou shalt know
      The sweet joy
   Nature doth allow
The ravished sense of man to cloy,
And cares in soft delight to waste.   *Anon.*

71. For date, see *op. cit.* note 3. The MS. l. 8, reads 'Whither,' for 'Whether.'

72. Cowley includes these three stzs. in the essay 'Of Myself,' remarking that they are 'the latter end of an Ode, which I made when I was but thirteen years old. . . . The Beginning of it is Boyish. . . . ' They were originally stzs. 9–11 of 'A Vote,' first printed in *Sylva*, 1636.

73. The play was registered, May 16th, 1631, as '*The Noble Spanish Soldier* by Thomas Dekker'; and was published 1634 as '*The Noble Soldier*, Written by S. R.,' but having *The Noble Spanish Soldier* as the running title. Both Dekker and Rowley seem to have had a hand in the writing; but the song is probably Dekker's. It appears in Colls. 98, 101, 116, 123.

74. Sir Julius Caesar's autograph copy of this poem, in *B.M. Add. MS. 34324*, is endorsed 'Dr. Dun Dean of Pauls his verses in his great sickness, Decemb. 1623.' Izaac Walton, in his 'Life' of Donne, written within nine years of Donne's death, says, 'He writ an Hymn on his deathbed, which bears this title: *An Hymn to God, my God, in my Sickness, March 23, 1630* [*i.e.* 1631, according to modern reckoning]. The Hymn was first printed in Donne's *Poems*, 1635.

77. In stz. 2, l. 2, Roxb. reads: 'And round about this airy welkin soon'; and in stz. 6, l. 6, 'And seems.' In these two places I have followed Bishop Percy (*Reliques of Ancient English Poetry*, 1765), in omitting 'And round,' and reading 'seem' for 'seems.' This poem has 12 stzs. in the broadsides; but there is a variant of 4 stzs. in *Bodley MS. Mal. 19* [c. 1630–40]; and another of 6 stzs. in *Windsor Drollery*, 1671. I print the eight usually chosen by modern editors, *i.e.* omitting the four which, in the broadsides, follow stz. 4. 'The merry pranks of Robin Goodfellow' was registered to Henry Gosson, the printer of the Roxb. ballad, on March 23rd, 1631. The poem is also to be found in Colls. 263 (*bis*), 276.

78. This appears in Colls. 14, 29, 37, 47, 63, 74a, 88, 90a, 95; some versions having two stzs. only.

79. 'Of his Mistress' appears in Colls. 26a, 29, 90a.

80. Towards the end of the century this was absurdly ascribed to Charles I. It appears with that attribution in Colls. 171, 219, 226, 248.

82. Strode's 'On Chloris,' was exceedingly popular. It is also found in many MSS., and the following Colls. 23, 24, 26, 26a, 29, 31, 42, 47, 50, 74a, 77, 83, 90a, 95, 110, 146a, 164.

82. Philipott was one of several who were inspired by the preceding poem to attempt a 'companion piece,' but was the most successful. His poem is often found with Strode's in the MSS., and may well have been written about the same time; for which reasons I place them together.

83. Also in several MSS., and Coll. 34.

90. Printed in Coll. 40, all editions.

91. Stz. 4. 'lengthens,' Willmott's emendation (1854); 'lengthen,' 1633.

95. The title of this book is *The Strange and Dangerous Voyage of Captain Thomas James, in his intended Discovery of the Northwest Passage into the South Sea. . . .*

96. For date of performance, see *D.N.B.*

97. Nabbe's song reappears in Coll. 94.

97. Of the 14 poems in Pestel's book, none of those which are dated are earlier than 1621, or later than 1634; I have therefore put this un-dated poem 'before 1634 ?' in which year the poet would be aged 50.

100. This and the following poem of Randolph's would seem to have been written before 1634; in which year he left London for good, harassed by creditors and broken in health, to stay with his father at Little Houghton, and later with W. Stafford at Blatherwick, where he died early in 1635. His engraved portrait, which appears in some editions, represents him at the age of 27, and the original may well have been the 'picture' of the second of these two poems. (See W. C. Hazlitt's edition of Randolph's *Works*, 1875.) In the 'Ode,' stz. 6, l. 2, 'Where, at' is misprinted 'Whereat,' in 1638.

101. For date, see G. E. Bentley.

103. Heywood's song appears in Colls. 47, 74a, 95.

104. 'Sweet Echo' was reprinted in Coll. 142.

110. Emendations of the 1646 text are as follows: Stz. 3, tread, MS.; to, 1646, 1648, 1670. Stz. 6, its duty, 1670; his duty, 1646, 1648, MS. Stz. 12, its being, MS.; his being, 1646, 1648, 1670. Stz. 15, displace, outface,

grace, MS.; displaces, outfaces, graces, 1646, 1648, 1670. Stz. 18, that dares, MS.; that dare, 1646, 1648, 1670: (but note, 'that dares' is the reading of 1646 in stzs. 29 and 38). Stz. 24, slight, MS.; flight, 1646, 1648, 1670. Stz. 40, merit dares, Mod. Eds.; merit dare, 1646, 1648, 1670, MS.: (but see next line where 'modesty dares' is the reading of all four texts). Date: this and the following poem appear in *B.M. Add. MS. 33219*, [written c. 1635]; see also *The Poems . . . of Richard Crashaw*, Ed. by L. C. Martin, 1927. A variant, 10 stzs. in length, appears in Colls. 24, 26; and 14 stzs. in Colls. 31, 42, 77, 83.

111. The 1646, 1670, and MS. (*B.M. Harl. MS. 6917*) texts of this poem omit ll. 11–14. For date, see preceding note. This poem appears in Colls. 31, 42, 77, 83.

112. Variants occur in Colls. 52, 73.

114. This poem in the broadside is followed by 'The second Part. To the same tune,' which space prevents me including. The broadside was printed for C. Wright, who ceased publishing in 1639. 'Original date c. 1635,'—J. W. Ebsworth, *Roxburghe Ballads*, Vol. VI, Pt. ii., 1887. Stz. 7, l. 4, 'doth blow,' is misprinted 'doe blow,' in the original.

114. I have been unable to find this song in any of Quarles' works, though Lawes specifically names him as the author. There is however one poem in the *Emblems*, 1635, Book IV, no. 5, the second stz. of which is practically identical with it in content but not in metre. Accordingly I have dated this, 'c. 1635 ?'

116. In the *Emblems* there is, as usual, a biblical text printed at the head of the poem: 'Job. xiii. 24: Wherefore hidest thou thy face, and holdest me for thine enemy?' It is not generally known that Rochester thieved this poem (*i.e.* he or another, for it was printed posthumously, like most of his work). He placed stz. 14 between stzs. 6 and 7, and omitting stzs. 8 and 10–13, he followed on with stzs. 9, 15 and 16, and ended with the last stz. of another of the *Emblem* poems, *viz.* Book III, no. 12; then writing 'Love' for 'Lord' and 'God' throughout, and making a few other slight alterations, he addressed the result *To his Mistress*. This sham has in the past imposed on many people, and quite recently has been included in general authologies and even in some exclusively devoted to XVIIth Century verse, as one of Rochester's finest poems.

118. Date: Wither's *Emblems* is divided into four Books, each with a separate title-page. Book I, is dated 1635; Books II–IV, 1634. There is no date on the engraved pictorial title-page to the whole volume.

120. Exact dates of writing are impossible to fix for much of Cartwright's work. But in the preliminary matter of the 1651 volume, *Comedies, Tragi-Comedies, with other Poems*, the following statement is made: 'Here is but one sheet was written after he entered Holy Orders [1635 ? D.N.B.]; some before he was twenty years old [1631], scarce any after five and twenty' [1636]. The earlier part of the section containing the *Poems* is apparently chronological; this and the following poem occur between two pieces dated 1634 and 1636 respectively. With these two I have therefore grouped the other selections, which were probably written at approximately the same period.

122. The title which I print is taken from the first line of dialogue following the song. The song appears in Colls. 45, 47, 74a, 92, 95, 262.

123. This song from *The Siege* was printed in Coll. 45.

124. This also appears in Coll. 45.

125. For date, see *D.N.B.*

126. Line 6, 'heat' is misprinted 'heart,' 1641. This song occurs in several MSS., and also in Colls. 36, 39, 63, 81, 88, 92, 100, 110, 262.

127. *Luminalia* is not included in Davenant's *Works*, 1673; but is now generally attributed to him, (see *A Short-Title Catalogue*, and 'Halkett and Laing,' new edn.).

127. The Epitaph appears in Colls. 26, 31, 42, 77, 83.

128. For date of acting, see G. E. Bentley. The song appears in Colls. 26a, 29, 90a, 94, 146a, 153, 258.

129. Berkley's song appears in Colls. 47, 95. For date, see G. E. Bentley.

130. This is to be found in Coll. 125.

132. Also found in several MSS., and in Coll. 93.

133. Lines 5 and 9, whither, 1651; whether, 1640 and 1642. This song gave rise to a number of imitations, parodies, and answers. It also appeared anonymously the same year, 1640, in *Poems . . . by Wil. Shake-speare. Gent.*; and, with the subscription 'P,' in Pembroke and Rudyerd's *Poems*, 1660,—a posthumous edition containing several poems of which they were not the authors. The song is also found in Colls. 26a, 29, 39a, 61, 64, 90a, 125, 146a.

133. Like the preceding poem, this was the inspiration of many later songs on the same theme, two or three of the more successful of which the curious reader may find in these pages. It appears in Colls. 37, 86, 88, 92, 262.

134. 'To my inconstant Mistress' is in Coll. 37.

134. Stz. 2, l. 5, 'And Sol . . . his way,' omitted in 1640, is now supplied from Coll. 29 (p. 228), which includes a number of Carew's poems. This song appears also in Colls. 86, 88, 91.

135. 'Persuasions to enjoy' was the most popular of Carew's songs; it is to be found in Colls. 36, 39, 47, 63, 74a, 88, 95, 128.

137. Possibly Herbert of Cherbury wrote this poem; it is more like his work than Carew's. (See G. C. Moore Smith's ed. of Lord Herbert's poems.)

137. This song occurs in Colls. 86, 88; and a variant in 133.

138. From *Poems on Several Occasions*, 1672, in *The Works*, 1673. This section, to judge from the poems which are dated, seems to be chronological. 'The Winter Storms' occurs between poems dated 1630 and 1639.

139. This poem was first printed in 1639 by Samuel Pick in *Festum Voluptatis*, a volume of poems of which he implicitly claims the authorship, though at least seven other hands are present. It next appeared in Carew's posthumous *Poems*, 1640, which includes a few pieces now known to be by other people. The poem in both these books contains four stanzas, and begins: 'O Think not, Phoebe, 'cause a cloud.' Our text, however, follows the three-stanza version beginning: 'Think not, my Phoebe, 'cause a cloud,' included by Shirley in his *Poems &c.*, 1646, the authorship of which volume he explicitly claims, though there is some doubt

about one or two pieces. Shirley would seem the most probable author.
The penultimate stanza he omitted reads—

> When thou dost touch the lute, thou may'st
> Think on my heart, on which thou play'st,
>   When each sad tone
> Upon the strings doth show my deeper groan;
> When thou dost please they shall rebound,
> With nimble air struck to the sound
>   Of thine own voice:
> O think how much I tremble, and rejoice.

142. This poem, expanded to more than twice its length, is often ascribed
to W. Cleland (1661 ?–1689), it having appeared in that form in his posthumous work, *A Collection of Several Poems and Verses*, 1697. Another
long variant was popular as a broadside. There were imitations or parodies
of it, one of them—written by R. Wild, with the burden 'Alas poor
Scholar! whither wilt thou go?'—is in *Iter Boreale*, 1668; this however
was not its first appearance, for it occurs in *Wit and Drollery*, 1656 and
1661; it is also found in other collections, and was, according to J. W.
Ebsworth (*Roxburghe Ballads*, VI, iii., 1888), written c. 1641. *Hollo, my
fancy* was apparently registered as a ballad, Dec. 30th, 1639, under the
title *Ha ha, my fancy etc.*, (the entries in the Registers frequently differ
from the printed titles of the publications concerned). The MS. itself was
written c. 1650, and represents, I believe, the original text. The various
expansions of the poem appear in Colls. 256, 264, 266.

142. 'Farewell, fair saint,' was first printed in *Poems: Written by Wil.
Shake-speare. Gent. 1640;* and is found in many MSS., of which at least
two are of approximately the same date, viz. *Bodley MS. Rawl. Poet. 160*,
and W. Lawes' autograph, *B.M. Add. MS. 31432*, where it is set to music
by Lawes himself, who died 1645. The poem is ascribed to 'Mr. T. C.' in
1647, and to 'Mr. Thomas Cary, Son to the Earl of Monmouth,' by
Henry Lawes in 1653. Lines 7–12 are sometimes omitted. The poem is
also found in Colls. 37, 50, 86, 88, 93, 125.

144. Date of writing: Fletcher would be on the verge of 60 years of age
in 1640; and as the 'Preface' says the book was written for the benefit of
his children and relations, it seems more likely to have been written earlier
than later.

144. The MS. from which this and the following song were taken, was
written c. 1650. That does not, of course, preclude an earlier date for the
songs themselves. And as these two are utterly unlike what was being
written after the Civil War, I have ventured to date them ten years earlier
than the actual transcription of the MS.

147. This poem was not included in the previous editions of 1634 and
1635.

149. Shirley included this in his *Poems*, 1646.

149. *The Discontented Colonel* was the original title of *Brennoralt*. There
is some doubt about its exact date.

150. 'Fatum Supremum' was reprinted in the 1641 edition (Coll. 24).

151. 'The Sympathy' appears also in Coll. 65, with ten additional stzs.

151. I have found this song, 'On a Lady Sleeping,' in the two MSS. cited, and nowhere else; and it is now, I believe, printed for the first time. The footnote shows my emendation in l. 7, which I think restores the original reading.

152. Felltham prints this in *Lusoria*, 1661, saying it was 'written by a Gentlewoman,' and below it gives his 'answer' to it.

152. Beedome's song appears in Colls. 39a, 55, 132.

153. The song is found with or without variants in Colls. 26a, 29, 63, 71, 88, 89, 90a, 100, 110, 190.

158. The wedding thus celebrated was that of Baron Broghill, later Earl of Orrery (one of our poets, see p. 288), who married Lady Margaret Howard, a daughter of the second Earl of Suffolk; and it is generally supposed that the 'Dick' of the 'Ballad' was the poet, Richard Lovelace. I have chosen the 1648 text as being the best of the three, both from the textual and narrative points of view. But, as a matter of fact, it really varies very little from the others, except for the transposition of stz. 14, which, in the other two editions, with the order of its first three and last three lines reversed, follows our present stz. 16. The poem was received with instant approbation, and, in spite of changing fashions, parodies, and imitations, retained its place in the public affection for the rest of the century. It appears in Colls. 31, 42, 68, 70, 77, 83, 89, 92, 135, 137, 148, 159, 190, 232, 235, 258, 262.

159. This nonsense rhyme is entitled 'Interrogativa Cantilena' in the text. It was probably inspired by the following little song of an earlier date which has survived in *B.M. Add. MS. 22601*, [c. 1603]:

> If all the Earthe were paper white
> and all the sea were incke
> 'Twere not inough for me to write
> as my poore hart doth thinke.   *Anon.*

The later verses appear also in Colls. 24, 26, 31, 42, 77, 83.

160. The 'Kiss' is found in Colls. 24, 26, 31, 42, 77, 83; and in an abbreviated form (omitting the last 14 lines) in Coll. 29.

162. 'Of thee, kind boy' appears in Colls. 36, 39, 63, 88, and twice in 47, 74a, 95.

162. This well-known song was not included in Suckling's works until 1659. It had previously appeared in Colls. 39, 47, and stzs. 1 and 2 in Coll. 56; in the first two it is anonymous, and in the third attributed to Hughes by H. Lawes, who must have known Hughes personally. The publisher of *The Last Remains*, 1659, did in fact include as Suckling's a poem by another author, namely Felltham (as I show in note 321); which does not add to one's confidence in his ascription of the present poem. Nevertheless, judging from the two men's work, I am inclined to think this is Suckling's, but have queried his name as author to draw attention to the above facts. The song also appears in Colls. 74a, 79, 95, 258; and a variant of stzs. 1 and 2 in Coll. 237.

163. Both Suckling's song and Mathews' answer are in Colls. 52, 73, 91, 94, 146a.

164. See preceding note. Date of writing unknown, but most probably this 'Answer' was written during Suckling's lifetime.

165. There is no title to the poem in the 1653 volume. I have adopted Browne's phrase which precedes and introduces the poem.

166. The song appears in Coll. 236.

170. 'To Chloris' is also found in *B.M. Harl. MS. 3991,* and with a variant first line: 'It is not, Chloris, your disdain,' in Coll. 103.

170. It is quite impossible to say when this and the following poem (supposing that to be Townshend's) were written. *D.N.B.* gives his date as '*fl.* 1601–43'; but some evidence has recently transpired to prove him still alive in 1651 (*Knole and the Sackvilles,* by V. Sackville-West, 1922). His period of greatest literary activity seems to have been c. 1632, when his masques were produced at Court; and as he must have been nearly 60 years of age in 1643, it is more than probable that these songs were written before, rather than after, that year.

171. For the attribution to Townshend (for which, however, no reason is given) see *Choyce Drollery,* Ed. by J. W. Ebsworth, 1876. The poem appears in Colls. 47, 48, 74a, 92, 95, 262.

173. The different texts of this famous poem contain many variant readings. In default of an authoritative text, I have chosen that which seems to me the best. The poem occurs in *B.M. Harl. MS. 3889;* and also in Coll. 264, where it is followed (as in Coll. 256) by a 'Second Part,' 13 stzs., beginning 'My dear and only Love, take heed.' According to W. Chappell (*op. cit.* note 30), and J. W. Ebsworth (*Bagford Ballads,* 1876, and *op. cit.* note 142), this 'Second Part' is not Montrose's, but an expansion of an earlier song, c. 1625, which, in its original form of 5 stzs., is to be found in Coll. 52. It is at least certain that several ballads, dating from 1618 to 1628, were written to the tune of 'I'll never love thee more;' and that Montrose in writing his poem adapted the older ballad form and its burden. His song is dated by the topical political references in it; *e.g.* 'synod' being an allusion to the Assembly of Divines held at Westminister in 1643. Stz. 4, l. 6, And go, MS. and Coll. 264; And goes, 1711.

173. This anonymous song was a great favourite, and is found in a number of MSS., amongst them one (*B.M. Sloane MS. 396*) written c. 1644, but which omits lines 7–10. It also appears in Colls. 36, 39, 47, 63 (*bis*), 65, 74a, 81, 88, 91, 95, 100, 110, 128, 133.

174. 'Gather ye rose-buds' was set to music by W. Lawes (who died 1645), and appears in his autograph, *B.M. Add. MS. 31432.* It was the most popular poem of the latter half of the century, and is to be found in Colls. 26a, 29, 35, 36, 39, 55, 63, 71, 77, 79, 81, 83, 87, 88, 89, 90a, 94, 100, 109, 110, 125, 128, 129, 133, 147, 162, 190; and in at least 13 different editions of *A Brief Introduction* [later *An Introduction . . .*] *to the Skill of Music,* between 1655 and 1700.

175. Strode's poem is to be found in several MSS., and in Colls. 29, 50, 61, and variants in 26a, 90a.

176. This poem of Strode's follows the reading of MS. 30982, except in

stz. 1, l. 3, where the MS. has: "Methought landscape here was spread'; instead of which I have printed the reading of MS. 19268. Both MSS. have
4 stzs.; I have omitted the third, which to my mind lets the whole poem
down. I print it here however (the text is the same in both MSS.)—

> The slender food upon the down
> Is all ways even, all ways bare,
> Which neither spring, nor winter's frown
> Can aught improve, or aught impare:
> Such is the barren eunuch's chin,
> Which thus doth evermore begin
> With tender down to be o'ercast
> Which never comes to hair at last.

176. 'A Catch' was set to music by W. Lawes (d. 1645). It is found in
Colls. 32, 34, 57, 68, 75, 79, 81, 89, 92, 100, 110, 190, 262.

178. In Howell's *Poems*, 1664, stz. 4, l. 5, is altered to 'And, by those spells
I am possessed'; otherwise the texts agree. The poem is in Colls. 48, 113.

179. The Lullaby occurs in a poem entitled 'An Alarm in 1645.'

180. 'The Secret' was written at the time of the Civil War, before the
Royalists' hopes began to fade: I have dated it accordingly. The poem was
first printed in my *Unfamiliar Lyrics*, and is a late arrival here. In l. 11, the
MS. reads, oft; and in l. 16, besides.

181. The MS. from which these four poems are taken is in the Duke's own
handwriting. It is entitled, *The Phanseys of the/Marquesse of Newcastle/
Sett by him in verse/att Paris the*. The second leaf is inscribed, 'These following Verses to Mrs:/Margarett Lucas before/hee Married her'. They were
married in Paris, 1645. The MS. contains the Duchess's writing in several
places; and the volume ends with some later poems by the Duke, which seem
to have been added from time to time; a number of these were included in
his plays, and were published in his lifetime. The poems of the betrothal
period have never, I believe, been printed before. See also Note 438.

181. I could not resist including these two stzs., but there is a third stz.
which is distinctly poor and not too intelligible. It runs thus in the MS.—

> You doe excell, Nature thought fitt
>> So too in witt
> And Judgment too, wher you doe come
>> Wee'r all struck dumme
> A mas'd with your discourse, when heare
>> Rauisht each eare
> So Orfious Harpe doth stringe your tongue of loue
> And when you Play, makes trees, and Rockes, to moue.

182. Stz. 3, l. 1, MS. reads 'sables.' Perhaps the line should be 'Your sables,
robe divine'; but the MS. has no comma, and 'sables' (see *O.E.D.*) seems to
have meant 'mourning garments' only. Here the poet is contrasting the ef-

fects of white, yellow, and black dresses, and there is no suggestion of bereavement. The *O.E.D.* cites 'sable' only as the adjective.

184. Walker's famous song appears in Colls. 46, 77, 83, 86, 88.

185. 'To a Lady singing' appears in Coll. 233.

186. This appears in Colls. 77, 83.

187. *Sighs* is evidently derived from a poem by Lady Mary Wroath. The first stz. is with variations the same as that of 'Song 2' of 'Pamphilia to Amphilanthus' in her *Urania*, 1621; though the two other stzs. differ completely from Lady Mary's remaining five stzs. The song is to be found in Colls. 26, 31, 42, 77, 83.

194. Slight variants of this appear in Colls. 31, 42, 77, 83; and in at least six edns of Cleveland's poems between 1659 and 1699.

196. The Hymn occurs in *The Second Book/of/Divine Poems*, 1647, which has a separate title-page, but the pagination and signatures are continuous with those of *Poems*, 1646, with which it is bound.

196. *Cock-throwing* was later reprinted in Colls. 31, 42, 77, 83.

199. The text of L'Estrange's famous poem presents many difficulties, no two early versions being alike. They may differ in the text, in the number or order of the stzs., or even in the title, which, in addition to the one I print, may read—'The Liberty of the Imprisoned Royalist' (or variations on it); 'Merry Thoughts in a sad Place'; or the later 'Loyalty Confined.' The poem was first printed, under the first title quoted above, with two other pieces in an anonymous and undated pamphlet in 1647 (*Thomason Tracts*, I, p. 532). The text I print is, however, that of the earliest MS. of the poem yet discovered, which is not only the best but hitherto has never been printed. There is also another MS. text (*B.M. Sloane MS. 1454*) of a little later date, having two more stzs and some variant readings. Only in two places has a slight emendation been necessary: the Harl. MS. (like the 1647 printed text) in stz. 1, l. 5, reads 'surely,' which I have corrected to 'surly' in accordance with the Sloane MS. and some 1656 printed texts; and in stz. 2, l. 5, the Harl. MS. omits 'walls,' which I have restored on the authority of practically all the other texts. The poem also appears in Colls. 50, 52, 73, 74, 93.

201. Of something like a score of editions of Cleveland's *Poems*, I have chosen the last one published in his lifetime, and have collated that text with the 1647 edition, *Optima & novissima Editio*, which included this poem (there were others that year without it), and also with *Poems*, 1653, and the *Genuine Poems*, 1677. Stz. 4, l. 7, art's; the MSS. cited in the footnote are *Bodley MS. Ashm. 47*, and *Bodley MS. Rawl. Poet. 147*. The poem appears in other MSS., and in Coll. 93.

201. 'My Diet' appears in Colls. 90a, 92, 127, 144, 149, 203, 262.

202. This is found in Coll. 127.

203. Reprinted in Colls. 84, 90a, 92, 94, 127, 146a, 262.

206. Settle, in his dramatization of *Pastor Fido*, 1677, includes Fanshawe's song, but substitutes 'time' for 'it,' l. 1. Fanshawe's 'it' refers to time, but the song being taken out of its context, the sense becomes obscure; so much so that 'it' has been taken by some editors to mean 'beauty,' and accordingly they have entitled the song, 'Of Beauty.' It appears in Coll. 162.

208. Herrick evidently intended *Noble Numbers* to be published before *Hesperides*, with which it was ultimately issued in 1648; for it has a separate title-page and pagination and is dated 1647. I have taken advantage of this fact to separate his religious from his secular poems.

212. Reprinted in Coll. 46.

215. This now famous poem was, of course, first discovered and printed by A. H. Bullen. The musical setting was composed by Thomas Forde, who died in 1648.

216. This poem was first printed in my anthology, *The Poets' Life of Christ*, 1922. It was set to music by Thomas Forde (died 1648).

216. This song was set to music by Forde (see note 215). A. H. Bullen was the first to discover this song, but in printing it, omitted 'bright,' in l. 3; and l. 5, printed 'these' instead of 'those'; in which oversights he has since been followed by other editors who have not collated their texts.

224. This appears in Colls. 36, 39, 47, 55, 63, 74a, 88, 95, 239.

225. It is rather interesting to compare stzs. 1 and 2 with Jonson's first 'Gipsy Song' on p. 1.

227. This appears in Colls. 29, 90a.

231. In the 2nd Ed., 1659, l. 1 reads 'Time is the feathered thing.' The song appears in Coll. 45.

232. The MS. was transcribed in the reign of Charles I, and the song was printed in Coll. 172.

232. 'On a Rosebud' is from the MS. mentioned in the preceding note, but it has not hitherto appeared in print.

237. *Bodley MS. Ashm.* 36–7, and Coll. 64, read 'birds' instead of 'gods' in stz. 1, l. 7. The poem also appears in Colls. 63, 64, 87, 88, 129, 147, 265, 276.

240. T. Beaumont is a new name among XVIIth Century poets, his work having never been printed before. His poems are taken from a MS., almost certainly the poet's autograph, written c. 1640–50.

242. There is a curious parallel in this poem (stz. 3, ll. 5–8) to W. Browne's 'Celia is gone,' stz. 4 (see p. 50); yet Browne's poem was not printed until 1815, and this never until now. In stz. 2, l. 6, the MS. reads 'darkning.'

243. The MS. was written c. 1650. The song is also found in *Bodley MS. Mus. b. 1*, written before 1656, and variants in Colls. 60, 159, 232, 252.

243. Date of MS.: c. 1650.

244. It is the opinion of Cotton's recent editors that this song was probably written on the death of Montrose, 1650. See *Poems of Charles Cotton*, Ed. by J. Beresford, 1923; and *The Life and Poetry of Charles Cotton*, by C. J. Sembower, 1911. But Mr. Beresford also mentions the possibility that 'Montross' may be the name of the tune; as such however I have been unable to trace it.

245. This song is ascribed to 'Phill. King' in the MS., and to Sir John Eaton in Dryden's *Examen Poeticum*, 1693. It appears in several MSS. and in Colls. 63, 88, 199.

246. Turnsole was the general name for any flower which turned with the sun, but at that date seems to have been most frequently applied to flowers of the heliotrope class. It may just possibly mean the sunflower.

246. This appears in Colls. 64, 73, 92, 262.

248. Subscribed 'G. Morley' in the MS. but is ascribed to Strode by B. Dobell (Poetical Works, p. 62) as the last part of a long poem. It is anonymous in Colls. 43, 49.

254. The original text has no title; I have therefore used l. 2.

259. I have found and collated six texts of 'The Hunting,' and none of them are completely satisfactory. I print the best (1672), but this has to be helped out with a few readings from *Bodley MS. Rawl. Poet. 147* (written c. 1650), and *Sportive Wit*, 1656, as follows. Stz. 1, l. 8, the hunting, 1656; once hunted, 1672. Stz. 3, l. 5, Who, MS.; And, 1672. Stz. 4, l. 8, With, 1656 and MS.; And, 1672. Stz. 5, l. 6, Maia, 1656 and MS.; May, 1672. Stz. 6, l. 2, Roused, 1656 and MS.; Raised, 1672. Stz. 7, l. 2, Harper MS.; Harpye, 1672. Stz. 7, l. 3, Rend, MS.; Rent, 1672. Stz. 9, ll. 7–8, Only I measure the jewel of pleasure,/Of pleasure the treasure is, MS.; Only as measures the jewel of pleasures,/Of pleasures the treasures of, 1672. For authorship, see the *Thurloe State Papers*, IV, 717–8, where, in an 'Examination' of one N. Brooks (April 19, 1656), it is definitely stated that Walter Wasse was the author of 'the hunting of the gods.' The poem also appears in *B.M. Add. MS. 27879* (dated, like the Bodley MS., c. 1650), and in Colls. 135, 199.

260. Patrick Carey has a song (date 1651) written to the tune of 'I'll have my Love, or I'll have on,' which must be the tune to which this song was originally sung. (See next note.)

262. Carey's poems remained for the most part in MS. until they were published by Sir Walter Scott in 1820 (Preface dated 1819); and the MS. from which Scott printed them seems to have disappeared. Having failed, in spite of a diligent search and many enquiries, to trace it, I have been compelled to print from the 1820 text. In addition to the London publication of a few of the poems in 1771, noted by Saintsbury (*Caroline Poets*, II.), the 'Hymn' appeared in *The Weekly Magazine*, Edinburgh, May 23, 1771.

268. 'The Vow' appears in Colls. 77, 83.

269. I have been unable to obtain a fresh collation of the texts of Beaumont's two poems; Prof. Palmer, of Harvard University, U.S.A., the owner of the MS., being away from home at the time of my application to him. He, however, vouches for the accuracy of Miss Eloise Robinson's text, from which I print the poems. I have, however, modernized Beaumont's antique spelling reproduced in her book: *The Minor Poems of Joseph Beaumont*.

270. 'Chode' is an old past tense of 'chide'; and 'prevent' means 'forestall.'

272. The 'Song' appears again in Coll. 39.

273. 'At Parting' is to be found in *Bodley MS., Mus. b. I*, which supplies 'Our nights' (stz. 2, l. 3) where 1652 reads 'Our eyes.' The song is in Colls. 39, 63, 64, 88.

274. This also occurs in *B.M. Harl. MS. 3991*, and in Colls. 39, 63, 88, 109, 162, and, expanded to 10 stzs., in Colls. 267, 268, 276.

275. For the date of Marvell's poems, see *The Poems of Andrew Marvell*, Ed. by G. A. Aitken, 1898.

281. Stz. 7, 'combs' was the original text, the 1726 ed. reads 'claps.'

285. Flecknoe included this song with slight variants in *Love's Dominion*, 1654, and *Love's Kingdom*, 1664.

288. Line 12, 'yon cloud,' misprinted 'you cloud,' 1665; 'yond cloud,' 1653. The poem appears in Colls. 37, 86, 88.

289. Orrery's song was reprinted in Colls. 63, 68, 88, 100, 110, 137, 148.

290. Shirley's song is also found in Coll. 130.

290. 'The Angler's Song' appears later in Colls. 63, 79, 81, 88, 100, 110.

291. 'To Celia' also occurs in Colls. 47, 63, 74a, 88, 92, 95, 262.

292. Although in the 1653 and 1658 volumes this song was followed by Carew's 'Ask me no more' as the 'answer' to it, that does not establish its priority of composition. Like the many other imitations inspired by Carew's lines, it was almost certainly written after his death. In addition to these two poems, the 1653 vol. contains another piece of the same kind, and 1658 has two others. The text follows that of *Wit Restored*, 1658.

295. The section of *The Works*, 1673, containing this poem, has a title-page—*Poems on Several Occasions Never before Printed*, 1672. The poem had appeared previously in Colls. 46, 48, 90a, 92, 94; and is found later in Colls. 146a, 153, 262.

296. This, the only XVIIth century text of Hammond, abounds with mistakes. 'Swift' (l. 4) could only be a possible reading if its meaning could be connected with the 'winds' of l. 2; but these 'winds forbear' to blow. Down is not of itself 'swift'; but the mental association of 'down' with 'soft' is instant and universal: 'soft as down' occurs repeatedly in the poems of the period. Further, in the antitheses in l. 7 (the whole point of the poem), 'rougher' is opposed to 'smooth' (l. 1); 'harder' is opposed to—'swift'? Surely the poet wrote 'soft.'

297. In all the reprints of this poem I have seen, stz. 2, l. 2 reads, 'the sharp arrows.' The 1655 Ed. has 'harrows,' which is obviously correct. The poem is called 'Husbandry,' and the metaphor is carefully worked out: 'plough,' 'furrows,' 'clods torn by the sharp harrows' and 'crumbled by pressing rolls,' sowing, springing grain, etc.

304. Stz. 1, l. 4, 'And to implore,' is misprinted 'And so implore' in 1673. Variant of song appeared earlier in Coll. 64, and is found earlier still in *Bodley MS. Mus. b. I* (see following note).

304. 'Away, away' and the seven poems following it, are from an un-published MS. in the handwriting of Wilson, who composed the musical settings of all the songs contained in it. The MS. was written c. 1650–5, and 'may have been given to the Library by Prof. Wilson when he entered on his professorship, for it was certainly referenced, if not acquired, about 1656,' *A Summary Catalogue of Western MSS., II*, Bodley. These eight songs are now printed for the first time.

305. L. 4, 'without'; Wilson has mistakenly written 'with one,' in the MS.

308. This also is in Wilson's MS., but with two more stzs. (see note 304).

308. This, expanded to two stzs., is also in Wilson's MS. (see note 304).

309. 'Chloris' appears in *B.M. Harl. MS. 3991*, and in Colls. 51, 62, 92, 109, 123, 153, 262.

310. 'The Swallow' appears in Coll. 127.

311. This occurs in Colls. 84, 127, 130.

313. Variants with one or two extra stzs. are also to be found in several MSS., and in Colls. 70, 73, 89, 109, 123, 130, 146a, 162, 190.

314. I have taken the 1671 text as being better than 1656. It appears also in Colls. 238, 258.

315. There was another issue of this book in 1658 with a different title: *Small Poems of Divers Sorts*. They seem otherwise identical.

315. Harington's 'Song' was reprinted in Coll. 88.

316. This also was reprinted in Coll. 88.

318. Line 4, Oppressèd, N.A.; Opprest, 1683.

319. 'To Sorrow' occurs in *B.M. Add. MS. 29396*, written 1678–82; but though the actual transcription is later than the printed volume, the text is so much better that I have followed it. This MS. text has not been printed before. In the same MS. is a little unprinted song, probably written 1670–80, as follows:

TO CLARINDA

No more, Clarinda, shall thy charms
Prevail against Camilla's arms:
She hath untied that knot at last,
And by another bound me fast:
   Nor think it strange
   To see this change;
Love cannot always last.   *Anon.*

320. The date of this famous poem, 'Of Death,' has not yet been established. The masque, of which it forms the conclusion, was first printed with Shirley's *Honoria and Mammon* in 1659, the title-page of which goes on to say—'Whereunto is added the Contention of Ajax and Ulysses As it was represented by young Gentlemen of quality at a private entertainment of some Persons of Honour.' Following the poem at the end of the play is a note saying—'This was afterwards sung in parts, the music excellently composed by Mr. Ed. Coleman.' The poem has been variously dated c. 1640, 1649, 1653, and c. 1658, on insufficient evidence, or none. The above note, however, seems to imply that some appreciable time had elapsed since the play had been performed; for it was 'afterwards' that the music was composed and the song 'sung in parts' on presumably other than dramatic occasions. I cannot find the music in print before 1667 (in Coll. 81), after which the song became one of the most popular of the period. With or without music, it is found in Colls. 81, 86, 88, 92, 94, 100, 110, 123, 125, 128, 146a, 253, 256, and, expanded to ten stzs. and issued as a broadside, in Coll. 264.

321. In *Lusoria* the poem is thus introduced—'This ensuing Copy the late Printer hath been pleased to honour, by mistaking it among those of the most ingenious and too early lost. Sir John Suckling.' Internal evidence also supports Felltham's claim rather than Suckling's, or, more precisely, 'the late Printer's' claim for Suckling (the latter had been dead 7 years before the poem was included among his works). The piece is now printed as Felltham's for the first time. It is also found, without ascription, in *B.M. Harl. MS. 6918.*

321. For date, see G. Saintsbury's *Minor Poets of the Caroline Period*, *III*, 1921.

322. This anonymous song was reprinted in Colls. 88, 138; and a variant, 'O fain would I before I die,' is found in Colls. 93, 94, 146a.

322. The 1670 text (*Merry Drollery complete*) seemed to me the best; accordingly I print from it. The poem, sometimes with an extra stz., sometimes with two, appears also in Colls. 74, 81, 100, 110, 190.

323. Though not published until 1689 when he was on the verge of 60, most of Cotton's love lyrics were undoubtedly written much earlier. In 1658 Cokayne wrote some verses praising Cotton for his excellent poems. Mr. C. J. Sembower (*op. cit.* note 244) thinks this and the four following pieces were written between 1650 and 1660.

326. Fairfax's poems were written 1650–60, at Nun Appleton, Yorks.— *D.N.B.*

327. The MS. has the only intelligible reading of the first two lines, besides being the earliest text. The song appears in Colls. 86, 88.

329. The earliest text is the best. It was reprinted in *Epigrams*, 1669 and 1670; *Epigrams of all Sorts*, 1671; and *A Collection of the Choicest Epigrams*, etc., 1673.

330. Howard's poem also appears in Colls. 109, 162.

332. A number of unpublished poems by Paman exist in various MSS. Of his shorter pieces, this is the best I have found; it is dated 1660 in the MS., and is now printed for the first time.

337. The MS. [temp. Chas. II] has the best text, and I have followed it accordingly. The song also appears in Colls. 87, 89, 92, 109, 129, 147, 162, 190, 262.

339. For date, see A. Nicoll. The poem is found in Colls. 86, 88, 89, 92, 94, 146a, 190, 262.

340. Date: 'a new play,' *Pepys*, Oct. 20th, 1662.

343. For date, see J. W. Ebsworth (*op. cit.* note 142). The poem appears also in Colls. 135, 137, 148, 235, 258, 262; and an expanded version in Colls. 263 (*bis*), 264 (*bis*), 266, 268, 276.

344. For date see A. Nicoll.

347. The song occurs in Colls. 92, 94, 146a, 262.

348. Date: 'to the Duke's house, and there saw *The Rivals*,' *Pepys*, Sept. 10th, 1664. Davenant never claimed this play, and it was not included in his *Works*, 1673; but it was acted by his company at his theatre in Lincoln's Inn Fields: *D.N.B.* The song appears in Colls. 89, 90a, 92, 94, 146a, 190, 262; and, expanded to 11 stzs., in Coll. 267; and to 12 stzs. in Coll. 264.

350. Although a contemporary ballad sheet of this famous song was undoubtedly published (it is entered in the Stationers' Register under the date, December 30, 1664), no extant copy of it has been recorded. The song was apparently lost sight of soon after the occasion it celebrated, and no more is heard of it until the turn of the century. The oldest surviving printed copy probably is the undated single music sheet in the B.M. (H. 1601, 428), which is tentatively dated [1707 ?]. The earliest dated copy is, I believe, that in Pope's first miscellany, *Miscellaneous Poems and Translations By Several Hands*, 1712; after which it was often reprinted, becoming very

popular and the model for many topical songs, the most famous imitation being Pope's *Court Ballad* published anonymously in 1716. The MS. version, from which I print the song, is thus easily the oldest surviving text by many years; it is now printed for the first time. The poem is headed *Shackley Hayes* in the MS., which is, of course, the name of the tune (there being ballads in Colls. 263, 264, 266, 276, 'to the tune of *Shackleyhay*'), but otherwise it has neither title nor attribution. The few errors of the MS. text I have corrected by the 1721 text, as follows. Stz. 2, l. 2, brain, 1721; brains, MS. Stz. 6, l. 6, men, 1721; MS. omits. Stz. 8, l. 4, MS. omits this line completely; it is supplied from the 1721 text. Stz. 8, l. 6, worthy, 1721; happy, MS. 'Ombre' is spelt 'Hambre' in the MS.; and variously elsewhere at that time, *e.g.* Umbre, Hombre, L'Ombre, are all contemporary. The date of the ballad is interestingly corroborated by Pepys' statement: 'I occasioned much mirth with a ballet I brought with me, made from the seamen at sea to their ladies in town,'—*Pepys*, Jan. 2nd, 1664–5. There can be little doubt that Pepys is referring to this poem; and it is now generally supposed that Dorset wrote it while serving under the Duke of York in his *first* cruise in November 1664; when the Dutch avoided an action by retiring into port; and *not*, as Prior says, on 'the night before the engagement' with the Dutch, in June 1665. The song is also found in *B.M. Lansd. MS. 852.*

350. Etherege's song also appears in *B.M. Harl. MS. 3991;* and Colls. 92, 262.

351. 'Duke of Buckinghā on his Mistress'—this statement in Anthony Wood's autograph referring to this poem (*Bodley, Wood 416*, f. 110) is a contemporary testimony of its authorship more trustworthy, one would suppose, than two anonymous, undated ascriptions of it to Lord Buckhurst (*i.e.* Dorset) written in two copies of Kemp's *Collection of Poems*, 1672 (Coll. 96), in which it appears (see V. de Sola Pinto's edition of Sedley's *Works*, I, p. xxiii). And its inclusion without evidence in Dorset's works in the following century, when it was also being attributed to Sedley, is no proof of either poet's claim to it. The Wood MS. ends with the words: 'Made by the Duke of Buckinham on the 20th of July, 1665. Addrest to his Mistris.' The text lacks ll. 3–4, 17–20, and its first line reads: 'Though Philis your prevailing charms.' The Harl. MS. [temp. Chas II] has the best text; but, in l. 23, reads 'Or for ever . . . '; the Ashm. MS. [c. 1670] supplies the reading I print; the Wood MS. has 'And there for ever.' Variants, from 16 to 24 lines in length, appear in Colls. 92, 96, 103, 146a, 198, 241, 251, 262.

352. For date of writing, see *op. cit.* note 321. Stz. 2 appears in Coll. 221.

353. Date: 'to the King's playhouse . . . and there did see a good part of *The English Monsieur*,'—*Pepys*, Dec. 8th, 1666.

356. Date: 'to the King's house to see *The Maiden Queen*, a new play of Dryden's,'—*Pepy's*, March 2nd, 1666–7. The play is called *Secret Love: or, The Maiden Queen.* The song occurs in *B.M. Harl. MS. 3991;* and in Colls. 92, 174, 262; and with the additions of one stz. at the beginning and seven at the end, as a ballad, 'The Bashful Virgin,' in Coll. 264.

356. Attributed to Etherege by W. Oldys, *Biographia Britannica*, 1750. Text from Coll. 96. The song is also printed with variants of 2, 3 or 4 stzs.

in some later edns of the music-book, and in Colls. 92, 94, 103, 128, 198, 241, 262.

357. A number of Wanley's poems have recently been published in an article, 'A Forgotten Poet of the XVIIth Century; by L. C. Martin, *Eng. Assoc. Essays and Studies*, XI, 1925. 'The Casket,' however, appears now in print for the first time. The poem is also found with other of Wanley's pieces in *B.M. Harl. MSS. 6646* and *6922*. It is here followed by a second poem from *B.M. Add. MS. 22472*.

359. A variant, 2 stzs. in length, had appeared earlier in J. Playford's *Catch that Catch can*, 1667, and also occurs in Colls. 81, 89, 100. It reads as follows:

> A fig for care, why should we spare?
> The parish is bound to find us:
> For thou and I and all must die,
> And leave the world behind us.
>
> The clerk shall sing, the bells shall ring,
> And the old, the old wives wind us;
> Sir John shall lay our bones in clay
> Where nobody means to find us.   *Anon.*

359. This famous 'Health' appears also in Colls. 89, 100, 110, 128, 133, 137, 148, 190.

360. Davenant's song is not in the 1643 and 1649 editions of the play; but the revision, in the 1673 volume, has an extra scene inserted in Act IV, where the song is found.

361. As originally printed, blanks were left where the names of 'Craven's,' 'Queen,' and 'Roper' occur in the poem. The 1704 text supplies them. The date is fixed by an amusing description Pepys gives of Lord Craven's endeavours to suppress an unruly mob of 'prentices who were 'taking the liberty of these holydays to pull down bawdy-houses . . . presently order was given for all the soldiers, horse and foot, to be in armes! and forthwith alarmes were beat by drum and trumpet . . . and all to their colours, and to horse . . . and my Lord Craven commanding of them, and riding up and down to give orders, like a madman,'—*Pepys*, March 24th, 1667–8. A. H. Bullen states that Christopher Roper was appointed page of honour to the Queen in 1667; and quotes Walpole for the identification of 'Black Bess' with Mrs. Barnes (*Musa Proterva*, 1889). The poem also appears in Colls. 104, 116, 120, 235, 258; and was included in the *Works of . . . Rochester and Roscommon*, etc. 1721.

362. Date: 'my wife and Deb . . . saw the new play, *Evening Love*, of Dryden's'—*Pepys*, June 19th, 1668. The song occurs in *B.M. Harl. MS. 3991*; and in Colls. 92, 93, 94, 262.

363. The song also appears in *B.M. Harl. MS. 3991*; and in Colls. 92, 93, 94, 108, 146a, 262; and expanded to 10 stzs., in Colls. 268, 276.

365. 'To Chloris' was reprinted in Colls. 92, 94, 135, 146a, 249, 262.

366. Since this anthology was first published, I have found an edition of

this song which gives it to Charles II. It is a music sheet (*B.M. H. 1601, 244*) entitled: 'The Phoenix. A Song the words by King Charles the 2ᵈ set to Musick by Mr. Humphres Under whom was Educated the late famous Mr. Henry Purcell.' The sheet is undated, but the printing cannot be earlier than Purcell's death in 1695, and may be as late as 1705; nevertheless, in the absence of any earlier evidence, it would seem to be the source of the persistent report of the King's authorship, to which (as my former note showed) Sir John Hawkins, Horace Walpole, and Thomas Park, not to mention several subsequent editors, in turn subscribed. Unfortunately, however, it does not settle the question, for the MS. (*B.M. MS. Harl. 3991*) still remains, in which it is entitled: '1st. Song in the Masque, 1670'; in addition to which I have found in another MS. (Longleat, Portland Papers, Vol, XIX, f. 123) a transcript headed: 'Mr. Dridens first Song at Court.' It would seem, therefore, that the King's name as its author must still be followed by a query. Besides the sources mentioned, the song occurs, with or without variants, in Colls. 92, 104, 108, 116, 120, 146a, 262.

367. For date of acting, see A. Nicoll. The song was very popular; it appears in *B.M. Sloane MS. 1487*, and in Colls. 92, 93, 94, 104, 116, 120, 123, 146a, 235, 258, 262.

368. Date by the title which, in 1704, concludes with the words, 'for his Gray Hairs, which he had at thirty.'

369. Dorset's poem appears also in Colls. 104, 116, 120, 146a.

370. The song appears in *The New Academy of Compliments*, 1671, and in Colls. 93, 94, 104, 116, 120, 146a, 235, 258.

371. Attributed to Etherege by Oldys (*op. cit.* note 356), and in Coll. 198 and later editions; this song is also found in Colls. 92, 103.

372. Settle's song appears in Colls. 94, 146a.

373. I have followed the earliest text to appear, as that seemed to me the best. The variations in Wycherley's 1672 text are as follows. Stz. 1, l. 1, A spouse; l. 3, give us a; l. 4, Who nothing will ask us or; l. 7, love for; l. 8, takes her kind. Stz. 2, l. 2, Without an act; l. 3, From wife; l. 5, When parents; l. 6, cannot is misprinted connot. According to John Dennis (*Original Letters*, 1721), it was this song, or rather, an 'allusion to the latter end' of it, which served as an introduction to the intimacy between the author and the Duchess of Cleveland, to whom he later dedicated the play on publication. The song also appears in Colls. 94, 98, 123, 143, 145, 146a, 258.

374. This anonymous song is also in Colls. 92, 94, 104, 116, 120, 146a, 262.

374. I supply the song's lack of title in the *Windsor Drollery* by printing that given in the same year in the *Oxford Drollery*, which on the other hand omits the last 5 lines. In *B.M. Harl. MS. 3991*, the song is entitled 'Mad Woman in The Pilgrim.' It is not in Fletcher's play *The Pilgrim*, 1647 and 1679 (though that has a mad woman who sings), neither is it in Vanbrugh's version of that play, 1700; nor in T. Killigrew's play of the same name, 1664. Langbaine, however, writing in 1691, mentions a revival of Fletcher's play 'some years since'; and *Covent Garden Drollery*, 1672, includes the Prologue which was presumably then spoken. This there-

fore was in all probability a song written especially for that revival, and, like so many others of the kind, survives only in the song books which collected such ephemeras of the stage and the court. It is to be found also in Colls. 92, 104, 108, 116, 120, 146a, 262; and as a ballad, expanded fore and aft to 12 stzs. and entitled 'The Sorrowful Lady's Complaint,' in Colls. 264, 276.

375. This song also occurs in Colls. 123, 262.

376. For date, see A. Nicoll. The song appears in Colls. 104, 106, 107, 116, 120.

377. Though this famous song was never owned by Dryden, it has frequently been assigned to him on the evidence of Buckingham's *Rehearsal*, 3rd Edition, 1675, where it is parodied as the work of 'Bayes,' who, in that scene at least, is identified with Dryden. Malone definitely attributes the song to him, and states that it was written on the death of Captain Digby, who was killed in a sea-fight with the Dutch, off Southwold Bay, May 28th, 1672; and he also identifies 'Armida' with Frances Stuart, Duchess of Richmond, (*Prose works of John Dryden*, 1800). 'Armida' is the spelling of *The Rehearsal*, and modern editors; but it was 'Armeda' in *New Court Songs*, and 'Arminda' and 'Amida' elsewhere. G. Thorn-Drury's argument against Dryden's authorship (*Covent Garden Drollery*, 1928, pp. 126–9) has been answered by C. L. Day, who, in *The Songs of . . . Dryden*, 1932, pp. 152–5, gives reasons for thinking Dryden wrote it. In addition to the two 1672 collections cited, the song appeared the same year in *Westiminister Drollery* and *Windsor Drollery;* and subsequently in Colls. 104, 108, 116, 120, 146a; and variants expanded to 10 stzs., beginning 'Farewell, my Callista,' are found in Colls. 264 (*bis*), 266 (*bis*).

377. 'Silvia' is also found in Colls. 98, 103, 104, 116, 120, 146a, 198, 234, 241.

378. Flatman's song first appeared in Colls. 98, 101; and again later in Colls. 171, 248.

379. Ravenscroft's song was reprinted in Colls. 98, 101, 104, 106, 116, 120, 146a, 249.

380. This poem, which appears thus in Sedley's *Works*, 1702 and 1707, has an extra stz. at the end in Colls. 96, 103, 198, 241, as follows:

> 'Tis fitter much for you to guess
> Than for me to explain;
> But grant, O grant that happiness
> Which only does remain.

381. Variants of this song of Sedley's appear in Colls. 96, 103, 180, 250.

383. 'The Rural Dance' is also found in Colls. 235, 258.

385. A great favourite, generally ascribed without evidence to Aldrich who wrote the music; it appears also in Colls. 135, 137, 148, 151, 153, 162, 163, 165, 174, 244, 257, 260.

386. This song was ascribed to Dr. Waldren (died 1702) by Nichols in his *Select Collection of Poems*, III, 1780, where it was printed, 'Fie, Celia!' &c. The song is also found in Colls. 116, 119, 120, 259.

389. In printing Traherne's poems, I have followed the text of the MS.

transcribed and prepared for the press by his brother Phillip (see *Traherne's Poems of Felicity*, Ed. by H. I. Bell, 1910), because this MS. contains many poems not in Dobell's edition, and corrects in many cases the readings of Dobell's MS.

396. This song is in Colls. 111, 112, 124,—the same collection with different titles.

397. For date, see A. Nicoll. The song was reprinted in Colls. 115, 119, 123.

397. Authorship fixed by Langbaine, 1691.

399. Variant, entitled 'The Tired Pilgrim,' in Coll. 113. The poem in the form as given appears also in Colls. 219, 226, 248.

400. 'Fading Beauty' appears in Colls. 111, 112, 124. (See note 396.)

400. The date ascribed to the actual writing of the MS. is the third quarter of the century. But as the country was very conscious of its sickness during the civil war, this poignant cry probably refers to the lax morality so widely prevailing under Charles II. It is now printed, I believe, for the first time.

402. Variants of this poem range from 6 to 11 stzs. which often occur in different sequence and contain different readings; and there are objections of various kinds to them all. To obtain the most satisfactory result I have printed the Rawl. text; but have included only those stzs. which appear in Playford's version, 1676, and arranged them in his order. In its various forms it appears in Colls. 120, 137, 148, 235, 258, 263, 264, 266, 267, 276 (*bis*).

404. For date see A. Nicoll. 'Love Armed' is in Colls. 122, 162; and, expanded to 9 stzs., in Coll. 276.

405. This poem is immediately followed by a 'sequel' of 4 stzs. in the same metre, in the 1676 volume, where the poems are numbered I and II respectively. The song leapt into immediate favour, and imitations of its novel metre appeared very early. It is to be found in Colls. 119, 120, 121, 122, 123, 135; and variously expanded, sometimes to as many as 52 stzs., in Colls. 264 (*bis*), 266, 267, 268.

405. Rochester's song appears also in Colls. 119, 122, 147.

406. In Etherege's play this song has a shoulder note, 'Song by Sir C. S.' The Prologue was written by 'Sir Car Scroope Baronet.' And a friend informs me that the song is definitely ascribed to Scrope in T. Coxeter's MS. notes on Langbaine's *English Dramatic Poets*, 1691; which attribution is now generally accepted. The song, however, was included in Sir Charles Sedley's *Works*, 1722 (Sedley died 1701), for which reason it is sometimes ascribed to him. It appears in *B.M. Sloane MS. 1009*, and in Colls. 119, 122, 123, 126, 147; and expanded to 10 stzs., in Colls. 266, 276.

406. *New Airs and Dialogues*, 1678 (i.e. Coll. 125) has the best text, which accordingly I print. The song also occurs in Colls. 122, 145, 147, 258.

407. For date, see *Sir Charles Sedley*, by V. de S. Pinto, 1927. Dorinda was Sedley's daughter, Katherine, later Countess of Dorchester, and mistress of James II. Early texts of 'Dorinda' are curiously rare. It seems to have been first printed in 1701; it reappeared as 'Belinda's sparkling wit' &c. in Bysshe's *Art of English Poetry*, 1702, but apparently was not again

reprinted before 'Johnson's Edition' of Dorset's works, 1779. I have, how-
ever, found it with three extra stzs. in a MS. written c. 1700 (*Bodley MS.
Add. A. 301*), and, with two extra stzs., in two early 18th century MSS.
(*B.M. Harl. MS. 7315*, and *Lansd. MS. 852*).

408. 'Love and Life' was first printed in the three books of *Songs . . .
by Henry Bowman*, 1677, 1678, and 1679, and later in Colls. 127, 156, 160,
201, 238, 258.

408. The authorship of this poem is not certain. The first printed text,
1677 (Coll. 122), has as title 'Song from *The Fool turned Critic*,' which
is a play by D'Urfey, printed 1678; it is not however in the printed edition
of that play. And in 1683 D'Urfey included it among his poems in *A New
Collection of Songs and Poems*, with the title, 'The Bully, a Song in the
Fool turned Critic.' In the meantime it had appeared in Rochester's posthumous *Poems upon Several Occasions*, [1680]; it was again reprinted in
the 1685 and 1701 Eds. of his *Poems;* and was included in the *Works of . . .
Rochester*, etc., 1709 and 1721. The poem also appears anonymously in Coll.
249.

411. This was reprinted in Rymer's poems appended to *Curious Amusements*, 1714, but except the alteration of 'Lucasia' to 'Celia,' l. 2; and
'that' being misprinted for 'shot' in stz. 2, l. 4, the texts are the same. The
song appears in Coll. 130.

413. Webbe's song is rather more than an echo of Carew's; see p. 133.

414. This song can also be found in Coll. 239.

415. This occurs in Colls. 130, 142; and, expanded to 10 stzs., in Coll. 276.

415. For date, see A. Nicoll. The song appears in Colls. 130, 135, 142,
258; and, expanded to 12 stzs., in Coll. 266.

416. 'Constancy' had been printed in the previous year in Coll. 126.

417. The 'Phyllis' song appears also in Colls. 135, 142, 238, 258; it is
found in *B.M. Add. MS. 19759*, and expanded to 10 stzs., in Coll. 266.

419. 'My dear Mistress' is also found in Colls. 153, 154.

419. This famous poem is frequently reprinted as Dorset's, to whom it
was for the first time ascribed, I believe, in *The Works of the most celebrated Minor Poets*, 1749. Mrs. Behn, however, had attributed it to Rochester in her *Miscellany*, 1685, while Dorset was still very much alive. To
judge from the song itself either might have written it. I print it from a
MS. text which is, I think, earlier than any yet recorded. The song also
occurs in Colls. 145, 154, 208, 251.

420. Subscribed in the MS. '—— Chambers,' this poem, which was thought
to have been first printed in these pages, appeared previously in a music
book of extreme rarity, entitled, *Songs set by Signior Pietro Reggio*. Part
II, [1680].

421. For date, see A. Nicoll. This is found in Colls. 135, 142, 258; and
expanded to 10 stzs. in Colls. 264, 276.

422. The 1681 text repeats a part of l. 5 of each stz. as a chorus; 1691 omits
them. For date, see A. Nicoll.

422. There can, I think, be little doubt that this is the original form of
the song. J. W. Ebsworth states that the tune (composed by Captain Pack)
to which it was sung, was written before 1680; and he also cites the

transformation of the text as a political song by the addition of 5 stzs., in 1681, which when re-issued was entitled *The Complete Citizen, or the Man of Fashion,* (*Roxburghe Ballads, IV,* 1883). I have myself found in Coll. 274 the same political song, beginning with this stz., entitled *The Complete Citt: or, The Man of Fashion. To the Tune of, Would you be a Man of Fashion.* That text, however, is dated 1683, and repeats the first two lines in each stz. In the same collection is another political ballad of the same date, written to the same tune. There were also imitations of the original song; one of which—*Would you be a Man of Favour, To the Tune of, Would you be a Man of Fashion,*—is in Coll. 276. In addition to the above issues, the song, in its original form, appears in Coll. 258, and, in its expanded form, in Colls. 149, 203.

423. I print this from the MS., that being the earliest text of the song I have discovered. A slight variant appears in Coll. 145.

426. There are three identical copies of this undated poem in *Wood 417,* which is meant to be chronological in arrangement. One occurs between poems dated 1682 and 1683; the second is in the 1685 section, and the third, among the 1688 pieces, is subscribed in Wood's hand—'bought at Oxon in Feb. 1688.' I believe the poem was only printed once and has never been reprinted. A fourth copy is in Coll. 276.

427. 'Kingston Church,' which as a title does not seem very relevant to the song, is probably the name of the tune to which it was sung, though I have been unable to trace it elsewhere. The song appears in Coll. 249; and, expanded to 10 stzs., in Colls. 264, 276.

428. The 1683 variants are:—Stz. 1, l. 4, of my woes; l. 8, shows pity, shows pity. Stz. 2, l. 5, Kind joys does ne'er. The poem is stated in *The Grove,* 1721, to be by Dr. Kenrick, and is there entitled 'The Melancholy.'

428. This, in the 1714 vol., follows a poem 'On her Going to London . . . Feb. 1683'; and as the same person, Clorinda, is the subject of both poems, it seems probable they were written about the same time.

429. 'To Silvia' also occurs in *B.M. Add. MS. 30303,* and in Colls. 149, 203, 258; and, expanded to 9 stzs., in Colls. 265, 266. It appears yet again as the three concluding stzs. of another ballad which commences, 'Cloe's face is heaven to me,' in Colls. 264, 266, and (I am told) 276,—but in the last mentioned Collection I accidentally omitted personally to verify its occurrence.

429. Colonel Sackville's song was included after my re-examination of the Collections. It appears in Coll. 160, and may be in one or two others.

430. 'A Farewell' also appears in Colls. 151, 163, 165, 244, 257, 260.

431. There are several variants of this very popular poem. They range from the 5 stzs. of its earliest printings in 1685, to the 20 stzs. of W. Pope's own elaborately annotated edition of 1697; between which dates other versions successively appeared with 6, 9, and 16 stzs. each. The 5 stzs. here printed, preserve, I believe, the form of the poem as it was first conceived and written—the nucleus round which the later stzs. collected, to the almost complete obliteration of its original charm. But while excluding the later accretions (some of which, especially those in the ballad form, are certainly not W. Pope's), I have followed the readings of his last re-

vision (1697) of the original stzs. The poem appears in varying forms in Colls. 149, 160, 163, 165, 203, 235, 250, 258, 264, 266, 272, 276.

432. I have been unable to trace a copy of *The Complete Academy of Compliments*, 1685, in which this song is said to appear (see *The Life and Letters of John Gay*, by L. Melville, 1921, Appendix I; 'Notes on the Sources of the Tunes of *The Beggar's Opera*,' by W. H. Grattan Flood; and *English Melodies*, Ed. by V. Jackson, 1910). I therefore follow the 1699 text. The song also occurs in Colls. 240, 258; and, in an expanded form, in Colls. 254a, 276 (*bis*).

433. 'Lucinda' occurs also in *B.M. Sloane MS. 3752*.

435. For date see A. Nicoll. H. Playford, in the book cited, prints at the end of the song, 'These words by Mr. Ousley.' Behn, who 'usually acknowledges her obligations' (A. H. Bullen, *op. cit.* note 361), includes this song in her play without comment as though it were her own. Who shall decide?

437. This jovial catch is also to be found in *B.M. Add. MS. 29386*, and in Colls. 165, 244, 257, 260.

437. This and the following poem were set to music by J. Gamble, who died 1687; and are now, I believe, printed for the first time.

438. 'When thou dost dance,' is curiously like the Duke of Newcastle's verses (see pp. 180–182), and may indeed be his.

440. The 'Serenade' also appears in Coll. 174.

442. Owing to inversion, the meaning of the sixth stz. is a little obscure. It is not 'men' who are 'o'ercome'; but the clash of weapons and the roaring drum and the trumpets' sound overcome the howls and yells of men, and rebound from the hills.

443. This well-known catch is usually attributed to Aldrich, but it is anonymous in the five early texts of it I have found. I have searched through a number of his music MSS. and have failed to discover it among them. The ascription, however, is quite probably true; for it is certainly in his vein, and, according to the *D.N.B.* the following epigram on the same subject is his:

> Si bene quid memini, sunt causae quinque bibendi;
> Hospitis adventus, praesens sitis atque futura,
> Aut vini bonitas, aut quaelibet altera causa.

The catch also appears in *B.M. Add. MS. 30982;* and in Colls. 244, 257, 260.

443. The 1690 text is found in Coll. 186.

444. Date: this poem is included in the *Winchilsea MS.* which was written before 1690 (see *The Poems of Anne Countess of Winchilsea*, Ed. by M. Reynolds, 1903).

445. This adaptation of Beaumont and Fletcher's *The Prophetess* as an opera, is attributed to Dryden by Langbaine, writing in the same or following year; and to Betterton by Gildon (1699), not to mention the *D.N.B.* and A. Nicoll. The song certainly shows a practised hand, and—as Saintsbury pointed out—has certain affinities with Dryden's song-writing. Whoever adapted the play, Dryden unquestionably wrote the Prologue for it,

and may have contributed this song as well. It appears without attribution in Colls. 238, 240, 254a, 258.

446. This song was printed in Shadwell's play, 1690, like his other songs in his plays, without comment. Gildon, however, in *Examen Miscellaneum*, 1702, includes it with the attribution, 'By the Earl D——' (*i.e.* Dorset). It is anonymous in Colls. 191, 238, 258.

446. Many of the songs in Southerne's plays are therein ascribed to various writers; of some others the authors are stated to be unknown; the few that remain, this among them, bear no ascription. I have therefore given Southerne's name as the author. For date, see A. Nicoll.

448. This also occurs in *B.M. Add. MS. 33234*.

449. This anonymous song appears also in Coll. 228, 255.

450. Cromwell's song, with the first line repeated after l. 5, is called 'A Rondeau' in Coll. 209; but the original form appears again in Coll. 252.

451. Crowne's song was reprinted in Colls. 197, 228, 255.

451. This appears in Coll. 258.

454. The misprint 'if ye,' l. 6, was corrected by Playford, who prints the song in Colls. 235, 258, and the later ed. of 1719–20.

454. 'Corinna' appears again in Coll. 255.

455. This was reprinted in Colls. 233, 241.

456. Congreve's song is in *Ch. Ch. MS. 580*, and in Coll. 210. For date see A. Nicoll.

457. 'To a Fair Young Lady' appears also in Coll. 233.

457. The 'Rondelay' occurs again in Colls. 212, 236.

458. The play is by Southerne. Henly's song is also in Colls. 211, 228, 255.

459. King's song appears also in Coll. 245.

459. The variants in the play are:—Stz. 1, l. 2, Still I presume; l. 4, Faintly repulsed; l. 9, With the citizen's; l. 10, received in Whitehall. Stz. 2, l. 5, 'Tis apparent; l. 6, Against love and reason; l. 8, He that knows. *The Gentleman's Journal* says 'The words by Mr. Southerne.' The song also appears in Colls. 189, 202, 258.

461. 'On Love' appeared in Wright's *Female Virtuosos*, 1693, and *The Gentleman's Journal* for the same year. It also occurs in Colls. 228, 255.

462. I have in this case preferred the earlier text to the revision. In *The Genuine Works*, 1732, the variants are as follows. Stz. 1, l. 4, Chloe so gently pressed complied; stz. 2, l. 1, With idle awe, an am'rous fool; l. 3, Say, Love; stz. 3, l. 2, the nymph be.

463. The 1721 vol. (the last in Prior's lifetime) is apparently chronological in arrangement. This poem occurs between two others dated 1694 and 1695 respectively. It appears in Coll. 251, where, I believe, it was first printed.

464. This well-known song appears also in Colls. 209, 213, 258.

466. Congreve's song appears in Coll. 214.

467. Date from A. Nicoll.

468. Prior's 'Ode' occurs between two poems dated 1695, in the 1721 edition. (See note 463.)

468. The play is by Southerne; and in the 1st Ed. 1696, and 2nd Ed.

1699, this song is said to be 'By an unknown hand.' It is however stated, in the first collected edition of Southerne's *Works*, 1774, to have been written by 'Sir Harry Sheers.' For date, see A. Nicoll. The song appears in Coll. 216.

469. *Woman's Wit* was acted 1696, see A. Nicoll.

470. This poem appears in Coll. 258.

472. John Dennis wrote the play in which Cheek's song appears.

473. For date, see A. Nicoll.

475. 'Diana's Hunting-Song' was first printed in *Twelve New Songs*, 1699.

479. This and the two following poems occur between others dated 1696 and 1700, in the 1721 edition. (See note 463.)

481. This poem follows a French version, 'By Monsieur Fontenelle,' of Adriani Morientis ad Animam Suam,' and is headed 'Imitated.' It occurs between two other poems dated 1700, in the 1721 edition. It appears in Coll. 251. (See note 463.)

482. I have failed to trace an earlier text of this famous song of Sedley's; but it was almost certainly written before 1700, at which date he was about 61 years of age. He died in 1701.

484. Entitled, *The Dying Damsel's Doleful Destiny: Or, True Love Requited with Evil*, this poem was issued as a ballad, without date. It was 'Printed for J. Deacon at the Angel in Giltspur Street, without Newgate'; from which address he was publishing c. 1694–1701 (*Dictionary of . . . Booksellers, 1668–1725*, by H. R. Plomer, 1922). From the style of the ballad it was almost certainly published before the end of the century; but it is impossible to fix a more exact date.

485. 'A Love Song,' Stz. 1, l. 7, fetters breaks, N.A.; fetters are, 1700. In stz. 2, l. 3, 'shaft' is misprinted 'shafts' in 1700.

486. With the name of Alexander Pope, appended to this Ode 'written when I was not twelve years old,' the doors of the Eighteenth Century spring apart—and this volume of Seventeenth Century Lyrics fitly closes.

A SHORT-TITLE LIST OF BOOKS
CONTAINING POETICAL COLLECTIONS
MAINLY ANONYMOUS AND OF THE
XVIITH CENTURY CONSULTED IN
THE COURSE OF THIS WORK

(Names or initials following the titles are those of composers, compilers, or publishers associated with the books concerned. Appended to the first edition of a book, or first volume of a series, are references to all the later issues,—e.g. 'see also Colls. 71, 89, 190'—each of which is in turn referred to the first. These are references to publication only, and not to contents, different editions of these collections being rarely identical.)

1621.	1. *A Help to Discourse.* 4th Ed. W. B. & E. P. And 6th Ed., 1627; and 7th Ed., 1628. (See also Coll. 17.)
	2. *A Help to Memory & Discourse.* 2nd Impr., enlarged.
1622.	3. *Songs, Of 3, 4, 5, & 6 parts.* T. Tomkins.
	4. *The First Book of Airs.* J. Attey.
1623.	5. *Remains, Concerning Britain.* 3rd Impr. W. Camden. (See also Colls. 11, 20.)
1624.	6. *Loves Garland.*
	7. *The Second Set of Madrigals & Pastorals.* F. Pilkington.
1627.	8. *Airs, or Fa La's for Three Voices.* J. Hilton.
1628.	9. *The Crumbs of Comfort.* 7th Ed. M. Sparke, And 10th Ed., 1629.
1629.	10. *French Court-Airs.* E. Filmer.
	11. *Remains, Concerning Britain.* 4th Impr. W. Camden. (See Coll. 5.)
1631.	12. *Ancient Funeral Monuments.* J. Weever.
	13. *The Crown Garlond of Golden Roses . . . With new additions.* R. Johnson. And Eds. 1659, 1683, & 1692; all reprints of 1631.
1632.	14. *Madrigals & Airs.* W. Porter.
1634.	15. *The Female Glory.* A. Stafford.
1635.	16. *A Description of the King & Queen of Fairies.* R. S.
	17. *A Help to Discourse.* 11th Ed. And 12th Ed., 1636; and 13th Ed. 1638 & 1648. (See Coll. 1)
1636.	18. *Annalia Dubrensia.* Mat. Walbancke.
	19. *Fasciculus Florum: or, A Nosegay of Flowers.*
	20. *Remains, Concerning Britain.* 5th Impr. W. Camden. And 5th Impr. 1637; and 6th Impr. 1657. (See Coll. 5.)
1638.	21. *The Seventh Set of Books.* M. East. (Music, with titles or first lines of songs only.)
1640.	22. *The Academy of Compliments.* (See also Colls. 26a, 29, 90a, 146a, 158.)
	23. *Wits Recreations.* (See also Colls. 24, 26, 31, 42, 77, 83.)
1641.	24. *Wits Recreations. Augmented . . .* (See Coll. 23.)

1642. 25. *Good and True, Fresh and New Christmas Carols.*
1645. 26. *Wits Recreations refined.* 3rd Ed. (See Coll. 23.)
1646. 26a. *The Academy of Compliments.* 7th Ed. (See Coll. 22.)
1648. 27. *Choice Psalms . . . With divers Elegies.* H. Lawes.
     28. *New Christmas Carols.* n.d. [*Temp.* Charles I.]
1650. 29. *The Academy of Compliments . . . last edition.* (See Coll. 22.)
     30. *The Dancing Master.* J. Playford. (Music, with titles of songs only.) And Eds. 1652, & 1665.
     31. *Wits Recreation refined.* (See Coll. 23.)
1651. 32. *A Musical Banquet.* J. Playford.
     33. *Reliquiae Wottonianae.* I. Walton. And 2nd Ed., 1654; 3rd Ed., 1672; & 4th Ed., 1685.
1652. 34. *Catch that Catch can.* J. Hilton. (See also Colls. 57, 75.)
     35. *Music's Recreation.* J. Playford. (Music, with titles of songs only.) And Eds. 1661, 1669, & 1682.
     36. *Select Musical Airs & Dialogues.* J. Playford. (See also Coll. 39.)
1653. 37. *Airs & Dialogues . . . The First Book.* H. Lawes. (See also Colls. 46, 56.)
     38. *Certain Verses . . . to be reprinted with the Second Edition of Gondibert.*
     39. *Select Musical Airs & Dialogues in Three Books.* J. Playford. (See Coll. 36.)
     39a. *The Card of Courtship.*
     40. *The Complete Angler.* I. Walton. And 2nd Ed., 1655; 3rd Ed., 1661, re-issued 1664; 4th Ed., 1668; & 5th Ed., 1676.
     41. *The Loves of Hero & Leander . . . with . . . other choice Pieces.* (See also Coll. 99.)
1654. 42. *Wits Recreations refined.* (See Coll. 23.)
1655. 43. *Musarum Deliciae.* Sir J. M[ennis]. & Ja. S[mith]. (See also Coll. 49.)
     44. *The Incomparable Poem, Gondibert, vindicated . . .*
     45. *The Marrow of Compliments.*
     46. *The Second Book of Airs & Dialogues.* H. Lawes. (See Coll. 37.)
     47. *Wits Interpreter.* J. C[otgrave]. (See also Colls. 74a, 95.)
1656. 48. *Choice Drollery.* R. P.
     49. *Musarum Deliciae.* 2nd Ed. Sir. J. M[ennis]. & Ja. S[mith]. (See Coll. 43.)
     50. *Parnassus Biceps.* A. Wright.
     51. *Sportive Wit.* J. P[hillips], or N. Brooke.
     52. *Wit & Drollery, Jovial Poems.* J. P. (See also Colls. 73, 135.)
     53. *Wit & Fancy in a Maze.* (Probably by one hand.)
1657. 54. *Mottets of Two Voices.* W. Porter.
     55. *Wit a Sporting.* H. B[old].
1658. 56. *Airs & Dialogues . . . The Third Book.* H. Lawes. (See Coll. 37.)
     57. *Catch that Catch can.* 2nd Ed., enlarged. J. Hilton. (See Coll. 34.)

58. *Naps upon Parnassus.*

59. *Poems consisting of Epistles & Epigrams.* J. Eliot. (By one hand?)

60. *The Mysteries of Love & Eloquence.* E. P[hillips]. (See also Colls. 159, 232.)

61. *Wit Restored.* J. S[mith].

1659. 62. *Airs & Dialogues . . . The Second Book.* J. Gamble (The First Book, 1656 & 1657, contains only T. Stanley's poems.)

63. *Select Airs & Dialogues.* J. Playford. (See also Coll. 86.)

1660. 64. *Cheerful Airs or Ballads.* J. Wilson.

65. *Le Prince d'Amour . . . with a collection of . . . poems & songs.* Sir B. Rudyerd.

66. *Rats Rhymed to Death.*

67. *The Muses Mistress.* J. C[otgrave]. (Only two hands in this.)

1661. 68. *An Antidote against Melancholy.* N. D.

69. *Choice Poems . . . By the Wits of both Universities.*

70. *Merry Drollery . . . The First Part.* W. N., C. B., &c. (See also Colls. 71, 89, 190.)

71. *The Second Part of the Merry Drollery.* W. N., C. B., &c. (See Coll. 70.)

72. *New Carols, For this merry time of Christmas.*

73. *Wit & Drollery . . . with additions.* E. M. (See Coll. 52.)

1662. 74. *Rump . . . Poems & Songs.*

74a. *Wits Interpreter.* J. C[otgrave]. 2nd Ed. (See Coll. 47.)

1663. 75. *Catch that Catch can: or, A New Collection . . .* J. Hilton. (See Coll. 34.)

76. *Robin Hood's Garland . . .* With new Additions. (See also Coll. 90.)

77. *Wits Recreations refined.* (See Coll. 23.)

1664. 78. *Poor Robin, 1664, An Almanack.* Also annually to 1700. (I have not been able to trace the issue for 1688.)

1666. 79. *Music's Delight on the Cithern.* J. Playford.

80. *Songs & Fancies . . . Second Edition . . . Enlarged.* J. Forbes. (The 1st Ed., 1662, is apparently not extant. See also Coll. 133.)

1667. 81. *Catch that Catch can: or, The Musical Companion.* J. Playford. (See also Colls. 100, 110, 151, 163, 165, 244, 247, 257.)

82. *Folly in Print: or, A Book of Rhymes.* (Apparently by one hand.)

83. *Wits Recreations refined.* (See Coll. 23.)

1668. 84. *Poems of Mr. Cowley and Others.* W. King.

1669. 85. *Miscellanea.* J. H.

86. *Select Airs & Dialogues . . . II.* J. Playford. (See Coll. 63.)

87. *The New Help to Discourse.* W. W. (See also Colls. 129, 147, 220.)

88. *The Treasury of Music . . . in Three Books.* J. Playford.

1670. 89. *Merry Drollery, Complete.* (See Coll. 70.)

90. *Robin Hood's Garland.* (See Coll. 76.)

90a. *The Academy of Compliments. Newly refin'd . . . and Enlarged.* (See Coll. 22.)

90b. *The Jovial Garland.* [1670?]

1671. 91. *Oxford Drollery.* W. Hicks.

92. *The New Academy of Compliments.* L. B., Sir C. S., Sir W. D. (See also Coll. 262.)

93. *Westminster Drollery . . . With Additions.* (I have not been able to examine the 1st Ed., 1671, and 3rd Ed., 1674. (See also Coll. 101.)

94. *Windsor Drollery.*

95. *Wits Interpreter.* 3rd Ed., with additions. J. C[otgrave]. (See Coll. 47.)

1672. 96. *A Collection of Poems . . . upon several occasions by several persons.* H. Kemp. (See also Colls. 103, 198, 241.)

97. *Covent Garden Drollery.* A. B[rome].

98. *New Court-Songs & Poems.* R. V.

99. *Ovid de Arte Amandi, and . . . The Loves of Hero & Leander,* etc. (See Coll. 41.)

100. *The Musical Companion, in Two Books.* J. Playford. (See Coll. 81.)

101. *Westminster Drollery, the Second Part.* (See Coll. 93.)

102. *Westminster Quibbles in Verse.*

1673. 103. *A Collection of Poems.* With additions. (See Coll. 96.)

104. *Choice Songs & Airs . . . The First Book.* J. Playford. (See also Colls. 116, 120, 126, 130, 138, 145.)

105. *Holborn Drollery.*

106. *London Drollery: or, The Wits Academy.* W. H[icks].

107. *Methinks the Poor Town . . . A Collection of all the New Songs.*

108. *The Canting Academy.*

109. *The Loyal Garland.* 4th Ed., with Additions. S. N. (This date is doubtful, it may be 1678. I have not been able to find any earlier edition. See also Coll. 162.)

110. *The Musical Companion, in Two Books.* With additions. J. Playford. (See Coll. 81.)

1674. 111. *A new Collection of Poems & Songs written by several Persons.* (See also Colls. 112, 124.)

112. *A new Collection of Poems & Songs written by several Persons . . . Collected by John Bulteel.* (This, except for title-page, is identical with Coll. 111. There was still another issue of the same book in 1674, entitled, *A New Collection of New Songs & Poems. None of them ever Printed before.*)

113. *Wit at a Venture: or, Clio's Privy-Garden.* C. F.

1675. 114. *A Perfect Collection of the several Songs now in mode.* (See also Colls. 115, 119, 122.)

115. *A Perfect Collection of all the Songs now in mode.* With additions. (See Coll. 114.)

116. *Choice Airs, Songs & Dialogues.* 2nd Ed., enlarged. J. Playford. (See Coll. 104.)

117. *Make Room for Christmas.* (By one hand?)

118. *Mock Songs & Joking Poems.*

1676.   119. *A New Collection of the Choicest Songs. Now in esteem . . .* (See Coll. 114.)

120. *Choice Airs, Songs & Dialogues . . . Newly reprinted with large additions.* J. Playford. (See Coll. 104.)

1677.   121. *New Songs, & Poems, a-la-mode . . .* P. W. (This is a re-issue of T. Duffett's *New Poems, Songs,* etc., 1676; with a new title-page, and preliminary pages omitted.)

122. *The Last and Best Edition of New Songs.* (See Coll. 114.)

123. *The Wits Academy: or, The Muses Delight.* W. P.

1678.   124. *Melpomene: or, The Muses Delight.* (A re-issue of Colls. 111 and 112, with a new title-page.)

125. *New Airs & Dialogues.* J. Banister & T. Low.

1679.   126. *Choice Airs & Songs . . . II.* J. Playford. (See Coll. 104.)

1680.   127. *Songs of Signior Pietro Reggio.* n.d. [1680.]

128. *Synopsis of Vocal Music.* A. B.

129. *The New Help to Discourse.* 2nd Ed. W. W. (See Coll. 87.)

1681.   130. *Choice Airs & Songs . . . III.* J. Playford. (See Coll. 104.)

1682.   131. *Grammatical Drollery.* W. H[icks].

132. *Loves School: or, A New Merry Book of Compliments.*

133. *Songs & Fancies.* 3rd Ed., enlarged. J. Forbes. (See Coll. 80.)

134. *The Shepherds Garland of Love, Loyalty, & Delight.*

135. *Wit & Drollery . . . with new additions.* (See Coll. 52.)

136. *Wit & Loyalty revived.*

137. *Wit & Mirth, An Antidote against Melancholy.* 3rd Ed., enlarged. H. Playford. (Earlier Eds. apparently not extant. See also Coll. 148; and another series beginning with Coll. 235.)

1683.   138. *Choice Airs & Songs . . . IV.* J. Playford. (See Coll. 104.)

139. *Cupid's Posies.*

140. *Loves Masterpiece.*

141. *Rome rhymed to Death.*

142. *The Complete Courtier: or, Cupid's Academy.* J. Shurley.

143. *Triumphs of Female Wit.*

1684.   144. *A Choice Collection of 120 Loyal Songs.* N. T.[hompson]. (See also Colls. 149, 203.)

145. *Choice Airs & Songs . . . V.* J. Playford. (See Coll. 104.)

146. *Miscellany Poems.* J. Dryden. (See also Colls. 157, 199, 208, 251.)

146a. *The Academy of Compliments.* (See Coll. 22.)

147. *The New Help to Discourse.* 3rd Ed., with additions. W. W. (See Coll. 87.)

148. *Wit & Mirth.* 3rd Ed., enlarged. H. Playford. (See Coll. 137.)

1685.   149. *A Choice Collection of 180 Loyal Songs.* 3rd Ed., with many additions. N. T[hompson]. (I have failed to trace the 2nd Ed. See Coll. 144.)

150. *A Collection of 86 Loyal Poems.* Nat. Thomson.

151. *Catch that Catch can, or the Second Part of the Musical Companion.* J. Playford. (See Coll. 81.)

152. *Cupid's Masterpiece.*

153. *Latin Songs, with their English: and Poems.* H. Bold.

154. *Miscellany . . . a Collection of Poems by several Hands.* A. Behn.

155. *Miscellany Poems & Translations, by Oxford Hands.* A. Stephens.

156. *Poems by several hands, and on several occasions.* N. Tate.

157. *Sylvae.* [*i.e.* 'Miscellany Poems,' II.] J. Dryden. (See Coll. 146.)

158. *The Academy of Compliments.* (See Coll. 22.)

159. *The Mysteries of Love & Eloquence.* 3rd Ed., with additions. E. P[hillips]. (I cannot trace the 2nd Ed. See Coll. 60.)

160. *The Theatre of Music . . . The First Book.* H. Playford. (See also Colls. 161, 164, 166.)

161. *The Theatre of Music . . . II.* H. Playford. (See Coll. 160.)

1686. 162. *The Loyal Garland.* 5th Ed., with additions (See Coll. 109.)

163. *The Second Book of the Pleasant Musical Companion.* J. Playford. (See Coll. 81.)

164. *The Theatre of Music . . . III.* H. Playford. (See Coll. 160.)

1687. 165. *The Second Book of the Pleasant Musical Companion.* 2nd Ed., enlarged. J. Playford. (See Coll. 81.)

166. *The Theatre of Music . . . IV.* H. Playford. (See Coll. 160.)

167. *Cupids Garland, set round about with gilded roses.* n.d. [Before 1688.]

168. *New Christmas Carols.* n.d. [Before 1688.]

1688. 169. *A Cabinet of Choice Jewels . . . New Christmas Carols.*

170. *Lycidus . . . Together with a Miscellany of New Poems.* A. Behn. (See also Coll. 225.)

171. *Harmonia Sacra.* H. Playford. (See also Colls. 200, 248.)

172. *The Banquet of Music . . . The First Book.* H. Playford. (See also Colls. 173, 180, 186, 191, 196.)

173. *The Banquet of Music . . . II.* H. Playford. (See Coll. 172.)

174. *The True Lover's New Academy*, n.d. [Before 1689.]

1689. 175. *A Collection of Poems on Affairs of State.* Parts I–IV. (See also Colls. 223, 224, 229, 250.)

176. *A Collection of the Newest . . . Poems . . . against Popery.* (See also Colls. 177, 178, 179.)

177. *A Second Collection of . . . Poems . . . against Popery.* (See Coll. 176.)

178. *A Third Collection of . . . Poems . . . against Popery.* (See Coll. 176.)

179. *The Fourth (and Last) Collection of Poems*, etc. (See Coll. 176.)

180. *The Banquet of Music . . . III.* H. Playford. (See Coll. 172).

181. *The Muses Farewell to Popery & Slavery.* (See also Colls. 182, 187, 188.)

182. *A Supplement to the . . . Poems against Popery & Slavery.* (See Coll. 181.)

183. *The Protestant Garland of Joy & Delight.*
184. *A New Garland . . . of . . . Songs & Catches.* n.d. [Before 1690 ?]

1690.   185. *Apollo's Banquet.* 6th Ed. H. Playford. (Music, with title of songs only.)
186. *The Banquet of Music . . . The Fourth & Last Book.* H. Playford. (See Coll. 172; and also Colls. 191, 196.)
187. *The Muses Farewell to Popery & Slavery.* 2nd Ed., with additions. (See Coll. 181.)
188. *A Supplement to the Muses Farewell to Popery & Slavery.* (See Coll. 181.)
189. *Joyful Cuckoldom.* n.d. [1690 ?–1696 ?] H. Playford.

1691.   190. *Merry Drollery Complete.* W. N., C. B., &c. (See Coll. 70.)
191. *The Banquet of Music . . . V.* H. Playford. (See Coll. 172.)
192. *The History of Adolphus, Prince of Russia . . . With a Collection of Songs.*

1692.   193. *A Present for the Ladies.*
194. *Miscellanea Sacra. Containing . . . Sacred Poems.*
195. *Miscellany Poems upon several occasions.* C. Gildon.
196. *The Banquet of Music . . . The Sixth & Last Book.* H. Playford. (See Coll. 172.)
197. *The Gentleman's Journal.* (See also Colls. 201, 209.)

1693.   198. *A Collection of Poems.* F. Saunders. (See Coll. 96.)
199. *Examen Poeticum.* [*i.e.* 'Miscellany Poems,' III.] J. Dryden. (See Coll. 146.)
200. *Harmonia Sacra . . . II.* H. Playford. (See Coll. 171.)
201. *The Gentleman's Journal.* (See Coll. 197.)
202. *Thesaurus Musicus . . . The First Book.* J. Hudgebutt. (See also Colls. 210, 213, 214, 221.)

1694.   203. *A Collection of One Hundred & Eighty Loyal Songs.* 4th Ed., with many additions. N. T[hompson]. (See Coll. 144.)
204. *A Posie for Lovers . . . in four Poems.*
205. *Chorus Poetarum,* MDCLXIXIV. [1694.] C. Gildon. (See also Coll. 230.)
206. *Miscellaneous Letters & Essays . . . in Prose & Verse.* C. Gildon.
207. *Poems on Several Occasions.* (Possibly by one hand.)
208. *The Annual Miscellany.* [*i.e.* 'Miscellany Poems,' IV.] J. Dryden. (See Coll. 146.)
209. *The Gentleman's Journal.* (See Coll. 197.)
210. *Thesaurus Musicus . . . II.* J. Hudgebutt. (See Coll. 202.)

1695.   211. *Deliciae Musicae . . . The First Book.* H. Playford. (See also Colls. 212, 215–218.)
212. *Deliciae Musicae . . . II.* H. Playford. (See Coll. 211.)
213. *Thesaurus Musicus . . . III.* J. Hudgebutt. (See Coll. 202.)
214. *Thesaurus Musicus . . . IV.* J. Hudgebutt. (See Coll. 202.)

1696.   215. *Deliciae Musicae . . . III.* H. Playford. (See Coll. 211.)

216. *Deliciae Musicae . . . IV.* H. Playford. (See Coll. 211.)
217. *Deliciae Musicae . . . The First Book of the Second Volume.*
     H. Playford. (See Coll. 211.)
218. *Deliciae Musicae . . . The Second Book of the Second Volume.*
     H. Playford. (See Coll. 211.)
219. *Miscellanea Sacra . . . Vol. 1.* N. Tate. (No more published.
     See also Coll. 226.)
220. *The New Help to Discourse.* 4th Ed., with additions. W. W.
     (See Coll. 87.)
221. *Thesaurus Musicus . . . V.* J. Hudgebutt. (See Coll. 202.)

1697. 222. *Miscellany Poems.* W. Rogers.
223. *Poems on Affairs of State.* Parts I & II. (See Coll. 175.)
224. *State-Poems Continued.* (See Coll. 175.)
225. *Poems . . . To which is added a Miscellany of New Poems.*
     A. Behn. (See Coll. 170.)

1698. 226. *Miscellanea Sacra.* 2nd Ed., with additions. N. Tate (See Coll.
     219.)
227. *Musica Oxoniensis.* J. Welldon & R. Goodson.
228. *Orpheus Britannicus.* H. Purcell. (See also Colls. 246, 255, 261.)
229. *Poems on Affairs of State.* Part III. (See Coll. 175.)
230. *The Poetical Remains of . . . Buckingham,* etc. C. Gildon. (See
     Coll. 205.)

1699. 231. *Devotional Poems, Festival & Practical.* (Possibly by one hand.)
232. *The Beau's Academy.* (A re-issue of Coll. 159, with a new
     title-page. See Coll. 60.)
233. *Mercurius Musicus, For . . . 1699.* H. Playford. (See also Coll.
     237.)
234. *Twelve New Songs.* W. Pearson.
235. *Wit & Mirth: or, Pills to purge Melancholy.* H. Playford. (See
     also Colls. 238, 258. And earlier series, Coll. 137.)

1700. 236. *Amphion Anglicus.* J. Blow.
237. *Mercurius Musicus.* Jan.–Oct. H. Playford. (See Coll. 233.)
238. *Wit & Mirth: or, Pills to purge Melancholy . . . The Second
     Part.* H. Playford. (See Coll. 235.)
239. *Venus Looking-glass . . .* n.d. [1700?] J. O[ldmixon].
240. *Wits Cabinet.* n.d. [1700?] (See also Coll. 249.)

1701. 241. *A Collection of Poems.* D. Brown. (See Coll. 96.)
242. *A New Miscellany of Original Poems.* C. Gildon.
243. *The Divine Companion.* H. Playford.
244. *The Second Book of the Pleasant Musical Companion.* 4th Ed.,
     enlarged. H. Playford. (See Coll. 81.)

1702. 245. *Examen Miscellaneum.* C. Gildon.
246. *Orpheus Britannicus . . . The Second Book.* H. Purcell. (See
     Coll. 228.)
247. *Supplement . . . to the Second Book of the Pleasant Musical
     Companion.* H. Playford. (See Coll. 81.)

1703. 248. *Harmonia Sacra. The First Book.* 2nd Ed., enlarged. H. Play-
     ford. (See Coll. 171.)

249. *Wits Cabinet.* 11th Ed., much enlarged. (See Coll. 240.)

1703–7. 250. *Poems on Affairs of State.* 4 Vols.: I & II, 1703; III, 1704; IV, 1707. (See Coll. 175.)

1704. 251. *Poetical Miscellanies.* [*i.e.* 'Miscellany Poems,' V.] (See Coll. 146.)

252. *The Theatre of Ingenuity.* N. D.

1705. 253. *Miscellanea Sacra: or, A Curious Collection of Original Poems.*

254. *A Collection of the most celebrated Songs.* n.d. [1705?] H. Purcell.

254a. *The Complete Academy of Compliments.*

1706. 255. *Orpheus Britannicus.* 2nd Ed. of Book I., with additions. H. Purcell. (See Coll. 228.)

1706–11. 256. *A Choice Collection of Comic & Serious Scots Poems.* Part I, 1706; Part II, 1709; Part III, 1711. J. Watson.

1707. 257. *The Pleasant Musical Companion.* 5th Ed. enlarged. H. Playford. (See Coll. 81.)

1707–9. 258. *Wit & Mirth: or, Pills to purge Melancholy.* 3rd Ed., in four vols. H. Playford. (I cannot find 2nd Ed. See Coll. 235.)

1708. 259. *Oxford & Cambridge Miscellany Poems.* n.d. [c. 1708.] E. Fenton.

1710. 260. *The Jovial Companions.* n.d. [1710?] H. Purcell & J. Blow.

1711. 261. *Orpheus Britannicus . . . The Second Book.* 2nd Ed., with additions. H. Purcell. (See Coll. 228.)

1713. 262. *The New Academy of Compliments.* L. B., Sir C. S., Sir W. D., etc. (See Coll. 92.)

ASSEMBLED COLLECTIONS OF BALLADS, &c.

263. B.M. Bagford Ballads. C. 40, m. 9–11.
264. ” Roxburghe Ballads. Roxb. Coll. I–IV.
265. ” A collection of English Ballads. C. 22. f. 6.
266. Bodley. Douce Ballads, I–IV.
267. ” Rawlinson Ballads. 4° Rawl. 566.
268. ” Wood E. 25.
269. ” Wood 401.
270. ” Wood 402.
271. ” Wood 416.
272. ” Wood 417.
273. ” Ashm. G. 15.
274. ” Ashm. G. 16.
275. ” Ashm. H. 23.
276. Magdalene Coll. Cambridge. Pepys 2505–9.

BIOGRAPHICAL NOTES

(The chief authority for the following notes is the D.N.B., though more recent 'Lives' have also been consulted when available.)

Behn, Aphra (1640–1689). Dramatist and novelist; said to have been born at Wye, her father's name being Johnson. Her early life was passed in the West Indies. On her return to England she married a city merchant of Dutch descent, and was received at court. During the Dutch war in 1665, Charles II employed her as a government spy in Flanders. When left a widow the following year, she took up writing for a livelihood, and is notable as being the first woman professional writer. She became a well-known figure, and was on friendly terms with the chief playwrights of the time. She wrote poems, novels, pamphlets, and plays, the last still retained their popularity on the stage in the eighteenth century.

Browne, William (1591–1643 ?). Poet; born and educated at Tavistock, Devon, later going on to Exeter College, Oxford, and the Inner Temple. He was for some time a member of the retinue of the Earl of Pembroke at Wilton, and his latter years were passed quietly in the country. He wrote eclogues and a masque, but his chief work was *Britannia's Pastorals*, in three books (though the last was not printed until 1852). He greatly admired Spenser, and ranks next to him as a writer of pastoral poetry.

Carew, Thomas (1595 ?–1639 ?). Poet; son of Sir Matthew Carew, Master in Chancery, was educated at Merton College, Oxford, and entered the Middle Temple in 1612; but was fonder of 'roving after hounds and hawks' than his legal studies. He soon left the law for the Diplomatic Service in which he was intermittently employed in Italy, Holland, and France over a number of years. Later he became attached to the Court, and in 1628 was appointed gentleman of the privy chamber, and subsequently sewer to Charles I. He was the intimate friend of contemporary writers like Jonson, Suckling and Davenant; and wrote a masque (printed in 1633) and songs for performance at Court; but his collected poems were not published until after his death.

Cartwright, William (1611–1643). Dramatist and poet; educated at Westminster School and Christ Church, Oxford. He took orders in 1638, and became well known as a preacher in the five years left to him before his death at thirty-two. He wrote plays and poems while still an undergraduate; and became a friend of Jonson and other poets of his day. His works were much commended in his lifetime, but were not published until 1651.

Congreve, William (1670–1729). Dramatist; a Yorkshireman by birth, educated in Ireland, at Kilkenny, and at Trinity College, Dublin, where he was a fellow-student of Swift. He entered the Middle Temple, but found writing more to his taste, published a novel, and wrote a play, *The Old Bachelor*, which was most successfully performed in January 1692–3, and was followed by other plays whose lasting popularity has been due to their vivacious and

528

faithful portrayal of the manners and society of the time. Congreve was also a poet and a contributor to Dryden's metrical versions of Latin poets. He was in comfortable circumstances through holding public offices (*e.g.*, the commissionership of wine licences), and took pride, to the point of affectation, in being considered a man of fashion.

Cotton, Charles (1630–1687). Poet and translator; born in Staffordshire; travelled on the continent while still young, gaining a wide knowledge of French and Italian literature. On his return he devoted himself to literature, though he served in the army in Ireland in 1670. He had many interests, and, besides burlesques of Latin poets and translations from French authors (his English version of *Montaigne's Essays* is a minor classic), wrote works on sport, fruit-growing, the Peak district, and a 'second part' of Izaak Walton's *Complete Angler*, Walton being his close friend. His poems were widely known in manuscript during his lifetime and were published after his death.

Cowley, Abraham (1618–1667). Poet; born in London, educated at Westminster School and Trinity College, Cambridge, where he held a fellowship, from which he was ejected when Cambridge fell into the hands of the Parliamentarians, whereupon he went to Oxford. Later he held office in the court of Charles I and was employed on various missions abroad. He was a royalist spy in London in 1656. Later he lived in France for a time. He enjoyed the patronage of the Earl of St. Albans and the Duke of Buckingham, who provided for his needs. At the early age of fifteen he published a volume of verse, *Poetical Blossoms*. He wrote pastoral drama, and Latin and English comedy, poems and sacred epics, *The Mistress*, published in 1647, being the best-known love-poems of the time. His Pindaric Odes set a fashion which was widely followed by poets for a century after.

Crashaw, Richard (1613 ?–1650). Divine and poet; educated at Cambridge, held a fellowship at Peterhouse, of which he was deprived through refusing to take the oath of the 'Solemn League and Covenant.' He joined the Roman Catholic church, and travelled in France and Italy, and shortly before his death he was appointed sub-canon of the Basilica Church of Our Lady of Loretto. His *Steps to the Temple* and *Delights of the Muses* appeared in 1646.

Davenant, Sir William (1606–1668). Dramatist and poet; reputed godson of Shakespeare, educated at Oxford. He wrote comedies and tragedies, poems and court masques. His comic masterpiece *The Wits* was acted in 1633. He was an active supporter of the Royalist cause and when threatened with arrest by Parliament fled to France. He was employed by Charles I and his queen, and was captured at sea by a Parliament ship while on a mission for the latter, and imprisoned in the Tower, 1650–2. He was in prison again in 1659 for taking part in Sir George Booth's rising. His *Siege of Rhodes*, written 1656, may be said to have founded English opera. He established the 'Duke's Theatrical Company' of Actors in 1660.

Dorset, Charles Sackville, Earl of (1638–1706). Courtier and poet; was educated privately, then travelled in Italy till the Restoration, when he returned to England and was elected member of Parliament for East Grinstead (1660). He lived the dissipated life of a courtier of the time; but volunteered and saw service in the navy at the time of the first Dutch war. He retired from the court during the reign of James II, but held the post of Lord Chamberlain of the Household from 1689–1697, and acted as Regent for William III more than once when the latter was absent from England.

Dryden, John (1631–1700). Poet and dramatist; was born in Northamptonshire and educated at Westminster School and Trinity College, Cambridge. He then went to London, but little is known of his early manhood there; for some time, however, he was clerk to his cousin, Sir George Pickering, chamberlain and close friend of Cromwell whose death he mourned in heroic stanzas, 1658. He became a member of the Royal Society in 1662 and the following year married a daughter of the Earl of Berkshire. The first of his many plays was produced in 1663, the best, *All for Love*, appearing in 1678. Owing to the great plague in 1665–6 Dryden withdrew to Wiltshire and, as the theatres were closed, temporarily ceased playwriting. While in the country he wrote *Annus Mirabilis* and his *Essay on Dramatic Poesy*, upholding the writing of tragedy in rhyme. He was made Poet Laureate in 1670, but it was not until 1681 that his great satires began to appear, invoked by the literary and political controversies of the time—*Absalom and Achitophel*, *The Medal*, and *McFlecknoe*. He became a Roman Catholic, in 1686, was patronised by James II, and for him wrote a further satire, *The Hind and the Panther*, 1687. At the Revolution in 1689 he lost his Laureateship; but he continued to write, and what with more plays and poems, translations from the Latin, and the famous *Fables*, the last ten years of his life compare well with any previous decade. He also edited the first four volumes of 'Tonson's Miscellany,' 1684–94; and was the acknowledged literary leader of the time.

D'Urfey, Thomas (1653–1723). Poet, dramatist and satirist; born at Exeter of Huguenot descent. His innumerable plays and songs were extremely popular among people with little pretension to learning or wit. As late as 1710, Pope could report from the country that D'Urfey was the 'only poet of tolerable reputation' there. Four successive monarchs were amused by him, and with two of them—Charles II and James II—he is said to have been on intimate terms. In addition to his own numerous publications, he compiled late in life a set of song-books called *Songs Compleat*, 1719 (reissued the same year under its better known title, *Wit and Mirth; or, Pills to Purge Melancholy*), in which his own songs fill the first two volumes.

Etherege, Sir George (1635 ?–1691). Dramatist and diplomatist; believed to have belonged to an Oxfordshire family and to have been educated at Cambridge, afterwards travelling on the continent. He advocated the use of rhyme in comedies, his first two plays (*The Comical Revenge*, 1664, and *She Would if She Could*, 1668) being amongst the earliest of the Restoration theatre. He was in the diplomatic service of both Charles II and James II, whom he represented in Holland and in Germany, thus gaining his knighthood. Like other poets of his day, he is said to have lived a dissolute life. He died abroad, most probably in Paris.

Felltham, Owen (1602 ?–1668). A writer of prose and poetry on a variety of subjects, of whom very little is known, except that he was chaplain to the Earl of Thomond. His earliest published work was a collection of essays, entitled *Resolves,* written at eighteen years of age, which ran through a number of editions, to the eighth of which, in 1661, he appended his poems, *Lusoria, or Occasional Pieces.* His book of travels, *A Brief Character of the Low Countries,* 1652, was likewise popular, several editions of it being issued in his lifetime.

Flatman, Thomas (1637–1688). Painter and poet; born in London, educated at Winchester School and New College, Oxford. He was well known in his own day both as a successful poet and a painter of miniatures of more than average merit, of which a number have survived, two self-portraits amongst them. His collected *Poems and Songs* was first published in 1674, new editions appearing in 1676, 1682, and 1686, each with additional matter.

Fletcher, John (1579–1625). Dramatist; born at Rye in Sussex (his father later becoming Bishop of London), and educated at Bene't (Corpus) College, Cambridge. He was probably living in London and already writing plays before 1607, when he is known to have been collaborating with Francis Beaumont. Their famous partnership lasted until Beaumont's death in 1616, after which, till his own death nine years later, Fletcher continued to write plays both alone and with other dramatists. His plays were still popular at the end of the century.

Habington, William (1605–1654). Poet; born in Worcestershire of a Roman Catholic family, and educated in France with a view to his entering the priesthood. He, however, returned home when he was twenty-one, and passed some time in the study of history. He married Lucy Herbert, daughter of Lord Powis, addressing many poems to her under the name of 'Castara,' by which name he also called his volume of poems. *Castara* was first published in 1634, but later editions contained many additional poems. He also wrote a play and two historical works.

Herbert, George (1593–1633). Poet and divine; brother of Lord Herbert of Cherbury; educated at Westminster School, and at Trinity College, Cambridge, of which University he became Public Orator in 1619, and held that office for eight years. Amongst his many friends was John Donne, whose verse influenced him to no small degree. After a breakdown in health, he decided to enter the Church; was ordained in 1630 and presented to the living of Bemerton, near Salisbury, where he died three years later well known for his saintly life; his biography being subsequently written by Izaak Walton. His most famous work, entitled, *The Temple. Sacred*

Poems and Private Ejaculations, was not published till after his death; it was read by Charles I while in prison, praised by Crashaw, Vaughan, and Baxter, and became very popular. His best known prose work is *A Priest to the Temple,* which was printed in his *Remains,* 1652.

Herrick, Robert (1591–1674). Poet and divine; son of a London goldsmith who died while he was still an infant. He was apprenticed to an uncle of the same trade, and lived in London until 1613, when he entered St. John's College, Cambridge. He graduated, however, from Trinity Hall in 1617; M. A., 1620. He took orders, and was presented to the living of Dean Prior, Devonshire, where he remained till ejected by the Commonwealth Government in 1647. He returned to London, where, the following year, he published a volume of his collected poems, *Hesperides,* which included his religious pieces under the title, *Noble Numbers.* After the Restoration his living was restored to him, and he remained at Dean Prior from 1662 till his death. Seventeen or more of his poems were set to music by William and Henry Lawes and other composers. He resembles Campion (see *Elizabethan Lyrics*) in having been practically forgotten for a long period after his death, but, more fortunate than he, was rediscovered early in the nineteenth century; Campion not until nearly its end.

Jonson, Ben (1572 ?–1637). Poet and dramatist; born of Scottish descent, his father having died a month previously; educated at Westminster School, then, after working for a short time at his stepfather's trade of bricklaying, escaped from it by volunteering for military service with the English troops in Flanders. On his return home he joined a company of actors and began to write plays, sometimes in collaboration with other writers working for Henslowe. Though the best of his plays were written between 1603 and 1615, he continued to write till almost the end of his life. In 1618–9 he visited Scotland, stayed with Drummond of Hawthornden, and was made a burgess of Edinburgh. In 1628 he became Chronologer to the City of London. Besides plays and masques he wrote a volume of prose essays and three volumes of poems. He was successful, arrogant, and didactic, and had definite theories about the drama, which tended to make him contemptuous of other writers and so led to quarrels. Of the dramatists of his age he ranks next to Shakespeare.

King, Henry (1591–1669). Poet and divine; educated at Westminster School and at Christ Church, Oxford. He entered the Church and filled many high offices previous to the See of Chichester, to which he was elevated in 1642. He was, however, deprived of his bishropric by the Parliamentarians from 1643 till the Restoration, but thereafter held it until his death. He was a friend of many famous men, amongst whom were Donne and Jonson; his poetical works were published in 1657, entitled, *Poems, Elegies, Paradoxes and Sonnets.*

Lansdowne, George Granville, Lord (1667–1735). Poet, dramatist, and statesman; educated in France and at Trinity College, Cambridge. He took no part in public life until the reign of Queen Anne, when he became member of Parliament for Fowey. In 1710 he became Secretary of State, following the fall of Walpole, and the next year was raised to the peerage. He held various high offices until the death of Anne; but after the accession of George I was imprisoned in the Tower for two years as a suspected Jacobite. He later lived in France for several years, but returned in 1732 and published a complete edition of his works, plays and poems, before his death. He was an early patron of Pope, who dedicated *Windsor Forest* to him.

Lovelace, Richard (1618–1658). Cavalier poet; he belonged to a wealthy Kentish family and was educated at Charterhouse and Gloucester Hall (now Worcester College), Oxford. He was a soldier and courtier of Charles I and was imprisoned by Parliament in 1642 for his support of the King. In 1646–7 he served in the army of the French King at the siege of Dunkirk and on his return to England was again imprisoned. In 1649 he published *Lucasta*, a collection of his poems, named after the lady who held his affections, but had married another, believing him to be dead. He is thought to have died in poverty in London.

Marvell, Andrew (1621–1678). Poet and satirist; born in Yorkshire, son of the Master of Hull Grammar School, where he was educated before going to Trinity College, Cambridge. He travelled on the continent, and in 1650–1 became tutor to the daughter of Lord Fairfax, whose influence led him to sympathize with the Commonwealth. Much of his best poetry was written while at Nun Appleton with the Fairfaxes. He later acted as tutor to a nephew of Cromwell; then became Milton's colleague in the Latin Secretaryship in 1657, and soon afterwards Member of Parliament for Hull, which seat he apparently retained till his death. After the Restoration he went to Russia and Scandinavia as secretary to the Ambassador, the Earl of Carlisle. He was independent, refused to receive favours from Court, hated intolerance, and was very vigorous in promoting the interests of his constituents at Hull. His poems preceded his prose works; several being written in honour of Cromwell, including an elegy on his death. His satires were many and bitter; he attacked the dissoluteness of the Court after the Restoration, and the mismanagement of national affairs, the only solution of which he felt to be a republic. He was the friend and champion of Milton until his death.

Milton, John (1608–1674). Poet and statesman; born in London, the son of a scrivener, who was also a musician. He was educated at St. Paul's School and then at Christ's College, Cambridge, where he remained for some years. Poems written at this time include the *Ode on the Morning of Christ's Nativity*. On leaving Cambridge he made his home with his father, retired and living comfortably at Horton in Buckinghamshire; here he passed his time in literary study, and wrote *Arcades, Comus, L'Allegro, Il Penseroso*, and *Lycidas*. In 1638 he started to travel in France and Italy, where he met many of the most enlightened men of the time, returning on the outbreak of civil war at home. He settled in London and took pupils; in 1643 he married a young wife who left him after one month, whereupon he published a pamphlet on divorce—but he and his wife were reconciled two years later. He was already taking part in the disputes in Church and State, was appointed Latin Secretary to the Commonwealth Council of State, and in spite of the blindness with which he was now afflicted was able with the assistance of Marvell and others to continue to hold the office. During this period most of his prose works, pamphlets, and tracts were written. In 1656 he married his second wife, who died two years later, about which time he is said to have begun to work in earnest on *Paradise Lost*, a scheme for which he had drafted as early as 1640–1. Shortly after the Restoration he was imprisoned and fined; he was soon released, however, and in due course finished the poem which was published in 1667, he having in the meantime married his third wife who outlived him. His last poems, *Paradise Regained* and *Samson Agonistes*, were published together in 1670, but post-dated 1671.

Newcastle, William Cavendish, Duke of (1592–1676). Royalist; educated at St. John's College, Cambridge, and then travelled abroad. He was a staunch Royalist and entertained both James I and Charles I at his home at Welbeck, Nottinghamshire. He lent large sums of money to Charles I and three times raised at his own expense troops which he commanded in the King's cause. After the defeat at Marston Moor in 1644 he went to France, where he met and married his wife, a maid of honour to Queen Henrietta Maria. He was in great straits for lack of money, and although he returned to England with Charles II at the Restoration he only regained possession of some of his land, in spite of the fact that he had spent almost £1,000,000 in aid of his Sovereigns. His later years were passed in retirement at Welbeck. He was a patron of both Ben Jonson and of Dryden, and his own writings include plays and poems, and two works upon the management of horses, one in French and one in English.

Prior, Matthew (1664–1721). Poet and diplomatist; educated at Westminster School and at St. John's College, Cambridge, where he later obtained a fellowship. He became secretary to the Ambassador at The Hague, and was later attached to the Embassy at Paris. He was also Secretary of State for Ireland and a commissioner of customs. On the accession of George I he was imprisoned for two years (1715–17), after which his friends published on his behalf an edition of his poems by which he benefitted to the extent of four thousand guineas. Further, Lord Harley gave him an estate in Essex, Down Hall, and there, well provided for, he spent the rest of his life. He wrote both poetry and prose, but it is owing to the excellence of his occasional verse that he is best remembered.

Quarles, Francis (1592–1644). Poet; educated at Christ's College, Cambridge, afterwards entering Lincoln's Inn. He subsequently held various appointments in court and city, and lay offices connected with the Church. For instance, he was for a time cup-bearer to the Queen of Bohemia;

later he accompanied Archbishop Usher to Ireland as his secretary, and in 1639 was appointed Chronologer to the City of London. He wrote a tract in defence of Charles I, which led Parliament to confiscate his property and to have his manuscripts destroyed. His health was completely broken by these misfortunes and he never recovered. He wrote much in prose and verse, mostly religious works, *Emblems*, published in 1635 being the best known, and containing some of his finest poetry. His popularity was so great that his books were still being reprinted in the eighteenth century.

Randolph, Thomas (1605–1635). Poet and dramatist; born in Northampton-shire and while still a child showed unusual literary talent. He was edu-cated at Westminster School and at Trinity College, Cambridge, where he held a Fellowship from 1629 onwards, and won distinction for his verse, both English and Latin. In 1632 he went to London and was the associate of Ben Jonson and his fellow poets. Two of his plays were published in 1630, and one in 1632, but his poems and the rest of his plays were not printed until after his death at thirty.

Rochester, John Wilmot, Earl of (1647–1680). Poet and courtier; educated at Wadham College, Oxford; he then travelled in France and Italy, and on his return was received at Court. In 1665 he served with the Fleet dur-ing the Dutch War; the following year he became Gentleman of the King's Bedchamber. He was several times dismissed in disgrace from Court, where he was, in spite of his youth, the most notorious of the King's profli-gate companions. He was a temporary patron of several poets and gained a reputation for his lyrics and satires in verse. His poems were published shortly after his death, and frequently reprinted in the following century.

Sedley, Sir Charles (1639?–1701). Dramatist and wit; born in Kent and educated at Wadham College, Oxford. After the Restoration he was one of the dissolute courtiers, 'the merry gang,' surrounding the King. He sat in Parliament as member for New Romney. He wrote tragedies, come-dies, translations, prose essays, and poems.

Shadwell, Thomas (1642?–1692). Dramatist; born in Norfolk, educated at Bury St. Edmunds and at Caius College, Cambridge, later entering the Middle Temple. *The Sullen Lovers*, his first play, was performed at Lin-coln's Inn fields in 1668. After a period of friendship with Dryden, a bitter feud broke out between them, each attacking the other in satires— he being the subject of Dryden's *MacFlecknoe*. After the Revolution, when Dryden was deprived of the Laureateship, Shadwell was appointed his successor, but died shortly afterwards.

Sherburne, Sir Edward (1618–1702). Clerk of the ordnance and poet; born in London, where he received his schooling, and then travelled abroad. He became clerk of the ordnance at the Tower, and was in charge of the Royalist artillery at the battle of Edgehill, 1642. He again travelled abroad, 1654–9. Regaining his office at the Restoration, he held it until the Revolution, thereafter living quietly in retirement. He translated many classical authors, wrote poems (which were published in 1651, entitled *Salmacis and Other Poems*) as well as technical works for the ordnance office.

Shirley, James (1596–1666). Dramatist and poet; educated at Merchant Taylors' School, and at both Oxford and Cambridge. After being ordained he became a Roman Catholic and spent some years teaching till 1625, when the successful production of his first comedy, *Love's Tricks*, encouraged him to give up teaching and go to London. There he became associated with Ford, Massinger, and other dramatists, and produced numerous plays and masques (some of them written during a visit to Ireland) before the closing of the theatres in 1642. He took part in the fighting of the Civil War under his patron, the Duke of Newcastle, and accompanied the latter when he retired to France. At length returning to England he became a schoolmaster again, and wrote books on education. He is generally regarded as the last of the Elizabethan dramatists.

Stanley, Thomas (1625–1678). Classical scholar; born in Hertfordshire and educated at Pembroke Hall, Cambridge. He was a wealthy man, travelled for some years on the continent and then settled in London, occupying himself with literary studies and with writing. He was generous to other literary men who were in need, including Sherburne and Shirley. He published original poems, translations from the Greek and Latin classics and the first English *History of Philosophy*, and wrote many other works which were still in manuscript at the time of his death.

Strode, William (1602–1645). Poet and dramatist; educated at Westminster School and Christ Church, Oxford; he took his degree of Bachelor of Divinity in 1631, and became a Canon of Christ Church in 1638. A dramatist as well as a poet, he wrote a tragi-comedy called *The Floating Island*, which was performed before Charles I and his queen at Oxford in 1636, the music being written by Lawes. Such of Strode's poems as were published were included in various collections of poems and miscellanies, his poetical works remaining uncollected until the present century.

Suckling, Sir John (1609–1642). Cavalier and poet; member of an old Norfolk family, educated at Trinity College, Cambridge. He inherited a large fortune from his father (1627), travelled in France and Italy, was knighted 1630, and served for a time in the army of Gustavus Adolphus. On his return to England in 1632, he joined his friends at Court, where he lived a gay and frivolous life. He wrote his first play, *Aglaura*, in 1637, and produced it himself in the most extravagant manner. He joined Charles I in his expedition to Scotland in 1639, leading a troop of horse which he himself had raised and lavishly equipped. He was later accused of being concerned in a Royalist plot, and fled to France, where he is believed to have committed suicide. Most of his works were published posthumously in 1646 under the title of *Fragmenta Aurea*.

Traherne, Thomas (1636–1674). Divine and poet; born in Hereford, and educated at Brasenose College, Oxford. He was presented to the living of Credenhill in Herefordshire in 1657, and for some years lived either there or in Oxford. He took his degree of Bachelor of Divinity in 1669. The latter part of his life was spent as chaplain to Sir Orlando Bridgeman, Lord Keeper between 1667 and 1672, in whose house at Teddington he was living at the time of his death. He wrote prose as well as verse; but the latter remained unpublished and unknown until the beginning of the present century.

Vaughan, Henry (1622–1695). Poet and physician; born in Brecknockshire and educated at Jesus College, Oxford. He studied law, and then medicine, which he started to practice in 1645. He wrote original poems, and translations of Latin devotional works; he is best known for his volume of poems on religious subjects, *Silex Scintillans*, which was published in two parts, in 1650 and 1655.

Waller, Edmund (1606–1687). Poet; born in Hertfordshire and educated at Eton and King's College, Cambridge. He became a member of Parliament, but was expelled from the House in 1643 for his part in a plot to gain control of London on behalf of Charles I; he was imprisoned, fined, and banished, and spent his exile in Paris. He was pardoned in 1651 and allowed to return to England; he gained the favour of Cromwell, whom he praised in verse, and was made a Commissioner of Trade. After the Restoration he again entered Parliament as member for Hastings, which he represented till his death. His best known verses, entitled *Poems*, were published in 1645, and *Divine Poems* in 1685.

Wither (or *Withers*), George (1588–1667). Pamphleteer and poet; born in Hampshire, educated at Magdalen College, Oxford. Later he entered Lincoln's Inn. When still a young man he was twice imprisoned in the Marshalsea on account of his satires; he was at the same time writing poems. In 1639 he served under Charles I in the war in Scotland; but later became an ardent Puritan, and fought in the Parliamentary army. He was given posts by Cromwell, which he held till the Restoration, when he was again imprisoned on account of his opinions. His best poems are contained in *Juvenilia*, published in 1622.

INDEX OF AUTHORS

(The references are to pages; but an italic figure in parentheses following a reference—e.g. 14(2), or 85–91(8),—denotes the number of the author's poems occurring on the page or pages indicated. The dates are taken, with a very few exceptions, from the D.N.B. A double-dagger ‡ placed in front of a name signifies that the poet was writing before 1621, and selections of his earlier work appear in the previous volume—'Elizabethan Lyrics'; and an asterisk * similarly indicates those poets who continued to write after 1700 and therefore reappear in the subsequent volume—'Eighteenth Century Lyrics.')

INDEX OF SUBJECTS

(The references are to pages on which the poems will be found—usually complete poems—on the theme indicated. There are, however, a few interesting exceptions where only a part of the poem is concerned with the particular subject.)

INDEX OF FIRST LINES

(A dagger † denotes poems printed for the first time)

550

PAGE